D0788845

LIBRARY
LEWIS-CLARK STATE COLLEGE
LEWISTON, IDAHO

UNDERSTANDING PSYCHOLOGICAL PREPARATION FOR SPORT

UNDERSTANDING PSYCHOLOGICAL PREPARATION FOR SPORT

Theory and Practice of Elite Performers

Lew Hardy
University of Wales, Bangor, UK

Graham Jones
Loughborough University, UK

Daniel Gould
University of North Carolina at Greensboro, USA

JOHN WILEY & SONS
Chichester · New York · Brisbane · Toronto · Singapore

Telephone (+44) 1243 779777

Email (for orders and customer service enquiries): cs-books@wiley.co.uk
Visit our Home Page on www.wileyeurope.com or www.wiley.com

Reprinted October 1997, December 1998, September 1999, July 2000, July 2001, August 2002, October 2003, July 2006, June 2007

Other Wiley Editorial Offices

John Wiley & Sons Inc., 111 River Street, Hoboken, NJ 07030, USA

Jossey-Bass, 989 Market Street, San Francisco, CA 94103-1741, USA

Wiley-VCH Verlag GmbH, Boschstr. 12, D-69469 Weinheim, Germany

John Wiley & Sons Australia Ltd, 33 Park Road, Milton, Queensland 4064, Australia

John Wiley & Sons (Asia) Pte Ltd, 2 Clementi Loop #02-01, Jin Xing Distripark, Singapore 129809

John Wiley & Sons Canada Ltd, 22 Worcester Road, Etobicoke, Ontario, Canada M9W 1L1

British Library Cataloguing in Publication Data

A catalogue record for this book is available from the British Library

ISBN 13: 978-0-471-95787-4 (P/B)
ISBN 13: 978-0-471-95023-3 (H/B)

Typeset in 10/12pt Palatino by Dorwyn Ltd, Rowlands Castle, Hampshire

This book is printed on acid-free paper responsibly manufactured from sustainable forestry in which at least two trees are planted for each one used for paper production.

CONTENTS

ABOUT THE AUTHORS

Lew Hardy is a Professor at the University of Wales, Bangor. He has been the psychological consultant to the British Amateur Gymnastics Association since 1983, and is currently serving his second four-year cycle as Chairperson of the British Olympic Association's Psychology Steering Group. Lew has been both Secretary and Chairperson of the Psychology Section of the British Association of Sport and Exercise Sciences; and both the Psychology and the Sports Performance Section Editor of the *Journal of Sports Sciences*. He is a Chartered Psychologist and a Fellow of both the British Association of Sport and Exercise Sciences, and the European College of Sports Scientists. He has written approximately 100 publications including the book he co-edited with Graham Jones entitled *Stress and Performance in Sport*, published by John Wiley.

Graham Jones is a reader in Sport Psychology at Loughborough University. He is a Chartered Psychologist with the British Psychological Society and also a Registered Psychologist with the British Olympic Association. He is a former Chairperson of the Psychology Section of the British Association of Sport and Exercise Sciences and currently sits on the British Olympic Association's Psychology Advisory Group. Graham has published widely in the areas of competitive anxiety and psychological preparation and has co-edited a book entitled *Stress and Performance in Sport*. He is also Editor of the international journal, *The Sport Psychologist*. Graham has also worked extensively as a consultant to numerous elite sports performers and teams, and he was one of four psychologists who worked with the Great Britain 1996 Olympic Team.

Daniel Gould is a Professor in the Department of Exercise and Sport Science at the University of North Carolina at Greensboro where he focuses his efforts on research, teaching and service activities in applied sport psychology. He has consulted extensively with numerous elite athletes and teams. Daniel has studied the relationship between stress and athletic performance, sources of athletic stress, athlete motivation, youth sports issues, and sport psychological skills training use and effectiveness. He has over 90 scholarly publications and over 50 applied sport psychology research dissemination-service publications. Daniel has co-authored three books, including *Foundations of Sport and Exercise Psychology* with Robert Weinberg.

PREFACE

This book has been written for sport psychologists, students studying sport psychology, and psychologists with an interest in sport or high level performance of any type. It arose from our concern about the gap which often appears to exist between research sport psychologists and practising psychologists working with (high level) sports performers. The book is therefore designed to advance both theory and practice in the psychological preparation of sports performers. An integrated approach is adopted in which research informs best practice, and practical experience informs research. Seven aspects of psychological preparation are considered in detail: basic psychological skills; self-confidence; motivation; arousal and activation; stress, anxiety and performance; concentration; and coping with adversity. For each topic, we have integrated the relevant qualitative and quantitative research literatures with quotations from elite sports performers and practical knowledge gained via our own personal experience of working with high level sports performers. Each of these discussions is then concluded with a summary of the implications for future research and best practice.

Following these integrated reviews, a unifying model is presented. This model organises the diverse range of variables that have been discussed in the previous chapters into a single functional framework which helps the reader to understand the context of each variable. The final two chapters of the book draw together the implications for research and best practice that have been identified in the previous chapters. Over 50 of the highest priority research questions are rated in terms of their importance and difficulty, and over 60 of the most important implications for best practice are identified together with a number of distinguishing characteristics of effective consultancy work with high level performers. At least two features of the book are unique: the research-to-practice orientation which is taken to preparation for high level sports performance; and the global perspective used by the authors in which evidence derived from the North American, European, Australasian, and other research literatures, in both general and sport psychology, is considered and utilised.

We have not found this an easy book to write and, as ever, the names which appear on the front cover do not reflect the contributions of a number of other people without whose support the book would not have been produced. In particular, Daniel would like to thank his wife Deb, and sons Kevin and Brian, for their patience and support throughout the duration of the project; Graham would like to thank his wife Sian, daughters Emma and Kellee, and son Ben, for their love, support and tolerance of his absence (both physical and mental) during the preparation of the book; and Lew would like to thank his parents, Derrick and Elsie, for always being there, his sons, James and Andrew, for making time for him, and his flat mates, Pete and Kim (plus a loving friend who remains anonymous), for helping him to remember how to laugh (long and hard). Other thanks, for their assistance during the preparation of this book and for helpful comments on earlier drafts, are due to Abi Cox, Sheldon Hanton, Ken Hodge, Deárbhlá McCullough, Murray Watson, Tim Woodman, and Eileen Udry.

Lew Hardy
Graham Jones
Daniel Gould

PART I

INTRODUCTION

1

WHY WRITE YET ANOTHER BOOK ON PSYCHOLOGICAL PREPARATION?

CONTENTS

RATIONALE

Sakumoto instilled in me the philosophy that when I trained in the gym it was as if I were in competition, as if every routine were competition . . . before every routine I ever did in my 12 years of competing, I raised my hand to my coach before beginning. Whether it was practice or competition, I raised my hand. And he raised his back to me, just like a judge. Doing that was like a trigger mechanism for me. I mean, I would raise my hand, he would raise his, and then with everything I had I would focus in on the routine. My routines in practice were just like real competition. (Peter Vidmar, Olympic Gold Medallist in men's artistic gymnastics; Ravizza, 1993, pp. 93–94)

In discovering the proper tension level . . . I found out there was a difference between winning and losing and took a while to zero in on it. It wasn't conscious until one time I went too far. Then I really noticed I'd gone overboard. I was way too nervous and I just blew the race. I thought, "Gee, I have to find that balance in there." Then I honed in pretty quickly. The way I did it, once I had an idea it was there, was to get really hyper for a race, and find out what reaction I got. Then be really laid back and see what the reaction was. Once you find out the outside limits you can get to, you can get quickly to the middle. (Highly successful alpine skier; Orlick and Partington, 1988, p. 119)

These statements from elite performers clearly indicate the importance that they attach to their psychological preparation for competition. This view is further reinforced by the fact that elite performers have been consistently shown to make greater use of psychological skills and strategies than their non-elite counterparts (Mahoney and Avener, 1977; Mahoney *et al.*, 1987; Orlick and Partington, 1988). Indeed, few sport psychologists would argue with the claim that psychological preparation is a most important part of sports performance. Nevertheless, there is a large (and ever-increasing) number of applied sport psychology texts that purport to describe how the necessary psychological skills can be acquired, so that critical readers could be forgiven for wondering why they should bother to read yet another "how to do it" sport psychology text.

The answer to this question is relatively simple. This is not just another "how to do it" text on the psychological preparation of sports performers; nor is it merely an examination of the scholarly research that has been performed in the area. Rather, the authors have attempted to explicitly relate current theory and research to personal understanding and experience gained from extensive consultancy work with high level performers and coaches from a variety of sports. In this way, the book adopts an integrated approach in which research informs best practice, and practical experience informs researchers about the most important questions to address. The primary aim of the book, therefore, is to advance both theory and practice of psychological preparation for high level performance. Each chapter deals with a separate aspect of psychological preparation, and reviews the quantitative and qualitative research literature which is relevant to that aspect. These reviews are integrated with personal experience via examples and quotations from elite sports performers, thus presenting qualitative evidence on the issues under consideration, and illustrating theory into practice. The quotations used come from a variety of sources, ranging from journalistic articles to refereed academic papers. In the authors' opinions, all these sources have some value. However, in line with normal practice in qualitative research (Lincoln and Guba, 1985; also see Chapter 10 in this book), the reader is left to judge the trustworthiness of the information contained in each quotation via reference to the methodological details reported in the original source. Following each review, the most salient research questions in that area are identified, together with practical implications for guiding psychological preparation for elite performance.

A number of features of the approach which has been adopted are unique. First, a research-to-practice orientation to preparation for high level sports performance has not been used before. Most applied practice texts do not explicitly link their recommendations and interventions to the research literature. Consequently, the reader is rarely given any real scientific justification for the interventions, and is often left with the feeling that they have been simply "plucked out of thin air". Second, a global perspective has been taken in which evidence derived from the North American, European, Australasian, and other, research literature in both general and sport psychology is considered and utilised. Most previous texts in this area have not made full use of knowledge generated from within general psychology or from outside North America. This situation may have arisen because the majority of the extant sport psychology literature has emanated from North America. However, it is the authors' contention that much can be learned from the adoption of a broader perspective. Third, both quantitative and qualitative research perspectives are integrated with practical experience to advance knowledge and understanding in the area; no one form of inquiry is elevated or denigrated with respect to others. Fourth, specific recommendations for both future research and best practice are derived from the reviews performed.

STRUCTURE AND OVERVIEW OF THE BOOK

The book is divided into three parts. The first Part contains only a single chapter—the present one. This chapter provides a rationale for the book and an overview of its structure. The second Part focuses on the Current State of Knowledge Regarding Psychological Preparation for Sports Performance. It contains seven chapters, each of which deals with a different aspect of psychological preparation for high level performance. The structure of these chapters is identical. The aspect of psychological preparation under consideration is first introduced via quotations from elite sports performers. The primary objective of this introduction is to highlight the importance of that aspect for elite performance. A critical analysis of the quantitative and qualitative research literatures which are of relevance to that particular aspect of psychological preparation is then undertaken. The quotations from elite performers, which are integrated into these reviews, are used to elaborate upon, and sometimes to challenge, the conclusions which are drawn from the research literature. The major implications for future research in the area are then presented, followed by the implications for best practice.

The aspects of psychological preparation which are considered in the seven chapters in this Part were selected by reference to the literature on distinguishing characteristics of elite performers, and psychological skills training for sport. Research examining the psychological differences between elite and non-elite performers has consistently shown that elite performers possess greater self-confidence, higher levels of motivation, and better arousal, anxiety and attentional control strategies than their non-elite counterparts (Fenz and Epstein, 1967, 1968; Mahoney and Avener, 1977; Mahoney, Gabriel and Perkins, 1987; Orlick and Partington, 1988). Similarly, reviews of the psychological skills training literature (Hardy and Jones, 1994a; Hardy and Nelson, 1988; Vealey, 1988) have also consistently identified these five skill areas as being the most important ones for practitioners to develop, although Vealey collapsed arousal and anxiety control into a single psychological skill in her content analysis. Consequently, five of the seven chapters in the second section focus upon these areas.

The first chapter in this Part focuses upon what Vealey (1988) has described as the psychological skills training methods of relaxation, goal-setting, imagery and self-talk (cf. Hardy and Jones, 1994a; Vealey, 1988). Whilst the present authors would not disagree with Vealey's argument that a distinction should be made between psychological skills (such as anxiety control) and the psychological methods (such as goal-setting and relaxation) which are used to achieve such skills, they would contend that these methods are also basic psychological skills in their own right. Consequently, rather than regard these psychological skills as *just* methods, the present text will regard them as *basic psychological skills*, which are sometimes used on their own and sometimes used as subcomponents of *more advanced psychological skills*. In view of this distinction, the chapter which examines these basic psychological skills appears as the first chapter in this Part, followed by the five chapters which examine the more complex psychological issues involved in self-confidence, motivation, arousal and activation, stress and anxiety, and concentration and attentional control.

The final chapter in this Part examines the ways in which elite sports performers cope with adversity. This area was selected partly because of the obvious need for elite performers to cope with a wide range of potential and actual problems, and partly because of the recent upsurge in research interest in the area (see, for example, Anshel, 1990; Gould *et al.*, 1993a, b; Hanson *et al.*, 1992; Krohne and Hindel, 1988; Smith *et al.*, 1990a). In conclusion, then, the aspects of psychological preparation which are addressed by the chapters contained in this Part are (in order of appearance):

- **the basic psychological skills** of relaxation, goal-setting, imagery, and self-talk;
- **self-confidence**, together with the relationship that exists between self-confidence and performance, and between self-confidence and anxiety, and strategies for the enhancement of self-confidence;
- **motivation**, including the motivational climate in which training and performance take place, attributions for success and failure, and issues associated with withdrawal from sport;
- **arousal and activation**, examining the conceptual distinction between these two constructs, theories of arousal and activation, and individual differences in arousal and activation;

- **stress and anxiety**, with a particular focus upon the antecedents of stress and anxiety, the relationship between competitive state anxiety and performance, and factors and strategies that influence anxiety responses;
- **concentration and attentional control**, with a critical analysis of several theories of attention, the relationship between anxiety and attention, and strategies for the enhancement of concentration and attentional control;
- **coping with adversity**, including primary and secondary appraisal, categories of coping, the measurement of coping, coping dispositions, coping outcomes, and an integrated model of coping.

The third Part of the book contains three chapters which focus upon the Implications and Future Directions issues that arise from the reviews performed in the preceding Part. The first of these chapters presents a unifying model of the factors that influence psychological preparation for elite performance. This model was originally proposed by Gould and Damarjian (in press); it organises the diverse range of variables that have been discussed in the preceding Part into a single functional framework. The second chapter in this Part identifies those Future Research Directions which are most likely to have a large impact upon psychological preparation for elite performance. The chapter rates the importance and difficulty of over fifty of the highest priority questions. A small number of research questions are then discussed in detail to highlight the principles underlying the selection of qualitative and quantitative methodologies for tackling such questions, given our current state of knowledge. The third chapter in this Part collates the Implications for Guiding Practice which have been identified in the previous Part, and builds them into the unifying model of psychological preparation for peak performance. The chapter then summarises more than 60 of the most important implications for best practice and identifies a number of important characteristics of effective consultancy work with high level performers. The book finishes with a short epilogue which briefly reviews the book and draws it to a close.

One limitation of the book is that, in focusing strongly upon the psychological preparation of *individual* elite performers, it does not seriously consider group dynamics, or other social and organisational factors, which might influence performance. Of course, this omission does not mean that the book is irrelevant to team sports, only that it does not really consider the functional integration of teams, and team performance. The decision not to include a detailed discussion of social factors was taken in light of the authors' view that the inclusion of such factors would have increased the length of the book by approximately 50 per cent. However, for further information on social factors and group dynamics, the interested reader is referred to reviews of these issues by Hardy and Jones (1994a), Sarason *et al.* (1991), and Widmeyer *et al.* (1993).

SUMMARY

This chapter has presented a rationale for writing the present book, together with an overview of the material that it contains. It has also provided a rationale for the approach which was adopted in writing the book, and has drawn attention to one limitation of this approach.

PART II

CURRENT STATE OF KNOWLEDGE REGARDING PSYCHOLOGICAL PREPARATION FOR SPORTS PERFORMANCE

2

BASIC PSYCHOLOGICAL SKILLS

CONTENTS

THE BASIC PSYCHOLOGICAL SKILLS UNDERLYING ADVANCED PSYCHOLOGICAL SKILLS

When considering the underlying principles involved in psychological skills training, Vealey's (1988) distinction between psychological "skills" and psychological "methods" is an appropriate starting point. In this context, psychological skills are the desired outcomes (e.g. increased self-confidence, reduced anxiety) associated with the implementation and practice of psychological methods. Vealey identified four methods which she demonstrated to figure prominently in sport psychology books published in North America between 1980 and 1988: imagery (discussed in 100 per cent of the books); thought control (93 per cent); physical relaxation (93 per cent); and goal-setting (70 per cent). Two modifications have been made to Vealey's terminology for the purposes of this book. Firstly, we contend that the four methods are more than just "methods"; they are psychological skills in their own right. However, they are often used, on their own or in combination, as the foundation for the advanced skills discussed in subsequent chapters. Thus, this book makes an important distinction between "basic psychological skills" and "advanced psychological skills". Secondly, we contend that the terms used to encapsulate the four basic skills, with the exception of goal-setting, are a little restrictive. The term "physical relaxation" is too limiting since research findings have shown that other forms of relaxation can also be beneficial in sport. The term "imagery" has been extended to include "mental rehearsal", and "thought control" is referred to as "self-talk".

This chapter, therefore, deals with the four basic psychological skills of relaxation, goal-setting, imagery and mental rehearsal, and self-talk. The basic principles underlying each skill are addressed, together with research findings. Finally, implications for research and best practice for each of the skills are proposed.

RELAXATION

Top level sports competition occurs in a highly stressful environment in which the ability to handle pressure is crucial. Performers use a variety of strategies and skills to enable them to cope in such situations, but a prominent one is relaxation. There are at least two major reasons why the ability to relax is important. Firstly, most performers will experience at least some anxiety during competition, but it is the ability to control the anxiety to manageable proportions, and even to use it to their advantage, which distinguishes elite from non-elite performers (Jones *et al.*, 1994; Mahoney and Avener, 1977; Orlick and Partington, 1988). Secondly, the literature on peak performance identifies being relaxed during performance as one characteristic of peak performance (Jackson, 1992; Ravizza, 1977; Williams and Krane, 1993). For example, Kerrin Lee-Gartner, winner of the 1992 Olympic Gold Medal in women's downhill skiing, described her own experience in the following way:

> *The focus is so clear that you shut your thoughts off, and you trust in yourself and believe in yourself. You've already prepared for years and years. All you do is go, it's very natural. You're very relaxed.* (Orlick and Lee-Gartner, 1993, p. 117)

In a series of interviews conducted with elite performers by Jones and Hardy (1990a), the use of relaxation emerged as an important strategy. All six performers used some form of relaxation technique, although it was also apparent that they had experienced little if any formal training in them. Their use of relaxation seemed to be part of the natural preparation which they had developed, and often appeared to take place in a fairly unstructured manner. The techniques they employed varied and included breathing, counting, and imagery. They appeared to have developed these skills in an instinctive way, trying out various innate methods until they had found something which worked for them. For example, former women's world champion trampolinist, Sue Challis, stated that she used relaxation techniques all the time during the pre-competition period, but that:

> *It's not a deliberate "now I'm going to sit down and relax for 10 minutes". It's much more innate. When I went to university I discovered that I was doing lots of things that have got names but I wasn't aware of it. I was just trying to prepare myself for the competition and it can be right the way through the complete build-up for the competition. I do it whenever I think it's necessary. But it's not a deliberate thing.* (Jones and Hardy, 1990a, p. 263)

Presumably, the assistance of a sport psychologist may speed up the learning process. However, the task of selecting and implementing a specific relaxation technique with an athlete is not straightforward, since there are many relaxation techniques from which to choose. These can be loosely grouped into "physical" and "mental" relaxation techniques. An example of physical relaxation is *progressive muscular relaxation (PMR)*, which is probably the most common form of relaxation used in sport. Modern progressive relaxation techniques are all variations of Jacobson's (1938) PMR. This entails the systematic focus of attention on various gross muscle groups throughout the body. The individual progresses through the body, tensing and then releasing the tension from each muscle group in turn. This basic procedure has been modified in different ways so that there are now many versions, including differential PMR, which requires partial relaxation of the muscles, enhancing greater self-awareness of degrees of bodily tension and their consequences for sporting performance (Rotella, 1985). Indeed, the skill of the sport psychologist is in enabling this technique to be used not only before, but also during, performance. Ost's (1988) applied relaxation technique (see Figure 2.1) is useful in this respect; the goal of applied relaxation training is to be able to relax in 20–30 seconds. The first phase of training involves a 15-minute progressive relaxation session practised twice a day, in which muscle groups are tensed and relaxed. The client then moves on to a release-only phase which takes between 5 and 7 minutes to complete. The time is reduced to a 2–3 minute version with the use of the self-instruction "relax". This time is further reduced until only a few seconds are required, and then the technique is practised in specific situations.

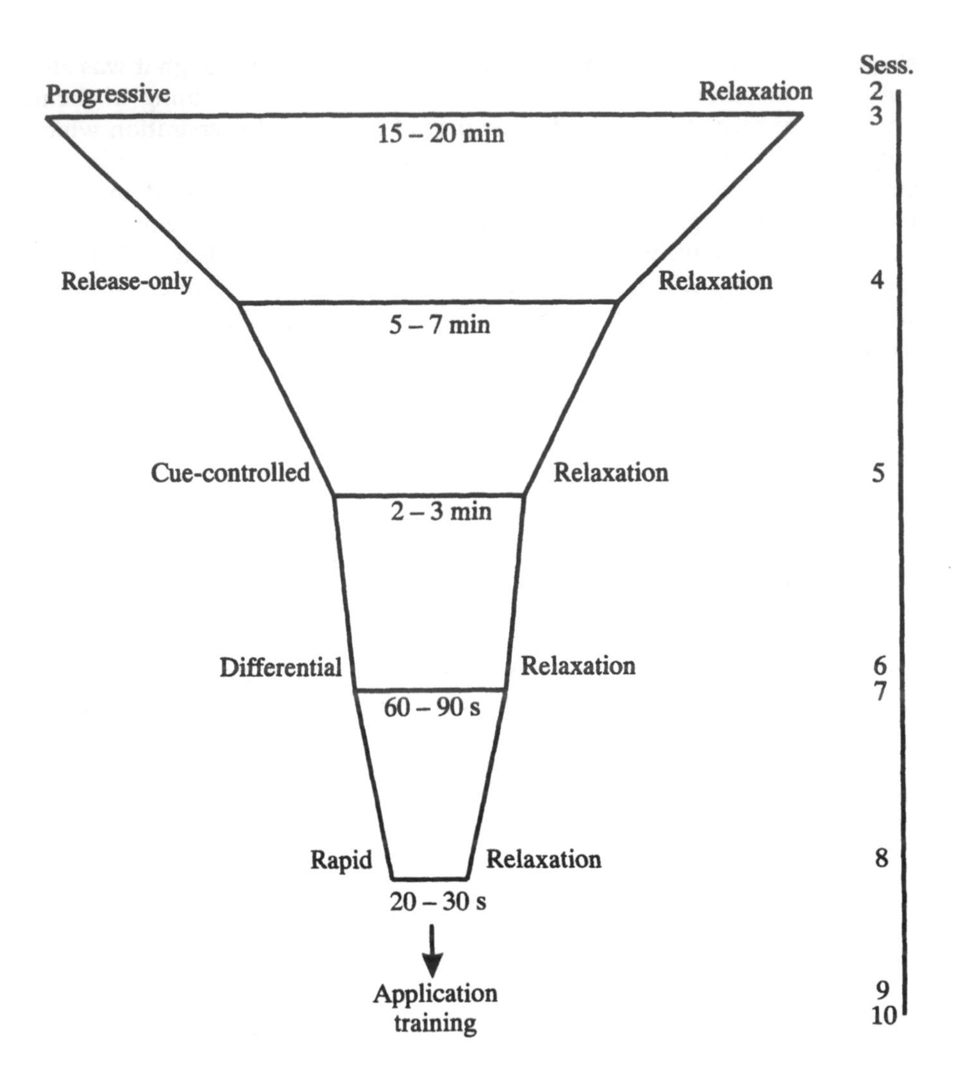

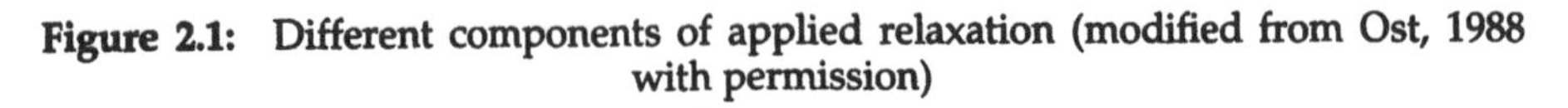

Figure 2.1: Different components of applied relaxation (modified from Ost, 1988 with permission)

Jones and Hardy (1990a) described how Mary Nevill, captain of the Great Britain women's hockey team which won a Bronze Medal in the 1992 Olympic Games, used a brief physical relaxation technique during performance

> *. . . by relaxing her shoulders by "just dropping them" and taking a deep breath. Mary usually tries to relax before stick-stopping a penalty corner, a time when she feels some pressure on her: "It would just be a moment to*

> *physically relax, and I also think I just need a quiet moment to prepare myself.*" (p. 263)

Ost's applied relaxation technique has received little research attention in sport, with the focus being mainly on general progressive relaxation techniques, and investigations ranging from case studies to group designs. Nideffer and Deckner (1970), for example, reported a case study in which progressive relaxation was implemented to improve a shot putter's performance. Using a group design, Kukla (1976) employed progressive relaxation with high school baseball players and reported a reduction in state anxiety as well as improved batting performance under stressful conditions when compared to a control group. Lanning and Hisanaga's (1983) study of high school volleyball players similarly found lowered state anxiety in a progressive relaxation group when compared to a control group, together with improved serving performance. However, whilst the findings have generally shown reductions in state anxiety, the findings relating to performance have not always shown improvements and tend to be rather inconsistent.

One example of mental relaxation is *transcendental meditation*. This technique has not been used as extensively in sport as PMR, but its benefits are well documented in other literatures. Transcendental meditation basically involves individuals assuming a comfortable position, closing their eyes, relaxing their muscles, focusing on breathing, and repeating a "mantra" or key word (Benson, 1976; Benson and Proctor, 1984). This technique has been shown to be associated with reduced oxygen consumption, decreased respiration, slower heart rate, lower blood pressure, and decreased responsivity of the sympathetic nervous system (Berger, 1994; Feuerstein *et al.*, 1986). Again, the benefits of this technique to the sports performer are dependent upon the skill of the sport psychologist in helping the athlete apply it to actual competition. Jones (1993) applied this technique with a world-ranked racquet sport player in the manner depicted in Figure 2.2. This is a modified adaptation of Ost's (1988) applied relaxation, substituting a meditative relaxation technique for PMR, and reducing the number of stages. The process employed by Jones (1993) involves learning the technique at a general level, with the aim of achieving a deeply relaxed state during a 20-minute session. Once learned, this technique is practised by the performer perhaps once or twice a week in order to reinforce the basic technique, but is not used on competition days. The technique is then modified to a 5-minute version which emphasises composure but not deep relaxation. This version can be used on competition days at any point up to within about an hour of performance initiation. The technique is finally modified to a few seconds' version which may involve only three or four breaths and repetition of a mantra, such as "relax", which can be used immediately prior to and during performance in order to regain composure and attention control (see Jones, 1993).

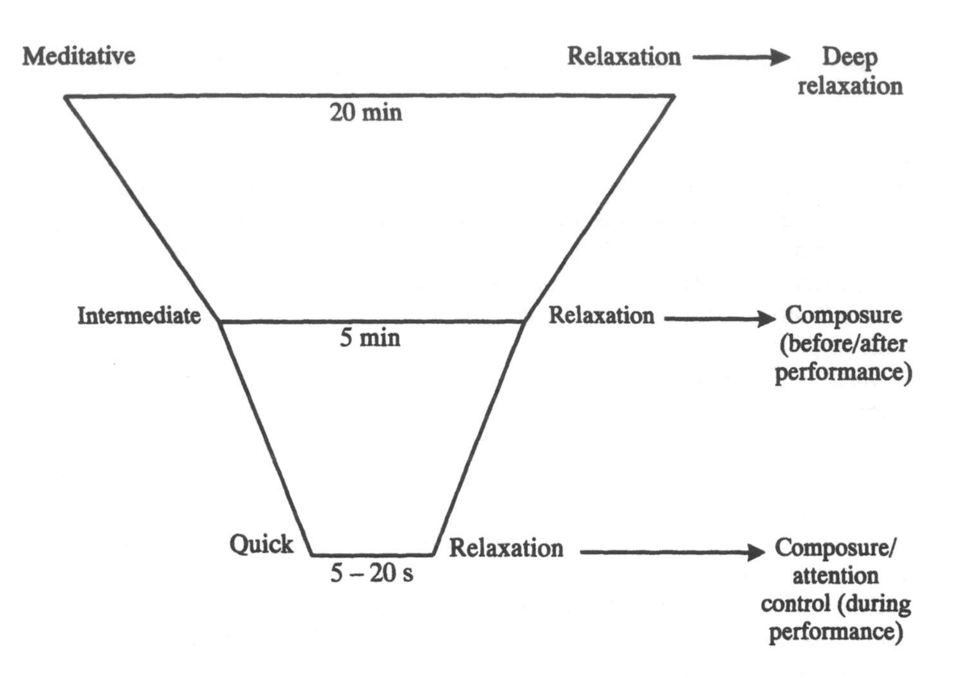

Figure 2.2: Three forms of meditation for use in sport (modified from Jones, 1993 with permission)

The gymnast James May, 1990 Commonwealth Games Gold Medal winner in the men's vault, described his use of meditative relaxation:

> *The relaxation technique that I have adopted over the past year is a mantra-type. I count down from three to zero and when I get to zero I can produce a calmer approach. I use that, say, if I have got to stand there and wait around for the judges and I feel a rush of nervousness that's too much. (Jones and Hardy, 1990a; p. 261)*

Research findings from investigations of meditation effects upon performance are relatively scarce and, as in the case of progressive muscular relaxation, have examined general techniques as opposed to the sport-specific one advocated by Jones (1993). Nevertheless, the available studies suggest that meditation may have a facilitative effect upon gross motor skills. Reddy *et al.*'s (1976) study showed that, when compared to a control group, athletes who meditated for twenty minutes a day during a six-week athletic conditioning programme showed significantly greater improvements in sprinting, agility, standing broad jump, and reaction time tasks. The meditators also showed greater improvements on cardiovascular and respiratory efficiency, systolic and diastolic blood pressure, and haemoglobin. Studies which have examined meditative relaxation effects on fine motor skills, on the other hand, have generally proved inconclusive (e.g. Williams, 1978; Williams *et al.*, 1977). A limitation with research on the use of meditative relaxation in sport is that it has generally been restricted to examining performance and physiological responses. Future researchers should focus more on examining the effects of this type of relaxation on the anxiety response.

The categorisation of techniques into mental and physical relaxation techniques is important in the context of treating different forms of anxiety. Basically, the anxiety response can be divided into at least two components: *cognitive anxiety* and *somatic anxiety* (Davidson and Schwartz, 1976; Liebert and Morris, 1967). Cognitive anxiety was defined by Morris *et al.* (1981) as "the cognitive elements of anxiety, such as negative expectations and cognitive concerns about oneself, the situation at hand and potential consequences" (p. 541); somatic anxiety was defined as "one's perception of the physiological–affective elements of the anxiety experience, that is, indications of autonomic arousal and unpleasant feeling states such as nervousness and tension". (p. 541) In examining relaxation intervention studies, Davidson and Schwartz (1976) suggested that certain types of relaxation technique seem to work better for specific types of anxiety. They therefore concluded that the relaxation treatment should be matched with the form of anxiety experienced; specifically, cognitive anxiety should be treated with a mental relaxation technique, and somatic anxiety should be treated with a physical relaxation technique. This recommendation is commonly known as the *matching hypothesis*.

The model that Davidson and Schwartz proposed also incorporated empirical research on the psychophysiological concomitants of the two anxiety components (e.g. Goleman, 1971) with the hemispheric specialisation literature indicating differential mediation of cognitive and somatic behaviour (e.g. Bogen, 1969; Kimura, 1973). Literature examining hemispheric lateralisation suggests that for most right-handed or mixed dominant individuals, the left hemisphere may be the site of sequential processing, verbalisation, logical reasoning, and problem-solving. The right hemisphere, on the other hand, is responsible for vision, spatial awareness, parallel processing, and performing automatically and intuitively (see, for example, Blakeslee, 1980; Davidson and Schwartz, 1976). On this basis, Davidson and Schwartz (1976) proposed that there are at least four types of anxiety that can be experienced: left hemisphere cognitive anxiety; left hemisphere somatic anxiety; right hemisphere cognitive anxiety; and right hemisphere somatic anxiety. These are depicted in the model in Table 2.1, together with suggested techniques for dealing with each type of anxiety.

Research examining the "matching hypothesis" has shown limited support for the basic tenets underlying it (e.g. Maynard and Cotton, 1993;

Table 2.1: Multimodal stress management model (modified from Burton, 1990 with permission)

	Left hemisphere		Right hemisphere	
	Anxiety problem	Intervention strategy	Anxiety problem	Intervention strategy
Cognitive anxiety	Sequential activation of verbal or analytical behaviours e.g. over-analysis or specific negative thoughts	Transcendental meditation Goal-setting Self-talk ● cue words ● counter-arguments Hypnosis—suggestion component	Parallel activation of multiple imagery/spatial behaviours e.g. automated images of disaster	Hypnosis—imagery/suggestion component Cognitive restructuring techniques that focus on changing self-images
Somatic anxiety	Sequential activation of specific somatic behaviour e.g. tension in specific muscles	Physical relaxation techniques EMG biofeedback Hypnosis—relaxation component Exercise/stretching	Parallel activation of global somatic behaviours e.g. butterflies in the stomach and cold, clammy hands	Zen meditation Hatha yoga breathing component Autogenic training Biofeedback ● skin temperature ● skin conductance

Maynard, Hemmings and Warwick-Evans, 1995; Maynard *et al.*, 1995b; Schwartz *et al.*, 1978), although Landers (1994) was quite critical of the hypothesis. However, his citation of one unpublished study which did not support the hypothesis is far from convincing evidence on which to refute the model. Admittedly, the basic model is probably too rigid in its prediction, since it appears that there are cross-over effects between the various forms of relaxation and their effects upon different forms of anxiety (Maynard *et al.*, 1995a; Maynard, Smith and Warwick-Evans, 1995). In the same way, cross-over effects have been reported in studies which have examined the effects of competitive anxiety upon performance, so that it is not merely a case of cognitive anxiety influencing the performance of cognitive tasks, and somatic anxiety affecting the performance of motor tasks (see Parfitt *et al.*, 1990). This led Burton (1990) to propose that a more appropriate approach was to use a multimodal stress management model which taught performers component parts to deal with multiple types of anxiety simultaneously.

A number of *multimodal stress management packages* are available and have been applied to sport. However, Burton (1990) argued that only two of them fulfil the major requirements of (a) alleviating both cognitive and somatic anxiety, and (b) providing systematic strategies for the rehearsal of coping procedures under simulated stressful conditions. These are stress inoculation training (Meichenbaum, 1975) and cognitive affective stress management (Smith, R.E., 1980). Both include training in relaxation skills combined with other skills such as imagery and positive self-talk (see Burton, 1990; Mace, 1990). A third package which has proved popular in sport is visuo-motor behaviour rehearsal (Suinn, 1972a, b). This combines imagery with physical relaxation. These three packages have received significant research attention in the sport psychology literature (e.g. Crocker *et al.*, 1988; Hall and Erffmeyer, 1983; Mace and Carroll, 1985). However, this attention to the combined effects of discrete treatments presents interpretational problems in evaluating the separate effects of relaxation (Neiss, 1988a).

Summary

The ability to relax is recognised at a practical level as an important aspect of achieving optimal performance in sport. Elite athletes generally appear to have developed strategies for achieving relaxed states in a "trial and error", almost instinctive, manner. However, a significant number of elite athletes have also benefited from a structured educational programme of relaxation training (cf. Jones, 1993).

The relative paucity of empirical investigations which have effectively isolated and examined the efficacy of different relaxation techniques in sport means that, at least at the research level, little is known about: (1) the specific effects of relaxation; and (2) the processes which underlie any beneficial effects. Indeed, several other limitations of relaxation-based intervention research have been identified, including: the inability to infer causal relationships between relaxation and performance (Greenspan and Feltz, 1989); the infrequent use of manipulation checks (Zaichowsky and Fuchs, 1988); and the failure to assess the long-term benefits of relaxation via retention tests (Gould and Udry, 1994). Gould and Udry (1994) have also emphasised the need for future researchers to examine the effects of relaxation on possible mediating variables, such as mastery and self-efficacy.

GOAL-SETTING

The following quote from a top collegiate tennis player in the United States emphasises the crucial importance of setting goals in sport:

> *The coach must have goals. The team must have goals—real, vivid, living goals . . . Goals keep everyone on target. Goals commit me to the work, time, pain and whatever else is part of the price of achieving success.* (Weinberg, 1988, p. 145)

Bell (1983) echoed such sentiments:

> *Floundering in the world of sports without setting goals is like shooting without aiming. You might enjoy the blast and kick of the gun, but you probably won't bag the bird.* (p. 64)

Goals have generally been viewed in very simple terms as "what an individual is trying to accomplish; it is the object or aim of an action" (Locke *et al.*, 1981, p.126). When used appropriately, goals set specific standards which are hypothesised to ". . . motivate individuals to take direct action by focusing attention, increasing effort and intensity, prompting development of new problem-solving strategies, and/or encouraging persistence in the face of failure" (Burton, 1992, p. 269).

Goal-setting as a motivational approach to enhancing task performance is one of the most thoroughly researched areas in *management and organisational environments* (see Locke and Latham, 1990). One of the earliest researchers to conduct detailed empirical work was Locke (1966, 1968). His programme of research laid the foundations for much of the subsequent research, both pure and applied, into the effects of goal-setting. His two major premises were that: (1) specific goals lead to higher performance than do general goals, "do your best" instructions, or no goals at all; and (2) difficult goals (if accepted) lead to a higher level of task performance than do easy goals. Goal proximity is also a major factor since short-term goals plus long-term goals have been shown to lead to better performance than long-term goals alone (Locke and Latham, 1985). Short-term goals are deemed to be particularly effective since they provide immediate incentives and feedback (Bandura, 1982; Carver and Scheier, 1982), and because the attainment of sub-goals provides indicators of mastery which will lead to enhanced confidence (Weinberg, 1993). Much of the research involving goal-setting in management and organisational environments has been described elsewhere in both traditional narrative reviews (Latham and Yukl, 1975; Locke, 1968; Locke *et al.*, 1981), and meta-analytic studies (Chidester and Grigsby, 1984; Locke *et al.*, 1980; Mento *et al.*, 1987; Tubbs, 1986). This work has consistently demonstrated that specific difficult goals have more beneficial effects upon performance than easy goals, no goals or "do your best" goals. Interested readers are directed to Locke and Latham (1990) for a detailed review and critique of this work.

Locke and Latham (1985) argued that the findings from organisational settings could be applied to the sport environment. They also suggested that more empirical tests of goal-setting should be undertaken within such settings. However, research into goal-setting within the sport psychology literature has provided somewhat equivocal findings. Some studies have provided support for Locke's (1968) proposals (Barnett and Stanicek, 1979; Burton, 1989a; Hall *et al.*, 1987; Tenenbaum *et al.*, 1991; Weinberg *et al.*, 1988). On the other hand, several investigators have reported no significant performance differences between specific difficult goals and "do your best" goals (Barnett, 1977; Hollingsworth, 1975; Weinberg *et al.*, 1985, 1987, 1990, 1991).

Locke (1991) addressed the issue of why established findings in other environments have not been replicated more convincingly within the *sporting environment*. He attributed this situation to methodological flaws in the sport psychology literature, and to three major problems in particular. First, he argued that "do your best" conditions have largely been contaminated by subjects setting their own specific goals. This situation is exacerbated in studies which have tested subjects in groups, in which competition and social comparison cause subjects who are assigned "do your best" instructions to begin setting goals (Hall and Byrne, 1988). Second, Locke emphasised a general failure to measure personal goals, assuming that some subjects will ignore externally assigned goals and will set their own covert goals. Third, he suggested that in many studies, the specific goals have not been sufficiently difficult to induce different levels of performance compared to "do your best" goals. Whilst acknowledging some of Locke's (1991) criticisms, Weinberg and Weigand (1993) provided counterarguments which suggested that methodological flaws are only partly responsible for differences in findings between the organisational and sport literatures. Weinberg and Weigand proposed, instead, that other factors such as the type of task and individual differences in motivation should be considered as important variables in helping to explain the discrepancy in findings from the different environments:

> *For example, subjects in many of the goal setting studies in sport and exercise voluntarily chose to be in specific physical activity classes or activities; thus, their motivation to perform physical fitness tasks (e.g. sit-ups) would be expected to be higher than subjects performing ordinary tasks in the industrial area (e.g. typing, card sorting, letter cancellation).* (p. 89)

Another, related factor is the proposal that athletes are operating closer to their performance potential than subjects examined in industrial settings (Burton, 1993). Studies in the sport domain which have failed to find significant goal-setting effects have included performance measures such as sit-ups (e.g. Weinberg *et al.*, 1985) and basketball free throw shooting

(Miller and McAuley, 1987). Locke and Latham's (1990) argument that the goal effectiveness curve reaches a plateau as individuals approach the limits of their ability would appear to be particularly salient to such performance tasks (see Burton, 1993).

Hall and Byrne (1988) earlier suggested that, in order to understand why the contradictions in the sport psychology literature had occurred, "... it is essential that we better understand the underlying processes" (p.185). Considerable attention has been directed towards understanding why and how goal-setting should produce enhanced task performance in organisational settings. Following the recommendations of Locke *et al.* (1981), several investigators have attempted to examine the theoretical framework underlying goal-setting. Erez and Zidon (1984) were among the first to examine the processes involved in such a framework. They investigated two processes which have been shown to be related to performance: *goal acceptance* and *goal difficulty* (Locke *et al.*, 1981). Erez and Zidon's examination of the hypothesis that goal acceptance moderates the relationship between goal difficulty and task performance showed that, when goals were accepted, the relationship between difficulty and performance was positive and linear, but that it changed to being negative and linear when goals were rejected.

In an earlier study investigating the relationship between goal acceptance and performance, Stedry and Kay (1966) suggested the existence of another process, *effort*, as being important in goal-setting. They suggested that a maximum tolerance level existed for the discrepancy between present and future goal difficulty. Within the tolerance limits, an increase in difficulty is followed by an increase in effort and hence performance but, beyond such a limit, further increases in difficulty have negative effects upon effort. In other words, if the future goal is perceived as difficult but attainable, increases in goal difficulty will be met with increases in effort. However, once the goal is perceived as too difficult, a reduction in effort will occur. Interestingly, Locke and Latham (1990) and Locke (1991) have since emphasised the importance of measuring self-efficacy (Bandura, 1977; see also Chapter 3) in goal-setting research, arguing that self-efficacy predicts goal choice, goal commitment, and performance. Locke and Latham (1990) recommended that future research should examine both magnitude and strength of self-efficacy since both have been shown to contribute to performance prediction (Locke *et al.*, 1984).

This work on perceived difficulty, goal acceptance, and effort, supports Locke and Latham's (1985) proposal that goals should be difficult and realistic to produce maximum performance benefits, but that unrealistic goals should be avoided since performance will drop off as a function of reduced motivation and effort. However, Garland (1983) questioned the goal attainability assumption on the basis that laboratory-based studies have generally shown monotonically positive relationships between goal difficulty and performance, even in the case of unattainable goals. Studies in the sport psychology literature which have examined performance as a function of specific goal difficulty levels have also generally failed to find performance decrements as goal difficulty increases beyond realistic levels of attainment (Weinberg *et al.*, 1987, 1990, 1991). Such findings might, at least in part, be explained via an examination of *task characteristics* in goal-setting research. Much of the work on goal-setting in the sport psychology literature has investigated relatively simple tasks, or performers who have been relatively skilled at the performance tasks under scrutiny. Wood *et al.*'s (1987) meta-analysis of the organisational literature showed that the attentional, effort, and persistence benefits of goals have a more direct effect on simple tasks, whereas more complex tasks require effective strategy development to occur before the motivational effects of goals can benefit performance. Within the sport psychology literature, Burton (1989b) similarly found some evidence suggesting that specific goals resulted in performance improvement in simple, but not complex, basketball tasks. Thus, it appears that the motivational benefits are greater upon simple tasks, possibly accounting for the failure to detect performance decrements in unattainable goal conditions. Such decrements would appear more likely to occur in situations where the performance task is complex.

The relatively inconsistent findings within the sport psychology literature have largely emanated from *experimental designs* in which a primary concern has been the rigorous control of key variables using tasks of relatively low ecological validity. Whilst such research has shed *some* light on the influence of key mediating variables, a natural side effect of this experimental focus has been the limited attention devoted to the application of goal-setting training programmes designed to enhance performance. However, the late 1980s witnessed some attempts to improve upon *ecological validity* by involving competitive athletes in competitive situations. Burton (1989a) conducted a field study investigating the effectiveness of a goal-setting training programme over the course of a season for a university swimming team. Findings indicated that swimmers who participated in the training programme demonstrated better performance than those who did not. Anderson *et al.* (1988) examined the interventions of publicly posted performance feedback, goal-setting, and praise as part of a behavioural management intervention package aimed at increasing the rate of legal body checking in a university ice hockey team. An on-the-baseline within-subjects procedure, which permitted a components analysis of the respective contribution of each treatment, revealed that goal-setting was associated with improvement. However, the findings also emphasised the importance of feedback as a moderator of goal-setting effects. Stitcher's (1989) study involved assigning members of a lacrosse team to either a goal-setting group or a "do your best" control group for different aspects of performance during a season. There were no statistically significant differences between the groups, but the mean difference indicated the superiority of the goal-setting group from a practical point of view. More recently, Swain and Jones (1995) used a single subject multiple baseline design to examine goal-setting in a sample of four university basketball players over 16 matches. The findings demonstrated positive consequences of goal-setting in three out of four targeted behaviours. Thus, although limited in quantity, the findings from the more applied and ecologically valid research on goal-setting in sport lead to the conclusion that goal-setting *is* a valuable tool for sports performers.

It is important to note, however, that when used improperly *goals can actually be dysfunctional* and a major source of stress (Beggs, 1990; Burton, 1989a, 1992; Earley *et al.*, 1989; Jones and Cale, in press). Although this notion has received little research attention in the sport psychology literature, there are a couple of studies which have provided interesting findings. Jones *et al.* (1990) identified what is a potentially interesting relationship between goal-setting and multidimensional competitive state anxiety. Jones, Swain and Cale examined the situational antecedents of competitive state anxiety in a sample of elite intercollegiate middle-distance runners. Their findings showed that the greater the difficulty of the pre-race goals set by the athletes and the lower their expectations of success, the higher the level of cognitive anxiety and the lower the level of self-confidence. However, the goal-setting variables did not affect somatic anxiety. This latter finding was not necessarily unexpected since cognitive anxiety and self-confidence have been predicted to be much more closely related to performance expectations than is somatic anxiety (Bandura, 1977; Martens *et al.*, 1990a; Morris *et al.*, 1981). In a second study in this area, Hardy *et al.* (1986) investigated levels of goal acceptance and performance on an ecologically valid sports task performed under two different conditions; first, in a low anxiety practice situation, and second, immediately before an important competition (i.e. high anxiety). Increases in cognitive and somatic anxiety were accompanied by a reduction in goal acceptance and a corresponding reduction in performance, leading Hardy and his co-workers to conclude that anxiety reduced the subjects' perceptions of their ability to achieve goals which they had previously accepted and achieved in low anxiety conditions. These are interesting findings with potentially important practical implications for goal difficulty levels assigned in high pressure competitive situations. However, further research is required in this area before firm conclusions can be drawn.

It is important to distinguish between at least three different types of goal that have been identified in the applied literature (Burton, 1989a; Hardy and Fazey, 1986; Hardy and Jones, 1994b; Hardy and Nelson, 1988). *Outcome goals* focus upon the outcomes of particular events and usually (but not always) involve interpersonal comparison of some kind; for example, finishing a 400-metre hurdles race in first place. *Performance goals* specify an end product of performance that will be achieved by the performer relatively independently of other performers; for example, running a race in a certain time. *Process goals* specify the processes in which the performer will engage during the performance; for example, maintaining a good lead leg technique over each hurdle. It is important to note that athletes will often set more than one type of goal for a particular event. Jones and Hanton's (1996) study of 91 swimmers showed that the vast majority of the sample set at least two types of goal, with nearly half setting a combination of all three types. Interestingly, none of the swimmers set outcome goals only. It is also important to recognise that different goals may be more salient at different times. Process-oriented goals are likely to be more prominent in training; outcome and performance goals, on the other hand, are likely to be more prominent before and during competition (cf. Burton, 1993).

Whilst outcome goals may possess great motivational value for performers in the short term, Roberts (1986) and others have argued that, ultimately, such goals are likely to lead performers to drop out from sport. Burton (1989a) has also shown that outcome goals are associated with higher levels of competitive state anxiety than are performance goals. Consequently, sports performers are usually encouraged to set performance, rather than, or at least in conjunction with, outcome goals (Gould, 1993a). So far, little research has been carried out on process-oriented goals, but Hardy and Nelson (1988) have suggested that they may exert their influence upon performance via the allocation of attentional resources. Recent findings reported by Kingston and Hardy (1994a) showed that golfers trained in the use of process-oriented goals were able to concentrate better, had increased self-efficacy, and were more able to control negative expectations than golfers trained in the use of performance goals. The process-oriented golfers also achieved significant reductions in their handicaps over a period of five months.

A further factor to consider in the goal-setting-performance relationship is that of *goal proximity*. This involves breaking long-term goals down into short-term goals, with feedback being available to the performer regarding goal achievement. Employed in this way, short-term goals should produce the more substantial and enduring self-regulated behavioural change (Bandura, 1982; Carver and Scheier, 1982). Unfortunately, this area has received little systematic research attention in the sport psychology literature. Two studies by Weinberg and colleagues (Weinberg *et al.*, 1985, 1988) showed no effects of setting short-term and long-term goals upon performance of a sit-up task. However, Hall and Byrne (1988) showed that subjects in a weight-lifting class who were set long-term and intermediate goals performed better than subjects who were set "do your best" goals; although the performance of subjects who were only set long-term goals did not differ from those in the "do your best" condition. Frierman *et al.*'s (1990) study of bowling performance over a five week period showed that the long-term goal group improved significantly more than the "do your best" group; however, no significant differences were revealed between the "do your best" and short-term goals groups. Finally, Tenenbaum *et al.* (1991) found sit-up performance over a ten week programme to be significantly improved by short-term and long-term goals when compared to a "do your best" condition. Importantly, the combined short-term and long-term goals condition produced the greatest improvements in performance when compared to short-term goals only and long-term goals only conditions. Although the empirical support to date is inconsistent, the intuitive sense in breaking long-term goals into intermediate and short-term goals is well documented in the applied literature (e.g. Bell, 1983; Gould, 1993a; Harris and Harris, 1984).

An important area within goal-setting which has thus far failed to attract research attention in the sport domain is that of *goal collectivity*. Research in the organisational literature has shown that group goals can be an important source of performance enhancement (Carroll, 1986; Locke and Latham, 1990). The literature on social loafing is important here. "Social loafing" refers to situations in which individuals working together on the same task exert less effort than when they perform the task alone (Jackson and Williams, 1985). Research findings have demonstrated that social loafing is reduced when individual efforts are identifiable (Williams *et al.*, 1981), and when individual performers perceive that they have made a unique contribution to the group's effort and performance (Harkins and Petty, 1982). Thus, setting group goals without setting accompanying individual goals may result in social loafing and sub-optimal performance (Burton, 1993). However, this prediction requires empirical investigation within the sport domain.

Summary

Goal-setting is an extremely important strategy employed in sport and it has been a prominent topic in the popular applied sport psychology literature. Several important practical implications for the use of goal-setting techniques in sport have been identified in this literature. In particular, goals should identify specific targets that lie within performers' control, that they are committed to, and that they perceive to be realistic and worthwhile. Furthermore, long-term goals should be broken down into short-term goals, with feedback being available to the performer regarding goal achievement. Unfortunately, goal-setting has been relatively under-researched in the more academically oriented sport psychology literature (Burton, 1993; Weinberg, 1994). Furthermore, the research which has been conducted in this area tends to provide rather unconvincing support for some of the practical implications just outlined. An important factor in this research has been the proliferation of design weaknesses and problems. Nevertheless, one important finding to emerge from this work is that setting goals does not always have benefits; in fact, goals can be dysfunctional (Burton, 1989a; Jones and Cale, in press). Further research is required to examine the notion of functional and dysfunctional goals in sport. This should be linked with the notion that athletes use several different types of goal. Examination of the effects of outcome, performance, and process goals upon cognitive and affect variables, as well as performance, could form the basis of this research. Finally, the notion of collective goals in team settings requires systematic investigation.

IMAGERY AND MENTAL REHEARSAL

Imagery forms a major component of every sports performer's preparation for performance. For some performers, imagery will be relatively unstructured and without appearing to serve any specific purpose; they "just do it" and may not be able to verbalise about the specific content of their imagery. For others, the use of imagery will be very structured and will be practised to satisfy a variety of needs, such as building confidence, enabling relaxation, learning new skills, focusing attention, etc. Elite performers report using imagery extensively and to great effect (e.g. Jones and Hardy, 1990a; Orlick and Partington, 1988). For example, a highly successful Olympic swimmer interviewed by Orlick and Partington (1988) stated:

> *I started visualizing in 1978. My visualization has been refined more and more as the years go on. That is really what got me the world record and the Olympic medals. I see myself swimming the race before the race really happens, and I try to be on the splits. I concentrate on attaining the splits I have set out to do. About 15 minutes before the race I always visualize the race in my mind and "see" how it will go . . . You are really swimming the race. You are visualizing it from behind the block. In my mind, I go up and down the pool, rehearsing all parts of the race, visualizing how I actually feel in the water.* (pp. 118–119)

Indeed, Orlick and Partington (1988) reported that 99 per cent of their sample of 235 athletes used imagery. Murphy (1994) reported findings from a survey of athletes training at the US Olympic Training Centre which showed that 90 per cent of them used imagery for training and competition, and 94 per cent of coaches used it with their athletes. Elite athletes have also been reported as being more proficient at imagery than non-elite performers (Hall *et al.*, 1991; Mahoney *et al.*, 1987). This section briefly examines the performance related effects of imagery and mental rehearsal, factors which mediate their effectiveness, and theoretical explanations of their effects.

There are several recent and very good critiques of the literature on imagery pertaining to sport (e.g. Murphy, 1990, 1994; Murphy and Jowdy, 1992). Unlike some previous researchers in the area, they have been very careful to distinguish between imagery and mental rehearsal rather than to use them synonymously. Imagery can be defined as a symbolic sensory experience that may occur in any sensory mode. Richardson (1969) referred to imagery as an awareness of quasi-sensory and quasi-perceptual experiences under conditions where the actual stimuli that produce the real sensorial and perceptual experiences are absent. As such, imagery is a mental process (Murphy and Jowdy, 1992) or a mode of thought (Heil, 1985). Mental rehearsal, on the other hand, is defined here as the employment of imagery to mentally practise an act. Thus, mental rehearsal is a *technique* as opposed to merely a *mental process*.

Major reviews of the mental rehearsal literature in the early 1980s (Feltz and Landers, 1983; Weinberg, 1981) suggested that there are three findings which appear to be robust: (1) mental rehearsal is better than no practice at all; (2) mental rehearsal combined with physical practice is more effective than either alone; and (3) the effects of mental rehearsal are greater for cognitive than for motor tasks. Some findings have also shown that the effects of mental rehearsal are greater when it is accompanied by the *physical simulation* of the target acts (Meacci and Price, 1985; Ross, 1985). This implies that a golfer's mental rehearsal of a seven-iron shot, for example, would be most effective if the rehearsal also involved physical simulation of the actual swing. Another factor which appears to be potentially important in determining the effectiveness of mental rehearsal is the *temporal pacing* of the imagery used in the rehearsal. However, this area has been virtually ignored in the research literature; only one study to date by Andre and Means (1986) has examined the pacing aspect of mental rehearsal. They reported no difference between slow motion and normal speed mental rehearsal.

Other variables which have been identified as mediating the effects of mental rehearsal include imagery ability, imagery perspective, and imagery outcome (Murphy and Jowdy, 1992). *Imagery ability* is commonly thought of in terms of performers' ability to form *vivid* images and also to *control* their images. However, the two skills do not necessarily go "hand-in-hand". For example, just prior to competing, an ice skater may be able to form very vivid images of herself performing a triple salco, but may not be able to control them, so that she imagines herself falling each time. Imagery ability has been found to influence the effects of mental rehearsal upon performance (e.g. Goss *et al.*, 1986; Housner, 1984; Ryan and Simons, 1982; Start and Richardson, 1964), and it also appears to be an important factor in distinguishing between elite and non-elite, and successful and less successful sports performers (Highlen and Bennett, 1983; Meyers *et al.*, 1979; Orlick and Partington, 1988). However, Orlick and Partington (1988) concluded that elite athletes have had to learn to image successfully and, initially, often do not have good control over their imagery. The quote below from a highly successful Olympic springboard diver illustrates how mental imagery skill is acquired through persistent daily practice:

> *It took me a long time to control my images and perfect my imagery, maybe a year, doing it every day. At first I couldn't see myself, I always saw everyone else, or I would see my dives wrong all the time. I would get an image of hurting myself, or tripping on the board, or I would "see" something done really bad. As I continued to work at it, I got to the point where I could see myself doing a perfect dive and the crowd yelling at the Olympics. But it took me a long time. I read everything I had to do and I knew my dive by heart. Then I started to see myself on the board doing my perfect dive. But some days I couldn't see it, or it was a bad dive in my head. I worked at it so much it got to the point that I could do all my dives easily.*
> (Orlick and Partington, 1988; p. 114)

Precisely how elite athletes learn and develop imagery skills is an important question for future researchers.

Imagery perspective refers to the basic distinction between "internal" and "external" imagery which Mahoney and Avener (1977) described as follows: "in external imagery, a person views himself from the perspective of an external observer . . . Internal imagery, on the other hand, requires an approximation of the real life phenomenology such that the person actually imagines being inside his/her body and experiencing those sensations which might be expected in the actual situation" (p. 137). A number of researchers have promoted the belief that internal imagery is superior since it closely allies the perceptual and kinaesthetic experience of performing in vivo (Corbin, 1972; Lane, 1980; Suinn, 1983; Vealey, 1986). Studies by Mahoney and Avener (1977), Rotella *et al.* (1980), and Mahoney *et al.* (1987) revealed that successful athletes adopted an internal imagery perspective to a greater extent than external imagery, although Meyers *et al.* (1979) failed to replicate this finding. Researchers adopting experimental designs to examine the relationship between imagery perspective and performance have generally failed to find differential effects (e.g. Epstein, 1980; Mumford and Hall, 1985). As Murphy and Jowdy (1992) and Murphy (1994) stated, the evidence in favour of internal imagery is far from conclusive, but this line of research may actually be relatively futile anyway, since it appears that performers often use a combination of imagery perspectives during mental rehearsal (Jowdy *et al.*, 1989). For example, a successful Olympic rhythmic gymnast interviewed in Orlick and Partington's (1988) study stated:

> *Sometimes you look at it from a camera view, but most of the time I look at it as what I see from within, because that's the way it's going to be in competition.* (p. 114)

Murphy (1994) suggested that researchers might be better advised to examine possible differential effects of internal and external imagery on factors such as confidence, or on identification of technique mistakes.

Fortunately, recent research by White and Hardy (1995) has clarified the position somewhat. They argued that much of the confusion that exists in the literature has arisen because researchers have not differentiated clearly enough between internal visual imagery and kinaesthetic imagery. In particular, Mahoney and Avener (1977) used the statement "when I am preparing to perform, I try to imagine what it will feel like in my muscles" as a measure of internal perspective imagery. Clearly, this statement does provide a measure of internal perspective imagery, but it does not provide the measure of internal *visual perspective* imagery which it was subsequently taken to imply. Nor is there any evidence in support of the common assumption that kinaesthetic imagery is easier to perform in conjunction with internal visual imagery as opposed to external visual imagery. In fact, White and Hardy (1995) showed that performers are capable of forming kinaesthetic images equally well with either visual perspective. They also showed that the nature of the task is an important variable which moderates the effects of internal and external visual imagery upon performance. More precisely, they found that internal visual imagery was more effective for a simulated canoe slalom task which required performers to make adjustments in response to changes in their visual field; but that external visual imagery was more effective for a simulated gymnastics task in which performance was judged according to technical execution (form). This latter finding has also been replicated by Hardy and Callow (1996).

A common recommendation made to sports performers by sport psychologists and coaches is to "think positive". Research findings in the *imagery outcome* area support the wisdom of this adage. Studies by Powell (1973) and Woolfolk *et al.* (1985b) found that mental rehearsal which involved negative outcomes degraded performance. Unfortunately, explanations for these findings have not proceeded much past the "educated guess" level and have generally concluded that negative outcome imagery may interfere with motor programmes. However, negative mental rehearsal is also likely to exert its influence via other mechanisms such as confidence and motivation (Murphy, 1994).

Paivio (1985) also proposed that different types of image might have different cognitive and motivational effects. For example, imaging a perfectly executed giant circle on rings may well enhance the activation of appropriate motor programmes in gymnastics, whilst imaging the crowd cheering as you stand on the winner's podium may well enhance performance via increased self-confidence and motivation. With this distinction in mind, Hall *et al.* (1996) devised the Sport Imagery Questionnaire to measure five different types of imagery: Cognitive General (e.g. imaging performance plans being executed successfully); Cognitive Specific (e.g. imaging specific skills being executed perfectly); Motivational General-Mastery (e.g. imaging staying focused when confronted by problems); Motivational General-Emotions (e.g. imaging the emotions that accompany major competitions); and Motivational Specific (e.g. imaging specific performance goals being achieved). Furthermore, using the Sport Imagery Questionnaire, Moritz *et al.* (1996) found that elite roller skaters who were highly confident prior to performing generally used more motivational mastery and emotional imagery than their less confident counterparts. Using the same subjects, Vadocz and Hall (in press) showed that the use of motivational mastery imagery was also associated with lower cognitive anxiety prior to performance. Thus, as Murphy (1994) observed, there is good reason to believe that imagery may well exert its influence upon performance via more than one mechanism. It will clearly need further research to unscramble the subtleties of these mechanisms, but Hall and associates' recent research is certainly suggestive that "what you see is what you get"; that is, performers become confident by imaging themselves being confident, not (necessarily) by imaging perfect performance.

It will be clear from the above discussion that much of the research literature on imagery effects is characterised by inconsistent findings. Furthermore, as Murphy (1990) has pointed out, this is at least partly attributable to inadequacies in the design of many studies. Murphy identified several *weaknesses in the research literature*, including:

1. Many studies have failed to describe the imagery intervention.
2. Relatively few studies have conducted manipulation checks to ensure that subjects performed the imagery intervention as instructed.
3. There is a paucity of adequate multidimensional assessment instruments.
4. Nomothetic designs have been employed in such a way that individual differences in imagery ability and style have been ignored.
5. There has been an over-emphasis on examining imagery effects upon performance at the expense of examining effects upon arousal control, motivation, confidence etc.
6. There has been a general failure to offer and examine theoretical explanations of imagery effects.

This final weakness is particularly evident in the sport psychology literature in which researchers have traditionally adopted a rather narrow perspective in debating the merits of only two theories of imagery effects:

psychoneuromuscular theory and symbolic learning theory. *Psychoneuromuscular theory* (Jacobson, 1930) suggests that during mental rehearsal the motor programme is actually loaded and run, but with "gain controls" turned down (Hardy and Wyatt, 1986). This results, it is claimed, in EMG activity which mirrors the EMG activity observed when the rehearsed movement is actually performed, but at a lower level of intensity. Unfortunately, most of the studies which might be used to test the theory have either lacked experimental control (e.g. Jacobson, 1930; Suinn, 1976), or have failed to demonstrate the appropriate patterns of action potentials during mental rehearsal (e.g. Hale, 1981; see Feltz and Landers, 1983).

The rival hypothesis debated in the sport psychology literature emanates from *symbolic learning theory* (Sackett, 1934). This theory argues that mental rehearsal allows the performer to rehearse the symbolic or cognitive aspects of the task; namely, task strategies, and the spatial and temporal sequencing of movements that is required. Thus, mental rehearsal should aid motor performance only to the extent that such cognitive factors play an important part in the task. For example, Schmidt (1975) has proposed that mental rehearsal should have a more pronounced effect during the early stages of motor learning when cognitive activity is more prevalent (Fitts, 1962). However, it should be noted that this proposal is directly contrary to previous conclusions that the efficacy of mental rehearsal is directly related to degree of familiarity with the task (e.g. Richardson, 1967).

The experimental studies which have tested symbolic learning theory have generally been supportive of it (e.g. Minas, 1980; Wrisberg and Ragsdale, 1979). Furthermore, the only published experimental study which has attempted to test symbolic learning theory against psychoneuromuscular theory (Johnson, 1982) also concluded in favour of the former. Murphy and Jowdy (1992) concurred that the available research does appear to support the notion of centrally based mechanisms in the effectiveness of mental rehearsal, as opposed to the peripherally based psychoneuromuscular hypothesis. However, Murphy and Jowdy also argued that symbolic learning theory is too simplistic and does not provide a rigorous explanation of where the beneficial effects actually occur. In response to this unsatisfactory situation, Murphy (1990) and Murphy and Jowdy (1992) have explored alternative explanations from the clinical area which have previously received little attention within the sport psychology literature. They have particularly focused on Lang's (1977, 1979, 1984) *bio-informational theory*.

Lang's model is an efferent-oriented view of imagery (Cuthbert *et al.*, 1991) and is based upon the assumption that an image is ". . . a functionally organised, finite set of propositions stored by the brain" (Murphy, 1990, p. 165). The model distinguishes between stimulus and response propositions. Stimulus propositions are statements that describe the content of the scenario to be imaged, and are sub-divided into two types of information (Lang, 1984). The first type of information includes the descriptive referents pertaining to elements of the external environment. In shooting a free throw in basketball, for example, stimulus information might include crowd noise, the sight of players around the key, the feel of the ball in the hands, etc. The second type of information involves semantic elaboration relevant to the event, such as "the game is important", "the score is tied", and "there are two seconds remaining" (Cuthbert *et al.*, 1991). Response propositions are statements that describe the imager's response to the particular scenario, and are designed to ". . . produce a relevant physiology during imagery" (Cuthbert *et al.*, 1991, p. 7). Responses might include those produced by somatomotor systems (e.g. limb flexion and eye movements) as well as autonomic activity (e.g. heart rate changes and muscle tension). Thus, responses in the free throw example might include a pounding heart, sweaty hands, etc., as well as the body movements involved in making the shot (Cuthbert *et al.*, 1991). The important practical implication of these proposals is that imagery scripts should include both stimulus and response propositions since this is more likely to create a vivid image than stimulus propositions alone (cf. Lang *et al.*, 1980). The proposal that imagery is accompanied by an efferent outflow which reflects the content of the image is evident in several psychophysiological studies (e.g. Hale, 1982; Lang, 1979; Lang *et al.*, 1983). Ahsen's (1972, 1984) *triple code model of imagery* is similar to that of Lang, but also includes a third essential aspect of imagery—the meaning of the image. "According to Ahsen, every image imparts a definite significance or meaning to the individual. Further, every individual brings his or her unique history into the imaging process, so that the same set of imagery instructions will never produce the same imagery experience for any two individuals" (Murphy, 1990, p. 167).

Summary

It is evident that imagery can be used to enhance athletic performance, but there is still relatively little known of the processes involved in imagery and mental rehearsal. An important factor here has been weaknesses in research designs which have also been rather constrained to addressing "does imagery work?" as opposed to "how and why does imagery work?" (Murphy, 1994). Theoretical perspectives have also been slow to develop. The sport psychology literature, in particular, has been devoid of any theoretical advances which might further our understanding, although the recent reviews by Murphy (1990) and Murphy and Jowdy (1992) will serve to broaden sport psychologists' theoretical horizons and hopefully stimulate quality research in the area. Such research should focus on establishing causal relationships and move away from correlational designs. In the mean time we are left with a rather mystical situation in that we know that imagery and mental rehearsal are often very effective, but we are unsure of why.

SELF-TALK

Bunker *et al.*'s (1993) view of the importance of self-talk in sport is captured in the following quote:

> *What athletes think or say is critical to performance. Unfortunately, the conscious mind is not always an ally. We all spend vast amounts of time talking to ourselves. Much of the time we are not even aware of this internal dialogue, much less its content. Nevertheless, thoughts directly affect feelings and ultimately actions. Inappropriate or misguided thinking usually leads to negative feelings and poor performance just as appropriate or positive thinking leads to enabling feelings and good performance.* (p. 225)

The importance of using positive self-talk is neatly captured in the following quote from an elite wrestler interviewed by Eklund *et al.* (1993) who reported using "... tons of positive self-talk" (p. 44), and further emphasised:

> *With everything that I'm thinking before the match—instead of thinking about anything else negative—I'm saying "o.k. what you gotta do is go out, you gotta move, you gotta get to the 'corner', you gotta stay on this guy for six minutes, go hard", telling myself, "I win" out loud so my subconscious gets it. Tell myself to win at all costs.* (Eklund *et al.*, 1993, p. 44)

Bunker *et al.* (1993) further stated that "the key to cognitive control is self-talk" (p. 226). This is not surprising given their conceptualisation of self-talk as "... anytime you think about something, you are in a sense talking to yourself" (p. 226). This all-embracing "thought content" definition reflects the often vague manner in which self-talk has been referred to in the sport psychology literature. However, Hackfort and Schwenkmezger (1993) have provided a more precise interpretation of self-talk:

> *In an internal dialogue, the individual interprets feelings and perceptions, regulates and changes evaluations and convictions, and gives him/herself instructions and reinforcement. As such, a central role is attached to language in the development of processes of thinking, and as thinking is part of actions (cf. Rubinstein, 1973), behavior can be modified by means of specific forms of external and internal talking.* (p. 355)

This interpretation emphasises the central role of language in the form of internal self-statements and dialogue. Thus, what athletes "say" to themselves is the central issue. However, as alluded to earlier, research in this area has not necessarily confined itself to self-statements, but has tended to adopt the more nebulous "thought content" approach.

Several researchers have shown that thought content and self-statements are important predictors of sports success (Klinger *et al.*, 1981; Mahoney and Avener, 1977; Orlick and Partington, 1988; Weinberg *et al.*, 1984). Mahoney and Avener's study, for example, found that the best discriminator of qualifiers and non-qualifiers for the US Olympic gymnastics team was the nature and content of their self-talk just prior to competition. Specifically, the successful gymnasts employed positive self-statements whilst the non-qualifiers exhibited negative self-talk. However, not all of the field-based, self-report research on self-talk is as enlightening. Rotella *et al.* (1980), for example, found that the content of more successful elite skiers' self-talk did not differ from less successful ones. Also, Highlen and Bennett (1983) reported elite divers as using less positive self-talk than their non-elite counterparts. The inconsistency in findings is further illustrated by Dagrou *et al.*'s (1991) report of athletes whose self-talk did not differ between their best and worst performances.

Findings from more experimental-based research have provided more convincing evidence of the efficacy of using positive self-talk (Van Raalte *et al.*, 1994). These generally indicate that negative self-talk is associated with worse performances (e.g. Dagrou *et al.*, 1992; Van Raalte, *et al.*, in press), whilst positive self-talk is prominent in better performances (e.g. Dagrou *et al.*, 1992; Johnston-O'Connor and Kirschenbaum, 1986; Van Raalte *et al.*, in press) when compared to control conditions. Recently, Van Raalte *et al.* (1994) have reported that negative self-talk by tennis players was associated with losing, and that players who reported believing in the utility of self-talk won more points than players who did not.

The precise reasons for the efficacy of positive self-talk are not known, although it seems likely that self-confidence (Feltz and Riessinger, 1990; Gould and Weiss, 1981; Wilkes and Summers, 1984) and anxiety control (Ellis, 1982; Mace and Carroll, 1986; Meichenbaum, 1977) are at least partially involved. Furthermore, despite the strong emphasis that mental training programmes often place upon the development of "appropriate" self-talk (see, for example, Kirschenbaum and Bale, 1984; Meyers and Schlesser, 1980; Rushall, 1984), relatively few controlled studies have been performed that would enable any sort of empirically based operationalisation of the word "appropriate" to be attempted. However, it is known that self-defeating self-statements have a negative effect upon performance (Rosin and Nelson, 1983; Rotella *et al.*, 1980); thought stopping techniques can be used to modify such statements (Meyers and Schlesser, 1980); self-statements can be used to trigger desired actions more effectively (Silva, 1982); and self-statements can be used to provide self-reward (Deci and Ryan, 1985). It is also thought that self-statements can be used to increase effort (Rushall, 1984), modify mood (Hardy and Fazey, 1990), control attention (Schmid and Peper, 1993), and aid the injury rehabilitation process (Ievleva and Orlick, 1991).

A common technique employed in altering self-statements is *cognitive restructuring*. The development of this approach is witnessed in the gradual shift in stance over the last 25 to 30 years towards a more cognitive approach by numerous clinical psychologists who formerly adopted behavioural techniques (Mace, 1990). Homme's (1965) work on *coverant control* provided a significant thrust since his technique involved the alteration of maladaptive thoughts by reinforcing alternative cognitions. Ellis' (1962, 1970) work on *rational emotive therapy* is another significant landmark. According to Ellis, irrational interpretations of objective reality are the fundamental cause of emotional disorders. Thus, it is important to recognise self-defeating irrational thoughts and to replace them with more constructive rational ones. Gould *et al.*'s (1993b) study of coping strategies, employed by elite figure skaters to deal with stress, highlighted this point. The skaters emphasised the importance of logically and rationally examining potential stressors, focusing on what could be controlled and viewing the stressor from a realistic perspective. A self-referenced focus was particularly prominent in this respect:

> *. . . I decided after our defeat that there was so much negativism going on, as far as judges and this and that and negative comments that I felt, "listen, if I want to skate, I have to skate, I have to do it for myself. I'm not out here to do it for anyone else but myself or for the USA. I am here to do it for myself. I've worked this hard". I kind of got angry about it and I think that's where my views changed.* (Gould *et al.*, 1993b; p. 456)

There are several variations of this type of approach. Meichenbaum's (1973) self-instructional training, for example, is focused on replacing anxiety-inducing cognitions with constructive problem-solving self-talk. Beck's (1970, 1976) work built on Ellis' basic premises in incorporating the concept of 'automatic thoughts', which can occur involuntarily when individuals think negatively. Again, the emphasis is on training individuals to become aware of such thoughts and employ effective coping strategies to replace them when they occur.

The importance of being able to identify inappropriate self-statements and thought patterns and restructure them is recognised as an important psychological skill in the applied sport psychology literature (e.g. Gould and Damarjian, in press; Jones, 1993; Weinberg, 1989b). Indeed, studies have shown that coaches, in particular, regard encouragement of the use of positive self-talk by their performers as being a very important component of their coaching style (Gould *et al.*, 1989; Weinberg and Jackson, 1990). However, employing positive self-talk is ultimately the responsibility of the performer who must be able to change negative statements into positive ones. This restructuring is referred to as 'countering' by Bunker *et al.* (1993).

Table 2.2: Changing negative self-talk to positive self-talk (modified from Bunker *et al.*, 1993 with permission)

Self-defeating thoughts	Change to self-enhancing thoughts
I can't believe it's raining. I have to play in the rain.	No one likes the rain, but I can play as well in it as anyone else.
You dumb jerk.	Ease off. Everyone makes mistakes. Shrug it off and put your mind on what you want to do.
There's no sense in practising. I have no natural talent.	I've seen good players who had to work hard to be successful. I can get better if I practise correctly.
This officiating stinks; we'll never win.	There's nothing we can do about the officiating so let's just concentrate on what we want to do. If we play well, the officiating won't matter.
Why did they foul me in the last minute of play? I'm so nervous. I'll probably choke and miss everything.	My heart is beating fast. That's OK, I've sunk free throws a hundred times. I'll take a deep breath to relax and then visualise the ball going in the basket "swish".
We'll win the meet only if I get a 9.0 on this routine.	Stop worrying about the score; just concentrate on how you're going to execute the routine.
The coach must think I'm hopeless. He never helps me.	That's not fair. He has a whole team to coach. Tomorrow I'll ask what he thinks I need to work on the most.
I don't want to fail.	Nothing was ever gained by being afraid to take risks. As long as I give my best, I'll never be a failure.
I'll take it easy today and go hard next workout.	The next workout will be easier if I go hard now.
Who cares how well I do anyway?	I care, and I'll be happier if I push myself.
This hurts; I don't know if it's worth it.	Of course it hurts, but the rewards are worth it.

Table 2.2 provides examples of how Bunker, Williams and Zinsser suggested that negative self-statements might be changed into positive ones by sports performers.

Summary

Given the important role of self-talk in sports performance, the amount of systematic research in this area is rather disappointing, but not surprising considering the obvious difficulties in carrying out empirical work in the area. A fundamental issue to be addressed in this area is precisely what constitutes self-talk. Past researchers have been too "loose" in their operationalization of self-talk; a debate and consensus over definitions is required. Amongst the issues which then need to be addressed are: the development of techniques for collecting and analysing self-statements in sports situations; the use of self-statements to cue psychological skills such as anxiety and attention control; the development of techniques for training athletes to use self-statements appropriately; and examination of the length of training required to bring about the habitual use of appropriate self-statements.

IMPLICATIONS FOR RESEARCH

Many of the research questions regarding the four basic psychological skills under scrutiny in this chapter actually relate to the advanced psychological skills addressed in later chapters in this book. Consequently, this section will consider only those questions relating to the basic principles underlying their effects.

Relaxation

The first observation that can be made about research into relaxation in sport is that there has been little of it. Of this scant amount, the majority has focused upon examining physical relaxation effects, or relaxation techniques which are incorporated within general stress management packages. More research is required which attempts to isolate relaxation effects from other components of these packages, and this research should examine mental as well as physical techniques. Causal effects of relaxation upon performance, cognitions, and affect, should be the focus of this research. Indeed, understanding the processes which underlie any relaxation effects should be an important goal of researchers in this area.

The matching hypothesis requires further examination, and researchers may wish to investigate whether some forms of relaxation are more suited to certain types of sport/task than others. The long-term benefits of practising relaxation is another question which begs attention. Linked to this is the issue of how relaxation techniques are best taught to athletes.

Goal-setting

Despite the fact that goal-setting is a topic which assumes a prominent position within the popular applied sport psychology literature, it remains relatively under-researched. Much of the sport psychology literature on goal-setting over the last few years has addressed the issue of why the findings from organisational and sport settings generally fail to "match-up".

Perhaps too much attention has been devoted to this issue, since the two contexts are clearly quite different and there is no reason to expect that findings from one should generalise to the other. Too much emphasis has been placed on experimentally based studies which attempt to control numerous variables in a manner which only hopes to replicate the findings from organisational settings, rather than understanding the processes involved in the "real" sport environment. Indeed, the more ecologically valid research on goal-setting in sport demonstrates its efficacy. More research of this type is required using elite performers to provide an important insight into the processes which underlie the effects of goal-setting.

One important issue which needs to be addressed regards goal proximity. The findings to date are inconsistent, but future research in this area should be carried out in the field. Another important question regards the use of different types of goal (i.e. outcome, performance, and process) and their relative effects upon performance, cognitions, and affect. Coaches' use of such goals would be an interesting line of research to pursue. Finally, the notion of dysfunctional goals and their antecedents is an area which requires urgent attention, since dysfunctional goal-setting probably occurs in sport more often than one would care to imagine.

Imagery and mental rehearsal

Future directions for research in the imagery and mental rehearsal area have already been expounded in recent critiques elsewhere (e.g. Murphy, 1990, 1994; Murphy and Jowdy, 1992). The overwhelming conclusion from this work is that we actually know very little about how imagery works. Since researchers in other areas of psychology have so far failed to unravel the "mystery", it appears unlikely that such a young academic discipline as sport psychology will contribute any dramatic advances in our knowledge in the short term.

However, there remain numerous practical issues which need to be addressed. Prominent amongst them is adopting research designs which allow causal rather than correlational relationships to be investigated. More idiographic approaches may offer some possibilities here. Researchers also need to devote more attention to examining imagery effects on cognitions and affect, rather than concentrating on performance as the dependent variable. Valid multidimensional assessment instruments should also be developed for use in research in the sport domain. Explicit methodological recommendations for future researchers have been provided by Murphy (1994), including: providing complete descriptions of imagery scripts employed; employing manipulation checks; assessing individual differences in imagery ability; and using psychophysiological methodologies.

In terms of how to implement imagery strategies with athletes, we need to know more about appropriate pacing or speed of mental rehearsal, and whether physical simulation produces more beneficial effects across all types of task, or whether these effects are unique to certain types of movement. Numerous issues emerge in the context of internal and external visual imagery. The issue most often raised relates to a comparison of effects of the two types, not only on performance but also on cognitions, affect, and motivation. A developmental approach might be adopted; for example, how have elite athletes developed their imagery and mental rehearsal skills? And what are the best approaches to adopt when teaching athletes imagery skills?

Self-talk

Self-talk is a difficult area to research. This situation has not been helped, however, by the fact that researchers to date have generally been too loose in their operationalisation of self-talk. As a consequence, findings across studies have not always been comparable. Thus, the first issue which researchers need to address in this area is to reach a consensus over a precise definition and operationalisation of self-talk. Only then can another very important issue be addressed: how can details about self-talk be captured? *In vivo* investigations are clearly desirable, but researchers run the risk of being over-intrusive. Retrospective analyses, on the other hand, carry with them their own problems of potential inaccuracy in recall etc. Researchers in this area are therefore confronted by serious challenges at both conceptual and methodological levels. Having resolved these issues, researchers may then wish to more rigorously address questions relating to: the nature of self-talk in elite and non-elite athletes; the nature of self-talk during successful and unsuccessful performances; how self-talk influences cognition, affect, and motivation; and how self-talk influences performance. As with other psychological techniques, the aim of researchers in this area should be to examine causal rather than correlational relationships.

IMPLICATIONS FOR BEST PRACTICE

The ways in which the basic psychological skills addressed in this chapter can be used to develop specific advanced psychological skills will be discussed in subsequent chapters in this book. For the moment, this section will highlight some of the implications for best practice of each of the four basic skills.

Relaxation

Many athletes have developed their own techniques for achieving a relaxed state prior to, and during, performance; this will have been achieved by rather unstructured, instinctive means by many of them. Other athletes may have developed their ability to relax through formal instruction in relaxation techniques. The sport psychologist has a potentially important role to play in structured relaxation training. An early, important decision in the process is whether to use a specific relaxation technique in isolation, or employ a technique as part of a general stress management training package. Whichever strategy is adopted, it is important to start at a basic, general skill level and to progress through the various learning stages until the technique is finely tuned to meet the demands of specific situations within the sports context. This obviously requires belief, patience, effort, and commitment on the part of the athlete.

The availability of different types of relaxation technique means that the decision over which specific one to implement is an important one. The distinction between mental and physical techniques is useful here, although a multimodal approach may be preferable. An additional consideration concerns the nature of the sport. If relaxation techniques are to be used during performance, then they are likely to be more easily incorporated into internally paced as opposed to externally paced sports.

Goal-setting

Although research findings within the sport domain have been equivocal in the area of goal-setting, the more ecologically valid, field-based work does emphasise the importance of setting goals in sport. Goals should be difficult but realistic, important, and accepted by the athletes so that they will commit themselves to them. Goals should also be broken down using a time-phased framework, so that feedback regarding goal attainment is available on a regular basis. It is also important to recognise that different types of goal exist, and that athletes should be encouraged to set combinations of outcome, performance and process goals depending upon circumstances and requirements. Athletes and coaches should also be wary of setting goals which may turn out to be dysfunctional. In this respect, goals need to be carefully negotiated and agreed between athletes and coaches, and also between team-mates, where applicable. Where team goals are set, it is important to also set individual goals to avoid social loafing.

Imagery and mental rehearsal

Like relaxation, the development and use of imagery techniques appears to be unstructured and instinctive in many athletes; in others, it is very structured and used for very specific purposes. It appears that elite athletes, in general, have not been born with highly tuned imagery skills, but have had to develop them along the way.

The most important implication for best practice is that imagery should be positive and successful. Also, imagery and mental rehearsal appears to be most effective when accompanied by physical simulation. A major prerequisite of effective imagery is that it is vivid and controlled. The available literature suggests that different visual imagery perspectives may be desirable for different tasks. Consequently, it may be safest to encourage most performers to learn how to use both perspectives. Finally, imagery scripts should use both stimulus and response propositions, in a way which conveys meaning to the performer.

Self-talk

The implications for best practice in the case of self-talk are that it is very important, and should be positive and rational in nature. Athletes should use self-talk to restructure cognitions and to alter maladaptive, irrational thoughts. Self-talk should also be employed to provide self-reward and can be used to increase effort.

SUMMARY

This chapter has made an important distinction between basic and advanced psychological skills. It has then focused on the basic psychological skills of relaxation, goal-setting, imagery and mental rehearsal, and self-talk. The basic principles underlying each skill have been addressed, together with major research findings relating to each skill. Finally, implications for research and best practice in each basic psychological skill have been proposed.

3

SELF-CONFIDENCE

CONTENTS

INTRODUCTION

One need look no further than the quote of tennis player, Jimmy Connors, in order to gain an insight into the enormous influence that confidence can play in sport:

> *The whole thing is never to get negative about yourself. Sure, it's possible that the other guy you're playing is tough, and that he may have beaten you the last time you played, and okay, maybe you haven't been playing all*

> *that well yourself. But the minute you start thinking about these things you're dead. I go out to every match convinced that I'm going to win. That is all there is to it.* (Weinberg, 1988, p. 127)

The importance of a high level of confidence is similarly highlighted in Jones and Hardy's (1990a) report of interviews carried out with several elite performers. For example, javelin thrower Steve Backley was in no doubt about the importance of maintaining the highest level of confidence possible when he said: "If you're slightly down and doubting yourself then you've lost . . . you've lost the battle with yourself to create a highly skilled performance" (p. 273). Indeed, it was clear from all of the interviews conducted by Jones and Hardy that in those athletes' minds, self-confidence was extremely important if they were to attain the levels of performance which they sought.

Hemery's (1986) investigation of 63 of the highest achievers from a wide variety of sports is equally enlightening; nearly 90 per cent of this particular sample had ". . . a very high level of self-confidence" (p. 156). Such levels of confidence are amply illustrated in Hemery's reports of several performers who were at one time the world's number one in their respective sports. For example, Daley Thompson, decathlete, stated "I've always been confident of doing well . . . I've never gone into a competition with any doubts" (pp. 156–157), whilst Shane Innes (formerly Gould), Olympic swimmer, ". . . said that she always had confidence in her ability" (p. 157).

To assume that all elite performers never doubt their ability to succeed would, however, be a gross misconception (Gould and Damarjian, in press). Several of Hemery's interviewees admitted to some self-doubt on occasions. Herb Elliott (middle-distance runner) actually viewed self-doubt as an asset: "I think one of my big strengths has been my doubts of myself: if you're very aware of the weaknesses and are full of your own self-doubts, in a sense, that's quite a motivation" (Hemery, 1986, p. 155). Another middle-distance runner, Steve Ovett, stated, "there's always a worry that I'd never live up to the expectations of my friends" (Hemery, 1986, p. 155). Some other elite athletes referred to feelings of apprehension and pressure which appeared to be associated with better performances. Thus, being confident does not mean that elite performers never have negative thoughts or feelings. Rather, in spite of any self-doubts, elite athletes seem still to believe in their ability to perform at very high levels.

In view of the importance the elite athletes referred to above attributed to confidence, it is not surprising that self-confidence has figured prominently in recent sport psychology research literature. This research is characterised by á number of different approaches which reflect a general lack of consensus over how self-confidence should be both conceptualised and operationalised. The aim of this chapter is not to present an exhaustive review of this work, but to be relatively selective in providing a framework within which the strategies used by elite performers to enhance self-confidence can be understood at both a theoretical and practical level. For the purpose of the following discussion, it is convenient to loosely categorise the relevant literature into four broad areas: (1) theoretical issues in the development of sport-specific self-confidence; (2) examination of the relationship between self-confidence, self-efficacy, and sports performance; (3) consideration of the relationships between self-confidence, self-efficacy, and anxiety; and (4) investigation into the effectiveness of various strategies used to enhance self-confidence.

THEORETICAL ASPECTS OF SELF-CONFIDENCE

The rather nebulous nature of the term "self-confidence" has resulted in its being operationalised in several different ways in the literature. These include the constructs of self-efficacy (Bandura, 1977), sport confidence (Vealey, 1986), perceived competence (Harter, 1982; Nicholls, 1984), outcome expectancies (Rotter, 1954), and movement confidence (Griffin and Keogh, 1982). The following discussion will focus upon two of these approaches, self-efficacy and sport confidence, which are particularly pertinent in the context of elite performers.

It is interesting to note an initial contrast between the self-efficacy and sport confidence approaches in the light of Feltz's (1988a) assertion that self-confidence should be viewed as:

> *. . . the belief that one can successfully execute a specific activity rather than a global trait that accounts for overall performance optimism. For example, one may have a high degree of self-confidence in one's driving ability in golf but a low degree of self-confidence in putting.* (p. 423)

"Self-confidence", as operationalised in the above quote in the case of very specific skills within golf, is essentially "self-efficacy" as identified and defined by Bandura (1977). Thus, self-efficacy theory represents a "micro-level" approach in that it investigates perceived ability to perform specific skills based upon the assumption that such perceptions of ability can vary greatly for individual skills within the same sport and within a specific competition. The sport confidence, "macro-level" approach (Vealey, 1986) is more concerned with the global level of self-confidence associated with overall performance expectancies in sport (trait sport confidence) and specific competitions (state sport confidence).

Self-efficacy

Bandura's (1977, 1982) theory of self-efficacy was originally developed within the framework of a social cognitive approach to behaviour causation which argues that behaviour, cognitive and physiological factors, and environmental influences operate as interacting determinants of each other (Bandura, 1986). The theory has since been adopted to explain behaviour within several disciplines of psychology, not least in sport psychology. Indeed, it has been the theoretical basis adopted for the majority of performance-related research in self-confidence in sport.

Self-efficacy refers to situation-specific self-confidence, as opposed to the global self-confidence referred to above. It is the performer's perception of his/her competence to succeed in a given task at a given time. The basic

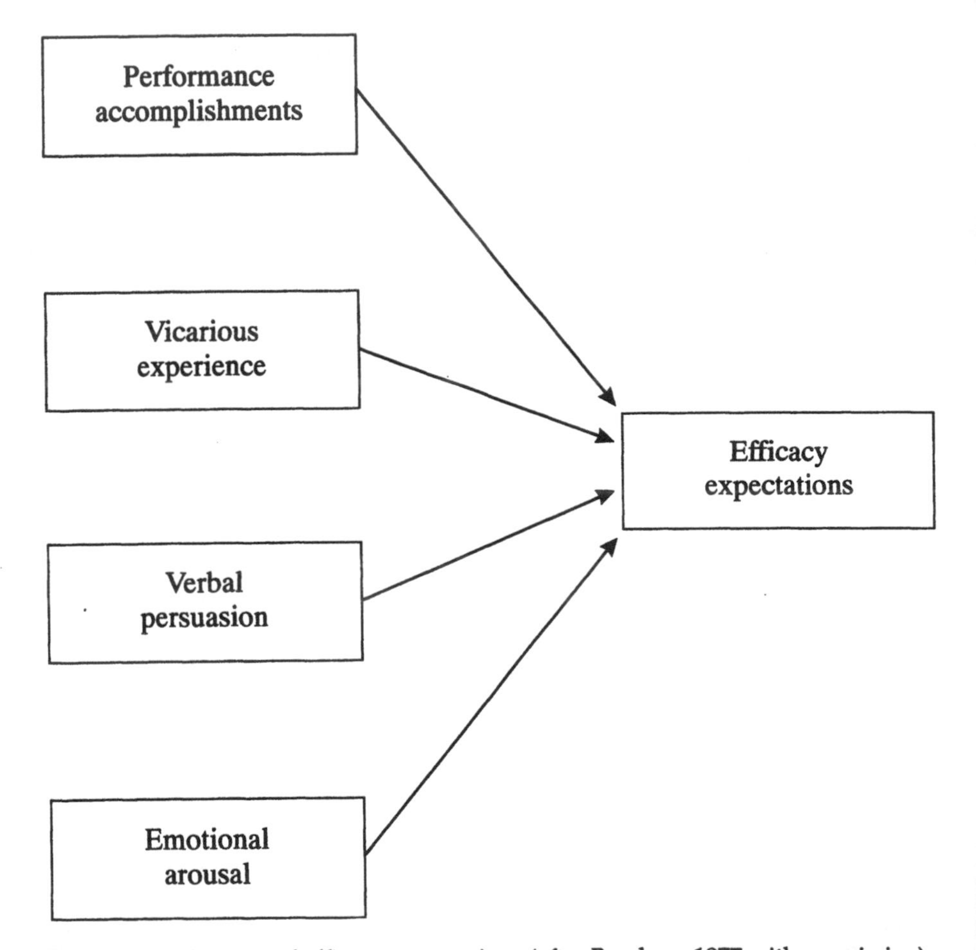

Figure 3.1: Sources of efficacy expectations (after Bandura, 1977 with permission)

premise underlying Bandura's theory is that self-efficacy will predict actual performance if necessary skills and appropriate incentives are present. Bandura further proposed that self-efficacy can be assessed along three dimensions: "level", concerned with the individual's expected performance attainment; "strength", reflecting the certainty with which the individual expects to achieve success; and "generality", referring to the number of domains in which the individual considers him/herself efficacious. According to Bandura's theory, and as depicted in Figure 3.1, efficacy expectations (i.e. one's belief that a certain level of performance can be attained) are predicted by four factors which are, in descending order of importance: performance accomplishments; vicarious experience; verbal persuasion; and emotional arousal.

The fact that the four sources of efficacy expectations identified in the theory are readily applicable to the sport context is largely responsible for the theory's popularity in sport psychology research. As will be expounded later in this chapter, the identification of such factors not only provides a theoretical underpinning for some of the strategies and techniques which have been proposed to enhance confidence in sport, but also provides a very useful indication to performers and coaches as to the most effective techniques and strategies for developing and maintaining confidence.

Performance accomplishments represent the most powerful effects upon self-efficacy since they are based upon personal mastery experiences. Obviously, the more positive the experiences, the higher the self-efficacy. However, the strength of this relationship will depend upon other factors such as the perceived difficulty of the task, effort exerted, the amount of physical guidance received, and the temporal patterning of success and failure. Specifically, success at a difficult task which is independently achieved early in learning will result in greater self-efficacy than success at a simple task with the help of others following the experience of early failures (Bandura, 1982; Feltz, 1988a). *Vicarious experience* refers to the information derived from seeing others perform the skill in question. This can be a particularly important source of efficacy information in performers lacking experience of the task at hand, relying upon others in order to judge one's own capabilities. *Verbal persuasion* refers to persuasive techniques used by self or others in order to manipulate behaviour. These techniques may include verbal encouragement and feedback, although important mediating factors include the credibility and expertise of the persuader. The final, and least powerful, predictor of self-efficacy is *emotional arousal*. This refers to performers' appraisals of their emotional arousal as opposed to their actual physiological states. Thus, it is the performer's cognitive appraisal or interpretation of the physiological response which will contribute to efficacy expectations, although Bandura (1986) also included factors such as levels of fatigue and pain in this self-efficacy source.

Self-efficacy theory has certainly not been without its critics. The major concern which has been expressed over the theory has been provided by anxiety reduction theorists (Borkovec, 1978; Eysenck, 1978; Wolpe, 1978) who argued that self-efficacy is merely a by-product of the anxiety response (see later section on Self-Confidence, Self-Efficacy, and Anxiety). The purely self-report nature of self-efficacy is also a source of criticism (Borkovec, 1978; Kazdin, 1978; Kirsch, 1985), although it is difficult to envisage how else this construct could actually be assessed.

Sport confidence

Vealey's (1986) more general conceptualisation of self-confidence was borne out of a dissatisfaction with the numerous different ways in which the construct had been operationalised in empirical investigations. She made the case for a much more parsimonious operationalisation which would be able to predict behaviour across a wide range of sport situations. In the model proposed by Vealey, self-confidence is separated into two constructs; trait self-confidence (SC-trait) and state self-confidence (SC-state). SC-trait was defined by Vealey as "... the belief or degree of certainty individuals *usually* possess about their ability to be successful in sport" (p.223). SC-state, on the other hand, was defined as "... the belief or degree of certainty individuals possess *at one particular moment* about their ability to be successful in sport" (p.223). A further construct included in the model is competitive orientation, which is essentially derived from Maehr and Nicholls' (1980) proposition that success means different things to different people. Indeed, Vealey's distinction between performance goal orientation (i.e. performing well) and outcome goal orientation (i.e. winning) appears to be not very far removed from Nicholls' (1980) earlier distinction between task orientation and ego orientation (see Duda, 1992; Nicholls, 1980; 1992; Chapter 4 in this book).

Vealey's model is an interactional one and is shown in Figure 3.2. The proposal is that SC-trait and competitive orientation interact with the objective sport situation to produce SC-state, which represents the most important mediator of behaviour. It is specifically hypothesised that SC-state is positively correlated with SC-trait and performance orientation, but negatively correlated with outcome orientation, especially in low SC-trait performers. The subjective outcomes construct in the model represents factors such as causal attributions, perceptions of success, and satisfaction with performance. The model predicts that SC-trait and competitive orientation both influence, and are influenced by, subjective outcomes. Vealey (1986) also reported the development of separate instruments to examine the hypothesised relationships in the model: the Competitive Orientation Inventory; the Trait Sport-Confidence Inventory; and the State Sport-Confidence Inventory.

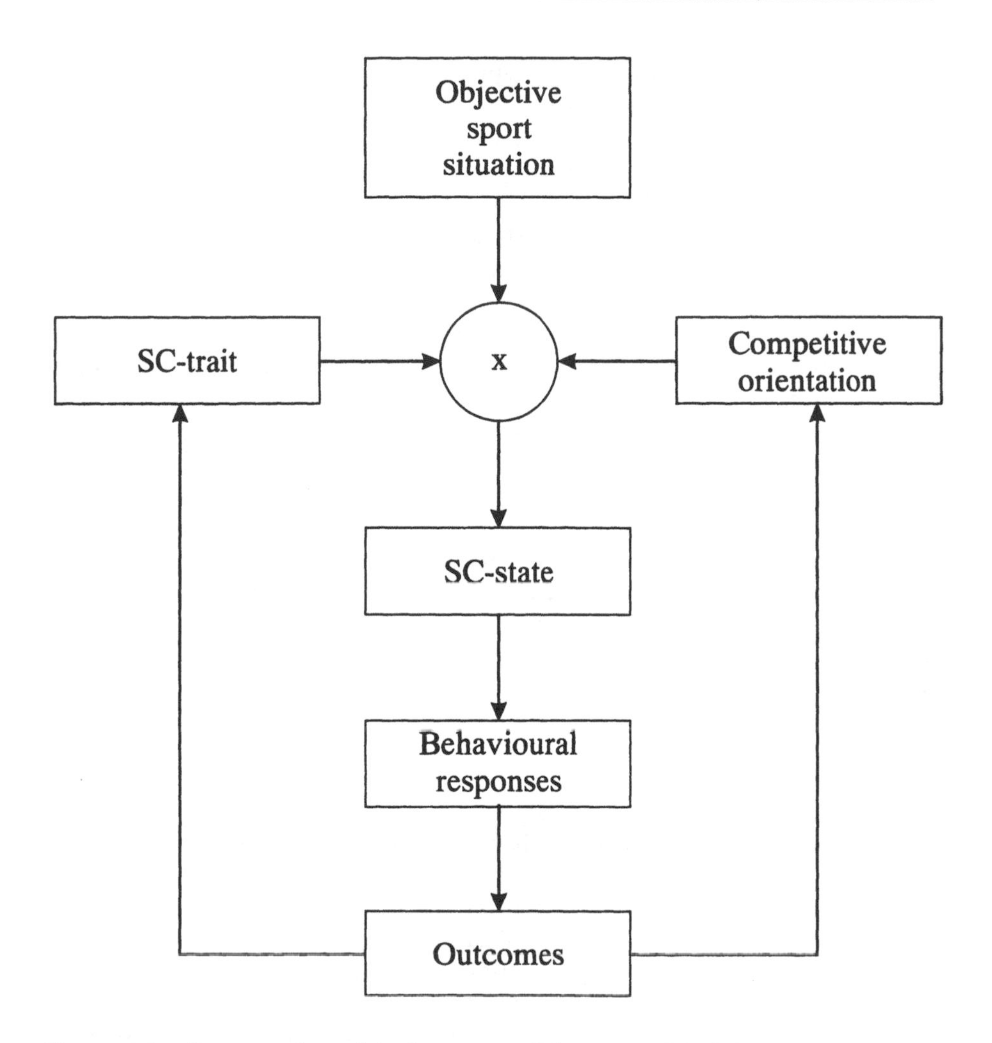

Figure 3.2: Conceptual model of sport confidence (modified from Vealey, 1986, with permission)

Relatively little research has been conducted on the predictions of Vealey's model. A recent study by Martin and Gill (1991) has offered partial support, although it failed to find a significant relationship between competitive orientation and SC-state. Indeed, Feltz (1988a) had earlier questioned the inclusion of competitive orientation in the model, and also argued that it lacks the predictive power of more situation-specific approaches such as self-efficacy. However, further research on this model is required to test its predictions adequately.

Martens *et al.*'s (1990a) Competitive State Anxiety Inventory-2 (CSAI-2) has also been employed to assess state sport confidence and has been the source of some interesting findings. Examination of the relationship between confidence and performance using the CSAI-2 will be discussed in the following section, but it is worth noting that the CSAI-2 has provided valuable information regarding several aspects of self-confidence. For instance, the temporal patterning of self-confidence during the period preceding competition has attracted notable research interest. Self-confidence is predicted to remain stable during the pre-competition period unless expectations of success change (Martens *et al.*, 1990), but several studies show that individual difference variables mediate this patterning. Krane and Williams' (1987) findings, for example, showed that as the competition approached self-confidence decreased in a sample of performers from a subjectively-scored sport (i.e. gymnastics) but increased in performers from an objectively-scored sport (i.e. golf). However, in addition to the sport-type difference, the authors also noted that the lesser experience and skill level of the gymnasts in the sample may have been important factors in the differential temporal patterning. Further studies by Jones and Cale (1989) and Jones *et al.* (1991) showed that pre-competition patterning differed in males and females; specifically, self-confidence remained relatively constant in males, whilst females reported a progressive reduction as the competition neared. More recently, Swain and Jones (1992) have shown that highly competitive athletes report higher confidence than low competitive athletes throughout the whole of the pre-competition period.

Summary

Bandura's (1977, 1986) self-efficacy theory and Vealey's (1986) sport confidence model represent conceptually quite distinct approaches to confidence. Self-efficacy is a micro-level, situation-specific conceptualisation of confidence; the sport confidence model, on the other hand, represents a more generalised, macro-level conceptualisation of perceptions of ability to be successful in sport. The greatest strength of the sport confidence model is its parsimonious approach. This is reflected in the fact that it is easily comprehensible and digested, and, as such, is a useful conceptual tool for sport psychology practitioners to employ in the process of educating coaches and athletes. At a more scientific, aetiological level, however, the greater specificity of self-efficacy theory keeps it ahead on points. In reality, of course, a combination of the two approaches is probably required.

SELF-CONFIDENCE, SELF-EFFICACY, AND SPORTS PERFORMANCE

Self-confidence and sports performance

The large majority of research in this area has emanated from North America. Mahoney and Avener's (1977) frequently cited study was among the earliest to demonstrate the importance of confidence, among other factors, in distinguishing between successful and less successful performers. They collected data from the 13 gymnasts involved in the final trial for the 1976 United States Olympic team via a questionnaire administered 48 hours prior to the competition, and also verbal interviews at various stages during the event. In comparing the data of those who qualified with those who did not qualify for the team, the questionnaire data showed that the qualifiers tended to be more self-confident. Mahoney and Avener also reported a higher frequency of gymnastic performance-related dreams among the successful gymnasts, within which they tended to see themselves being successful. However, it should be noted that these findings are derived from a correlational design and a small sample.

A later study by Mahoney *et al.* (1987) examined psychological skills in elite, pre-elite and non-elite performers. They administered a questionnaire, the Psychological Skills Inventory for Sports (PSIS), to 713 athletes from 23 sports. Of this sample, 126 performers were identified as elite, the criterion being that they had been placed fourth or above in national championships or recent Olympic or World Championship events. The 141 pre-elite performers comprised mainly athletes attending special training camps or junior national events. The remaining 446 non-elite performers were members of major university athletic teams. Item analysis of the PSIS showed that, among other findings, the elite performers had higher and more stable levels of self-confidence than the non-elite athletes, although no differences emerged between elite and pre-elite performers. Subsequent regression, factor, and cluster analyses also showed that confidence was a major differentiating factor between elite and non-elite performers. A cautionary note in interpreting these findings is necessary, however, since the measure on which they are based is, as yet, an unvalidated inventory of psychological skills (for criticisms of the PSIS, see Chartrand *et al.*, 1992).

Other studies which have shown self-confidence to be an important discriminating factor between successful and less successful performers include ones on wrestling (Gould *et al.*, 1981; Highlen and Bennett, 1979; Meyers *et al.*, 1979); international rifle shooting (Doyle *et al.*, 1980); and swimming (Jones *et al.*, 1994). As Feltz (1984) emphasised, however, these findings are the result of correlational designs so that causality cannot be inferred. *Thus, one is left pondering over the inevitable debate as to whether elite athletes owe their status to an underlying high level of self-confidence, or whether they are highly confident because of their previous high levels of performance.*

The studies discussed above have essentially sought to describe the psychological characteristics of groups of athletes divided into different skill/ability levels on a sometimes rather arbitrary basis. A number of other studies which have examined the relationship between confidence and performance have adopted a different approach in that they have operationalised performance as a continuous variable. Studies which have used the CSAI-2 as the central measuring tool have generally supported the hypothesised positive relationship between confidence and performance (e.g. Burton, 1988; Jones *et al.*, 1993; Martens *et al.*, 1990a), although Gould *et al.*'s (1987) finding of a negative correlation for pistol shooters is a notable and unexplained exception in the literature.

Self-efficacy and sports performance

The relatively few studies that have been carried out to examine the relationship between self-efficacy and performance in actual sports situations (e.g. Feltz *et al.*, 1989; Gayton *et al.*, 1986; Weiss *et al.*, 1989) and in laboratory-based studies which have incorporated competitive conditions (e.g. Feltz and Riessinger, 1990; Weinberg *et al.*, 1979) have generally shown positive correlations. However, as Feltz (1988a) emphasised, such studies do not necessarily demonstrate a causal relationship between confidence and performance, and really offer nothing in the way of providing information as to the direction of the relationship. In light of this criticism, a few studies have been conducted to specifically examine causal relationships within the context of Bandura's (1977) theory of self-efficacy (e.g. Feltz, 1982; Feltz *et al.*, 1979; Feltz and Mugno, 1983; George, 1994; McAuley, 1985; Weinberg *et al.*, 1979). Although the findings are by no means clear-cut, the path analyses used in such studies have generally supported the proposal that self-efficacy is a major determinant of sports performance. Feltz (1992) has pointed out, however, that researchers need to move away from "nonmicroanalytical" (p.105), global measurements (e.g. win/loss) of sports performance. She argued that the relationship between self-efficacy and sports performance can only be properly examined if researchers adopt the same microanalytic approach to measuring performance as is employed to examine the concept of self-efficacy itself.

A limitation with previous research is that it has largely focused upon performance as the dependent variable, and has failed to examine the processes and mechanisms underlying self-efficacy effects. As depicted in Figure 3.3, these can be categorised into "behaviour patterns" (i.e. choice, effort, persistence) and "thought patterns" (i.e. goals, worry, attributions) (Bandura, 1977, 1982, 1986; Feltz, 1992). Research findings from the mainstream psychology literature have highlighted the valuable insight which can be gleaned from this approach. For example, when in stressful situations, individuals low in self-efficacy will tend to give up, attribute failure internally, and experience greater anxiety (Bandura, 1982). In the context of goal intentions, research has shown that high self-efficacy leads to more difficult goals being selected and greater commitment to those goals, once selected (Locke *et al.*, 1984). Furthermore, where individuals experience negative discrepancies between aspirations

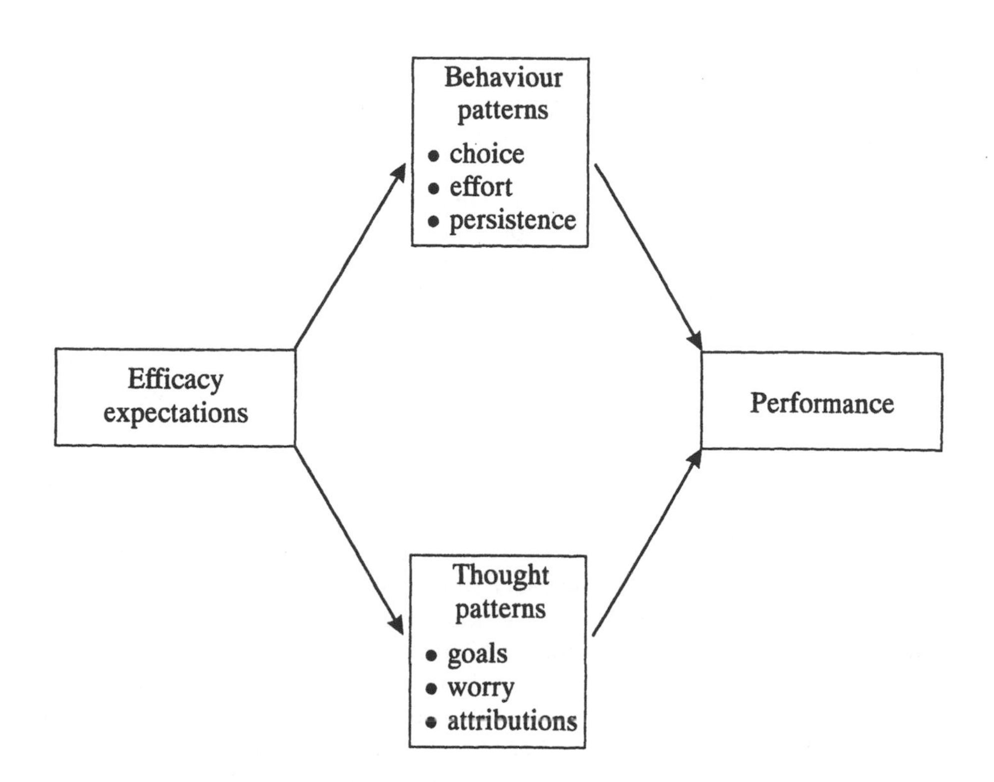

Figure 3.3: Processes underlying self-efficacy effects

and actual level of achievement, high self-efficacy performers will increase their level of effort and persistence, whilst low self-efficacy performers will give up (Bandura, 1986, 1989). Bandura also cited evidence from Collins (1982) which suggests that efficacy beliefs bias causal attributions. Specifically, high self-efficacy performers were found to attribute failure to lack of effort, whilst low self-efficacy performers attributed it to lack of ability (see also Chapter 4).

Extrapolating from these findings, and based upon the assumption that elite sports performers generally have high self-efficacy, it is possible to predict that elite performers, when compared to their non-elite counterparts, will: select more difficult goals to which they are highly committed; increase their level of persistence and effort when goals are not achieved; and attribute failure to lack of effort rather than ability. Such tentative predictions clearly require further empirical investigation.

Collective efficacy and sports performance

Research in the area of efficacy and sports performance has been almost exclusively targeted at examining self-efficacy and sports performance at an individual level. Given that many sports involve teams of individuals who operate closely together, it is surprising that the area of collective efficacy (Bandura, 1986) and team performance has attracted so little research attention (Feltz, 1992; McAuley, 1992).

Initial investigations have generally demonstrated that collective, or team, efficacy is not equivalent to simply summing the efficacy beliefs of the team's individual members. Lirgg and Feltz (1994) showed that a female basketball team's collective efficacy predicted team performance in four of six basketball skills, but aggregated self-efficacy scores failed to predict any of the team performance measures. Chase *et al.* (1994) showed that collective and individual efficacy were predicted by different sources, again in a female basketball team. Specifically, sources outside basketball were more important than vicarious experience in predicting self-efficacy, whilst vicarious experience was more important than other sources outside basketball in predicting collective efficacy. In an earlier study, Spink (1990) found that collective efficacy was positively related to group cohesion in elite volleyball teams. This further suggests that a conceptual distinction is required between collective and individual efficacies, since Bandura (1977) made no reference to group unity as a source of efficacy expectations.

The importance of group cohesion in the relationship between collective efficacy, self-efficacy and performance is highlighted in a recent study of male rugby players from a number of teams (Swain *et al.*, 1995). The results revealed that in low cohesion teams, self-efficacy predicted more performance variance (18.3 per cent) than collective efficacy, which contributed only a further 0.9 per cent of the variance. In contrast, in high cohesion teams collective efficacy predicted 40.2 per cent of performance variance, with self-efficacy contributing an additional 0.5 per cent.

Group cohesion is only one aspect of group motivation which is likely to mediate the relationship between collective and individual efficacies and performance. Other mediating constructs may include group attributions, desire for group success, and social loafing (Feltz, 1994). Collective efficacy in sport is clearly a relatively uncharted area of research, and is therefore likely to form the focus of considerable research attention in the future.

Summary

This section has examined the findings of studies which have investigated self-efficacy and the more generalised conceptualisation of confidence as predictors of sports performance. These findings lead to the conclusion that both constructs are important predictors, but the correlational nature of much of the research precludes any proliferation of valid claims for causal relationships. Future researchers should employ designs which allow causal relationships to be examined. They should also devote more attention to studying the processes and mechanisms underlying confidence and efficacy effects.

SELF-CONFIDENCE, SELF-EFFICACY, AND ANXIETY

Bandura's original work on self-efficacy theory in 1977 also included proposals regarding the relationship between self-efficacy and anxiety. Specifically, Bandura argued that behavioural change is determined by efficacy expectations and that efficacy cognitions result in reduced anxiety. These proposals were in direct conflict with those of anxiety reduction theorists (Borkovec, 1978; Eysenck, 1978; Wolpe, 1978) who argued that the anxiety response is the direct cause of both efficacy expectations and behavioural change. Indeed, Eysenck (1978) referred to self-efficacy as merely a by-product of anxiety. Unfortunately, research which has compared the self-efficacy model with the alternative anxiety-based model in predicting behaviour has proved inconclusive, with neither model gaining clear support (Feltz, 1983; McAuley, 1985).

The work of Martens *et al.* (1990a) is pertinent here, but in relation to a more general conceptualisation of confidence than is embraced in the self-efficacy approach. Martens and his colleagues' work on the CSAI-2 was originally intended to develop a multidimensional measure of cognitive and somatic anxiety. During the validation of this measure, factor analysis effectively split cognitive anxiety items into two separate factors; one that included negatively phrased items, and the other that comprised positively phrased items. The latter factor was subsequently labelled "self-confidence", so that the CSAI-2 comprises three as opposed to two factors.

Martens *et al.*'s (1990) validation work on the CSAI-2 led them to propose that self-confidence and cognitive anxiety represent opposite extremes of a cognitive evaluation continuum, thus echoing the basic principles of the debate described above but providing no hint as to any directional cause. However, Martens *et al.*'s proposal is questionable considering that the cognitive anxiety and self-confidence factors were derived from factor analyses with the purpose of identifying orthogonal (independent) factors. Furthermore, it is evident from some elite athletes' experiences described in the introduction to this chapter that they can be confident but also aware of some self-doubts (i.e. cognitive anxiety) at the same time. In addition, studies which have reported correlations between these two factors generally demonstrate their relative independence, sharing less than 40 per cent common variance (e.g. Gould *et al.*, 1984; Jones and Cale, 1989; Martens *et al.*, 1990), whilst Hardy (1996) has offered clear evidence of self-confidence significantly predicting golf performance over and above the variance in performance predicted by cognitive and somatic anxiety. Furthermore, recent work which has examined the pre-competition temporal patterning and antecedents of cognitive anxiety and self-confidence also suggests that these two factors are relatively independent (Jones *et al.*, 1990, 1991). Interestingly, Jones *et al.* (1993) showed that performers' interpretations of the debilitative or facilitative consequences for performance of the intensity of their cognitive and somatic anxiety symptoms correlated more strongly with self-confidence than did the actual intensity of cognitive and somatic anxiety symptoms. No causal or directional influences are possible, of course, but this finding does allow the intriguing proposition that self-confidence may, in some way, protect against anxiety effects.

Summary

The situation regarding the relationship between anxiety and confidence, and subsequent relationships with performance is clearly a complex one in which numerous issues remain to be addressed. An important issue at a conceptual level is whether anxiety and confidence are independent, or if not, the degree to which they are related. Another issue currently being investigated is whether cognitive anxiety and confidence have additive or interactive effects upon performance. The results of recent theorising and empirical work suggest that a fair degree of performance variance can be explained by a very complex interaction between the two constructs. This issue is beyond the bounds of this chapter but will be re-visited in greater detail in Chapter 6.

STRATEGIES FOR ENHANCING SELF-CONFIDENCE

Relatively few studies have examined the precursors of global self-confidence in terms of overall performance optimism. Gould *et al.* (1984) found that perceived ability predicted self-confidence in intercollegiate wrestlers. Perceptions of physical and mental readiness have also been shown to be consistent and important predictors (Hanton and Jones, 1995; Jones *et al.*, 1990), with perceptions of the external environment also being significant (Jones *et al.*, 1990). However, Hanton and Jones (1995) reported that perceived readiness predicted much more of the variance in confidence in elite swimmers when compared to non-elite swimmers. Also, Jones *et al.* (1991) found that self-confidence in males and females had different antecedents. Their findings showed that the major predictors of self-confidence in females were the perceived importance of a good personal performance, and perceived mental and physical readiness. Predictors in the males, on the other hand, related to the extent to which they were likely to win, together with their perception of their opponents' ability in relation to their own. These findings provide general support for Gill's (1988) proposal that females focus more upon personal goals and standards whilst males focus more upon personal comparison and winning. Further research is required in this area since the identification of the precursors of overall performance self-confidence is likely to prove valuable in the search for achieving optimal pre-competition states.

A considerably greater amount of research attention has been devoted to the predictors of self-efficacy. Although not developed within the specific context of sport, Bandura's (1977) theory of self-efficacy is by far the most popular theoretical approach adopted to explain the effectiveness of the various strategies employed to enhance self-confidence in athletes. As stated earlier in this chapter, this popularity is largely due to the fact that the four predictors of efficacy expectations are readily applicable to the sporting context, although, as will be illustrated below, some adaptation of the techniques advocated by Bandura is necessary. Thus, the discussion now returns to a consideration of performance accomplishments, vicarious experience, verbal persuasion, and emotional arousal, in order to gain an understanding of how and why various strategies and techniques are effective.

Performance accomplishments

Research which has examined the role of performance-based information in determining self-efficacy has shown it to enhance both efficacy expectations and performance (e.g. Brody *et al.*, 1988). Empirical findings also support the proposal that performance-based information is superior to the other three sources in predicting self-efficacy (e.g. Feltz *et al.*, 1979; McAuley, 1985).

The importance of achieving repeated success for the development of self-confidence is clearly evident in the small sample of quotes below from Jones and Hardy's (1990a) interviews with elite athletes:

> *Sue Challis (trampolinist) said that she builds her confidence by "training very hard. I like to do what I'm going to do in competition over and over again."* (p. 272)
>
> *James May (gymnast) perceived the primary determinant of his self-confidence to be his previous experiences of success at performing his routines: "the more times you go through a routine successfully, then you are going to feel more confident about going through the performance on the day."* (p. 274)

Hemery's (1986) observations of elite athletes allowed him to gain an insight into the role of achieving success early in life in establishing perhaps a more global type of confidence for sport in general:

> *Chris Evert Lloyd (tennis player) said that winning when young brought self-confidence, supporting the view that those who win reasonably consistently from an early age see themselves as winners, and believe in most cases that they can and will win. . . .* (p. 156)

The role of a third person in helping to enhance self-confidence is clearly crucial in the process described in the quote above. In the context of elite athletes, the third person would for the most part be the athlete's coach. The role of the coach in enhancing self-confidence has been acknowledged in the literature (Feltz and Doyle, 1981; Feltz and Weiss, 1982), but has only very recently been addressed at an empirical level (Gould *et al.*, 1989; Weinberg *et al.*, 1992; Weinberg and Jackson, 1990). The importance of this role will become evident as the following discussion progresses.

One of the most valuable strategies employed for the purpose of enhancing self-confidence within the mechanism of performance accomplishments is goal-setting (Beggs, 1990; Feltz, 1984). Again, the documented experience of an elite athlete serves to emphasise the importance of this technique:

> *In the long term, David Hemery (400 metre hurdler) identified that his self-confidence was most strongly determined by his long history of achieving performance improvement goals and by the confidence that he gained from beating other competitors. He described his history of goal achievement as being a self-perpetuating spiral, with every step making him feel "stronger, fitter, faster".* (Jones and Hardy, 1990a, p. 272)

Hemery's classic use of structured goal-setting throughout his career fits in neatly with the findings of Bandura and Schunk (1981) and Schunk (1983) who demonstrated that improvements in self-efficacy accompany very carefully planned goal-setting. According to the findings of this research, the use of proximal as well as distal goals is particularly important. Bandura and Schunk (1981) proposed that proximal goals provide markers of increasing competence as distal goals are approached, and it is this increase in perceived competence which leads to an increase in self-efficacy.

The fundamental principles of goal-setting have already been described in Chapter 2, but it is worth re-emphasising the importance of setting goals at an appropriate difficulty level (Locke and Latham, 1985) if they are to form the basis of increases in self-confidence. For example, if goals are too difficult and beyond the performer's attainability then they are likely to be dysfunctional in that they will result in increased anxiety and reduced self-confidence when they are not achieved (Earley *et al.*, 1989; Jones and Cale, in press). They are also unlikely to be achieved when performers get anxious (Hardy *et al.*, 1986).

A further crucial factor identified in the literature is the specificity of the goals that are set. In view of the fact that it is the achievement of success which is hypothesised to be the dominant predictor of confidence, it is argued that it is important for the performer to be aware that the goals have been achieved. Thus, the literature on goal-setting is characterised by a strong recommendation to set goals that are easily measurable (Locke and Latham, 1985). The natural conclusion is that only performance and outcome goals should be assigned in an attempt to enhance confidence since they can provide the degree of measurability required.

It would be unwise to move on to another strategy for enhancing confidence without briefly re-visiting the "conclusion" drawn above. The implication is that process goals are likely to be unhelpful in increasing confidence to any significant extent. This is potentially misleading and denies the contribution which process goals can make to increasing confidence, particularly in the short term (Kingston and Hardy, 1994a, b). This is aptly reflected in the following quote of Kerrin Lee-Gartner, 1992 Olympic Gold medallist in the women's downhill ski race, during rehabilitation from injury:

> *The obvious struggles were my knee injuries and each one took six months to about a year and a half to recover form. It wasn't just the physical recovery. The mental recovery was the hardest part. There are always waves in life, and when you're down in ski racing, with a physical disability like my knees were, it was most important to keep my goals set, to always believe in myself and to look at the reasons why I was going through these struggles, to look at the end result really. I made little tiny goals for myself—little tiny steps, focused on little things. I stayed focused, stayed focused, stayed focused. I think that's the only way through it, to go gradually and continue believing in yourself the whole way.* (Orlick and Lee-Gartner, 1993, pp. 113–114)

The use of participant modelling (i.e. demonstration plus guided performance) has also been identified as an important source of performance-based information (Bandura and Adams, 1977; Bandura *et al.*, 1977). Feltz *et al.* (1979) and McAuley (1985), for example, found participant modelling to be superior to vicarious experience techniques such as video and live demonstrations. This suggests that coaching techniques designed to emphasise performance accomplishments should use physical supports or aids and should modify the skill in order to guarantee the performer's success during participant modelling (Feltz, 1984), although it is also important that this guidance be removed gradually (as opposed to abruptly) until successful performance is achieved unaided (Feltz *et al.*, 1979).

One factor that appears to be common across the vast majority of elite performers is that they train hard. As stated earlier in the quotes of Sue

Challis and James May, repeated success in training is an important source of pre-competition confidence. Coaches also appear to be convinced of such practice, as evidenced by the findings of Gould *et al.* (1989). They administered a questionnaire to 124 Olympic, Pan American and/or National team coaches in order to examine the strategies elite coaches use to enhance self-confidence in their athletes. The strategies most often used and considered most effective included performance-based instruction drilling and hard physical conditioning. Successful performance during well-structured simulation training has also been reported by top athletes as enhancing confidence during the run-up to competition (Jones and Hardy, 1990a; Orlick and Partington, 1988). Via this technique, the performer is able to achieve the desired outcome in conditions which, if appropriately structured, closely approximate the conditions that will be encountered in competition. Success in such conditions appears to have a very positive effect upon self-confidence.

Vicarious experience

Although information derived from vicarious experiences is hypothesised to be less powerful in enhancing efficacy expectations than information derived from past performance accomplishments, several studies have demonstrated that it is a very important means of enhancing confidence (e.g. Feltz and Riessinger, 1990; Lirgg and Feltz, 1991; Weinberg *et al.*, 1981b). As stated earlier, according to self-efficacy theory, vicarious experience refers to information gained from seeing others perform. The use of demonstrations or modelling is particularly important in this context, and several studies within sport psychology confirm that modelling enhances self-efficacy (e.g. Gould and Weiss, 1981; McAuley, 1985; Weinberg *et al.*, 1979).

The degree of influence of modelling on self-confidence is dependent upon a number of factors. For example, Gould and Weiss (1981) showed college females' self-confidence and performance on a muscular endurance task to be enhanced when viewing a model of similar age, sex, and athletic ability. Lirgg and Feltz (1991) examined the influence of skilled and unskilled teacher, and peer models, on motor performance. Results showed that subjects who observed an unskilled model had lower efficacy expectations than subjects who observed a skilled model. The use of multiple models, of widely differing performance and personal characteristics, is also proposed to enhance the modelling effect (Bandura, 1977).

Empirical work carried out by Gould *et al.* (1989) and Weinberg *et al.* (1992) has demonstrated that coaches view their own modelling of confidence as an important source of confidence in their athletes. Indeed, the coaches judged peer models to be much less effective than acting as models themselves which is perhaps rather surprising in view of the evidence supporting the effectiveness of peer models cited above. This has yet to be empirically verified, although Orlick and Partington's (1988) reports of Canadian Olympic athletes certainly offer some support for the importance of the coach's role in terms of their seeming to remain calm just prior to an event.

The use of symbolic modelling (i.e. imagining others performing a task) is also advocated within Bandura's self-efficacy theory. Little empirical work has been conducted in sport psychology, but this technique has been shown to be effective in the area of clinical psychology. However, a note of caution is required at this point since the majority of studies have examined the effectiveness of symbolic modelling in performers who are relatively unskilled at the criterion task. Since this book is concerned with highly skilled elite athletes, the use of another person as a symbolic model, either physically or mentally, is unlikely to be used to any great extent or to have a great effect upon confidence. Such athletes are much more likely to focus upon themselves as models and, in the context of vicarious experience, to use mental imagery as a major source of enhancing self-confidence (Jones and Hardy, 1990a).

The key to using imagery as a source of confidence is to see oneself demonstrating mastery (Moritz *et al.*, 1996). Jones and Hardy (1990a) reported that ". . . imagery played an important part in enhancing and maintaining Steve's (Backley) self-confidence" (p. 273). Backley reported practising imagery "absolutely all the time—it's almost an obsession . . . I sometimes visualise myself throwing 90 metres" (the world record was then 87.6 metres) (p. 265). The longer-term confidence-enhancing benefits of using imagery are highlighted in the following quote from a highly successful Olympic pistol shooter:

> *As for success imagery, I would imagine to myself, "How would a champion act? How would a champion feel? How would she perform on the line?" This helped me find out about myself, what worked and didn't work for me. Then as the actual roles I had imagined came along, and I achieved them, that in turn helped me believe that I would be the Olympic champion.* (Orlick and Partington, 1988; p. 113)

Empirical evidence regarding the effectiveness of imagery in enhancing confidence has been provided by Feltz and Riessinger (1990) and Moritz *et al.* (1996), although this is an area which requires further research attention. However, studies by Gould *et al.* (1989) and Weinberg *et al.* (1992) have shown that the elite coaches in their samples had doubts regarding the effectiveness of imagery in enhancing self-confidence. Such a finding could well reflect a relative lack of knowledge of imagery and its implementation on the coach's part.

Verbal persuasion

Verbal persuasion refers to persuasive techniques usually used by self and others to manipulate confidence. Verbal persuasion is an important technique used by coaches (Gould *et al.*, 1989; Weinberg *et al.*, 1992) in the form of encouraging exhortations (e.g. "come on, you can do it") and rewarding statements (e.g. "well done"). The Olympic athletes in Orlick and Partington's (1988) study reported that ". . . the coach expressing confidence in the athlete, saying positive things like 'You look good, you can do it'" (p.125) helped their performance. Other research similarly indicates the importance of coaches' expectations and feedback in enhancing their athletes' confidence levels (Horn, 1984; Rejeski *et al.*, 1979; Smoll and Smith, 1984).

A further form of persuasion which is at the coach's disposal is that of deception (Feltz, 1984). Ness and Patton (1977), for example, found that weightlifters who were deceived into thinking they were attempting to lift less than was actually on the bar improved on their previous maximum performance. Mahoney (1979) was unable to replicate this finding, but a recent study by Fitzsimmons *et al.* (in press) found that false positive feedback increased both self-efficacy and performance in weightlifters. It is important to emphasise, however, that the use of this technique is accompanied by the obvious danger of undermining trust, particularly if used excessively.

Of particular importance within this verbal persuasion mechanism for enhancing confidence is the nature of the athlete's own self-persuasion, via self-talk. The following quote from Janel Jorgensen, 1988 Olympic Silver medallist in the 100-metre butterfly, illustrates how verbal persuasion might be used to manipulate levels of confidence:

> *. . . you have to believe that it's going to happen. You can't doubt your abilities by saying, "oh, I'm going to wake up tomorrow and I'm going to feel totally bad, since I felt bad today and yesterday". You can't go about it like that. You have to say, "O.K., tomorrow I'm going to feel good. I didn't feel good today. That's that. We will see what happens tomorrow."* (Ripol, 1993, p. 36)

Olympic downhill skier, Kerrin Lee-Gartner, is another elite athlete who emphasised the importance of her self-talk:

> *Just by believing in myself and always talking to myself very positively, and putting positive thoughts in my mind, it only encouraged the belief I already had . . . I would turn anything negative into a positive . . . On race day at the Olympics, it was very light, very foggy, which is not very pleasant in downhill. The first positive thing was to say to myself, "you're good on flat*

light, you're one of the best skiers in flat light, this is your opportunity right now, go for it." (Orlick and Lee-Gartner, 1993; p. 115)

Several researchers have shown that thought content and self-statements are important predictors of success in sport (Klinger *et al.*, 1981; Mahoney and Avener, 1977; Orlick and Partington, 1988). The precise reasons for this relationship are unknown, although its effects upon confidence are likely to be prominent (Hardy and Jones, 1994b). The few studies which have attempted to investigate the contribution made by positive self-talk to efficacy expectations (e.g. Weinberg, 1986: Wilkes and Summers, 1984) have proved inconclusive (Feltz, 1988a). Wilkes and Summers (1984), for example, found positive self-talk to enhance performance but efficacy-related cognitions did not appear to mediate this relationship. Feltz (1992) proposed that the inconsistent findings in this area may be due to performance having a confounding effect. Since the research is characterised by multiple performance trials, Feltz argued that subjects' perceptions of their performance experience might mask any effects of the self-talk treatment upon self-efficacy (see also Feltz and Riessinger, 1990).

Emotional arousal

Bandura (1977) proposed that the effects of arousal upon performance, instead of being the product of a direct relationship, are the result of efficacy expectations derived from the performer's cognitive appraisal of perceived arousal levels. Thus, according to Bandura, it is not the actual physiological arousal level, or even the perceived level of arousal, which is important. Instead, it is how the performer views the experienced arousal in terms of its consequences for performance (Jones, 1995b; Jones and Swain, 1992; Jones *et al.*, 1993). For example, the Olympic gymnast, James May, reported a relatively high level of arousal as being facilitative for the performance of tumbling in the floor routine, but debilitative for the more delicately-balanced motor skills required on the pommel horse (Jones and Hardy, 1990a).

Relatively few studies have examined the relationship between emotional arousal and self-confidence (Feltz, 1982, 1988b; Feltz and Mugno, 1983; Kavanagh and Hausfeld, 1986). Although these studies offer relatively inconsistent findings, the study by Feltz (1982) on diving performance is interesting. As would be expected following the proposals above, the subjects' actual levels of physiological arousal did not predict efficacy expectations; *perceived* autonomic arousal, on the other hand, was a significant predictor. However, previous performance accomplishments still provided the best prediction, although this study did not examine the perceived facilitative/debilitative consequences of the arousal for performance. A recent study by

Jones *et al.* (1993) of female gymnasts suggests that this is an important factor. Their findings showed that perceived intensity of somatic anxiety (physiological arousal) did not correlate significantly with confidence, but there was a significant correlation between confidence and how somatic anxiety was perceived in terms of its consequences for subsequent performance. Recent studies on elite swimmers (Jones *et al.*, 1994) and elite cricketers (Jones and Swain, 1995) also revealed that higher levels of confidence were associated with more positive perceptions of physiological arousal.

The practical implications for dealing with performers who perceive themselves to have inappropriate levels of physiological arousal are numerous, and are addressed in more detail in Chapters 5 and 6. To briefly summarise, two basic strategies can be adopted: firstly, by changing the symptoms via some form of relaxation technique in the case of perceived over-arousal, or by some method of increasing activation in the case of perceived under-arousal; and, secondly, by leaving the symptoms largely unchanged and inducing a reappraisal, or reinterpretation, of the consequences of those particular symptoms through some form of cognitive restructuring. Unfortunately, the findings of Gould *et al.* (1989) and Weinberg *et al.* (1992) show that such techniques are low on elite coaches' priority lists as methods for enhancing confidence. Again, as with imagery, this may be due to a relative lack of knowledge and experience in using such techniques on the part of the coaches.

Summary

This section has employed self-efficacy theory, and the four sources of efficacy expectations, as the framework for discussing strategies for enhancing confidence, since relatively little work has been conducted on the precursors of more global self-confidence. In order to understand the strategies used by elite athletes, it has been necessary to adapt recommendations for some of the techniques advocated within the theory. It is clear that there are numerous strategies which might be employed to enhance confidence. Goal-setting and imagery appear to be particularly prominent amongst them. The importance of the coach as a confidence enhancer has also been emphasised, although it seems that further education of coaches is required regarding the variety of strategies that they might employ.

IMPLICATIONS FOR RESEARCH

Two major research issues should be immediately apparent from the discussion thus far. The first relates to the relationship between confidence and elite performance. The research in this area is characterised by correlational designs which show quite a strong association between the two, but preclude any inference regarding causal relationships (Jones *et al.*, 1994). Future investigators should employ causal designs to address this issue. The other somewhat obvious research implication to emanate from this chapter is that the relative contributions of the self-efficacy and sport confidence approaches to understanding confidence in sport need to be directly compared. Is one of them more appropriate for examining elite performance? Or is a combination of the two the way forward? However, there remain numerous issues which also need to be addressed within the approaches themselves. Furthermore, attempts to resolve some of the more major issues within the self-efficacy and sport confidence approaches may well provide some important and more detailed answers to the issues raised above.

Self-confidence, self-efficacy, and sports performance

Given that it is generally accepted that elite performers are able to maintain control over self-doubts in high pressure situations, relatively little is known about the details of the strategies elite athletes employ to this effect. This needs to be explored in the context of both the micro-level approach of self-efficacy theory, and the more macro-level approach of the sport confidence model.

Within the self-efficacy approach, one research strategy might be to examine the incentives elite performers use to ensure that their self-efficacy will facilitate their performance. In reality, little is known about the relationship between self-efficacy and motivation in elite athletes since research activity has been perhaps limited by devoting too much attention to examining performance. There is an urgent need to investigate the processes which underlie the effects of self-efficacy upon performance. This research could be initiated by examining the predictions that in stressful situations elite athletes, when compared to non-elite ones, will maintain their commitment to difficult goals, will increase their persistence and effort when goals are not achieved, and will attribute their failure to lack of effort or poor strategy choice rather than to ability. Further research along these lines should conduct detailed examinations of the thought and behaviour patterns associated with self-efficacy effects. In the context of performance, Feltz (1992) is quite correct in urging future investigators to use the same micro-analytic approach employed to examine self-efficacy to also examine performance itself. This may facilitate the explanation of greater performance variance than in previous studies.

The sport confidence model, and its predictions, clearly requires the same level of scrutiny afforded to the older self-efficacy theory. Its predictive power in relation to the self-efficacy approach has been questioned, but this is perhaps a little premature since it has received very little examination.

Future researchers may wish to examine the pre-competition temporal patterning and antecedents of confidence in elite athletes, as well as the extent to which these are predicted by trait sport confidence. Attempts to merge self-efficacy theory and the sport confidence model may best be directed at Feltz's (1992) postulation that self-efficacy beliefs may be generalisable.

Perhaps the most exciting area for research over the next few years will be the examination of confidence levels, their antecedents and effects upon performance in elite sports teams. There is a need for more detailed investigation of the relationship between individual and collective efficacies and their effects upon group performance. Preliminary research findings suggest different antecedents of individual and collective efficacies (Chase *et al.*, 1994). These require substantiation and examination across different types of sport; for example, interactive versus coactive team sports. The processes which underlie collective efficacy should not receive the belated research attention that has characterised self-efficacy research. Initial findings suggest that group cohesion may be an important moderator of the collective efficacy–performance relationship (Swain *et al.*, 1995). This and other potential mediating variables, such as social loafing and group attributions, require careful scrutiny (Feltz, 1994).

Self-confidence, self-efficacy, and anxiety

It is probably expecting a little too much of future investigators in sport psychology to resolve the issue of the precise nature of the relationship between anxiety and confidence since this has proved elusive to numerous eminent theorists in the past. Research within the self-efficacy framework has thus far failed to make a substantial contribution to the debate, and it is actually the more generalised approach to confidence which may provide more cause for optimism. Confidence and its relationship to control over internal and external factors may provide the key here (Jones, 1995; Jones and Hanton, 1996). Researchers need to examine the proposition that self-confidence may protect against anxiety effects (Hardy, 1996b; Hardy and Jones, 1990), and the mechanisms which might underlie such a relationship. An important related issue is whether cognitive anxiety and confidence have additive or interactive effects on performance. Such questions will be revisited in Chapter 6, but represent a major challenge for investigators in this area.

Strategies for enhancing self-confidence

As will have been evident in previous sections, a considerable amount of work has been devoted to examining the antecedents of self-efficacy. Relatively little research activity, on the other hand, has focused on the antecedents of more generalised confidence. Do the antecedents of confidence in elite and non-elite performers differ? Hanton and Jones' (1995) study of elite and non-elite swimmers showed perceived readiness to be the only predictor of confidence in both groups, but it predicted a much greater percentage of the variance in the elite group, suggesting some potential differences.

Returning to the self-efficacy approach, performance accomplishments have been shown to be an important predictor of self-efficacy in elite performers; but what about the relative contributions of the various related strategies which are available? For example, do goal-setting and actual success result in higher levels of self-efficacy than imaging success? Dealing with goal-setting in isolation, does the achievement of different types of goals, or combinations of them, produce higher self-efficacy in elite athletes? Do elite athletes set different types of goal or more difficult goals than their non-elite counterparts in order to enhance self-confidence?

The coach has been identified as an important party in enhancing self-efficacy in athletes. Coaches perceive their own modelling of confidence as an important source of confidence for their athletes, but do the athletes perceive this in the same manner? In teams, how important is the confidence modelling of other team members to individual efficacies, and also to collective efficacy? Research is required to examine the effects of coaches' verbal persuasion techniques on their athletes' self-efficacy. And what about their deception strategies; how are these perceived by the athletes?

Imagery has been identified as a vital source of confidence, but much of the research to date has concentrated on the extent of imagery effects upon performance. Future research should focus more on the processes underlying any effects, and particularly the relationship between imagery and confidence. Little is also known about how self-talk interacts with confidence. This is mainly due to the methodological problems associated with data collection so that initial research should be directed towards developing suitable methodologies.

Finally, perception of control has been consistently flagged in this chapter as being of primary importance in the process of enhancing confidence. Perception of control can be increased through any of the performance accomplishments, vicarious experiences and verbal persuasion channels, but it is particularly pertinent within the context of the emotional arousal channel. Perception of control is concerned with control over external factors, but also over the internal environment (Jones, 1995b). Thus, positive perceptions of physiological arousal and the ability to manipulate physiological arousal where appropriate are important. Comparisons of cognitive restructuring versus relaxation techniques in situations in which physiological arousal is perceived to be too high, and comparisons of techniques such as cognitive restructuring against imagery when physiological arousal is perceived to be too low, are a high priority for future researchers.

IMPLICATIONS FOR BEST PRACTICE

This section summarises the major implications of the content of the previous sections for best practice in the preparation of athletes for elite performance. Inevitably, there will be significant individual differences in how elite performers prefer to enhance and maintain their confidence levels, but there are some generalisations which can be identified. As emphasised early in the chapter, the nebulous nature of the term "self-confidence" has resulted in its being operationalised in several different ways in the literature. This has meant a variety of theoretical approaches to the study of the construct. Two approaches, self-efficacy theory and the sport confidence model, have been examined in this chapter. Whilst these are in conflict in some respects, there are also commonalities across the approaches. Potential differences in terms of implications for best practice will be highlighted where relevant.

Self-confidence, self-efficacy, and sports performance

One of the underlying premises of self-efficacy theory is that efficacy expectations will not predict performance unless necessary skills and incentives are present. The necessary skills, by definition, are present in elite athletes, but incentives represent an important variable. The motivation of elite athletes, and the incentive systems which underlie it, are addressed in detail in the following chapter. For the moment, it can be vaguely generalised that elite sports performers have developed strategies for enhancing motivation which serve to harness their self-efficacy in the direction of good performance.

The sport confidence model proposes that trait sport confidence is important in predicting state sport confidence and subsequent performance (Vealey, 1986). This highlights a potential conflict with self-efficacy theory in terms of the implications for best practice. Should athletes direct their efforts towards developing a generalised sport confidence? Or should they focus on developing strategies for enhancing and maintaining their confidence in specific situations when performing specific tasks? For example, is it more important for a golfer to begin a tournament round with a high level of confidence about returning with a good score? Or should the golfer's confidence be more specifically related to playing each and every shot well? A golfer who is driving and playing approach shots well but putting poorly is unlikely to begin the round with a high level of generalised confidence. The golfer will almost certainly need to raise efficacy expectations about putting before a high level of generalised pre-round confidence can be established. Thus, the implication speculated here is that athletes primarily need to develop efficacy regarding all the most important sub-components of performance.

Whilst the processes underlying the effects of self-efficacy upon performance are relatively poorly understood at the present time, the research findings (e.g. Bandura, 1989; Collins, 1982; Locke *et al.*, 1984) from general psychology suggest some important implications. Specifically, it appears that elite athletes' high levels of self-efficacy in pressure situations should allow them to maintain their commitment to difficult goals, increase their persistence and effort when goals are not achieved, and attribute their failure to unstable rather than stable factors. Such attributes in highly self-efficacious performers may be crucial in enhancing their probability of success in highly stressful situations.

It is important to emphasise that elite performance is often the result of athletes coacting or interacting as a group. Although in its relative infancy, research in the area of collective efficacy suggests that collective efficacy is more than just the sum of individual efficacies (Lirgg and Feltz, 1994). This has the obvious implication that the role of the leader (e.g. team captain, coach, etc.) is crucial in generating team efficacy since it cannot simply be left to individual team members to generate their own level. It has been suggested that there are several factors which may mediate or modify the effects of collective efficacy upon performance, but group cohesion has been demonstrated empirically to be an important moderator of the effects of collective efficacy upon performance (Swain *et al.*, 1995). Specifically, it appears that collective efficacy only predicts performance to any great extent in highly cohesive groups. Consequently, it is important that coaches and sport psychologists attempt to develop both collective efficacy and group cohesion in tandem with one another.

Self-confidence, self-efficacy, and anxiety

The inconclusive debate amongst self-efficacy and anxiety reduction theorists means that it is unclear whether elite athletes in high pressure situations should devote their efforts primarily towards increasing their confidence or reducing their anxiety (cf. Feltz, 1983; McAuley, 1985). The evidence discussed in previous sections seems to imply that anxiety and confidence may be relatively independent. Elite athletes have described how they can be confident but also have some self-doubts at the same time; and some even say that the combination of anxiety and self-confidence facilitates their precompetitive state and subsequent performance. This suggests that elite athletes may have strategies at their disposal for dealing separately with both anxiety and self-confidence, thus allowing them to maintain the level of control they seem capable of in stressful situations.

Strategies for enhancing self-confidence

Findings from research into the antecedents of macro-level self-confidence suggest that perceptions of appropriate readiness are an important predictor of self-confidence in elite athletes (Hanton and Jones, 1995; Jones *et al.*, 1990). The research also suggests that antecedents of self-confidence may differ between male and female athletes. The specific implications are that males should be encouraged to focus not only on their perceived readiness but also on their own ability being superior to that of their opponents; the implications for females, on the other hand, are that their levels of physical and mental readiness, together with thoughts about a good personal performance, should be their major focus.

Self-efficacy theory implies that focusing on past performance accomplishments will be the major source of efficacy expectations. Empirical findings do indeed support the crucial importance of this factor (e.g. Feltz *et al.*, 1979; McAuley, 1985). Structured goal-setting is an important strategy employed by elite athletes. This includes using proximal as well as distal goals, and setting goals which are difficult but also realistic. Interestingly, elite athletes appear to use a combination of different types of goal. They will inevitably set outcome goals, but also use performance and process goals, particularly in the short term (possibly due to the greater perception of control they generate), as an important means of enhancing and maintaining confidence. "Quality training" and repeated success in training during the run-up to a major competition are also major sources of self-efficacy which operate through the performance accomplishments channel. Elite athletes clearly require their coaches to structure the training environment, as well as competitions during the lead up to major competitions, to be conducive to this type of achievement.

Coaches also have an important role to play in the area of vicarious experience. Elite coaches perceive their own modelling of confidence as an important source of confidence for their athletes (Gould *et al.*, 1989; Weinberg *et al.*, 1992). However, the available research suggests that coaches remain unconvinced about another vital source of confidence to the athletes; imagery. Almost without exception, elite athletes repeatedly attest to the crucial role imagery plays not only in their confidence prior to and during competition, but also during their training. A factor which may distinguish them from their non-elite counterparts is that they practise imagery on a daily basis and appear to be able to exert a level of control over their images which may not be achievable by other athletes.

Elite athletes generally appear to be very efficient at manipulating their confidence levels through their own verbal persuasion techniques. Using self-talk to remain positive in high pressure situations when there is the potential for self-doubts to overpower self-confidence is a valuable means of maintaining the necessary control. Being able to restructure cognitions from negative to positive in such situations is also likely to be an important factor distinguishing elite athletes from their less successful counterparts. As with the other sources of efficacy, coaches can have a valuable role to play in using verbal persuasion techniques to "encourage" their athletes to be confident (Gould *et al.*, 1989; Weinberg *et al.*, 1992). However, it seems likely that elite performers may be more dependent upon their own self-talk due to the control they appear able to exert over it.

The available research suggests that elite athletes have more positive perceptions of their pre-performance physiological arousal than non-elite athletes (Jones *et al.*, 1994; Jones and Swain, 1995). This seems to be important in determining higher levels of confidence in elite sports performers. Research has also shown that athletes who have high levels of self-confidence will perceive their physiological states as being facilitative to performance (Jones, 1995b). Task demands are important in this context. As James May (gymnast) stated, a high level of physiological arousal is facilitative for explosive tasks such as tumbling, but debilitative for the more finely-balanced skills required on the pommel horse (Jones and Hardy, 1990a). Being able to alter levels of physiological arousal by, for example, increasing it through imagery or decreasing it through relaxation, are skills which are important to elite performance; but the skill of restructuring the cognitions associated with high or low levels of physiological arousal may be equally important.

SUMMARY

This chapter has employed the constructs of self-efficacy (Bandura, 1977) and sport confidence (Vealey, 1986) to examine self-confidence in sport. It has reviewed the findings of studies which have investigated self-efficacy and the more generalised conceptualisation of confidence as predictors of sports performance. The chapter has also discussed the relationships between self-efficacy, confidence, and anxiety in sport. Finally, a number of implications for future research and best practice have been proposed.

4

MOTIVATION

CONTENTS

INTRODUCTION

To say that elite performers must be highly motivated is a statement of the obvious. However, *extremely* high levels of motivation may be necessary to repeatedly produce the kind of high quality training sessions that are required for elite performance (Hardy and Parfitt, 1994; Mahoney *et al.*, 1987; Orlick and Partington, 1988). Furthermore, maintaining motivation throughout the duration of a gruelling season, during periods of enforced rest through injury, and following setbacks in competition and training, may be a characteristic which distinguishes elite performers from those who are "only" very good. Consider, for example, the following statements:

> *In retrospect my training wasn't to improve my physical strength or stamina; those came as a secondary result, but the primary purpose of every training session was to toughen up mentally. A training session was totally useless until it started to hurt. That was the point when it started to be worthwhile.* (Herb Elliott, 1960 Olympic Gold medallist and World Record holder for the mile; Hemery, 1991, pp. 8–9)

> *Everything I do, whether it is weights, or running, or the normal training things, or the leisure activities I do, it is all geared toward how it's going to affect my paddling. . . .* (Highly successful Olympic canoeist; Orlick and Partington, 1988, p. 110)

> *Just seventeen days before the Olympic trials Joan Benoit underwent knee surgery. On waking from the anaesthetic her first words to Bob Sevene, her advisor, were, "Can I start tomorrow?" Joan said, "The trials were on 12 May and a week before them I couldn't even run. The ups and downs, it was a nightmare. I didn't say 'Why me?' but I said, 'Why the timing?' Things were going so well and all of a sudden, 'Boom'. I was stressed and I was questioning what was going on but I dealt with it and I just tried to find different things to keep me occupied and alternative exercises." This included pedalling the exercise bike with her arms prior to clearance to do so with her legs. Her determination was awesome. Joan admits that winning the trial so soon after this operation was tougher than winning the Olympics.* (David Hemery on Joan Benoit Samuelson, 1984 Olympic Gold medallist for the Marathon; Hemery, 1991, pp. 197–198)

This chapter explores the factors which are thought to underlie and maintain such phenomenal levels of striving for success and persistence in the face of failure. The chapter commences with a review of some of the intrinsic and extrinsic factors which might promote prolonged motivation for high level involvement in a sport. The second section explores the different goal-setting skills that elite performers may utilise in order to sustain high levels of performance during training and competition. The third section considers the ways in which attributions may influence motivation for high level performance. The fourth section discusses the literature on burnout, overtraining, and injury. The implications of these reviews for both the practice of sport psychology with elite performers, and future research into motivation, are then summarised in the final sections.

INTRINSIC AND EXTRINSIC MOTIVATION

Traditionally, motivational theories have attempted to explain the reasons for people's behaviours in terms of their biological and social needs (Deci and Ryan, 1985). However, some explanations of people's behaviour do not depend upon needs for their explanatory power; for example, Weiner's (1972) attribution theory proposes that the nature of performers' explanations for their success or failure will influence their subsequent motivation. These more recent theories which rely on people's cognitions, rather than their needs, to explain the reasons for their behaviours are known as social cognitive theories. In the present chapter, motivation will be defined in its broadest sense to encompass all potential explanations of behaviour, regardless of their social cognitive, or more traditional, origin.

Much recent research on motivation has focused upon the study of young people's motives for participating in sport, and their reasons for "dropping out" (see, for example, Weiss and Chaumeton, 1992). Whilst such research does not focus directly on elite performance, it is still relevant to the present chapter, because prolonged participation is clearly a necessary minimum requirement for elite performance to occur.

There seems little doubt that most elite performers participate for a variety of different reasons (Bakker *et al.*, 1990), some of which are intrinsic and some of which are extrinsic. The following quotations give some feel for this:

> *. . . Ever since I saw John Wood win a silver medal, I wondered, does he dream all the time about being the best in the world? I have always dreamed about doing that. Maybe that's different from other people.* (Highly successful Olympic canoeist; Orlick and Partington, 1988, p. 110)
>
> *I just did it because I wanted to . . . getting the best out of myself for all the effort I'd put in.* (Steve Ovett, 1975 World Cup 800 m champion, and 1977 and 1980 World Cup 1500 m champion; Hemery, 1991, p. 142)

Despite the fact that elite performers' primary motivation for involvement in sport may be either intrinsic or extrinsic, it appears most unlikely that they would be able to sustain high levels of motivation throughout all the setbacks and "lean periods" that they appear to experience if they did not have high levels of intrinsic motivation for their sport. Furthermore, anecdotal and other evidence (Hardy and Parfitt, 1994; Mahoney *et al.*, 1987; Orlick and Partington, 1988) suggests that elite performers do indeed sustain high levels of intrinsic motivation throughout their careers.

Cognitive evaluation theory

One of the most commonly cited theories of intrinsic motivation is Deci and Ryan's (1985) cognitive evaluation theory (see Figure 4.1) which proposes that individuals have an innate need to feel personally competent and self-determining. Consequently, the theory predicts that specific events will increase intrinsic motivation only to the extent that they enhance performers' perceptions of personal competence and self-determination. Conversely, if events lead to a reduction in performers' perceptions of *either* their personal competence *or* their self-determination, then intrinsic motivation will be decreased. A word or two about the term self-determination is perhaps in order at this stage. In the context of cognitive evaluation theory, self-determination is usually operationalised in terms of *locus of causality*. Individuals are said to have an internal locus of causality when they perceive their actions to have been initiated by themselves, but an external locus of causality when they

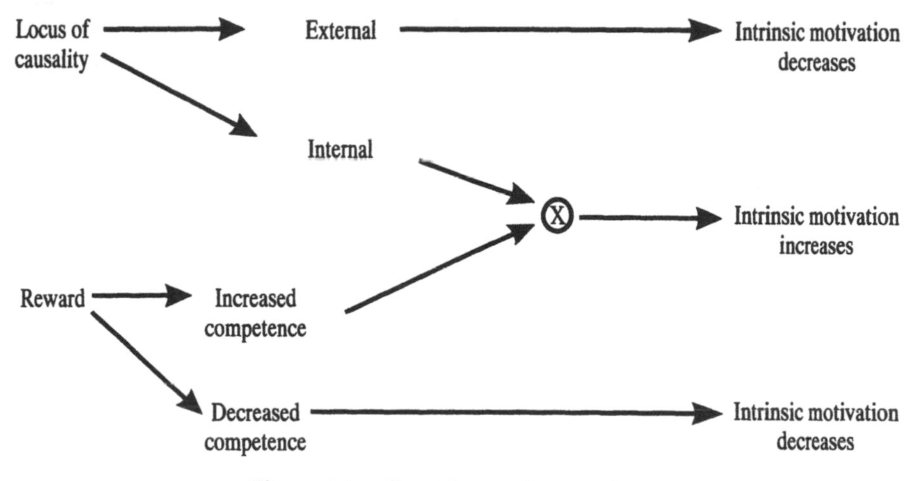

Figure 4.1: Cognitive evaluation theory

perceive their actions to have been initiated (or forced upon them) by events external to themselves (De Charms, 1968). In crude terms, the perception of choice is the important factor here. The basic predictions of cognitive evaluation theory have received considerable empirical support in the general psychology literature (Deci and Ryan, 1985, 1991; Deci *et al.*, 1991).

According to Cognitive Evaluation Theory, elite performers have a strong need to demonstrate their personal competence and self-determination. Consequently, they choose, and commit themselves to, difficult and demanding goals, the achievement of which confirms their feelings of competence and self-determination, thereby enhancing their intrinsic motivation for sport. Anecdotal support for these implications can also be found:

> *I had worked very hard in the winter before the Tokyo Games, and in May I won the Inter-Counties for the first time with over 26ft 4in (8.03m) and the 100 yds in 9.5 sec and I achieved a new level of esteem as an athlete. I walked into the Tokyo stadium feeling I had a right to be there, whereas at the European Championships two years before, I was letting things happen, I wasn't controlling the situation at all.* (Lyn Davies, 1964 Olympic Gold medallist at the long jump; Hemery, 1991, p. 154)

A further implication of cognitive evaluation theory is that any disruption to the achievement of performers' personal goals (through injury, for example) should lead to reductions in perceived competence, and a corresponding reduction in intrinsic motivation. However, it is worth noting the potential involvement of self-efficacy in this motivational process (even though cognitive evaluation theory does not consider self-efficacy). Greater self-efficacy means that athletes are likely to set and achieve more difficult goals (Bandura, 1986; Locke *et al.*, 1984), which therefore lead to even greater increases in intrinsic motivation, and possibly a stronger resistance to the disruption of motivation during setbacks (Bandura, 1986). Again, anecdotal support exists for such a view:

> *The commitment is more than 100%. It's commitment through the ups and downs. Committed through the good results and the bad results, when you're coming 50th and it looks like there's never an end to the bad results. You still have to be committed and still focused and still trying to win every race. I think that the day you let your commitment go, is the day you don't have a chance to win. . . . A lot of people assume it's an overnight success story. It's taken me nine years of hard work in international competition and many years before that.* (Kerrin Lee-Gartner, 1992 Olympic Gold medallist in the Women's Downhill Ski Race; Orlick and Lee-Gartner, 1993, p. 111)

There are at least two obvious implications of cognitive evaluation theory for sustaining the high levels of motivation that are necessary for elite performance: athletes must receive positive feedback about their personal competence; and athletes must feel that they are (at least partially) responsible for the initiation of the training (and performance) behaviours which have led to their success. In line with the first of these implications, athletes are often encouraged (Burton, 1989b; Duda, 1992) to set performance-oriented goals, as opposed to outcome-oriented goals. The logic behind this recommendation is that performance-oriented goals allow the performer much greater control over their reinforcement schedule. This issue has already been mentioned in Chapter 2, and will be discussed further in the next subsection.

As a consequence of the need for highly motivated athletes to feel that they are at least partially responsible for their own training and performance, one might expect that elite performers would perceive themselves to have been coached in a relatively liberal and democratic environment, where they experienced choice and had some input into the decision-making process. Furthermore, one might expect this to be particularly the case in sports where a successful career normally spans a substantial number of years; for example, in gymnastics, swimming, soccer, tennis, golf, or track and field athletics. There is also some qualitative evidence to support this view (Hemery, 1991).

Goal orientations

Other research from a more social cognitive perspective has focused on the effects of different goal perspectives upon various motivational variables (see Duda, 1992, for a review). Goal perspectives refer to the comparisons which performers make in order to formulate their perceptions of competence. Thus, *task-oriented* performers make self-referenced comparisons in which their perception of competence is based on improvements in their own level of performance on the task in question. *Ego-oriented* performers, on the other hand, formulate their perceptions of competence by comparison of their own ability against that of others.

A number of devices exist for the measurement of individual differences in the goal perspectives of sports performers (Duda, 1989a; Gill and Deeter, 1988; Vealey, 1986). However, the Task and Ego Orientation in Sport Questionnaire (TEOSQ; Duda, 1989a) is probably the most commonly used. The TEOSQ has been shown to possess a stable factor structure with two internally consistent orthogonal (independent) factors reflecting the hypothesised ego and task orientations (see Duda, 1992). The orthogonality of task and ego orientations is important, since it implies that performers may be high (or low) on both task and ego orientation, as well as having a dominant orientation. Unfortunately, despite this orthogonality of task and ego orientations, a substantial proportion of the empirical literature from the area has invested in reporting comparisons between subjects who are high in ego orientation and subjects who are high in task orientation, instead of between subjects who are for example high in ego orientation and low in ego orientation. Such comparisons are not really logical, since they confound two independent variables and amount to a comparison of "apples and oranges". However, their occurrence stems from the use of instructional sets to attempt to manipulate goal orientations. Typically, these instructional sets have involved one manipulation which emphasises competition against some specific opposition; and another which emphasises the learning opportunities present in the situation (rather than competition). These instructions therefore confound the experimental design by manipulating two independent variables (ego and task orientation) simultaneously. Nevertheless, studies which have manipulated goal orientation using this approach suggest that ego-oriented environments are likely to lead to high anxiety (Duda *et al.*, 1990), low self-efficacy (Nicholls, 1989), and a denigration of the role of effort in performance (Duda and Chi, 1989; Hall, 1989), *in subjects who have a low perception of their own ability*. Thus, performers who doubt their own personal competence are likely to feel highly anxious, believe that they are unable to cope, and refuse to believe that there is any point in trying, when they are confronted by a situation which emphasises the need to win. Conversely, correlational studies have suggested that performers who are high in task orientation are likely to practise more during their free time (Duda, 1988), and exert more effort in order to achieve high levels of performance (Duda *et al.*, 1989) than performers who are low in task orientation. Other retrospective studies have shown that drop-outs from sport report higher levels of ego orientation than continuers (Duda, 1989b; Ewing, 1981); although whether or not these drop-outs had low perceptions of their own competence when they were performing remains unknown.

In conclusion, ego orientations are often denigrated by goal orientation researchers, a position that is certainly not in accordance with the view received from coaches and performers that "you don't get to be a world champion by not wanting to beat other people". Indeed, if goals really do motivate one's behaviour (Locke and Latham, 1985), then it is difficult to see how one could become a genuinely elite performer without having a strong ego orientation. Furthermore, all the elite wrestlers interviewed by Gould *et al.* (1992a, b) had outcome goals, and qualitative studies of other elite performers appear to confirm the same view:

> *In the Olympics I was aiming to make the final and possibly the bronze. I went in thinking there was no beating the American Ralph Boston or the Soviet Igor Ter-Ovanesyan. The weather conditions were really bad and the performances were all down. I thought I could jump further than was being jumped in those conditions, and suddenly I felt a perception of their vulnerability. I was sitting there watching them, perceiving that it was possible to beat them. It was my fifth out of six jumps and I jumped into a six-inch lead. It showed that the bad conditions had been having more of a psychological than a physical effect, and the others came back to within two or four inches, but it was too late; I'd seen the opportunity and snatched it.* (Lyn Davies, 1964 Olympic Gold medallist at the long jump; Hemery, 1991, p. 154)

> *The biggest confidence I have is in my will power, my ability to race. I haven't met anybody who wants to race more than I do. One competitor*

> *and team-mate of mine, one of the best compliments he ever gave me was during this one workout. I was just dead tired and he knew it, so he was trying to take advantage of it and we just killed each other. It was at the end of the sets and we were racing. He gets done and he can't believe I'm doing this, and he said, "Man, you are the best damn competitor I've ever seen".* (Mike Barrowman, 1992 Olympic Gold medallist and World Record holder for the 200-metre Breaststroke; Ripol, 1993, pp. 36–37)

In view of the contradiction that exists between the arguments that have just been presented, and the view that ego orientations are to be discouraged, it is perhaps worth noting some of the limitations in the current literature on goal orientations. First, there is virtually no evidence that ego orientations *per se* have detrimental motivational consequences. *Rather, the available evidence shows only that high ego orientations combined with low perceived competence may have serious negative motivational consequences.* Elite performers presumably have quite high levels of perceived competence and self-efficacy (see Chapter 3). Second, although generally little is known about the combined (interactive) effects of high task and ego orientation, there is some evidence that a high level of both task and ego orientation is associated with a positive motivational climate and higher levels of performance (Goudas *et al.*, 1992). Third, elite performers may channel their ego orientation into long-term goals such as winning a World Championships or an Olympics in order to sustain their motivation over long and difficult training periods. Similarly, they may channel their task orientation into performance and process-oriented goals for competitive performances (see Chapter 2 and the following section in this chapter; also Burton, 1989b; Jones and Hardy, 1990a). Alternatively, elite performers may focus on outcome goals in certain situations, for example, during monotonous training sessions; but on performance and process goals in other situations, for example, during major competitions (Kingston and Hardy, 1994a).

Finally, a number of the findings in the goal orientation literature could be viewed as being "over interpreted". For example, Nicholls (1989) proposed that ego orientation would be more strongly related than task orientation to a willingness to cheat. The basis for this hypothesis was that

> . . . *A preoccupation with winning* (beating others) *may well be accompanied by a lack of concern about justice and fairness . . . When winning is everything, it is worth doing anything to win.* (Nicholls, 1989, p. 133)

Duda *et al.* (1991) tested this hypothesis by presenting subjects with scenarios from sport which portrayed different acts of cheating and violence. Following the presentation of each scenario, subjects were asked "Is this OK (legitimate) to do if it was [sic] necessary in order to win the game?" The results showed the predicted positive relationship between ego orientation and cheating, but not between task orientation and cheating. In discussing these findings, Duda (1992) suggested that

> *Athletes who tend to be ego- or task-involved in sport seem to have very different conceptions of the long-term value of sport involvement and what is considered acceptable or "fair" behavior within the athletic arena . . . Based on initial research in this area, it appears that athletes who are high in ego orientation focus on two questions, namely "What's in it for me?" and "What do I need to do to win?"* (Duda, 1992, p. 84)

So, people who want to compete (i.e. have an ego orientation) are the "bad guys", and people who "play nicely" (i.e. have a task orientation) are the "good guys" . . . strong words indeed! This does not sit very comfortably with qualitative evidence obtained from elite performers which suggests that "the figure for those who would not intentionally foul or cheat is over 80%" (Hemery, 1991, p. 238). However, Duda *et al.*'s (1991) results do not actually offer any evidence in support of the view that performers with a high task orientation would not cheat *in a situation which was important to them*. The question to which the subjects responded asked whether it was legitimate to cheat *in order to win*. Winning is by definition irrelevant to someone with a high task, but low ego, orientation. It is quite possible that anyone who is very highly motivated to achieve a particular objective might be tempted to cheat in order to obtain it, even if they were only "cheating on themselves". As Duda *et al.*'s (1991) findings show, it is possible that high, compared with low, levels of ego orientation are associated with a greater willingness to cheat in order to win. However, it also seems plausible that this correlation is as much due to the importance of the goal as it is due to the goal orientations that might underlie motivation. As such, the whole issue of individual difference variables underlying cheating and aggression is overshadowed by other, much more fundamentally moral variables than goal orientations. How many of us can honestly say that we have never cheated in the weight training gymnasium by "cutting corners" in terms of quality in order to achieve a new personal best? Yet such goals are clearly task-oriented, and we are indeed only cheating ourselves.

Summary

Elite performers are likely to compete for a variety of reasons, some of which will be intrinsic and some extrinsic. However, it is difficult to see how they could sustain the very high levels of motivation that are necessary to perform at that level if they did not have at least fairly high levels of intrinsic motivation. According to cognitive evaluation theory, elite performers have a strong need to demonstrate their personal competence and self-determination. Consequently, they commit themselves to difficult and demanding goals, the achievement of which confirms their feelings of self-competence, thereby increasing their intrinsic motivation provided that they feel they were (at least partially) responsible for the initiation of the training and performance behaviours which led to that success. Furthermore, actions which are perceived as facilitating goal achievement will generally result in a corresponding increase in intrinsic motivation, whereas events that are perceived as leading to a disruption in goal achievement (e.g. injury, or a poor training environment) will result in a corresponding loss of intrinsic motivation. However, the possible moderating influence of self-efficacy in this latter relationship is noteworthy.

The literature on goal orientations suggests that performers who have a strong ego orientation, but are low in perceived competence, are likely to experience serious motivational difficulties, particularly when they are required to perform under pressure. However, it is difficult to see how elite performers could get to where they are without ever wanting to beat the opposition. Furthermore, it is at least plausible that a lack of perceived competence is not usually a major problem for elite performers. Consequently, it seems likely that elite performers are high in both task and ego orientation, but use these different orientations for different motivational purposes.

GOAL-SETTING SKILLS

Earlier, in Chapter 2, we made a distinction between outcome, performance, and process goals. Furthermore, it was emphasised that performers might utilise all three types of goal for any particular event, but that different goals might be more salient at different times. For example, a gymnast might have an outcome goal of winning a competition, and might have identified that in order to win he must perform twelve "clean" routines (a performance goal). However, prior to performing on parallel bars, he might have the process-oriented goals of relaxing his trapezius and latissimus dorsi muscles in order to swing freely. The distinctions between outcome goals on the one hand, and performance and process goals on the other, parallels the distinction which was made in the previous section between ego and task orientations. More precisely, predominantly ego-oriented performers are more likely to set outcome-oriented goals, whilst predominantly task-oriented performers are more likely to set performance- or process-oriented goals. A natural consequence of this line of reasoning is that performers who are strong in both task and ego orientation should set all three types of goal.

Quality training

Following a qualitative study of 235 Canadian Olympians, Orlick and Partington (1988) concluded that two of the characterising features of highly successful Olympians were the quality of their training and their use of clear daily goals. They quoted a highly successful Olympian, who was a rhythmic gymnast, as saying:

> *I've seen a lot of girls train, and I've seen them think of practice only as practice. They go out on the floor and do repetition after repetition, you know, "Oh well, it's only practice, it doesn't matter." What I've learned to do is if I'm going to take the energy and go out on the floor to do a routine, it's got to count, and so I'd be better off to go out and do 4 perfect routines than to do 20 that are just mediocre. It's quality not quantity. When I walk out around the floor in practice, that's what I would do at a competition. At a competition, I wouldn't just sort of drag myself onto the floor, get into position, wait around, talk, and then go. Once I decide to do my routine, I set the mood exactly, as closely as it could be to competition.* (Orlick and Partington, 1988, p. 111)

Clearly, if performers are required to train for 30–40 hours per week, their motivation to maintain the quality of their training throughout these sessions is an important issue. From Orlick and Partington's study, it seems highly likely that performers set themselves clear daily goals in order to maintain the quality of their training. For example, another of Orlick and Partington's interviewees, a highly successful pistol shooter, said:

> *I would write what I wanted to do and say to myself, "What am I going to do this training session?" I wouldn't just get on the line and pump rounds down the range, but would actually go to the line with an intent, a goal, even if it was just to make sure everything was smooth. When I go to the line, and set everything up, and take up the gun in my hand, I also mentally go through my shot plan checklist before I shoot. This strategy started out very mechanically with a physical list of words which I have on the shooting table, and which I read exactly. These words represented every single step involved in shooting a shot. Then I reduced these to key words so that I could go through the list faster. Finally I didn't need the list anymore. I would usually write one word to emphasise what I wanted, such as "trigger" or "smooth". Then this shot-plan rehearsal became a mix of simple verbal reminders and images which I ran before each shot.* (Orlick and Partington, 1988, pp. 111–112)

It is worth noting at this stage that most of the goals that have been mentioned by these performers are not outcome goals, or performance goals; they are process goals. Yet the extant empirical literature on goal-setting focuses almost exclusively on outcome and performance goals (for reviews, see Beggs, 1990; Burton, 1993). Even authors who have considered process-oriented goals (e.g. Hardy and Nelson, 1988; Kingston and Hardy, 1994a, b) have suggested that the value of such goals may lie in their attention-directing capabilities, rather than their motivational properties. Herein lies a problem.

Although the evidence is not as strong in sport settings as it is in organisational and industrial settings, the goal-setting literature generally supports the view that specific, optimally difficult short-term product-oriented goals (i.e. outcome or performance) will exert a beneficial effect on the performance of relatively simple tasks (Beggs, 1990; Burton, 1992, 1993; Locke *et al.*, 1981). However, as was noted in Chapter 2, the results of this literature are much more equivocal regarding the effects of goal-setting strategies upon more complex tasks (Burton, 1992; Mento *et al.*, 1987). Burton (1992) concludes that

> *for complex skills, strategy development is necessary in order to first develop a way to execute the technique correctly; then the motivational effects of goals can facilitate performance by focusing attention and increasing effort and persistence.* (p. 282)

But this conclusion ignores the possible beneficial effects that *process-oriented* goals might have on strategy and technique development (Kingston and Hardy, 1994a, b). Certainly, Orlick and Partington's (1988) highly successful performers appear to have used such goals to maintain their motivation for *quality* training. Perhaps the problem lies in the fact that the literature seems to view motivation as being concerned only with the quantitative aspects of performance, whereas *for elite or high level sports performers motivation is concerned with both the quantity and the quality of performance, particularly during routine training.*

Relative salience of different types of goal

In line with the goal orientation literature, Burton's (1992) competitive goal-setting model (see Figure 4.2) predicted that performers with an outcome orientation will tend to set outcome-oriented goals which, depending upon their performance expectancies, may lead to anxiety, poor performance, and a subsequent reduction in motivation. On the basis of these predictions, Burton argued that performers should be encouraged to set performance, rather than outcome, goals. However, the implicit assumption that performance goals will not lead to anxiety, poor performance, and a subsequent reduction in motivation, appears to be unsubstantiated. Deci and associates

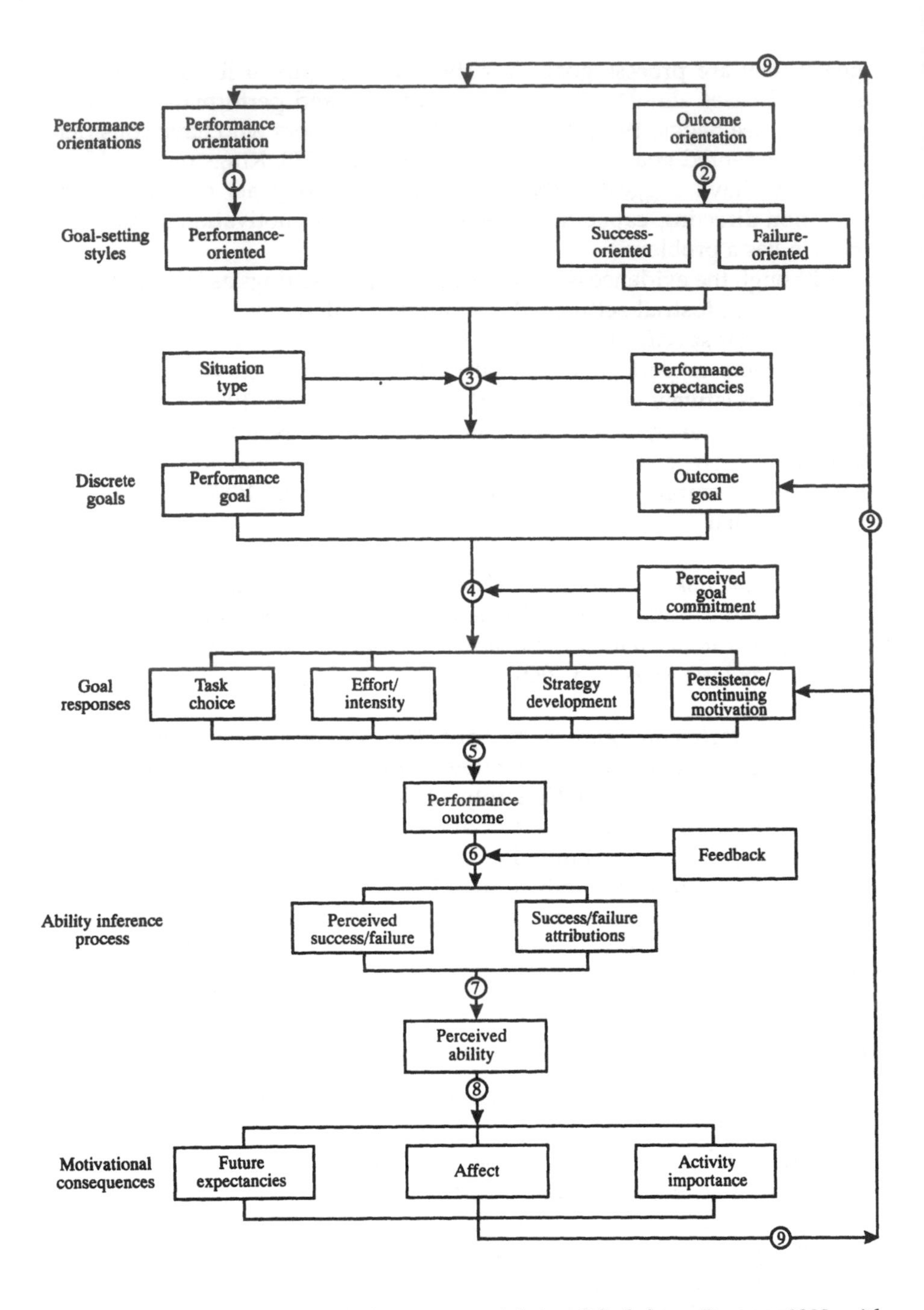

Figure 4.2: A competitive goal-setting model (modified from Burton, 1992 with permission)

(see, for example, Deci and Ryan, 1985) have repeatedly argued that such goals can become internally controlling events which have all the same negative motivational consequences as have been argued to be associated with outcome goals. For example, a female runner might have the performance goal of running a 1500 metres race in under four minutes. Furthermore, the runner might gradually become so committed to this goal that she feels that she has no choice but to continue to strive towards it regardless of the lack of real progress that she is experiencing in terms of race times. In effect, the goal has become an internally controlling event which signals a lack of self-determination and personal competence to the athlete. According to cognitive evaluation theory, such an athlete would show all the negative affective, motivational, and performance characteristics which have been claimed by Burton (1992) and others to be the consequences of outcome goals.

Beggs (1990) has also argued that all goals can be perceived as something of a "double edged sword". On the one hand, realistic and worthwhile goals may motivate the performer to invest the effort and resources necessary for their achievement. On the other hand, emphasising the importance of achieving any criterion may be a source of considerable stress and anxiety when performers have doubts about their ability to do so (cf. Bandura, 1977; Earley *et al.*, 1989; Hardy *et al.*, 1986; Jones and Cale, 1989; Lewthwaite, 1990).

This line of reasoning has an interesting implication at an applied level. Erez and Zidon (1984) have shown that goal acceptance and commitment are necessary conditions for goals to exert a positive effect upon performance. Furthermore, it is well known that performers generally do experience doubts (cognitive anxiety) as competitions approach (Martens *et al.*, 1990b; Parfitt *et al.*, 1990). Thus, talented and ambitious performers are likely to set themselves difficult goals which they may subsequently have doubts about. When this happens, they are likely to reject goals which previously seemed entirely realistic, and performance will quickly follow the same downward spiral. Clearly, this suggests a need to achieve some sort of balance between goal commitment and flexibility in adjusting goals when they become unrealistic. Consultancy experience of working with high level performers suggests that this is a fairly common problem, since such performers have high expectations of themselves and are highly committed to their goals (see also the earlier section on cognitive evaluation theory). They therefore often find it difficult to adjust their goals when circumstances change, for example, through missing training due to injury.

Burton (1989, 1992) commences a similar "double edged sword" argument to Beggs' (1990), but then seems to attribute this property solely to outcome goals. It may well be logically correct to argue that performance goals provide greater opportunity for performers to exert control over their goal difficulty levels and, therefore, their goal achievement (Burton, 1989b). However, as has already been noted, this does not imply that performance goals are without their problems, or that outcome goals are without value. Rather, anecdotal reports (Hemery, 1991) and experiences from professional consultancy suggest that outcome goals may help performers sustain their motivation during setbacks and throughout many hours of gruelling training:

> *I didn't consciously choose to endure pain. I just did whatever it took to achieve and I realized afterwards that I'd shredded myself sometimes. I'd just been so focused that I didn't feel the pain. I once got out of a car and saw that I'd ripped the hands out of my gloves and my hands were bleeding, and I hadn't felt them at the time.* (Sir John Whitmore, 1965 World GT and European Saloon Car Racing Champion; Hemery, 1991, p. 10)

What does appear to be a problem is focusing solely on outcome goals, particularly close to important events when they are naturally very salient. *Perhaps the answer is that elite performers need to have outcome, performance, and process goals in order to progress and perform optimally; but they need to emphasise the relative salience of each goal type in different situations* (Jones and Hanton, 1996; Kingston and Hardy, 1994a, b). Such an argument would also help to explain the rather equivocal findings in the goal proximity literature. For example, some studies (Bandura and Schunk, 1981; Bandura and Simon, 1977; Manderlink and Harockiewizc, 1984) have found that short-term goals are more effective than long-term goals because, it is argued, they provide more opportunity for (positive) feedback. However, Kirschenbaum *et al.* (1982) found that moderately specific planning and longer-term goals were more effective than highly specific short-term goals for the acquisition of self-regulatory skills. Furthermore, as was reported in Chapter 2, studies of the effects of goal proximity upon performance in sport settings have also yielded very mixed findings. Perhaps the problem is that performers are not being asked to set the most effective *type* of goal for the specific circumstances involved in some of these studies.

Summary

Whilst much of the literature has argued that performers should be discouraged from setting outcome goals, it has been shown that elite performers utilise outcome, performance, and process oriented goals in order to maintain their high levels of motivation and performance. However, the relative salience of each of these different types of goal may change in different situations. It is also clear that, for elite performers, motivation is as much concerned with quality as it is with quantity, and that this is reflected in their use of process-oriented goals to maintain their commitment to high quality training on a daily basis. A number of researchers and practitioners have argued that performance-oriented goals overcome all the problems which they have argued to be associated with outcome goals. However, there is good evidence that many of these problems can also be caused by performance-oriented goals under certain circumstances. In particular, it has been shown that performance goals which were previously considered realistic and acceptable become completely unacceptable when performers become very anxious, and also that difficult performance goals lead to anxiety. It is possible that self-confidence is an important factor here which may be relatively independent of anxiety (see Chapters 3 and 6). Nevertheless, it seems clear that the subtleties of goal-setting are rather more complex than has previously been recognised in the literature.

ATTRIBUTIONS

Attributions concern people's perceptions about the causes of events. According to the social cognitive view of the world, individuals' perceptions about the causes of events will be a major determinant of their feelings, expectations, and general motivation towards similar events in the future. This view also hypothesises that certain personality and situational variables will influence the attributions that people make. Thus, a highly confident elite performer might reasonably infer that she beat another competitor because she had a lot of ability, whereas a less confident and less talented performer who had also just won a competition might reason that she had done so because the conditions suited her, but did not really suit her

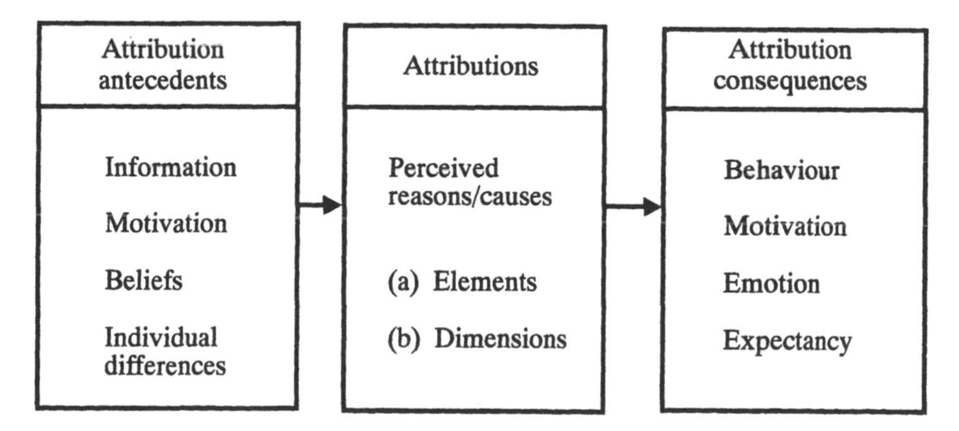

Figure 4.3: An attribution process model (modified from Biddle, 1993 with permission)

opponents. Some of the possible antecedents and consequences of the attributional process are shown in Figure 4.3.

A number of attributional models and theories have been proposed (Heider, 1958; Jones, 1979; Kelley and Michela, 1980; Weiner, 1985). However, attributional research in sport has been dominated by the use of Weiner's model of achievement attributions (Weiner, 1985).

Consequences of attributions

Weiner's early work proposed that achievement attributions could be classified along two attributional dimensions: *stability* and *locus of causality* (Weiner, 1972). The stability dimension is relatively straightforward and refers to the extent to which the attributed quality is stable across time. The locus of causality dimension is also relatively straightforward to define in the context of attributions; however, rather confusingly, this definition differs from that used by cognitive evaluation theorists (cf. Deci and Ryan, 1985). In the attribution literature, locus of causality refers simply to whether the cause was internal or external to the individual concerned. For example, the attribution of a given success to innate ability would be classified as internal and stable, because innate ability is clearly internal to the performer and should not change a great deal across time. Other stereotypical attributions for success and failure are shown in Figure 4.4.

STABILITY	LOCUS OF CAUSALITY: Internal	LOCUS OF CAUSALITY: External
Stable	Ability	Coaching Difficulty
Unstable	Effort Practice Form (unstable ability)	Luck Task ease Officials

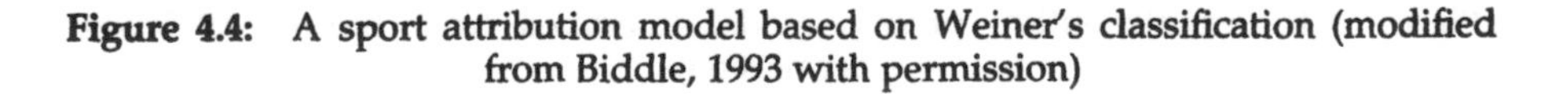

Figure 4.4: A sport attribution model based on Weiner's classification (modified from Biddle, 1993 with permission)

Later theorising by Weiner (1979, 1986) proposed a third attributional dimension, *controllability*. This made it possible to distinguish between attributions which were potentially controllable and those which were not. It is perhaps worth noting here that controllability does not refer only to internal attributions. External attributions could also be controllable by someone else. For example, a gymnast might feel unprepared for a competition because his coach had failed to individualise his training programme sufficiently to meet his personal requirements during the latter stages of his preparation for the competition. Such an attribution by the gymnast would clearly be to a cause which was both external and controllable.

One of the most fundamental predictions of Weiner's (1986) theory is that the stability of attributions should determine expectations regarding future success. More precisely, Weiner predicted that *stable attributions will lead to a greater degree of certainty regarding future outcomes than will unstable attributions; thus, stable attributions will lead to an increased certainty regarding future outcomes*, whereas unstable attributions will lead to reduced certainty about the future or the expectation that the future will be different from the past. Given that self-confidence and self-efficacy are thought to be important determinants of high level performance, these are important predictions of attribution theory for sport psychologists to examine. It is therefore rather surprising that they appear to have been addressed by only a very small number of studies.

Rudisill (1988, 1989) showed that, following failure feedback on a stabilometer balancing task, expectations regarding future success, persistence, and performance were all enhanced in subjects who perceived themselves to have high self-competence and used attributions that were internal, controllable, and unstable. This is consistent with Weiner's (1986) predictions and is, of course, perfectly reasonable, since one would expect that attributions which allowed the possibility of future success would be beneficial following failure. However, Grove and Pargman (1986) found that attributions to effort predicted future expectations, whilst attributions to ability did not. Taken together, these findings suggest that controllability may be the key attributional dimension in predicting future expectations, not stability.

Weiner's (1986) predictions regarding the emotional consequences of attributions are rather more complex. They state that emotional reactions which are related to self-esteem, such as pride and shame, will be associated with internal attributions; emotional reactions which are related to future expectations, such as hope and dejection, will be associated with attributions to stability; and social emotions, such as pity and guilt, will be associated with the controllability dimension. Furthermore, research by Weiner and associates outside the sport context has generally supported these predictions (for a review, see Weiner, 1986). However, other research by Russell and McAuley (1986) suggests that attributional elements may exert a direct influence upon emotional reactions, over and above that exerted via the attributional dimensions of stability, locus of causality, and controllability. Vallerand (1987) took this finding a stage further and proposed an attributional model which distinguished between two different types of appraisal when examining the emotional consequences of sport outcomes. *Intuitive appraisal* is the immediate and relatively automatic appraisal that naturally occurs following the outcome of any important event. On the other hand, *reflective appraisal* involves greater thought being given to the event, and the consideration of attributional processes. A similar distinction has also been made by Weiner (1986). These are important distinctions to make, because recent research by Vallerand, Biddle, and others, has shown that the primary determinant of emotional reactions to success and failure is the intuitive appraisal of the subjective success or failure, and that attributions following reflective appraisal generally play only a supplementary role (see Biddle, 1993 for a review).

Antecedents of attributions

A number of individual difference variables have been studied as potential influences upon the different attributions that people give for success and failure. These include self-esteem, self-efficacy, goal orientations, gender, and attributional styles. For example, individuals high in self-esteem tend to attribute success to internal, stable, and controllable factors more than individuals low in self-esteem (Marsh *et al*, 1984; Weiss *et al.*, 1990). Similar findings have also been reported for self-efficacy (McAuley, 1991; McAuley *et al.*, 1989); whilst Eysenck (1982) has reviewed evidence which suggests that highly anxious performers tend to attribute failure to more internal and stable causes.

Research on goal orientations and attributions has generally confirmed the prediction that strong ego orientations lead to a greater emphasis on ability attributions. Conversely, strong task orientations lead to a greater emphasis being placed on effort attributions (for a review, see Duda, 1992). However, attributional research on gender has failed to provide clear support for the prediction that women would show "attributional modesty" by offering less stable and internal attributions for success than men (for a review, see Biddle, 1993). Deaux (1984) proposed that attributional modesty is mediated by expectations of success. Consequently, she argued that the equivocal findings regarding attributional modesty may be due to the failure of researchers to take into account the nature (sex-typing) of the activity in question, and whether or not subjects are performing in same- or mixed-gender situations, since women are not necessarily expected to have low expectations for success in feminine activities, or when they are competing against other females. On the basis of these arguments, one would not expect to observe attributional modesty in female elite sports performers.

Research on attributional styles has been somewhat controversial. The concept of attributional styles was proposed by Abramson *et al.* (1978) following their introduction of *globality* as a fourth attributional dimension concerned with the Generalizability of causes to other areas of behaviour. Using this as a starting point, Peterson *et al.* (1982) developed the Attributional Style Questionnaire. This questionnaire purported to measure attributional style along three attributional dimensions: locus of causality, stability, and globality. It was developed to test Abramson *et al.*'s (1978) reformulation of the learned helplessness model of clinical depression. This proposed that the primary cause of depression was the repeated attribution of uncontrollable failure to stable, internal, and global causes. Thus, individuals become depressed because they perceive themselves to be caught up in a situation where failure is inevitable, where this failure is brought about by their own actions, and where their actions are likely to be similarly unsuccessful in most other situations; that is to say, because of repeated exposure to such situations, they have learned that they are indeed helpless.

Peterson *et al.* (1982) found support for the hypothesis that depressives should show the characteristic attributional style of attributing uncontrollable failure to stable, internal and global causes. Furthermore, Sweeney *et al.*'s (1986) subsequent meta-analysis of 104 such studies also supported this prediction, thereby providing support for the notion of attributional styles. However, Cutrona *et al.* (1984) found that the Attributional Style Questionnaire did not predict attributions for actual events "very well". Of course, given the fact that attributional styles are almost certainly influenced by situations, the phrase "very well" may simply reflect the age-old paradox of whether a one litre glass containing half a litre of water is half empty or half full!

Modest support has been presented for the involvement of attributions in the development of learned helplessness in sport (Johnson and Biddle, 1988; Prapavessis and Carron, 1988; Seligman *et al.*, 1990). It has also been argued (Biddle, 1993; Dweck and Leggett, 1988) that performers who have strong ego orientations and low perceptions of their own competence will be particularly vulnerable to such learned helplessness. Whilst one would obviously not expect elite sports performers to demonstrate a learned helplessness attributional style, it would be a mistake to assume that they never demonstrate such an attributional pattern or enter the "learned helplessness spiral", especially if they are in a "slump". Rather, it seems likely that elite performers may possess strategies that enable them to change their attributions in order to get out of this spiral when they do enter into it.

Learned helplessness is also of interest because, in some senses, it represents the opposite of autonomous self-regulation, which is what most sport psychologists try to help their performers to achieve. The literature on the attributional retraining of learned helplessness (see, for example, Dweck, 1980; Forsterling, 1988) is unequivocal in advocating the use of ability attributions for successful outcomes. However, the use of effort attributions for failure outcomes is not without its problems. For example, Covington and Omelich (1979) have indicated that individuals who invest greater effort following failure, but still fail, are even more likely to attribute this second failure to ability than they were for the first. Consequently, the preferred attribution for failure in sport may be to strategy rather than to effort (Biddle, 1993).

Factors influencing the attributional process

One of the most widely reported phenomena associated with attributions is the self-serving bias of performers in attributing their successes to more internal, controllable and stable causes than their failures. Research has generally confirmed that this phenomenon does exist at least in terms of the stability dimension (Grove *et al.*, 1991; McAuley and Goss, 1983; Mullen and Riordan, 1988; Watkins, 1986). However, it is not clear exactly why such a bias occurs. It has been argued that it reflects a strategy to protect or enhance self-esteem (Miller, 1976); but it has also been argued that it is a function of differential memory for information related to one's own, as opposed to others', performances (Brawley, 1984). There is evidence to support both positions (for reviews, see Kelley and Michela, 1980; Mullen and Riordan, 1988). It is unclear whether or not the self-serving bias is stronger or weaker in elite performers when compared to their non-elite counterparts. However, theoretical arguments and qualitative reports suggest that a bias should exist in terms of the locus of causality dimension of attributions, since elite performers do appear to take considerable personal responsibility for their failures as well as their successes:

> *If you learn from your mistakes, you become a better person. If you don't learn from what you've done wrong, then you're defeating the purpose.* (Wayne Gretzky, Canadian ice hockey centre, and the only man in NHL history to score 2000 points; Hemery, 1991, p. 212)

> *If I've given up a goal and the other team has gone one up, that's a different situation. It's like I was saying earlier; the longer the game goes on, that goal is costing you the match. All you can do now is your best not to give up another one. If at the end of the day that mistake is the one that cost your team, well that hurts, and I think it has to hurt! . . . you can't expect to be 100 percent every day. At the same time, it's not as if just because you've made a mistake once, that's eliminated it, that you're not going to make the mistake again. Football doesn't happen like that. In some situations, it's*

> *only after you make the mistake over and over again that you realize what you are doing and you learn from it.* (Pat Jennings, capped 119 times as Northern Ireland's goalkeeper, and voted Footballer of the Year by the English Professional Footballers' Association in 1976; Newman, 1992, p. 81)

Other research (McAuley and Duncan, 1989; Weiner, 1986) has suggested that causal searches are more likely, and emotional reactions more intense, when performers' expectations regarding the outcomes of events are disconfirmed than when they are confirmed. Thus, the relationships between attributions, subsequent emotional reactions, and expectations, may be stronger when the outcome is unexpected than when it is expected. This may relate to Vallerand's (1987) distinction, discussed earlier, between intuitive appraisal and reflective appraisal. Similarly, Biddle and Hill (1988) have shown that emotional reactions are more strongly related to attributions when the outcome in question is important to the performer than when it is not.

Finally, as Kelley and Michela (1980) indicated, many of the antecedents and consequences of attributions are bound together in cyclical relationships. For example, high self-efficacy leads to more internal, controllable, and stable attributions for success (McAuley, 1991; McAuley *et al.*, 1989), which in turn lead to stronger expectations regarding future success (Bandura, 1990; Weiner, 1986). Hence, there is a need for more longitudinal studies which explore the possibly interactive and cyclical nature of the relationships that exist between such variables as perceived competence, goal orientation, outcome rewards, attributions, emotional reactions, self-efficacy, and subsequent motivation.

Cultural effects on attributions

In a rather different direction, Bond (1983) has presented strong arguments to support the view that cultural factors may have an important influence upon attributions. In particular, Bond (1983) identified three ways in which attributional processes may differ across cultures. First, performers may make spontaneous attributions more or less frequently, depending upon the cultural context. For example, elite performers from western cultures may be more likely to ask themselves the question "why?" following success or failure than elite performers from eastern cultures. Second, performers from different cultures may attach a different meaning to success and failure, and may consequently make use of different attributional elements and dimensions. For example, objective success may be less important in some cultures than in others. Third, cultural differences may influence the attributions that are made in private and in public. For example, Bond (1983) reported that research had shown that the self-serving bias does not exist in Hong Kong Chinese because of their need to appear modest. Furthermore, Bond and others (e.g. Duda and Allison, 1989) have argued that attributional research has been dominated by a western perspective. Such a bias could easily lead to false conclusions regarding the generalizability of results to other cultures. Although research into cultural differences in attributions is very limited, such differences may prove to be very important at a time when an increasing number of national coaches are imported from other countries.

Summary

A number of implications for elite performance can be drawn from the attributional research which has been discussed in this section. First, elite performers are more likely than most to make internal, controllable and stable attributions for success, and internal, controllable, unstable attributions for failure. This attributional style may be independent of gender in elite performers, and has a self-serving bias in that it is likely to help elite performers avoid getting into "learned helplessness spirals". Second, elite performers are likely to need and possess good restructuring strategies, so that whenever they do get into "learned helplessness spirals" they can modify their attributional patterns for failure in order to get out of them. Furthermore, from an applied practice point of view, there is good evidence to suggest that it may often be better to encourage performers to attribute failure to poor strategy rather than to lack of effort. Third, the intuitive appraisal which immediately follows success or failure has a much stronger effect upon emotional reactions (and presumably therefore future expectations) than does the more reflective appraisal which may take place later. Consequently, the need for extensive success during the build-up to major competitions should not be underestimated, even for elite performers. Fourth, there may well be important cultural differences in attributions and the relationships that they have with other variables. Such differences have been little explored, but may be important given the international mobility of top level coaches. Finally, there is an urgent need for more longitudinal studies which explore the possibly cyclical relationships which may exist between the antecedents and consequences of attributions.

WITHDRAWAL FROM SPORT

Although it may not be immediately obvious to the reader that withdrawal from sport is an important aspect of elite performance, at least three forms of withdrawal appear to have important motivational consequences for elite performers; these are withdrawal due to burnout, overtraining, and injury.

As will become clear from the literature reviewed, the first of these forms of withdrawal has both motivational antecedents and motivational consequences, whereas the latter two have only motivational consequences.

Burnout

Burnout in sport has been brought to public attention by the sudden withdrawal from sport of such elite tennis players as Bjorn Borg and Andrea Jaeger, apparently because of intolerable levels of stress associated with continued involvement in their sport. Burnout is generally regarded as a syndrome brought about by continuous exposure to stress associated with performing some particular activity (Chernis, 1980; Freudenberger, 1980; Smith, 1986). It is characterised by physical and emotional exhaustion, together with a lowered level of functioning. Ultimately, burnout leads to psychological, and sometimes physical, withdrawal from some previously enjoyed activity. Smith (1986) has stated that when people are burned out they typically experience chronic fatigue, poor sleep patterns, increased vulnerability to viral infections and other illnesses, depression, and helplessness. Not surprisingly, their performance is markedly impaired.

There is an established psychological literature on burnout in the service professions, and even some literature on burnout in coaches and sports officials (Dale and Weinberg, 1990; Farber, 1983; Kelley, 1994; Kelly and Gill, 1993; Taylor *et al.*, 1990). However, there is as yet very little empirical literature on burnout in sports performers (for exceptions, see Gould *et al.*, 1995a, b). Nevertheless, a number of theoretical models of athlete burnout have been proposed which offer some guidelines for both best practice and future research in the area (e.g., Coakley, 1992; Fender, 1989; Schmidt and Stein, 1991; Smith, 1986).

Smith (1986) drew on Thibaut and Kelley's (1959) social exchange theory to construct a model of athlete burnout which paralleled typical models of the human response to stress (cf. Lazarus, 1982; Selye, 1976). According to Smith's (1986) model, performers' continued participation in their sport is determined by the balance that exists between the rewards that are available from continued involvement and the costs of that involvement. This balance is called the *outcome* of continued involvement. If this outcome exceeds a certain level, called the *comparison level,* then the performer will experience satisfaction from continued involvement. On the other hand, if the outcome is less than the comparison level, then performers will be dissatisfied with their involvement. The rewards which may be taken into account in these comparisons include trophies, money obtained from performing, satisfaction and feelings of self-competence at the achievement of personal goals, and the admiration of (significant) others. Conversely, the costs that might be considered include the amount of time required for training, the experience of anxiety and other negative emotions at major competitions, feelings of failure or disapproval following defeat, and a lack of opportunity to engage in other potentially interesting activities or relationships.

Although the comparison level determines how much satisfaction performers will obtain from continued involvement in their sport, it is not the sole determinant of whether or not performers will continue their involvement in that activity. Sometimes, for example, a performer leaves a sport despite obtaining satisfaction from it. According to social exchange theory, this occurs because performers also have a *comparison level for alternatives*, which is defined as the minimum outcome that the performer will accept without abandoning current involvement in favour of some other activity. Clearly, the comparison level for alternatives will be somewhat influenced by the outcomes that the performer expects to obtain from these alternatives. However, these may not be the only determinants of the comparison level for alternatives; for example, individual difference variables (such as persistence and impulsivity) may also exert an influence. At any rate, if the outcome for the current activity exceeds the comparison level for the performer's best alternative, then the performer is said to be dependent upon their current activity, and will continue to be involved in it. However, if the outcome for the current activity drops below the comparison level for alternatives, then there is no longer any dependence and the performer will withdraw from their current activity. Thus, *an important feature of social exchange theory is that it has the potential to explain why performers who enjoy their sport sometimes withdraw*: the outcome for their current activity exceeds the comparison level, but the anticipated outcome for some alternative activity raises the comparison level for alternatives above the outcome currently obtained. *Equally, it has the potential to explain why performers who are dissatisfied with their sport sometimes continue to be involved in it*: the outcome for their current involvement is less than the comparison level, but the outcomes that they anticipate from other activities are so low that their current outcome still exceeds their comparison level for alternatives.

In essence, Smith's (1986) model suggests that performers may withdraw from a sport for at least four reasons: the potential rewards to be obtained from involvement in some other activity increase; the potential costs from involvement in some other activity decrease; the anticipated rewards of continued involvement in the current activity decrease; or the anticipated costs of continued involvement in the current activity increase. According to Smith (1986), performers *drop out* from sport when the outcomes expected from other activities raise the comparison level for alternatives above the outcome level for their current involvement. However, *performers burn out as a result of "an increase in stress-induced costs" (Smith, 1986, p. 39) associated with continued involvement, without any compensatory increase in rewards.* Using former American football coach Dick Vermeil as an example, Smith (1986) argued that "there was no indication that the reward value of coaching had decreased; rather, it appeared that the positives became outweighed by the stress-induced costs to the point that the outcomes dropped below the comparison level for the alternative of discontinuing activity" (p. 39).

Smith's (1986) model of athletic burnout is useful in that it draws attention to the distinction that needs to be made between drop-out and burnout. However, Schmidt and Stein (1991) have argued that both Smith's model of burnout, and Gould and Petlichkoff's (1988) subsequent model of drop-out and burnout, suffer from two weaknesses. The first of these revolves around evidence from Gould *et al.* (1982) which suggests that drop-out may occur because of rising outcomes associated with alternatives (e.g. performers wanted to play other sports) *or* lowered satisfaction with their current involvement (e.g. performers were no longer having fun, experienced too much pressure, etc.). Thus, Smith's distinction between drop-out and burnout in terms of rising rewards associated with alternatives and rising costs associated with current involvement may not stand up to empirical examination. However, Schmidt and Stein's (1991) second criticism is much more serious. Smith (1986, p. 37) defined burnout "as a reaction to chronic stress", thereby implying a temporal component to burnout in which the performer experiences high stress and lowered satisfaction over a prolonged period of time prior to burning out. However, according to Thibaut and Kelley's (1959) definition of dependence, burnout could not then occur because the performer would leave the sport *as soon as* the outcome dropped below the comparison level for alternatives. In view of these criticisms, together with anecdotal evidence that elite sports performers often stay involved in their sport long after they have ceased to obtain satisfaction from it, Schmidt and Stein (1991) argued that Thibaut and Kelley's (1959) social exchange theory could not provide an adequate explanation of burnout from sport without the addition of a temporal component. They found this temporal component in Kelley's (1983) model of commitment in close relationships, together with Rusbult and associates' extension of this work to investment (Rusbult, 1980; Rusbult and Farrell, 1983; Rusbult *et al.*, 1986). Kelley (1983) defined commitment to a relationship behaviourally as membership stability, whilst Rusbult (1980) proposed that commitment is determined by a combination of satisfaction (rewards minus costs), alternatives, and investments (resources put into the relationship).

Schmidt and Stein (1991) used the notions of commitment and investment to argue that the reason why some performers remain involved in their sport after they have ceased to gain any satisfaction from it is that they have invested too much in it to feel able to withdraw. This enabled Schmidt and Stein to distinguish between enjoyment-based commitment, entrapped commitment, and drop-out from sport. More precisely, according to Schmidt and Stein, enjoyment-based commitment is characterised by high (or

Table 4.1: Investment model predictions of two types of commitment and drop-out (modified from Schmidt and Stein, 1991 with permission)

	Commitment (enjoyment-based)	Commitment (burnout)	Drop-out
Rewards	Increasing (or high)	Decreasing	Decreasing
Costs	Low	Increasing	Increasing
Satisfaction	High	Decreasing	Decreasing
Alternatives	Low	Low	Increasing
Investments	High	High (or increasing)	Decreasing

increasing) rewards, low costs, high satisfaction, few alternatives, and high investment. Entrapped commitment is characterised by decreasing rewards, increasing costs, decreasing satisfaction, few alternatives, and high (or increasing) investment. Furthermore, according to Schmidt and Stein, entrapped individuals are prone to burnout. Finally, drop-out is characterised by decreasing rewards, increasing costs, decreasing satisfaction, an increase in alternatives, and a decrease in investment (see Table 4.1). Early research on the expanded Sport Commitment Model which has been developed from Schmidt and Stein's (1991) model has proved encouraging (Carpenter *et al.*, 1993; Scanlan *et al.*, 1993a, b). On the basis of this, Schmidt and Stein's model (see Table 4.1) seems to offer much promise for future empirical research into burnout. In summary, it argues that performers burnout because: they experience a sharp increase in the cost of their involvement in sport; they perceive no increase in the rewards associated with this involvement; they perceive themselves to be required to increase an already large investment in their sport; and they perceive themselves to have few alternatives to continued involvement in that sport. If confirmed, this explanation might offer some important predictions regarding psychological interventions for minimising the risk of burnout occurring in high level sports performers.

Most of the models of athlete burnout that have been proposed so far focus upon the athlete's response to chronic stress as the cause of burnout. Coakley (1992) has proposed a rather different, sociological model of burnout. Coakley does not disagree that burnout is stress induced, but places much more emphasis upon the organisational causes of this stress, rather than the athlete's response to it. More precisely, Coakley (1992) used data obtained from a set of 15 interviews with former athletes who were thought to have burned out to argue that burnout occurs because the social organisation of high level sport constrains athletes to such an extent that it takes away their personal control, disempowers them, and stops them from achieving their full developmental potential as human beings. Clearly, there are links with self-determination and cognitive evaluation theory here (see earlier section in this chapter).

One of the few well-designed empirical studies of burnout in athletes was a combined qualitative and quantitative study of 61 junior elite tennis players conducted by Gould *et al.* (1995a). They examined organisational, personality, and coping response variables, and found that burnout was predicted by all three types of variables. In particular, the major reasons given for withdrawal included competitive pressure, subtle parental pressure, time pressures, and a desire to develop a social life outside sport. The major personality variables that predicted burnout were related to perfectionism, and the need for external organisation. Finally, burned out players tended to use planning and cognitive restructuring as coping strategies less than non-burned out players. Gould *et al.*'s (1995a) findings, therefore, offer some support for both Coakley's disempowerment model and the cognitive appraisal/coping response models that have been proposed by Smith (1986) and others. Consequently, Gould *et al.* (1995a) proposed that future research should utilise more integrated interactional models of burnout.

The major differences between burnout and enjoyment-based commitment revolve around the reward–cost balance (outcome) of involvement in sport. One of the more potent rewards available to performers is the satisfaction and self-approval which come from successfully meeting internal standards of performance (Bandura, 1977; Smith, 1986). However, this success is largely determined by the goals that performers set (cf. Bandura, 1977; Spink and Roberts, 1980). Furthermore, as has already been observed, self-efficacy, goal-setting, and attributions seem to be irrevocably bound together in a cyclical relationship. High self-efficacy increases the likelihood that performers will set, and achieve, more difficult personal goals (Bandura, 1986; Locke *et al.*, 1984), and also the likelihood that they will accept personal responsibility for these successes (McAuley, 1991; McAuley *et al.*, 1989). Consequently, high self-efficacy performers should obtain more satisfaction from their involvement in sport. However, the primary determinant of performers' self-efficacy is their previous experience of success and failure, which is largely determined by the personal goals that they set. High levels of goal-setting and attributional skill should therefore increase satisfaction and reduce the risk of mid-career burnout occurring.

A rather different situation may prevail when elite performers have achieved extremely important long-term goals, such as peak performances at an Olympic Games or other lifetime ambitions. Following the achievement of such goals, it seems natural to expect that the anticipated reward–cost balance associated with future involvement may be considerably reduced, essentially because there is nothing left that the performer really wants to achieve. Under such circumstances, Schmidt and Stein's (1991) model would suggest that performers' enormous investments in their sport may make them extremely vulnerable to burnout. Furthermore, consultancy experience of performers' attempts to deal with these situations would seem to support this position. Perhaps this is a time when performers should be encouraged to reappraise the alternatives that are available to them (for example, coaching, further education, and other careers), and see that their previous investments in sport may be more portable than they had previously realised (Ogilvie and Taylor, 1993). Performers should then be much better placed to identify future aims and objectives, either in their current sport (leading to continued enjoyment-based commitment), or in some other direction (leading to withdrawal and drop-out). Either way, they should be able to avoid the anguish and distress of burnout.

Overtraining

So far in this section, the discussion has focused upon the psychological concomitants of burnout. However, burnout is recognised as a multidimensional syndrome which contains physiological and behavioural components, as well as psychological ones (Silva, 1990; Smith, 1986). There is also a well-established literature indicating that increases in physical training loads, or *overtraining*, can lead to staleness and burnout (see, for example, Hackney *et al.*, 1990; Murphy *et al.*, 1990; Silva, 1990); although it seems to be generally accepted by sports scientists and medical doctors working in the field that staleness and burnout more often result from the total sum of stressors which come to bear upon the athlete, rather than from just the training load.

Early research on the psychological symptoms of staleness in performers following "overtraining" (e.g. Morgan *et al.*, 1988) relied largely on the measurement of mood disturbances from the so-called "iceberg" profile that elite performers were argued to possess (see Figure 4.5). The idea behind this research was that training loads could be titrated against psychological mood disturbance so as to minimise the risk of placing too great a training load on athletes. However, some research has questioned the desirability of "iceberg" profiles for high levels of performance (see, for example, Cockerill *et al.*, 1991), and more recent research on overtraining (e.g. Murphy *et al.*, 1990) has adopted a more complete profiling approach which includes mood state as just one of a number psychological variables.

The effects of overtraining upon the immune system are fairly well documented (Fitzgerald, 1988; Jakeman *et al.*, 1994; Noakes, 1986). Low intensity and short duration exercise are thought to enhance immune system functioning (Keast *et al.*, 1988; Oshida *et al.*, 1988), whilst high intensity and long duration exercise are thought to impair immune system functioning (Parry-Billings *et al.*, 1990). In view of these effects, overtrained athletes may possess reduced wound-healing capability, and be particularly susceptible to a number of allergies and upper respiratory infections (Noakes, 1986).

Quite how much training elite performers lose as a result of such problems is not known, but one could reasonably infer that it is more than one

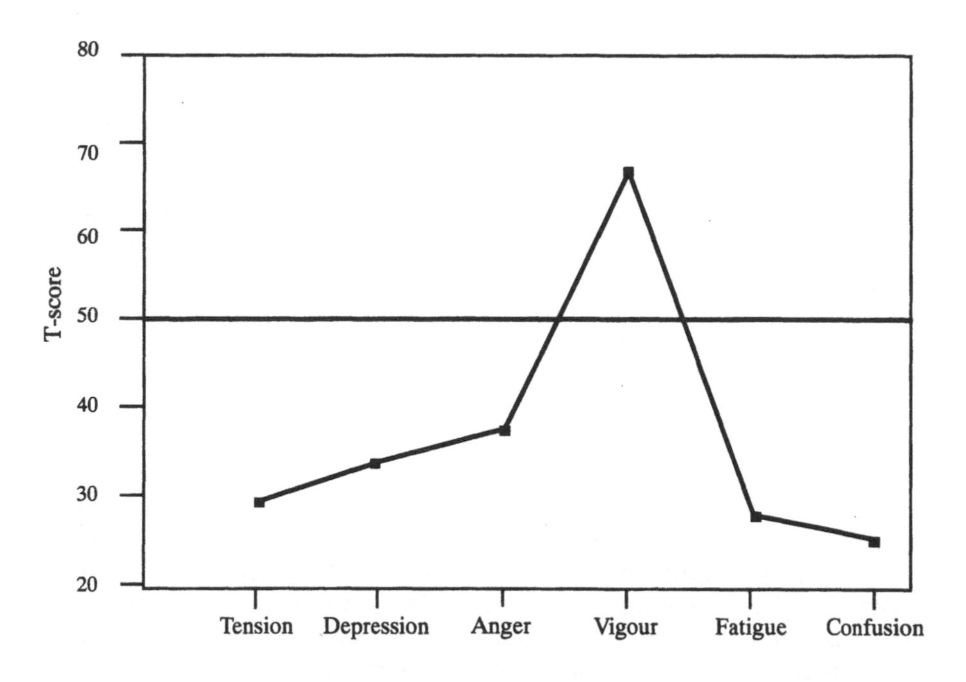

Figure 4.5: The iceberg profile

would like it to be. Consequently, any technique that could enhance immune system functioning following high intensity training would be of considerable benefit to elite performers. At least two branches of research present themselves as possible candidates for this role. First, Paikov (1985) suggested that the restorative effects of active regeneration techniques such as massage, sauna, and hydrotherapy may be up to three times greater than those of passive rest. Second, research outside the sport and exercise context (Dillon and Minchoff, 1985; Hall, 1983; Olness *et al.*, 1988) indicates the possibility that hypnosis and other stress management techniques may increase the psychological resources that are available to self-regulate immune system functioning. Taken together, these findings suggest that *active regeneration, stress management training, and social support, might all be useful in trying to help athletes avoid overtraining and burnout.*

Coping with injury

Very little research appears to have directly addressed the motivational consequences of injury, although a number of studies have touched upon these tangentially. The stress of enforced withdrawal from sport through injury has been likened to a grief response in which between three and six stages or phases can be identified (Averill, 1968; Kubler-Ross, 1969;

Pederson, 1986; Wehlage, 1980). The most commonly referred to of these models is Kubler-Ross' (1969) five-stage model which was derived from interviews with over 200 terminally ill patients. According to this model, the first stage of grief is characterised by denial that the illness (injury) has serious consequences. This is replaced by anger, feelings of rage, envy, and resentment. Extreme emotionality is to be expected at this stage, and is hypothesised to help performers accept that an injury has occurred. The third stage is characterised by bargaining, which represents the performers' attempt to regain their lost fitness. Next follows hopelessness and depression, thought to be brought about by acceptance that the injury has occurred, and realisation that it cannot be reversed. During this stage, performers are hypothesised to become socially detached, and preoccupied with all the things that they will not be able to do as a result of their injury. Kubler-Ross' final stage is acceptance that death is about to occur. This stage should not be thought of as a contented or "positive" stage, as Kubler-Ross describes it as being almost completely devoid of feelings; a stage in which the patient has completely "given up" might be a better way to think about it. In line with Averill's (1968) model of grief through the loss of significant others, this phase is often replaced by reorganisation or recovery in grief models of injury (Pederson, 1986; Wehlage, 1980). During this stage of injury, performers are hypothesised to come to terms with their losses and restructure their lives so that they can gradually return to (a perhaps new form of) normal life.

Although grief models could clearly be used as a basis for the development of intervention programmes with injured performers, there are a number of differences between loss of self through death, loss of loved ones, and loss through injury, not the least of which is the degree of recovery that is possible. Furthermore, within the clinical psychology literature on grief through death and loss of loved ones, there is considerable controversy over the linearity of progression through the various stages or phases proposed. A number of researchers have suggested that progression through these phases is circular or accompanied by frequent relapses to earlier phases rather than strictly sequential. Unfortunately, well-designed tests of grief models of injury have rarely been conducted; although following a review of the available sport psychology literature, Brewer (1994) concluded that such models held less promise than the alternative cognitive appraisal models (see Figure 4.6) that have been proposed by a number of other researchers (e.g. Anderson and Williams, 1988; Wiese-Bjornstal and Smith, 1993). However, given the generality of cognitive appraisal models, the fact that athletes' emotional responses to injury represent an important part of such models, and the paucity of good quality data, this conclusion seems to be somewhat premature. Furthermore, a detailed review of the clinical psychology literature on grief (as opposed to just the sport psychology

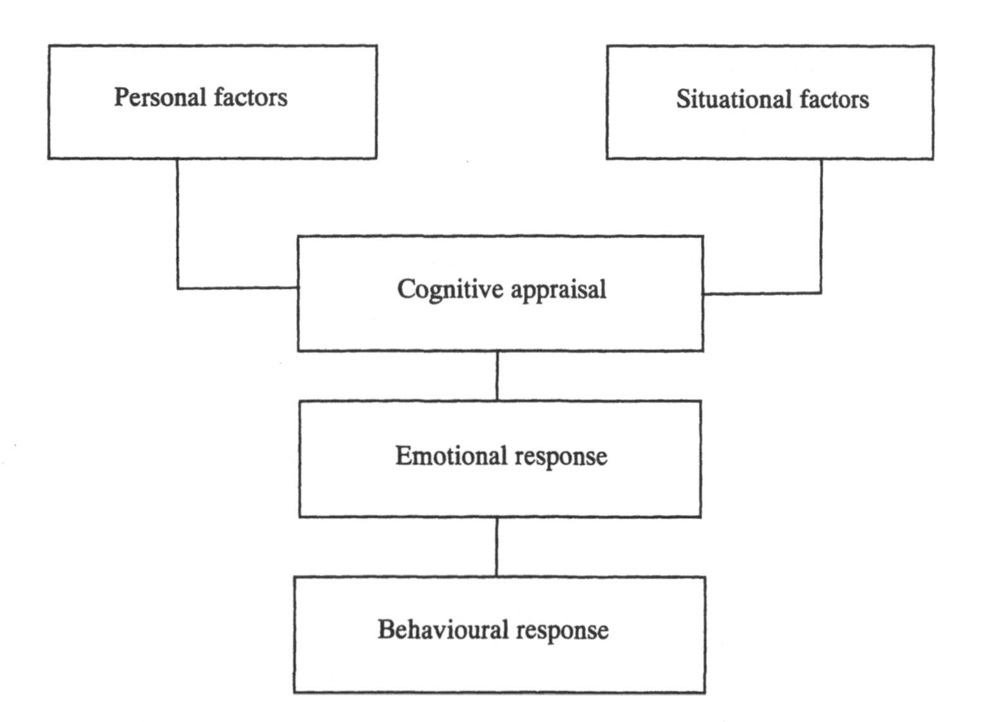

Figure 4.6: Cognitive appraisal model of psychological adjustment to athletic injury (after Brewer, 1994 with permission)

literature) by Evans and Hardy (1995) did not agree with Brewer's conclusion, but concluded instead that grief models of injury were worthy of further research provided that more appropriate designs and measurement instruments were used.

The extent of performers' emotional responses to injury and the speed with which they recover psychologically may be a distinguishing characteristic of elite performers. Following interviews with over 50 elite sports performers, Hemery (1991) concluded:

> *Several of the top achievers have had the good fortune of not being injured, but those who were often competed with it if they could, or else worked around the problem. There seems to be a quality of not giving in to a negative happening. It's just seen as an obstacle to overcome or a challenge to be accepted. There are no, "Poor me!" attitudes. If they do have negative thoughts they catch themselves immediately and turn their mind to what they can control; the best they can do with where they are.* (p. 17)

Borrowing from the literature on adherence to health-related exercise, psycho-immunology, and psychological factors in the progression of disease, Wiese and Weiss (1987) proposed a number of psychological skills that might help injured performers adhere to their rehabilitation programmes and cope with the stress of being injured. These included:

- goal-setting to assist motivation;
- imagery and self-talk to enhance self-efficacy;
- relaxation to reduce worry and excessive muscle tension at the site of injury;
- communication skills to enable performers to discuss concerns about their injury and rehabilitation with the medical support team.

Wiese and Weiss also suggested that social support could help the performer to maintain a positive attitude towards injury, particularly if it was provided by other performers who had recovered from similar injuries. In a survey of athletic trainers (physiotherapists), Wiese *et al.* (1991) found support for the view that goal-setting, positive self-talk, and good communication skills, were significant determinants of a performer's ability to cope with the stress of being injured. Furthermore, in a retrospective study of recovery from soft tissue injuries, Ievleva and Orlick (1991) confirmed Wiese *et al.*'s findings for goal-setting and positive self-talk, but also found a beneficial effect of imagery upon speed of recovery from injury. Finally, Pearson and Jones (1992) found that high level sports performers often felt that athletic trainers should be trained in the use of psychological skills so that they could contribute more to both the psychological and the physiological rehabilitation of performers.

Summary

The research reviewed in this section suggests that elite performers are most vulnerable to burnout when they have perfectionist tendencies, are personally disorganised, have poor cognitive restructuring strategies, and their sport is organised in such a way as to disempower them by giving them few choices and little self-determination. Burned out athletes are likely to perceive their involvement in sport as being characterised by decreasing rewards, increasing costs, decreasing satisfaction, few alternatives, and high or increasing investment. Furthermore, because of the involvement of self-efficacy and attributions in the processes of self-reward that underlie the reward–cost outcome, it seems likely that high levels of goal-setting and attributional skill would help to protect elite performers against burnout. The psychological literature on overtraining is somewhat sparse. However, overtraining does seem to be quite a serious problem for elite performers, and it has been suggested that active regeneration and other stress management strategies might offer some protection against reduced immune system functioning and the motivational consequences of overtraining. Similarly, the empirical literature on psychological aspects of injury is still somewhat underdeveloped. Certainly, the ability to deal with the stress of being injured does seem to be a distinguishing characteristic of elite performers, and there is some suggestion in the literature that goal-setting, self-talk, and imagery skills may have important roles to play in this coping. However, it is as yet unclear exactly what role the athlete's emotional response to the stress of being injured plays in the total rehabilitation process.

IMPLICATIONS FOR RESEARCH

Motivation appears to be a rather under-researched area in the context of elite performance. Consequently, areas of motivation in need of research abound; only the most urgent needs for elite performance will be identified here.

Intrinsic and extrinsic motivation

There is a need for longitudinal studies of the (possibly cyclical) relationship that exists between goal perspectives, performance, rewards, attributions, self-competence, and (intrinsic) motivation in elite performers. In particular, this research might attempt to shed some light on the need to achieve in elite performers, the roles that are assumed by extrinsic rewards at different stages during elite performers' development, the influence of coaching behaviours and parental behaviours upon the motivational climate of elite performers, and the moral development of elite performers.

Goal orientations

There is an urgent need to better understand the goal orientations of elite performers. Most of the available literature is focused squarely on participation rather than high level performance. What little evidence is available suggests that elite performers are likely to have both strong ego and strong task orientations. This proposal requires further examination together with the consequences of such orientation patterns. Furthermore, in view of the finding that ego and task orientations are independent constructs, the research strategy which has dogged the goal orientations literature of comparing high task-oriented subjects with high ego-oriented subjects amounts to a comparison of "apples and oranges". Rather than persist with this approach, researchers should explore the ways in which task and ego orientations interact to influence other motivational and performance-related variables.

Goal-setting skills

As has already been mentioned, goal-setting skills appear to underlie many of the motivational phenomena that have been discussed in this chapter. Nevertheless, the empirical literature on goal-setting for high level performance on complex tasks remains weak. Future research should examine the motivational consequences of emphasising the relative salience of outcome, performance, and process goals at different stages during preparation for major competition.

In a rather different direction, the internally controlling nature of goals suggests a need to explore the trade-off that may exist between setting goals that are perceived to be realistic and setting goals that are perceived to be worth while. Similarly, future research should also explore the trade-off that may exist between the need for performers to commit to goals in order for them to exert a motivational (or any other) effect, and the need for performers to be flexible about their goals should the circumstances in which they find themselves change.

Attributions

It seems likely that elite performers attribute success to internal, controllable, stable causes, and failure to internal, controllable, unstable causes. However, this proposal awaits confirmation, as does the suggestion that they may attribute failure more to strategy than to effort. The extent (if any) to which elite performers take more personal responsibility for both success and failure than non-elite performers is also worthy of further investigation. If confirmed, the acceptance of personal responsibility for failure would be interesting, if only because it begs the question "why?" Perhaps the self-esteem of elite performers is so high that they do not need any self-serving bias. Alternatively, it is possible that elite performers have a very strong internal locus of control with respect to their involvement in sport. Either way, there may be important coaching implications for the development of such dispositions if they were shown to underlie elite performance. Another issue that is worthy of further investigation is the relative contribution of intuitive and retrospective appraisal to emotional reactions and subsequent efficacy expectations in elite performers, together with the possible moderating influence of goal orientations upon this relationship.

Withdrawal from sport

There is an urgent need to generate an empirical knowledge base on burnout, psychological aspects of overtraining, and the maintenance of motivation during injury. Schmidt and Stein's (1991) model of enjoyment, burnout, and drop-out is certainly worthy of further investigation, as is its parent, the Sport Commitment Model. One interesting hypothesis which stems from Schmidt and Stein's (1991) model is that elite performers should be more burned out after competitions in which they achieve lifetime ambition goals than before them. Coakley's (1992) disempowerment model and Gould *et al.*'s (1995a) interactive model also offer much promise for increasing our understanding of how personality and situational variables might interact to increase athlete vulnerability to burnout. Furthermore, there is a need for research into the roles of active regeneration, stress management training, and social support in avoiding burnout during overtraining. This research might be enhanced by taking account of the totality of stressors which are brought to bear upon elite performers, rather than just their training load.

Rigorous empirical investigations of cognitive appraisal and grief models of injury, together with explorations of the interventions that they predict, should also be a high priority for future research. Researchers in this area should take much more care to control confounding variables and use theoretically relevant measurement tools than they have done in the past. Other models of injury could also be developed; for example, motivational models of injury based upon cognitive evaluation theory. Generally speaking, current theoretical models of the psychology of injury are rather crude and loosely formulated. Future research should attempt to refine these models so that *specific* predictions can be made about the influence of different psychological strategies upon different aspects of the recovery process.

IMPLICATIONS FOR BEST PRACTICE

This section summarises the implications of the evidence discussed in the previous sections for best practice in the preparation of athletes for elite performance. Perhaps inevitably, the available research seems to throw up as many questions as it does answers, so that sometimes the authors have been forced to take "educated guesses". However, the text indicates where this is the case.

Intrinsic and extrinsic motivation

The fundamental prediction of cognitive evaluation theory is that performers' intrinsic motivation for their sport will be enhanced or maintained as long as their involvement fulfils their need to feel competent and self-determining. Furthermore, perceptions of competence are largely determined by goal achievement and positive feedback. Consequently, one would expect elite performers to have good goal-setting skills, good self-reward strategies, and a positive coaching environment. Self-determination, on the other hand, is primarily concerned with choice in the initiation of behaviours. Consequently, one would also expect elite performers to enjoy a relatively democratic coaching environment.

The implications of the goal orientation literature for elite performance are difficult to interpret. However, the available evidence suggests that elite performers probably have high levels of both task and ego orientation. It also suggests that, when things are not going well, a strong ego orientation without a strong task orientation may present some problems for high level performers. Consequently, one might infer that elite performers are likely to have a very strong desire to win, but are also able to put this desire into some sort of personal development perspective. For example, an elite female gymnast might have winning the World Championships as a long-term outcome goal, but might also have performance- and process-oriented goals which help her to train with sufficient quality and intensity to produce routines of the required standard to achieve this outcome goal (cf. Orlick and Partington, 1988). Furthermore, she might use process-oriented goals to help maintain her concentration throughout the duration of the competition. However, *it seems likely that these process-oriented goals have such salience immediately prior to performing that the gymnast would be able to use her outcome and performance goals to help focus her attention on the process-oriented goals, rather than distract her from them* (cf. Kingston and Hardy, 1994a, b). This point is highlighted in the following report from an interview with 400 m hurdler David Hemery.

> *He reported regularly mentally rehearsing "every lane and condition that I could conceivably think of: drawn in lane one and having people hare off, but maintaining my control; drawn in the outside lane and not being able to see and still having sufficient confidence in my going for World Record pace, so that if I couldn't see anyone I would still go for it, not letting them determine my aim. It was my aim, and if it was good enough then fine . . . If it wasn't then I had done the best I could".* (David Hemery, 1968 Olympic Gold Medallist and World Record holder for the 400 metres hurdles; Jones and Hardy, 1990a, p.269)

Taken together, these findings suggest that coaches of potentially elite performers should be encouraged to adopt a relatively democratic and positive style of coaching which emphasises personal development as well as the need to win (cf. Weiss and Chaumeton, 1992). They also suggest that sport psychologists should ensure that potentially elite performers acquire relatively subtle goal-setting and good self-reward strategies. Having said this, it should be noted that the recommendation to adopt a relatively democratic style of coaching is somewhat at odds with research which has been conducted on preferred leadership styles in team sports, but may apply equally well to individual sports (Chelladurai, 1993).

Goal-setting skills

Considering so much research has been performed on goal-setting, we do not seem to know as much as one might reasonably expect about setting goals for high level performance on complex tasks such as sports skills. Nevertheless, goal-setting skills seem to underlie many of the motivational phenomena that have been considered in this chapter, and some educated guesses can be made regarding best practice. Elite performers should be encouraged to use a variety of different types of goal: outcome goals for ultimate aims and objectives; performance goals in order to ensure controllability and goal achievement; and process goals to help them focus on the "here and now". Furthermore, the strong emphasis on quality training that seems to be required for elite performers means that process goals will frequently play an important motivational role during training as well as their preparation for competition. Other issues which seem to be important, but about which there appears to be little available evidence, include helping elite performers strike a balance between the need for goals to be realistic and the need for them to be perceived as worthwhile; and between the need for commitment and the need for flexibility should circumstances change once a goal has been set (for example, the performer gets injured). Perhaps the key here is to have review sessions built in to the goal-setting programme at regular intervals.

Attributions

There are a number of implications for applied practice which can be drawn from the literature on attributions. First, it would appear to be a good strategy to encourage potentially elite performers to take personal responsibility for both their successes and their failures. More specifically, it would seem to be a good strategy to encourage such performers to attribute success to internal, controllable and stable causes, and failure to internal, controllable but unstable causes. There is also a suggestion that it may be more effective to encourage them to make attributions for failure to incorrect strategy choice, rather than lack of effort, although this suggestion requires confirmation. Second, research on attributional styles and learned helplessness suggests that potentially elite performers should be taught cognitive restructuring strategies, so that they can modify their attributional patterns if they do start to slip into learned helplessness spirals. For example, a slalom skier might be encouraged to attribute a fall to poor choice of line, rather than lack of aggression or inability to turn early enough.

Third, although elite performers may be better equipped (attributionally) than their non-elite counterparts to deal with failure, the literature suggests that the intuitive appraisal which immediately follows success or failure exerts a much more powerful effect upon emotions (and possibly future expectations) than does the retrospective appraisal which may take place later. The one exception to this "rule" may be when the outcome is unexpected. Then, retrospective appraisal may exert rather more influence upon emotions (McAuley and Duncan, 1989; Weiner, 1986), although, depending upon exactly how unexpected the outcome was, this influence may or may not extend to changing future expectations. For example, if a track and field athlete is unexpectedly beaten by an opponent she will likely experience strong negative emotions as a result of losing, but she will also be more likely to experience emotions associated with her perceived reasons for losing than if her defeat was expected. These emotions may be more or less negative, depending on the athlete's perceived reasons for the defeat. Furthermore, the strength of the emotions may influence the degree to which the athlete's attributions impact upon her future expectations regarding performance. However, the major conclusion to be drawn here is that it remains important for coaches of elite performers to plan training and lead-up competitions prior to a major event in such a way that their performers experience success.

Finally, the vast majority of attributional research has been conducted on western populations, and little is known about the effects of cultural context upon attributions or their relationships with other variables. Furthermore, in recent years, there has been considerable international mobility amongst elite performers and their coaches in sports such as soccer and gymnastics. Consequently, sport psychologists who work with such multicultural teams and squads need to be aware of the fact that the implications that can be drawn from the attributions literature may not always apply to their clients.

Withdrawal from sport

The finding that performers are most prone to burnout when they have perfectionist tendencies, are personally disorganised, and have poor cognitive restructuring strategies, obviously implicates the need for sport psychologists and coaches to help potentially elite performers develop good goal-setting and restructuring skills. Furthermore, the key role that the outcome (reward–cost balance) of involvement appears to play in burnout and drop-out also highlights the importance of success, and the attribution of that success to performers' own ability and efforts. This, in turn, re-emphasises the importance of teaching potentially elite performers good goal-setting and attributional skills. However, another implication of Schmidt and Stein's (1991) model of sport commitment is that whilst performers whose commitment is enjoyment-based and performers whose commitment is burned out both perceive themselves to have few alternatives, they hold this perception for different reasons. Performers whose commitment is enjoyment-based perceive themselves to have few alternatives because they get so much satisfaction from their current involvement in sport; whilst performers whose commitment is burned out perceive themselves to have few alternatives because they don't have any choice. When the stress (costs) of involvement becomes too great and elite performers start to burn out, it may therefore be important to help them identify and explore alternatives to their current career path even though they may then choose not to take those alternatives. This may be particularly important in the later stages of a performer's career, or following the achievement of a major long-term goal.

Other research which was reviewed identified the importance of the social organisation of sport as a contributing factor to burnout (Coakley, 1992; Gould *et al.*, 1995a). The major implication of this research is that sport psychologists should help and encourage coaches of elite performers to structure the organisational climate so as to empower performers and increase their self-determination. Ways in which this could be achieved include: adopting a relatively democratic coaching style; encouraging performers to have interests outside of their sport; placing emphasis on the personal development opportunities that arise from their performers' involvement in sport (in particular, keeping winning in perspective); and, at appropriate intervals, helping their performers to explore and evaluate the pros and cons of continued involvement in their sport.

The psychological literature on overtraining is somewhat sparse. However, it does suggest the possibility that active regeneration strategies, stress management training, and social support, may all have some potential for the reduction of negative side effects during periods of heavy training. Examples of active regeneration strategies include massage, sauna, hydrotherapy, relaxation sessions, and playing alternative sports provided they are not too strenuous.

Another major stressor which regularly confronts potentially elite performers is injury, and ability to cope with injury may constitute a distinguishing characteristic of the truly elite performer. This resistance is probably best developed by ensuring that potentially elite performers possess good stress management skills, and receive good social support from their peers and coaches. Group work on the development of social support networks would clearly be of benefit here. It is unclear whether encouraging performers to get involved in alternative activities is a good thing or not. On the one hand, such involvement might help to maintain motivation and a "positive mind set", but on the other it might distract performers from maintaining their focus on their own sport and the rehabilitation process. Perhaps the answer to this question is partially determined by the severity of the injury. If a swift return to normal training can be reasonably expected, then it might be better to encourage performers to stay focused; but if the injury is likely to be a lengthy one then it might be better to encourage them to become involved in other activities.

SUMMARY

This chapter has discussed a number of factors which may have an influence upon the motivational state of elite performers. These included the influence of perceived self-competence and self-determination upon the development of intrinsic motivation; the influence of goal orientations upon a range of motivational variables; the roles of goal-setting and attributional skills in the motivational process; the causes of burnout; and the motivational effects of withdrawal from sport through overtraining or injury. The applied and research implications of the literature considered in this discussion were also presented.

AROUSAL AND ACTIVATION

CONTENTS

INTRODUCTION

Athletes and coaches often think of arousal and activation as being about "psyching up" or "psyching down". Later on in this chapter, we will argue that such a view of arousal and activation is something of an oversimplification; however, for now, it will serve perfectly well as a starting point.

Even a cursory glance at the available literature indicates that there are large individual differences in the way that elite performers prefer to prepare themselves for major events. For example, in a retrospective study of Olympic wrestlers, Gould *et al.* (1992a, b) found that the wrestlers reported having had high levels of arousal and activation prior to their best matches. Similarly, Jones and Hardy (1990a) reported that former world champion javelin thrower Steve Backley sometimes used a breathing technique to "psych" himself up: ". . . it would usually be because I was underaroused, if I needed perking up" (p. 262). However, other performers have reported using "psyching down" strategies prior to their best performances. David Hemery reported deliberately relaxing and slowing his pulse as part of his pre-performance strategy prior to his world record, Gold Medal winning 400 metres hurdles run in the 1968 Olympics (Jones and Hardy, 1990a). Nick Faldo, winner of many of the world's major golf championships, also reported using a similar strategy prior to big golf competitions:

> *As a youngster I heard that you should lie perfectly motionless—deep breathing—for eighteen minutes or twenty minutes or something like that. I did this first thing in the morning and I didn't play till 2 o'clock in the afternoon . . . I still do that sometimes, going to sleep, letting my body go like lead, absolutely still to relax, and sure enough, it usually knocks me off to sleep.* (Hemery, 1991, p. 185)

In the same vein, former Welsh rugby union scrum-half Gareth Edwards, and ice-dancing world champions Jane Torvill and Christopher Dean, reported feeling detached prior to major events, and preferring to prepare for them quietly on their own (Hemery, 1991).

One important issue that arises from a more detailed consideration of the anecdotal evidence that has been presented above is that "psyching up" or "psyching down" formed only a small part of the overall preparation strategy that these elite performers used. Another issue relates to variables that might predict the individual differences in optimal preparation strategies that these elite performers reported using. It seems likely that many of these individual preferences reflect differences in both task and personality variables. For example, gymnast James May (1990 Commonwealth Games Bronze Medal winner in the all-round apparatus finals) reported that high levels of arousal usually helped him on floor "because that bit of tension seems to produce an extra bit of lift for the tumbles", but did not help on pommel horse because "your body tightens up and pikes. Of course, that brings your feet closer to the horse on every circle, and your hips closer to the handles, and you are off before you know it" (Jones and Hardy, 1990a, p. 256).

This chapter takes a broad view of arousal and activation, regarding them as being concerned with both the intensity of performance, and readiness to perform. It also explores some of the task and personality variables that might influence the optimal preparation strategies that elite performers use.

CONCEPTUAL ISSUES

Traditionally, psychologists used the words "arousal" and "activation" synonymously to refer to a single unitary construct which embodied both physiological and psychological characteristics and was concerned with the intensity of behaviour. For example, Duffy (1962) defined arousal as "the extent of release of potential energy, stored in the tissues of the organism, as this is shown in activity or response" (p. 179). Arousal was hypothesised to have an inverted-U shaped relationship with performance (see Figure 5.1), whereby performance was best at moderate levels of arousal (Broadhurst, 1957; Hebb, 1955).

Over the years, a number of researchers have criticised the conceptualisation of arousal as a single unitary construct (Hockey and Hamilton, 1983; Jones and Hardy, 1989; Lacey, 1967; Neiss, 1988b). Initial criticisms were formulated by Lacey (1967), who presented evidence that it was possible to distinguish between at least three different types of activation (arousal): *electrocortical*, referring to the degree of electrical activity in the cortex and measured by electroencephalogram; *autonomic*, referring to the degree of

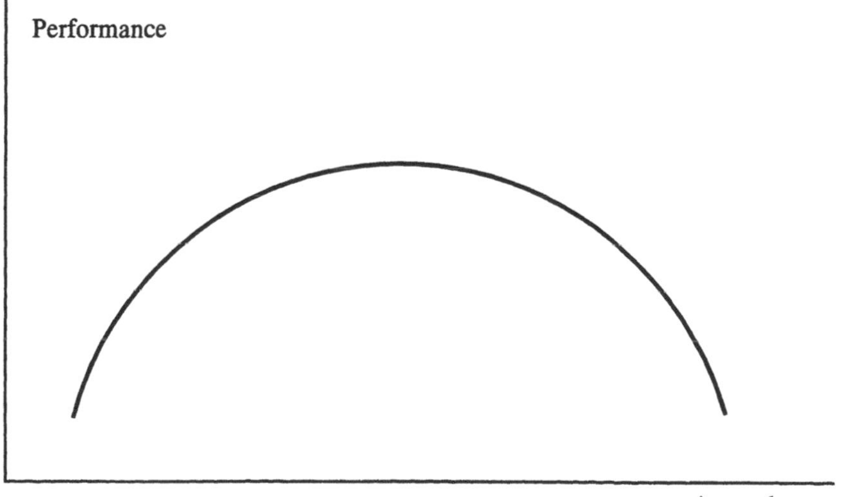

Figure 5.1: The inverted-U hypothesis

physiological activity taking place in the autonomic nervous system, and measured by such indices as skin conductance, heart rate, and blood pressure; and *behavioural*, referring to the overt activity of the organism. Furthermore, Lacey (1967) showed that it was possible for activity in one of these systems to be elevated, whilst activity in another was depressed, a phenomenon which he called *directional fractionation*. He also showed that different patterns of activity within each system could be reliably reproduced across different situations. For example, in stressful, choice reaction time situations (such as saving a penalty at soccer), heart rate is typically depressed, whilst skin conductance is typically elevated. However, when performers are engaged in stressful cognitive activity (such as deciding how to play a difficult shot at golf), both heart rate and skin conductance are typically elevated (Lacey, 1967). Lacey called this phenomenon *situational stereotypy*.

Lacey's work clearly does present some serious problems for any explanation of arousal effects which is based upon a simple unidimensional conceptualisation of arousal. Nevertheless, the inverted-U hypothesis has retained its popularity with many sport psychologists (see, for example, Gill, 1986; Landers, 1994). For example, based on the inverted-U hypothesis, Oxendine (1970, 1984) proposed that different levels of optimal arousal could be predicted for different sports dependent upon the task characteristics involved in the sport. He argued that: (1) a slightly above average level of arousal was necessary for optimum performance on all motor tasks; (2) a high level of arousal was necessary for optimal performance on gross motor activities involving strength, endurance, or speed; and (3) a high level of arousal interfered with performance on tasks involving complex skills, fine muscle movements, co-ordination, steadiness, and general concentration. While this attempt to match different types of sports performance to different levels of optimal arousal may be intuitively appealing, a number of criticisms have been levelled at it (Jones, 1990; Jones and Hardy, 1989). Firstly, Oxendine's classification is oversimplified in that it assumes that one particular level of arousal is appropriate for all skills within a particular sport. For example, he classified basketball skills as requiring an intermediate level of arousal. However, a basketball player may require high levels of arousal when rebounding, but low levels of arousal when performing a free throw. Similarly, it is not clear that the complexity and power requirements of kicking a field goal remain the same regardless of whether the kick is being made from 15 metres or 50 metres. Thus, Oxendine's classification fails to take into account situational factors which may require sports performers to be able to quickly change arousal levels to suit the specific demands of different tasks within a particular performance.

Secondly, Oxendine did not seriously consider the cognitive requirements of different sports skills. For example, he made a distinction between football blocking as a gross, low complexity skill requiring strength, speed, and endurance, and golf putting as a more complex skill requiring fine muscle control, co-ordination, and steadiness. However, this distinction between "simple" and "complex" skills completely ignores the information processing demands of the different tasks. In golf putting, the performer, the object to be struck (the ball), and the target (the hole), are all stationary, and the performer is effectively under no external time constraints. In football blocking, however, both the tackler and the target are moving, the external environment is constantly changing, and the tackler is under serious time pressure. In short, football tacklers must process large amounts of information quickly and have little chance of recovery should they be deceived by their opponent "throwing a dummy". This is not a simple task!

Weinberg (1989a) also argued that Oxendine's approach was far too simplistic and took little account of perceptual and decision-making factors. Landers and Boutcher (1986) proposed an alternative system for estimating the complexity of sports performance which addressed some of these issues by summating the perceptual, decision-making, and motoric demands of the task. Nevertheless, *many cognitive psychologists seriously question the meaningfulness of attempts to define complexity in unidimensional terms, by arguing that such attempts are tantamount to trying to "equate apples and oranges"* (Eysenck, 1992; Hockey and Hamilton, 1983). For example, passing a soccer ball to a team mate requires the passer to use complex perceptual information about the speed and direction of both players and the distance of opponents from the line of the pass in order to arrive at decisions about whether the ball should be passed, and the speed and direction in which the ball would need to be kicked if it were passed. On the other hand, the perceptual demands of performing a flared circle on the pommel horse in gymnastics are minimal, whilst the complexity of the motor response to be output is considerable. It is therefore not at all clear that it is meaningful to even ask which one of these two skills is the more complex. The obvious, if rather glib answer, is that it depends upon whether you are a soccer player or a gymnast. The tasks are simply different!

A number of researchers (for example, Hockey and Hamilton, 1983; Naatanen, 1973; Neiss, 1988b; Parfitt *et al.*, 1990) have suggested that it may be necessary to take a much more "fine-grained" view of arousal, in which all the different subsystems that support performance are identified. For example, Naatanen (1973) and Neiss (1988b) have argued that arousal is best considered not as a unitary quantitative state, but as a patterning of different physiological parameters. Furthermore, according to this position, performance efficiency is affected by the appropriateness of this pattern with respect to performance on the task at hand (Hockey and Hamilton, 1983). If the current physiological arousal pattern is appropriate for the task, then performance is maintained or even enhanced; if not, then performance is impaired (cf. Neiss, 1988b).

The present chapter takes an even stronger stance and adopts Pribram and McGuinness' (1975) definitions of arousal and activation in which a clear distinction is made between the (cognitive and physiological) activity that occurs in response to some new and external input to the system, and the (cognitive and physiological) activity that is geared towards preparing a planned response appropriate to the current situation. Consider a gymnast who is waiting to perform her beam routine in an important international competition. She has had her two minute warm-up, has stretched and mentally rehearsed whilst waiting for her turn to perform, has "chalked up", and is now standing in front of the beam waiting for the chief judge's signal to start. She has performed this routine a hundred times or more in training and other competitions, and is both mentally and physically tuned to perform it once again with relatively little attempt to *consciously* control any of the movements. In short, she has an appropriate activation pattern. The chief judge signals; the gymnast salutes back, and commences her approach run for a complex mount. Just as she is about to land on the springboard, a balloon which was being held by a member of the audience bursts with a loud bang. The gymnast experiences an involuntary startle (arousal) response which disrupts her activation pattern, so that she is no longer ready to perform the mount. She misses it.

This hypothetical example should give the reader some feel for the distinction that is being made between arousal and activation. *Activation* refers to cognitive and physiological activity that is geared towards preparing a planned response to some anticipated situation (Pribram and McGuinness, 1975). It is therefore more logically correct to talk about *appropriate* activation states than it is to talk about the *level* of activation, since for any given task there may be high levels of activity in some subsystems but low levels of activity in others. For example, an appropriate activation state for golf putting might include high levels of alpha brain wave activity, but low levels of electrical activity in the muscles of the forearms. An appropriate activation state also implies some degree of preparation on the part of the performer and a relatively long time frame (essentially because preparation takes time, and most performers seem to prefer to be prepared some time before they actually have to perform). Another important feature of (appropriate) activation states is that they are task-specific, since different tasks presumably make use of different cognitive and physiological subsystems (Fleishman and Hempel, 1955; Hockey and Hamilton, 1983; Parfitt *et al.*, 1990). Readers might like to convince themselves of this by imagining what would happen if they prepared themselves to perform a maximum bench press in the weights gymnasium, but were then asked to hole a ten foot golf putt instead.

Arousal, on the other hand, refers to cognitive and physiological activity which takes place in response to some new input to the system (Pribram and

McGuinness, 1975). It therefore implies a lack of planned preparation (for that stimulus) on the part of the performer and a relatively short time frame (essentially because arousing agents lose their effects across time). Notice that arousing stimuli do not have to be surprising or intense; for example, a leaf gently blowing across a golf putting surface might gradually become a visual distraction to a golfer who is about to putt. It is also worth noting that arousal may not always be detrimental to performance; for example, weight trainers often use loud music to help them train (and presumably lift heavier weights). Whether an arousing agent is detrimental or beneficial to performance appears to depend very much on the nature of the activation pattern that is required to perform the task at hand, and the nature of the arousing agent (Hockey and Hamilton, 1983; Parfitt *et al.*, 1990).

Another construct which is often linked to arousal is anxiety, and it may surprise some readers that no mention has yet been made of anxiety in this section. However, in just the same way as progress in understanding arousal and activation has been impeded by researchers' inability to clearly differentiate between the two constructs, so anxiety research has also been impeded by poor conceptualisation which has occasionally even equated anxiety with arousal. The present authors would argue that anxiety is a meta-cognitive emotion which should be clearly distinguished from the cognitive and physiological states which underlie arousal and activation. The effects of stress and anxiety upon performance will therefore be discussed later in Chapter 6.

Summary

Early research on arousal and activation was held back by a lack of conceptual distinction between arousal and activation. This section has attempted to remedy this shortcoming by arguing that activation is a complex multidimensional cognitive and physiological state or pattern which reflects the organism's readiness to respond. Arousal, on the other hand, is the organism's response to new stimuli or input, and may affect performance by altering the performer's activation state (for better or for worse).

THEORIES OF AROUSAL AND ACTIVATION

A number of cognitive theories can be identified in the literature which relate the effects of arousal and/or activation to performance (see, for example, Easterbrook, 1959; Hockey and Hamilton, 1983; Sanders, 1983). However, only Easterbrook's cue utilisation theory appears to have been seriously considered by most sport psychologists.

Cue utilisation theory

Easterbrook's (1959) cue utilisation theory was one of the earliest cognitive theories of arousal and performance. It viewed arousal as a single unitary construct, and argued that high levels of arousal reduced the range of cues to which performers would attend. According to the theory, this narrowing of attention should therefore initially lead to a rejection of irrelevant cues and an improvement in performance. However, with further increases in arousal, continued attentional narrowing would lead to relevant cues also being ignored, so that performance would be impaired. In this way, cue utilisation theory was used to explain the inverted-U hypothesis (see, for example, Landers, 1981).

Easterbrook's (1959) hypothesis has been tested using dual task paradigms, the prediction being that under conditions of high arousal, performance on secondary tasks should be impaired, whilst performance on the primary task should be maintained or even enhanced. However, as Eysenck (1982) has pointed out, this paradigm is biased towards the acceptance of Easterbrook's hypothesis, since only three of the nine possible combinations of primary and secondary task performance are incompatible with the hypothesis. Nevertheless, there is certainly some evidence to support a hypothesis of attentional narrowing under conditions of high arousal (for a review, see Eysenck, 1982).

More recent laboratory research by Hockey and Hamilton (1983), and Shapiro and Lim (1989), has refined Easterbrook's hypothesis by suggesting that attentional selectivity is governed more by the subjective importance of different cues than by their spatial location in the visual field. Unfortunately (for sport psychologists), this research has used auditory noise as an environmental stressor, rather than emotional arousal. Nevertheless, findings such as these have led Eysenck (1988) to argue that the processes which underlie attentional narrowing are more likely to be under the strategic control of the performer than the relatively passive response that was envisaged by Easterbrook (1959). A good example of arousal-induced attentional narrowing would be a soccer defender who consistently fails to mark opponents when he is "psyched up" in "big games" because he "ball watches"; i.e. focuses all of his attention on the ball, instead of on the players he is supposed to be marking. However, if Eysenck's arguments about the strategic control of attentional narrowing are correct, it should be possible to re-educate such a player by helping him to understand the importance of the spatial relationship that exists between the player in possession of the ball, himself, and the opponent he is supposed to mark.

Multidimensional activation states

Hockey and Hamilton (1983) reviewed research which extended Easterbrook's work by examining the effects of different environmental stressors, such as auditory noise, monetary incentives, and lack of sleep upon different aspects of information processing in what they called a "broad band" approach. Essentially, Hockey and Hamilton argued that different environmental stressors create qualitatively different activation states in which the operation of some processes will be enhanced whilst the operation of others will be impaired. Thus, Hockey and Hamilton argued that in order to obtain a complete picture of the effects of a given stressor, it was necessary to examine its effects upon a wide range of different (cognitive) indicator variables; for example, vigilance, selectivity of attention, short-term memory capacity, short-term recall, long-term recall, and speed of information transfer. Hockey and Hamilton's (1983) approach is important because it highlights the importance of examining the processes that underlie performance, as opposed to just global measures of performance. Furthermore, whilst Hockey and Hamilton's approach is limited by the fact that it considers the effects of laboratory stressors upon mainly cognitive tasks, this approach has also been used to examine the effects of the physiological arousal that is associated with performance anxiety upon sports tasks. The most reliable

Table 5.1: The type of processes and their expected effects upon performance in basketball (modified from Parfitt *et al.*, 1990 with permission)

Process	Effect	Example
Perception	Attentional narrowing (Hammerton and Tickner, 1968), and selectivity leading to hyperdistractability (Deffenbacher, 1978)	Tunnel vision and ball watching leading to: failure to see free players (own and opposition); distraction by refereeing decisions niggling and self-distracting
Working memory or short-term memory	Impaired working memory with large memory loads (Humphreys and Revelle, 1984; Jones and Cale, 1989; Parfitt, 1988)	Time penalties in attacking key. Slow to release early balls when there is a choice of passes. Failure to drive at the basket when there is a space
Long-term recall	Impaired for difficult tasks? Improved for easy tasks—rebound shooting (Parfitt, 1988)	Failed critical set shot. Accurate rebound shooting
Anaerobic power	Enhanced in simple tasks—Sargent jump (Parfitt, 1988)	Good height on backboard defending
Manual dexterity	Impaired (Baddeley and Idzikowski, 1985)	Poor ball handling under pressure
Fine control	Impaired, e.g., pursuit rotor (Matarazzo and Matarazzo, 1956)	Failed lay-ups. Lack of touch
Dynamic balance	Unknown	Clumsy challenges in the air. "Flat-footed" defending

findings so far obtained suggest that such physiological arousal impairs: working memory and the ability to make decisions (Jones and Cale, 1989; Parfitt and Hardy, 1993); movement fluidity (Weinberg and Hunt, 1976); and manual dexterity (Baddeley and Idzikowski, 1985). However, this physiological arousal enhances anaerobic power (Parfitt *et al.*, 1995) and simple reactions (Jones and Cale, 1989; Parfitt and Hardy, 1993). Table 5.1 is a hypothetical plan summarising these effects.

Another important feature of Hockey and Hamilton's approach is that it completely rejects the notion of a single unitary arousal system which mediates the effects of different environmental stressors upon performance, and therefore it suggests that the inverted-U hypothesis is rather meaningless. It also suggests that the use of interventions which globally reduce (physiological) arousal in sports performers may be akin to "throwing the baby out with the bath water", since both the beneficial and the detrimental effects of such arousal will be lost (cf. Burton, 1990; Parfitt *et al.*, 1990). Rather, Hockey and Hamilton's theory suggests that sport psychologists should help performers to develop task-specific strategies which will facilitate appropriate activation states. A very simple example of such a strategy is mental rehearsal of the task to be performed. A number of researchers have offered evidence that mental and physical practice may be functionally equivalent in establishing appropriate activation states (for example, Ainscoe and Hardy, 1987; Hall and Schmidt, 1992; Johnson, 1982; Marks and Isaac, 1992; Shepard and Podgorny, 1978; Weiss *et al.*, 1987). It could therefore be argued, on both empirical and theoretical grounds, that the successful mental rehearsal of a given skill should provide a most efficient means of establishing an appropriate activation pattern prior to performance.

A rather more subtle way of enhancing activation states might be to use music, self-talk and other inductions to help performers create an appropriate "recipe of emotions" (Gould and Udry, 1994), whereby the associated arousal state facilitates the desired activation state. Thus, for example, anger might be expected to facilitate tasks requiring powerful output, whilst enjoyment and empathy might be more appropriate for tasks requiring delicate "touch".

A limitation of Hockey and Hamilton's (1983) theory is that it does not specify the number of different subcomponents of performance that need to be considered, or how these different subcomponents are resourced. Consequently, whilst Hockey and Hamilton are quite explicit in declaring that a single unitary arousal system is insufficient, they do not actually specify how many dimensions of arousal are necessary to energise performance.

Humphreys and Revelle's model

One model of arousal and performance which does specify the number of arousal systems required to energise performance was devised by

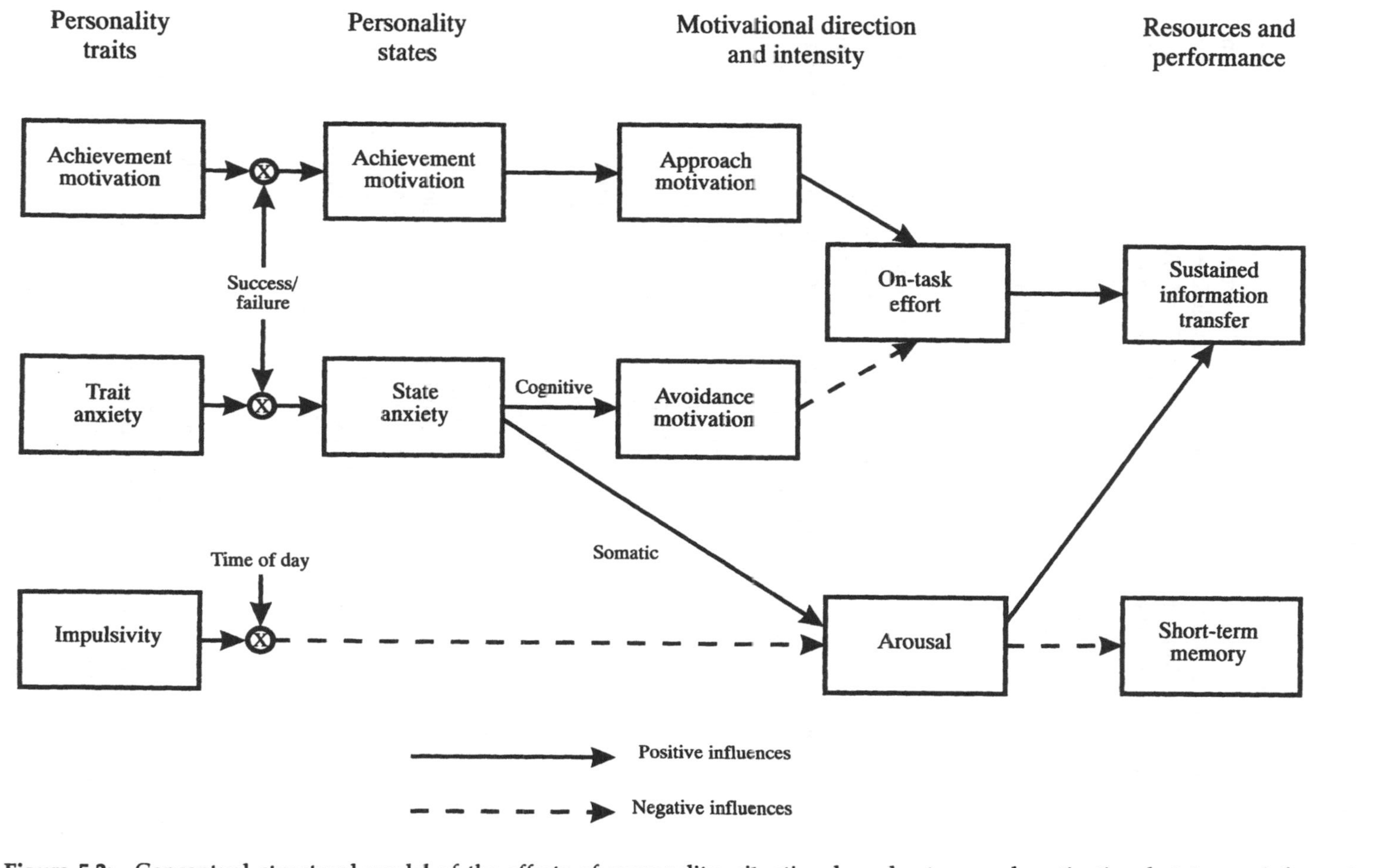

Figure 5.2: Conceptual structural model of the effects of personality, situational moderators, and motivational states on information processing and cognitive performance (modified from Jones, 1990, with permission)

Humphreys and Revelle (1984). This model attempted to predict the combined effects of personality and motivational variables upon performance using two arousal systems, called arousal and on-task effort. In Humphreys and Revelle's terminology, *arousal* was defined as "a conceptual dimension . . . that factor common to various indicants of alertness" (Humphreys and Revelle, 1984, p. 158), whilst *on-task effort* was defined as the allocation of available attentional resources to the task at hand. Although Humphreys and Revelle's definition of arousal could be severely criticised (essentially because of its unidimensional nature), their model is presented here because it has some interesting predictions, and was the first to explicitly include personality, motivational, situational, and cognitive variables, in a single arousal model. A simplified version of the model is shown in Figure 5.2.

The model attempts to predict performance on two types of task: sustained information transfer (SIT) tasks, and short-term memory (STM) tasks. SIT tasks involve rapid throughput of information with no attempt to hold that information in memory; whilst STM tasks require information to be either held or retrieved from memory. Thus, a tennis rally close to the net would be a good example of an SIT task, since the performer has to perform a series of choice reaction type movements in quick succession. Making a strategy decision about what sort of serve to make next would be a good example of an STM task from the same sport. Here information about the opponent's preferences, strengths, and weaknesses, must be held in memory whilst the decision is made. Humphreys and Revelle (1984) recognised that these may not be the only subcomponents of performance, but argued that most tasks contain elements of one or both of them.

A major prediction of the model is that performance on SIT tasks is a monotonically increasing function of arousal, whilst performance on STM tasks is a monotonically decreasing function of arousal. Humphreys and Revelle (1984) also presented arguments which show how such a pair of relationships could account for an inverted-U hypothesis, assuming that the task contained elements of both SIT and STM. Thus, in line with Hockey and Hamilton's (1983) approach, Humphreys and Revelle's (1984) model predicts that certain aspects of performance may be enhanced by arousal-inducing agents, whilst others may be impaired. The model also makes predictions about impulsivity and anxiety. However, these predictions will be discussed later in this chapter, and in Chapter 6.

Sanders' model

Another model which specifies the number of resource pools required to energise performance was devised by Sanders (1983). This was based on a linear stage model of information processing and had three energetical (arousal) systems. The model was derived using Sternberg's (1969) additive

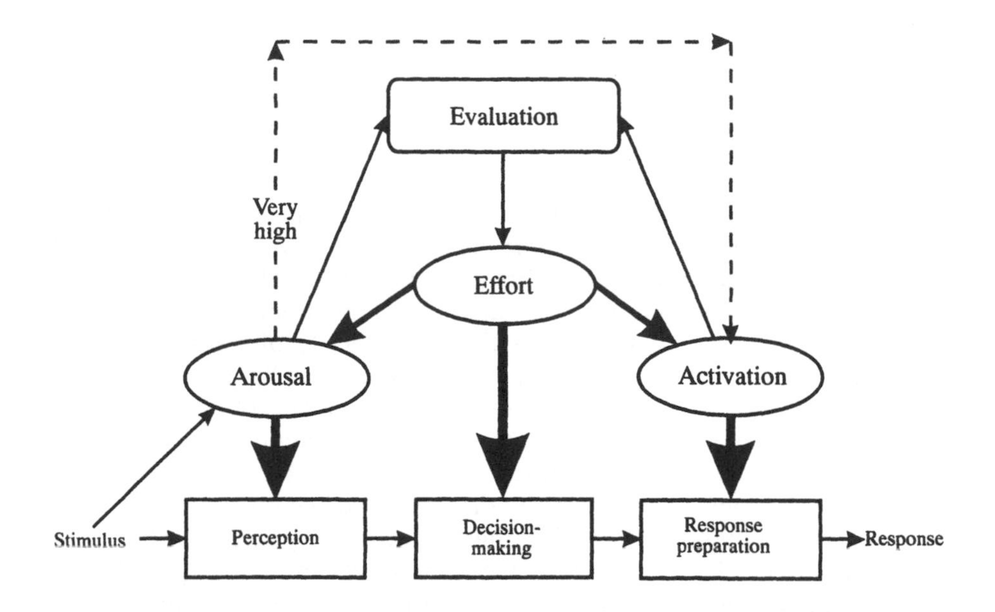

Figure 5.3: A simplified and modified version of Sanders' (1983) model of stress and human performance (modified from Jones, 1990 with permission)

factor analysis of choice reaction time, and as such can be applied only to those aspects of sports performance which require such rapid responses; for example, reaction saves from a goalkeeper, or receiving a tennis service (Note: even here there may be problems—see Jones, 1990). The three energetical systems proposed by Sanders (1983) were arousal, activation, and effort. In line with Pribram and McGuinness (1975), *arousal* was defined as the organism's immediate response to input and was hypothesised to energise perceptual processes; whilst *activation* was defined as the organism's readiness to respond and was hypothesised to energise motor programming. Sanders' third energetical system was responsible for decision-making, and the co-ordination of arousal and activation when the link between perception and action was complex or difficult. This co-ordination was viewed as requiring effort on the part of the organism, and so the co-ordinating mechanism was named *effort* by Sanders (1983). Sanders' model is depicted in Figure 5.3.

The general idea behind Sanders' model is similar to that which underlies the whole of this chapter. In anticipation of the stimuli that may arise, the organism prepares responses which are ready to be triggered. When the stimulus appears, it arouses the perceptual system which then triggers the appropriate response, provided the stimulus–response link is well established. For example, a field hockey defender who is "jockeying" an attacker is programmed to tackle as soon as the attacker lets the ball get too far away.

The defender is primed ready to tackle, and just waits for the signal to go. When the stimulus–response relationship is more difficult, the co-ordination (effort) system may be required to ensure that the correct response is activated. This takes longer and requires effort on the part of the organism.

It is clear that Sanders' (1983) model is far removed from the inverted-U hypothesis with its predictions about general arousal affecting general performance. The emphasis is much more akin to Hockey and Hamilton's (1983) approach in which different stressors exert differential effects upon different aspects of performance. Consider a tennis player attempting to make a return of service. Sanders' model predicts that the intensity of the stimuli in the performing environment (for example, crowd noise and light conditions) will affect the player's level of arousal, which will in turn affect the player's effective perception of the ball in flight. Appropriate decision-making with regard to shot selection will then be influenced by effort, and the cognitive preparation of the shot will be influenced by the state of activation.

Sanders also proposed that when the stimulus is very intense or the activation system is highly energised, the arousal system can bypass the co-ordination system and trigger a response from the activation system directly. In such cases, a faster response will result, but there will be a correspondingly greater risk that the response will be ill-considered and inappropriate, particularly when stimulus–response compatibility is low; for instance, when the skill is not well learned or the performer has to choose a response from a large number of alternatives. Jones and Hardy (1989) suggested that this situation is analogous to a sprinter whose arousal level is so high that he responds prematurely to a slight movement from the runner in the next lane before the starting gun fires, thereby giving a "false start".

Conversely, baseball players may sometimes fail to get a hit when receiving from a very fast pitcher because they take too long to select the appropriate swing. However, on big pressure pitches, they may also fail because they trigger an inappropriate hit which can be easily fielded. Sanders' model predicts that the accurate perception of the ball is affected by the player's arousal state (which will be partially determined by the external environment); the choice of an appropriate swing is affected by effort; and the cognitive preparation (programming) of the swing is affected by the state of activation of the player. More generally, Sanders' model can be summarised as making the following predictions (Jones and Hardy, 1989):

(1) high levels of arousal speed up perception;
(2) high levels of activation speed up motor preparation;
(3) high levels of effort speed up decision-making.

Sanders' model has yet to be tested in a sport setting. However, some support for the model has been generated using threat of shock (Van der

Molen *et al.*, 1987), time pressure (Jaskowski *et al.*, 1994), and sleep loss and stimulant and depressant drugs (Sanders, 1983).

Summary

This section has reviewed four models of arousal and activation. Easterbrook's (1959) cue utilisation theory predicts that highly aroused performers will progressively attend to a narrower and narrower range of cues as they become more and more aroused. However, more recent work (Hockey and Hamilton, 1983) suggests that the focus of such attentional narrowing may be more determined by the subjective importance of different cues than by their spatial location. Research on multidimensional activation states suggests that different arousing agents will have differential effects upon performance which are mediated by changes in the activation patterns that underlie performance. A corollary of this research is that different aspects of performance may be differentially affected by the same arousal conditions. For example, Olympic gymnast James May reported that he found the physiological arousal associated with big competitions to have a negative effect upon his pommel horse performance, which requires precision and dynamic balance, but a beneficial effect upon his tumbling and vaulting, which requires considerable explosive power (Jones and Hardy, 1990a).

Humphreys and Revelle (1984) proposed a two-arousal system model which makes predictions about the effects of various personality, situational, and motivational variables, upon two aspects of (cognitive) performance: sustained information transfer and short-term memory. In particular, the model predicts that high levels of arousal will enhance SIT performance (for example, reaction saves by an ice hockey goalkeeper), but impair STM performance (for example, a quarterback deciding which play to choose). Finally, Sanders (1983) proposed a three-arousal system model of choice reaction time which differentiates between arousal, activation, and effort. The model predicts that high levels of arousal increase perceptual speed, high levels of activation speed up motor preparation, and high levels of effort are required for quick decision-making. It also predicts that very high levels of arousal can overflow into activation, thereby enabling fast responses to be made, but with a correspondingly greater risk that the response is incorrect when the task is complex.

It is difficult to say which of the four models that have been discussed in this section possesses the greatest potential for application to high level sports performance, because each of them has something unique to offer. Having said that, cue utilisation theory is somewhat superseded by Hockey and Hamilton's (1983) broad band approach; Sanders' (1983) theory has a limited domain of application, and has yet to be tested in the sport domain; whilst Humphreys and Revelle's (1984) praiseworthy attempt to explain the interactive effects of certain motivational, personality, and situational variables may be a little premature, given the probable complexity of these interactions and the rather limited empirical database that currently exists in this area (cf. Eysenck, 1986). In light of these criticisms, Hockey and Hamilton's (1983) broad band approach would seem to have the most to offer sport psychology at this moment in time. The most important feature of this model is that different arousing agents are predicted to facilitate different activation states and therefore exert differential effects upon different aspects of performance.

STRATEGIES INFLUENCING AROUSAL AND ACTIVATION

As should by now be clear, one of the major problems with previous discussions of arousal and sports performance is that they have usually been based on the assumption that arousal and activation are the same thing, and that pre-performance strategies exert their influence upon performance via changes in this single arousal construct and the inverted-U hypothesis. However, *the present chapter has presented activation as a complex multidimensional state or pattern of readiness to perform which may be altered by changes in arousal as a result of new input to the organism* (cf. Hockey and Hamilton, 1983; Jones and Hardy, 1989; Neiss, 1988b; Pribram and McGuinness, 1975). "Psych-up" and "psych-down" strategies should therefore be viewed as examples of such input which may differentially affect the efficiency of the organism depending upon whether they induce a more, or a less, appropriate activation pattern for the task at hand. In practice, psych-up and psych-down strategies frequently involve goal-setting, imagery, self-talk, physical activity, and relaxation components. For example, tennis players such as John McEnroe are seen to talk themselves into a state of high excitement; weight lifters sometimes ask their coaches to slap them to make them angry; whilst shooters almost always employ relaxation strategies to calm themselves down prior to shooting. As has already been suggested, it is possible that the arousal states which are associated with these different "recipes of emotions" help performers to create more appropriate activation states for the task at hand (cf. Gould and Udry, 1994).

Mental preparation strategies

A number of early studies (Caudill *et al.*, 1983; Shelton and Mahoney, 1978; Weinberg *et al.*, 1980, 1981a) explored the effectiveness of performers' preferred psych-up strategies as a means of enhancing performance. This research found that most performers reported employing multimodal psych-up strategies which typically included some combination of positive self-talk, attention control, arousal manipulation, and imagery. Furthermore, this research also suggested that such strategies were generally effective in enhancing performance. Unfortunately, as Murphy (1990) has pointed out, studies of this type do not enable any inferences to be drawn regarding the processes that underlie such facilitatory strategies. However, more recent research by Whelan *et al.* (1990) has shown that psych-up strategies can exert a beneficial effect upon performance without any corresponding change in physiological arousal, as measured by heart rate. This finding was interpreted by Whelan *et al.* (1990) as suggesting that the process underlying the performance effect was probably not change in some *unitary* arousal construct.

Research has also examined the effectiveness of various experimenter-prescribed pre-performance strategies for enhancing sports performance on a number of different criterion tasks. Gould *et al.* (1980) found that "preparatory arousal" enhanced performance on a leg kick strength-endurance task; whilst Murphy and Woolfolk (1987) found that "elevated arousal" depressed performance on a golf putting task. Lutkus (1975) found that visual imagery enhanced performance on a mirror drawing task; Hardy and Wyatt (1986) also found that visual imagery enhanced performance on a reaction catching task; whilst Woolfolk and associates (Woolfolk *et al.*, 1985a, b) found negative outcome imagery to have a negative effect upon a golf putting task when compared with positive imagery and control conditions. Aside from the obvious motivational explanations, this latter finding is consistent with previous research implicating the functional equivalence of mental and physical practice (Johnson, 1982). Finally, Ainscoe and Hardy (1987) showed that a multimodal (visual, kinaesthetic, and acoustic) imagery strategy was beneficial to performance on a gymnastic double leg circling task. The most obvious conclusion to be drawn from this literature is that *imagery-based strategies appear to be a highly effective means of generating an appropriate activation state.*

Pre-performance routines

Many athletes whose sport requires them to perform self-paced tasks employ systematic, routinised behaviours and sequences of movements that they follow prior to performing those tasks. For example, tennis players often bounce the ball a fixed number of times in a specific fashion prior to serving; whilst golfers may "waggle" their club prior to driving. Some performers appear to have quite sophisticated pre-performance routines that involve relaxation, imagery, and other cognitive strategies, as well as physical acts. Several researchers have examined the pre-performance routines that performers use in more detail. Orlick and Partington (1988) performed a qualitative study on Canadian Olympians, and concluded that the use of pre-performance routines was a distinguishing characteristic of successful Olympians. Crews and Boutcher performed a series of studies on golf putting (Boutcher and Crews,

1987; Crews and Boutcher, 1986, 1987) with collegiate and novice golfers. Their conclusions were that pre-performance routines could be taught, and that such routines were likely to enhance the putting performance of golfers significantly, particularly if the golfers were experienced. Similarly, Lobmeyer and Wasserman (1986), and Southard and Miracle (1993) found that free throw performance in basketball was also significantly enhanced by the use of pre-performance routines. The following example of a professional golfer's pre-performance routine was adapted from Boutcher (1990). It should be clear from this example that such routines are in essence just a sequence of process-oriented goals (see earlier discussions in Chapters 2–4).

(1) Shot analysis, involving the choice of the appropriate club to use for the shot;
(2) setting, involving the use of strategies for controlling physiological arousal, such as physical relaxation techniques;
(3) imagery, in the form of the ball in flight and then landing in the desired position on the fairway or green;
(4) kinaesthetic coupling, concerned with establishing the feel of the upcoming shot in the form of practising the feel of the shot whilst mentally rehearsing it;
(5) set-up, in the form of addressing the ball and checking on factors such as stance, grip, posture, alignment etc.;
(6) waggle, which involves small movements of the hands and club away from the ball just prior to swinging;
(7) swing thought, such as "tempo", which is aimed at focusing attention on the overall rhythm and timing of the shot rather than on specifics of the swing.

The precise means by which pre-performance routines exert their influence are not well understood. However, in essence, the mechanisms that have been proposed (Boutcher, 1990; Boutcher and Crews, 1987) all involve the performer establishing some sort of appropriate activation state. Furthermore, although our understanding of what constitutes an appropriate activation state is still very crude, psychophysiological studies support the view that such states are task-specific (Collins *et al.*, 1990, 1991; Gannon *et al.*, 1992; Salazar *et al.*, 1990), and may be enhanced by the use of pre-performance routines (Boutcher and Zinsser, 1990).

Summary

The literature that has been reviewed in this section suggests that mental preparation strategies and pre-performance routines are used by elite performers and do seem to help them to achieve high levels of performance.

Although self-talk, goal-setting, imagery, and arousal manipulation frequently play an important part in mental preparation, pre-performance strategies and routines are often intuitively constructed, and appear to be somewhat idiosyncratic in nature. Consequently, Gould and Udry's (1994) recommendation that athletes need to try to find the right recipe of emotions for *their performance* in *their sport* seems to be a reasonable one.

INDIVIDUAL DIFFERENCES IN AROUSAL AND ACTIVATION

Experience

Several psychophysiological studies have examined the effects of experience upon activation by comparing the pre-performance activation states of expert performers with those of less experienced performers. This research has shown that expert performers exhibit cardiac deceleration: between the "get set" and the "go" phases in simulated race starts (Stern, 1976); immediately prior to putting in golf (Boutcher and Zinsser, 1990); immediately prior to squeezing the trigger in rifle shooting (Landers *et al.*, 1980); and immediately prior to releasing the arrow in archery (Wang and Landers, 1986). This research also suggests the possibility that there may be identifiable patterns of electroencephalographic (EEG) activity which are indicative of appropriate activation states for particular activities (Collins *et al.*, 1990, 1991; Crews, 1989; Gannon *et al.*, 1992; Hatfield *et al.*, 1984; Salazar *et al.*, 1990). Finally, Landers *et al.* (in press) have shown that the ability to produce such activation states can be learned via biofeedback techniques and that, when activation control has been enhanced in this way, performance is also enhanced.

Taken together, these findings suggest that *the ability to generate appropriate activation states is an acquired skill that may be enhanced by appropriate experience.* However, it is perhaps worth emphasising the word *appropriate* here, since it is known that experience which leads to failure feedback can cause increases in anxiety about performing the task on subsequent occasions (Gaudry, 1977; Morris *et al.*, 1981). The effects of such changes in anxiety will be discussed in much more detail in Chapter 6. However, it can be argued that when anxiety exerts a negative effect upon performance, it does so because it disrupts the activation state that is necessary to perform the task (Hockey and Hamilton, 1983; Parfitt *et al.*, 1990).

Personality variables

The dimension of personality that is most frequently argued to be related to arousal states is introversion–extroversion. According to Eysenck's (1967) theory of personality, introverts are chronically over-aroused individuals who should therefore prefer a less-arousing environment for optimal performance. Such an argument would suggest that introverts should not stand up well to the pressures of elite competition. Furthermore, on the assumption that more cognitively complex tasks require lower levels of optimal arousal (Eysenck, 1982; Humphreys and Revelle, 1984), even fewer introverts should achieve elite levels of performance in sports that have large memory demands. There is some laboratory evidence to support the contention that extroverts perform better than introverts on complex tasks (Eysenck, 1982); and there is also some correlational evidence that elite sports performers are more extravert than their less elite counterparts (Bakker *et al.*, 1990). However, there is other laboratory evidence which suggests that introverts' performances are actually *less* affected than extroverts' by arousing factors such as noise, incentives, and knowledge of results, despite the fact that they are more prone to be physiologically aroused by them (for a review, see Eysenck, 1982). Similarly, Eysenck (1982) also presents evidence that introverts are less affected than extroverts by de-arousing factors, such as sleep loss and prolonged performance. All of these arousing and de-arousing factors could, of course, be thought of as examples of exactly the sort of distractions which elite performers have to cope with during their most important competitions (for example, the World Championships, or the Olympic Games). Consequently, one could also argue that, because of their greater performance stability, introverts should stand a better chance than extroverts of becoming elite performers. As Eysenck (1982) points out, paradoxical findings and arguments such as these clearly cannot be accounted for by a unitary arousal model of personality. They could be accounted for by postulating the existence of a higher level arousal mechanism, such as Sanders' (1983) effort mechanism, particularly if one assumed that this higher level mechanism exerted an inhibitory effect upon the lower level arousal-activation connection. According to such an account, introversion would be equated with a strong compensatory effort mechanism, whilst the other arousing and de-arousing factors discussed above would affect the lower level arousal and activation mechanisms (cf. Broadbent, 1971; Eysenck, 1982). Unfortunately, a more detailed discussion of this issue is beyond the scope of this book. However, one implication of such a position is that introversion would probably be an advantage in situations which strongly punished "false positives" or bad decisions (e.g. a soccer goalkeeper taking a high cross 12 metres from the goal line), but would be a disadvantage in situations which strongly punished procrastination (e.g. a soccer goalkeeper making a short-range save). Clearly, many sports require performers to be able to deal with both these different types of situation, and this fact may in part account for the somewhat equivocal findings that have been reported above.

Humphreys and Revelle (1984) argued that impulsivity, rather than introversion–extroversion, was the crucial personality variable as regards arousal-related performance effects. Impulsivity is a combination of extraversion and neuroticism in Eysenckian personality terminology, so that high impulsives are characterised by a tendency to act somewhat rashly and without due consideration. There is strong evidence that low impulsives are more highly aroused than high impulsives early in the day, but that they are less aroused than high impulsives later in the evening (for reviews, see Eysenck, 1982; Humphreys and Revelle, 1984). Consequently, according to Humphreys and Revelle, low impulsives should be more likely to experience over-arousal induced deficits in performance early in the day, while high impulsives should be more likely to experience them later in the day. Furthermore, these effects should be particularly pronounced when the task has a large memory demand. One obvious implication of this line of reasoning is that elite performers should modify their pre-performance strategies for competitions that take place at different times of day. Alternatively, they may fail to do this and only perform at their best when competitions take place at certain specific times of the day.

Summary

The research reviewed in this section suggests that, with appropriate experience, performers might acquire the ability to generate task-specific activation states, although the precise form that such appropriate experience should take is not at all clear. The literature also predicted a number of interesting differences that could be explored between introverts and extroverts (or between high and low impulsives). More specifically, biological theories of introversion–extroversion suggest that introverts and extraverts might need to employ different activation strategies in order to achieve peak performance; they might be differentially suited for high levels of performance on different types of task; and they might need to employ different activation strategies in order to achieve peak performance at different times of day. Future research might profitably examine these predictions.

IMPLICATIONS FOR RESEARCH

It seems clear that the inverted-U hypothesis does not offer a tenable explanation of the effects which arousal and activation manipulations have upon different performance tasks. There is therefore an urgent need to explore alternative explanations of these effects.

Theories of arousal and activation

The extent to which emotion-induced changes in arousal influence activation states and subsequent performance is certainly worthy of direct examination. Such research could gainfully employ psychophysiological measures to assess changes in activation states. It should also adopt Hockey and Hamilton's (1983) broadband approach, but using sports-based criterion tasks which are relatively "pure" in nature, so that the performance data can be used as secondary evidence of changes in activation states (cf. Parfitt *et al.*, 1990). Furthermore, both Sanders' (1983) model and Humphreys and Revelle's (1984) model provide testable predictions which are worthy of examination in sports settings.

Strategies influencing arousal and activation

It is also important to understand the means by which psych-up strategies, psych-down strategies, and pre-performance routines, exert their influence upon performance. In particular, there is a need to examine the extent to which such effects are mediated by changes in emotion, arousal, and activation. As a starting point, Hockey and Hamilton's (1983) broadband approach could again be gainfully employed, as could psychophysiological mapping of the activation states associated with successful performance on different sports-related tasks.

Individual differences in arousal and activation

There is a need to examine the personality-by-situation interactions which may moderate the effects of arousal and activation manipulations upon performance. Personality variables that could be considered include introversion–extroversion and impulsivity; whilst situational variables include time of day, and task requirements. Finally, when conducting any of the broadband research that has been called for in this section, it is important that researchers bear in mind the calls of ecological psychologists (for example, Whiting, 1987) for criterion tasks that do not separate out the perception–action link. Such researchers would argue that the use of laboratory–based choice reaction time tasks can tell us little about the way a tennis player might respond to a choice reaction type situation in a tennis match because the laboratory-based task has removed choice reaction from its perceptual context (see also Hardy and Jones, 1994a; Parfitt *et al.*, 1990).

IMPLICATIONS FOR BEST PRACTICE

Conceptual issues and theories of arousal and activation

The first important implication of the literature reviewed in this chapter is the conceptual distinction that needs to be made between activation and arousal. According to this distinction, activation is a complex multidimensional state which reflects the organism's anticipatory readiness to respond; whilst arousal refers to the organism's immediate response to new stimuli or input. Activation states are therefore task-specific, and arousal-manipulating strategies will exert beneficial effects upon performance only to the extent that they induce a more, rather than a less, appropriate activation pattern for the task at hand.

Although the empirical database on several of the theories discussed in this chapter is still relatively weak, a number of implications can tentatively be drawn from the literature. First, performers are quite likely to demonstrate "tunnel vision" when they become physiologically aroused, which will lead them to focus only on those perceptual cues that they perceive to be important. These may or may not be the perceptual cues that are actually important. Before trying to deal with this potential problem, coaches and sport psychologists might first explore the magnitude of the problem by identifying which cues the performer perceives to be important. Some sort of educational re-training might then be necessary. Performers could also be taught quick relaxation strategies which they can use *during* performance to lower levels of arousal if necessary (see, for example, Jones, 1993; Ost, 1988). Furthermore, coaches and sport psychologists could encourage performers (and their team mates) to learn task-specific cues which will help them to maintain an appropriate focus of attention when they are highly aroused.

Second, high levels of physiological arousal are likely to benefit certain aspects of performance (for example, powerful movements and simple reaction time), but impair others (for example, complex reaction time and decision making). Coaches and sport psychologists therefore need to be very aware of the precise technical demands which confront their performers. The value of extensive overlearning should not be underestimated; but global relaxation strategies should be used cautiously, as they may remove the beneficial effects, as well as the detrimental ones, associated with high levels of physiological arousal. Similar comments could also be made about global activation strategies.

Strategies influencing arousal and activation

A number of strategies have been identified that performers could be taught to use in order to modify their activation states. These include: psych-up and psych-down strategies, mental rehearsal strategies, and performance routines. Psych-up and psych-down strategies frequently involve self-talk, imagery, physical activity, and other arousal manipulation components. Furthermore, it seems likely that creating the right recipe of emotions is the key to exerting beneficial effects upon the cognitive and physiological activation states of performers (cf. earlier comments and Gould and Udry, 1994).

Name: Debbie Downhill

MENTAL PREPARATION PROFILE

These questions are designed to help you reflect on your competitive ski experiences over the last two seasons and develop your Competition Preparation Plan.

A. Think of your <u>best</u> performance within the last two seasons and respond to the following:

1. How did you feel just before skiing?

No determination to achieve goal	0 1 2 3 4 5 6 7 8 9 10	Completely determined
No physical activation	0 1 2 3 4 5 6 7 8 9 10	Highly physically activated
No worries or fears	0 1 2 3 4 5 6 7 8 9 10	Extremely worried or afraid
Mentally calm	0 1 2 3 4 5 6 7 8 9 10	Mentally uptight
No confidence	0 1 2 3 4 5 6 7 8 9 10	Complete confidence

2. What were you saying to yourself (thinking) or focusing on **just before** the race?
Remembering past quiet times skiing alone.

3. What were you saying to yourself (thinking) or focusing on **during** the race?
Nothing special; just skiing gate to gate.

4. How much were you focused on the race as compared to the result of the race?
Not focused at all on the results. Just maintaining a good line and arcing my turns.

B. Think of your <u>worst</u> performance within the last two seasons and respond to the following

1. How did you feel just before skiing?

No determination to achieve goal	0 1 2 3 4 5 6 7 8 9 10	Completely determined
No physical activation	0 1 2 3 4 5 6 7 8 9 10	Highly physically activated
No worries or fears	0 1 2 3 4 5 6 7 8 9 10	Extremely worried or afraid
Mentally calm	0 1 2 3 4 5 6 7 8 9 10	Mentally uptight
No confidence	0 1 2 3 4 5 6 7 8 9 10	Complete confidence

2. What were you saying to yourself (thinking) or focusing on **just before** the race?
I kept wondering what the coach and my dad would say if I didn't place well at this race.

3. What were you saying to yourself (thinking) or focusing on **during** the race?
I was worried about a jump at the top bowl.

4. How much were you focused on the race as compared to the result of the race?
Not at all focused - more worried about making the top three to qualify for Europe.

C. Compare your responses from your best and worst performances and then respond to the following by indicating how you want to feel in the future before and during a big competition.

No determination to achieve goal	0 1 2 3 4 5 6 7 8 9 10	Completely determined
No physical activation	0 1 2 3 4 5 6 7 8 9 10	Highly physically activated
No worries or fears	0 1 2 3 4 5 6 7 8 9 10	Extremely worried or afraid
Mentally calm	0 1 2 3 4 5 6 7 8 9 10	Mentally uptight
No confidence	0 1 2 3 4 5 6 7 8 9 10	Complete confidence

2. What will you be saying to yourself (thinking) or focusing on **just before** the race?
Staying loose and visualising what it feels like to ski all by myself.

3. What were you saying to yourself (thinking) or focusing on **during** the race?
Thinking about how fast and fluid I can be.

4. How much were you focused on the race as compared to the result of the race?
First things first - focus on being fluid, fast and feeling a good line, then the results.

Figure 5.4: Mental preparation profile (modified from Udry and Gould, 1992, with permission and based on Orlick, 1986)

Performance routines can also be used to help performers generate appropriate activation states. Activation control may not be the only function that such routines serve, but it is nevertheless an important one. Most of the research that has been conducted on performance routines has focused on the use of pre-performance routines in tasks which are closed, in the sense that they are self-paced, and have relatively few perceptual and decision-making demands; for example, archery, golf, gymnastics, and serving in tennis. However, there seems no reason why such routinised plans should not be used in other situations; for example, as part of a global competition preparation strategy (as opposed to preparation for a specific shot or performance); to re-focus attention after a distraction; or to recover following a mistake (cf. Gould *et al.*, 1993a, c, d; Orlick, 1986; Orlick and Partington, 1988).

Orlick (1986) and others (e.g. Hardy and Fazey, 1990; Udry and Gould, 1992) provide detailed guidelines on how a sport psychologist or coach might help a performer to construct an appropriate competition plan. Udry and Gould (1992) suggest that performers should first of all perform a retrospective analysis of what they did and how they felt (recipe of emotions) prior to their best and worst performances over the last one or two seasons (see

Name: Debbie Downhill

COMPETITION PREPARATION PLAN

	Day before	**Preparing to leave (day of event)**	**Arriving at site**	**Warm up and final minutes**	**During event**
Physical preparation	Good sleep and cut down on activity	Double checking all equipment	Stretching in lodge	Keep moving and warm. Warm-up for 30 minutes prior to race	Focus on good turns (outside ski)
Mental preparation	Listen to my relaxation tapes	Listening to tapes. Listen to some music	Staying away from others who get me too keyed up	Good inspection. Relaxing - deep breathing. Visualise myself skiing well - loose, fast, fluid	Doing my race - 'loose' and 'fluid'

My back plan is to:
find a place to get away to if there are delays or if I am one of the last runs of the day.

Figure 5.5: Competition preparation plan (modified from Udry and Gould, 1992, with permission)

Figure 5.4). The sport psychologist or coach can then help the performer to use these profiles to construct a competition plan which specifies what the performer should do: the day before the event; when preparing to leave for the competition; on arrival at the competition site; during warm-up and the countdown to performing; and during the event (see Figure 5.5). Like pre-performance routines, such competition plans are, of course, just a sequence of process-oriented goals. Examples of re-focusing and recovery routines can be found in Orlick (1986).

Individual differences in arousal and activation

The above discussion of individualised performance routines leads naturally to another implication of the research which has been reviewed. Whatever activation control strategies are used, it seems likely that their appropriateness will depend upon both personality and situational variables. Introverts may be starting from lower levels of baseline arousal than extroverts; optimal preparation strategies may be different for different performers depending upon the time of day of the competition; and in American football, for example, a blocker may require a completely different activation state to a kicker. Furthermore, performers in sports such as speed skating may need to retain a relatively stable activation state because thecognitive and physiological demands of their sport remain relatively stable. Conversely, performers in other sports may need to constantly modify their activation state as the demands of their sport change; for example, biathletes alternate between cross country skiing and rifle shooting. This situation is made still more complex for coaches and sport psychologists who work with certain team sports, where the demands that are placed upon different players within the same team are drastically different; for example, American football, netball, rugby, and soccer. Clearly, the changing room strategies that are adopted in such situations need to be highly individualised.

SUMMARY

This chapter has made a clear distinction between the terms arousal and activation, and has presented extensive evidence of their inherent multidimensionality. It has also: presented several, largely cognitive, theories of arousal and activation; discussed the arousal and activation control strategies that have been studied in the sport-related literature; and considered individual difference variables that influence arousal and activation. Some of the material that has been presented is quite complex, particularly the material on cognitive theories of arousal and activation. Nevertheless, it was felt important to include this material because it raises a number of important conceptual issues that have not previously been considered in the sport psychology literature.

6

STRESS AND ANXIETY

CONTENTS

INTRODUCTION

It doesn't take much technique to roll a 1.68 inch ball along a smooth, level surface into, or in the immediate vicinity of, a 4.5 inch hole. With no pressure on you, you can do it one-handed most of the time. But there is always pressure on the shorter putts . . . 90 per cent of the rounds I play in major championships, I play with a bit of a shake. . . . (Jack Nicklaus on golf putting; Patmore, 1986, p. 75)

Standing behind my blocks, I put my hands on my knees and tried to take as deep a breath as I could. I could not completely fill my lungs. There was a cold constriction between my stomach and my throat. My mouth and throat were dry, it was impossible to swallow . . . I wished I could be anywhere else. Why was I doing this anyway? I had never before felt such dreadful pressure. I walked forward to put my hands on the track in front of my blocks. Take your marks! No turning back. I kicked each leg out and placed it against the block. Still I felt weak. Did I feel ready to run the fastest quarter of my life? I was not sure. . . . (David Hemery prior to his World Record and Olympic winning 400 m Hurdles run at the Mexico Olympics in 1968; Hemery, 1976, p. 4)

You have no idea how important this match was to me. It's not only about winning and losing when people get that emotional about something. For six weeks before it felt like life and death. . . . (Billy Jean King talking about her 1973 tennis match against the self-confessed "male chauvinist pig" and 1939 triple Wimbledon champion Bobby Riggs before a crowd of over thirty thousand with fifty million more watching on television. She won; (Hemery, 1991, p. 196)

The ability to cope with intense pressure and anxiety is an integral part of all competitive sport, particularly at the highest levels (Gould *et al.*, 1992a, b, 1993a; Jones and Hardy, 1990b; Orlick and Partington, 1988; Patmore, 1986; Scanlan *et al.*, 1989; Scanlan *et al.*, 1991). The above statements from elite performers clearly indicate that they were experiencing considerable stress and anxiety at the times to which they refer. Such a view is reinforced by Murphy's (1988) breakdown of the problems on which he was consulted at the United States 1987 Olympic Festival. Over 50 per cent of these consultations addressed stress- or anxiety-related problems. Nevertheless, elite performers generally manage to control their anxiety, and somehow generate an appropriate activation state that enables them to perform at their very best at least most of the time. This chapter will review the available literature on anxiety and performance in order to identify its predictions for the preparation of elite performers and future research into elite performance. The first section deals with conceptual issues and developments which have taken place over the past twenty to thirty years. The second section explores the literature on sources of stress and antecedents of anxiety in sports performers. The third section critically appraises a number of theories and models which have attempted to describe the relationship between stress-related affect and performance. The fourth section discusses some of the factors which may influence anxiety responses in elite performers. The implications of this work for research and best practice are then summarised in the final two sections.

CONCEPTUAL ISSUES

Our understanding of the effects of stress and anxiety upon performance has been greatly impaired by the failure of researchers to make a clear distinction between the basic constructs of stress, anxiety, arousal, and activation (see previous chapter on Arousal and Activation). Following Cox (1978) and Lazarus (1966), stress will here be regarded as a state in which some demand is placed upon the individual, who is then required to react in some way in order to be able to cope with the situation (Jones, 1990). In consequence of this definition, stress may or may not impose a "strain" upon the individual (Jick and Payne, 1980; Lazarus, 1966), depending upon whether the individual perceives him- or herself to be able to cope with the demands of the stressor in question. Doubts about one's ability to cope with a given stressor are likely to be reflected in feelings of anxiety.

As was the case with arousal research (see Chapter 5), psychologists traditionally have attempted to explain the effects of stress upon performance in terms of the inverted-U hypothesis. According to this explanation, increased stress leads to increases in arousal, which in turn leads to enhanced performance up to some point of optimal arousal, after which performance deteriorates. Some of the limitations of the inverted-U hypothesis and unidimensional conceptualisations of arousal have already been discussed in Chapter 5. However, this explanation of stress effects was further confounded by the fact that researchers often used the words "stress", "arousal", and "anxiety" interchangeably; the limitations imposed by this failure to distinguish between separate constructs should be readily apparent.

Multidimensional trait and state anxiety

One of the earliest developments in anxiety research was Spielberger's (1966) distinction between state and trait anxiety. Spielberger (1966) defined *state anxiety* as "subjective, consciously perceived feelings of tension and apprehension, associated with . . . arousal of the autonomic nervous system" (p. 17). High state anxiety is the response that individuals make when they are confronted by a threatening situation; high *trait anxiety* refers to a general disposition that certain individuals possess to respond to a variety of (relatively unthreatening) situations with high levels of state anxiety.

Spielberger and others (Magnusson and Ekehammar, 1975; Martens 1977) subsequently argued that since anxiety responses were situationally specific, better predictions of performance would be obtained using situationally specific measurement devices.

Recent research on anxiety and performance in sport has followed this lead and developed two sports anxiety scales. The Competitive State Anxiety Inventory-2 (CSAI-2) was developed by Martens *et al.* (1990a), and contains three relatively independent subscales: cognitive anxiety, somatic anxiety, and self-confidence. *Cognitive anxiety* is characterised by fear of failure and negative expectations about performance; whilst *somatic anxiety* refers to individuals' perceptions of their physiological state in response to the stressful situation in which they find themselves. The majority of items in the *self-confidence* subscale of the CSAI-2 have the stem "I feel confident . . ." followed by an achievement oriented statement. The identification of self-confidence as a separate subscale, independent of cognitive anxiety, is interesting, because these two constructs have often been viewed as lying at opposite ends of the same continuum (Bandura, 1977; Eysenck, 1978). This issue has already been discussed in some detail in Chapter 3, and will not be revisited here.

The Sport Anxiety Scale (SAS) is a competitive sport trait anxiety scale devised by Smith *et al.* (1990b). It measures trait cognitive anxiety, somatic anxiety, and concentration disruption. Self-confidence items were not identified as a separate factor, independent of cognitive anxiety, in the development of the Sport Anxiety Scale.

Summary

As was the case with arousal and activation, early research into stress and anxiety was held back by the lack of clear distinction that was made between basic constructs such as stress, arousal, activation, and anxiety. More recent research has attempted to overcome this problem by distinguishing between state and trait anxiety; and between cognitive anxiety, somatic anxiety, and self-confidence as subcomponents of the state anxiety response to stressful situations.

ANTECEDENTS OF STRESS AND ANXIETY

Most of the current intervention literature focuses upon anxiety management strategies which are aimed at reducing, or coping with, high levels of competitive state anxiety. This literature has undoubtedly provided useful knowledge about how to modify inappropriately high anxiety states. However, it has also been argued that identification of the major causes of competitive state anxiety would enable sport psychologists to tailor interventions so that performers avoided becoming excessively anxious in the first place (Gould *et al.*, 1984). Of course, a major constraint upon this kind of research is the ethical problem of manipulating variables which are thought to cause anxiety. Consequently, most of the studies that have been performed in this area have essentially employed correlational techniques to try to identify factors which apparently precede the state anxiety response and predict the intensity of that response. These factors are usually referred to as the *antecedents* of state anxiety.

Antecedents of unidimensional anxiety

Early studies did not consider the different components of anxiety, but did attempt to identify predictors of anxiety in (generally young) performers. Simon and Martens (1977) found that competitive state anxiety was higher for young participants in individual sports compared with team sports, and in individual contact sports compared with individual non-contact sports. Lowe and McGrath (1971) showed that the importance of a particular game within the season was a significant predictor of physiological arousal in young performers with more critical and important games being associated with higher levels of physiological arousal; while Hanson (1967) showed that children's physiological arousal was significantly higher when they were at bat during baseball matches than at other phases in the game. Thus, both the criticality of the game and the immediate situation within the game are situational predictors of stress-related physiological arousal. Personality, as well as situational, variables were also considered; Scanlan and Passer (1978) showed that trait anxiety, self-esteem, and performance expectancies were all significant predictors of competitive state anxiety.

This research gathered momentum when Kroll (1979) attempted to identify more specific sources of psychological stress in higher level adult performers. Using factor analytical techniques, he identified five sources of psychological stress that were experienced by adult performers: fear of failure (e.g. making a foolish mistake); feelings of inadequacy (e.g. getting tired); loss of internal control (e.g. unfair officials); guilt (e.g. at hurting an opponent); and current physical state (e.g. sore muscles). Using a sample of junior wrestlers, Gould *et al.* (1983) confirmed the first four of Kroll's factors, and identified social evaluation as an additional source of stress. Another study by Gould and Weinberg (1985) which examined sources of stress in intercollegiate wrestlers, also found the most frequently experienced sources of stress to be worry about not performing well, improving on the last performance, what the coach will think or say, losing, not performing up to ability, and the performer's physical condition. However, only concerns about what the coach would think or say, losing, and making mistakes (which was not a frequently cited worry) were significant predictors of performance. Feltz *et al.* (1992) replicated these sources of stress with young distance runners.

Antecedents of multidimensional anxiety

More recent research has examined the antecedents of multidimensional anxiety as measured by the CSAI-2. Martens *et al.* (1990) hypothesised that the antecedents of cognitive anxiety and self-confidence should be those factors in the environment which might influence the performer's expectations of success. These include perceptions of one's own ability and that of one's opponent. Antecedents of somatic anxiety, on the other hand were hypothesised to be non-evaluative, of a shorter duration, and consist mainly of cues which signal the proximity of the competition, such as changing room preparation and pre-competition warm-up, or fear of physical harm. It is perhaps worth noting even at this early stage that the latter assumption that somatic anxiety is not affected by performers' expectations of success does not sit very comfortably with the findings of Hanson (1967), and Lowe and McGrath (1971), reported above.

Gould *et al.* (1984) considered trait anxiety, perceived ability, wrestling success, and "years of experience" as predictors of the three CSAI-2 subcomponents. The strongest predictor of cognitive anxiety was "years of experience" (high experience was associated with low cognitive anxiety), whilst the strongest predictor of self-confidence was perceived ability. However, the only significant predictor of somatic anxiety was trait anxiety.

Jones *et al.* (1990) investigated the antecedents of the CSAI-2 components in high level, male, middle distance runners in more detail. They found that cognitive anxiety was predicted by performers' perceptions of their readiness to perform, their attitude towards previous performances, and their use of outcome goals. In the case of outcome goals, cognitive anxiety was positively related to the difficulty of the goal, and negatively related to the athlete's perception of whether or not he could achieve the goal. This finding extended other research (Burton, 1989b; Hardy *et al.*, 1986; Jones and Cale, in press; Pendleton *et al.*, 1995) which also suggests interesting relationships between goal-setting skills and state anxiety (see Chapter 2). The major predictors of self-confidence in Jones *et al.*'s (1990) study were perceived readiness to perform, and the external environment (e.g. the weather and the condition of the running surface). Somatic anxiety was not predicted by any of the antecedents considered.

Taken together, the above findings are important because they offer some explanation of why cognitive anxiety and self-confidence sometimes seem to separate into two factors, and sometimes seem to behave as though they are opposite ends of the same factor. More precisely, the results suggest that cognitive anxiety and self-confidence may share some common antecedents, but also may possess certain unique antecedents. Thus, if perceived readiness to perform is the most salient variable when anxiety data are collected, then self-confidence and cognitive anxiety would be expected not to separate; but if attitude towards previous performances and environmental conditions are particularly salient, then one would expect self-confidence and cognitive anxiety to behave independently. Jones *et al.*'s (1990b) results also indicate an important role for the coach in helping to determine the performer's perceived readiness for competition.

In a follow-up, Jones *et al.* (1991) examined the antecedents of cognitive anxiety and self-confidence in male and female performers. In line with previous research by Gill (1988), Jones *et al.* (1991) found that females focused more on personal goals and standards than did males. Furthermore, the cognitive anxiety and self-confidence of the females were mainly determined by their readiness to perform, and the importance of "doing well" personally. On the other hand, the cognitive anxiety and self-confidence of the males were more strongly influenced by the ability of their opponents in relation to themselves, and their perceptions of the probability of winning.

Qualitative research on elite performers

Few of the studies that have been reported above have examined the antecedents of stress and anxiety in elite, or even national level, performers. However, several researchers have used qualitative techniques to examine sources of anxiety in elite performers (Gould *et al.*, 1991; Gould *et al.*, 1993c, d; Scanlan *et al.*, 1989; Scanlan *et al.*, 1991). Furthermore, these studies are particularly interesting because they have started to unearth some of the organisational and occupational stressors that confront elite performers. These include: readiness and performance problems; refereeing decisions and competition organisation; coach and team-mate problems; coaching and management decisions; social support; accommodation, transport, food, and training facilities; and financial and time pressures.

> *I just got set up . . . they kind of tricked us on that one and we fell for it. On the bout sheet they had me wrestling last when actually I was wrestling first . . . it caught me off guard. I thought when (the coach) came and told me I was wrestling, I thought he was joking. It just caught me off guard.* (Olympic wrestler; Gould *et al.*, 1991, p. 32)

> *He could not handle the frustration, and he would really freak out and blame me for my injury. That was a really hard thing to deal with. It's like, "Yes, of course I know we are supposed to be training hard, and yes, I want to defend the title, too, but I don't need you putting more stress*

> *on me".* (United States pairs ice skating Champion; Gould *et al.*, 1993d, p. 150)
>
> *Worrying about finances, about the money. How could my family pay for all this? That was a constant worry for me.* (United States figure skating Champion; Gould *et al.*, 1993d, pp. 140–141)

Summary

Whilst much of the research on antecedents of anxiety has focused upon the undifferentiated unidimensional anxiety responses of young performers, recent studies have begun to identify the antecedents of multidimensional state anxiety and some of the sources of stress in high level performers. Antecedents of cognitive anxiety include: attitude towards previous performances; perceived readiness to perform; and the nature of the personal goals set for the competition. Antecedents of self-confidence include: perceived readiness to perform; and the performing (external) environment. Sources of stress include: readiness and performance problems; competition organisation and officiating problems; interpersonal and management problems within the team; poor facilities; and financial and time pressures.

COMPETITIVE STATE ANXIETY AND PERFORMANCE

As has already been mentioned, the anxiety–performance relationship was traditionally discussed in terms of the inverted-U hypothesis (Hebb, 1955; Yerkes and Dodson, 1908). In essence, this approach advocated that anxiety affected performance *because* changes in anxiety were associated with corresponding changes in arousal. Furthermore, whilst moderate levels of such arousal were supposed to be beneficial to performance because they energized the organism in some way, higher levels of arousal were thought to be detrimental because they produced too much energy which could not be controlled. One characteristic of this approach was that the energy demands of the task to be performed should at least partially determine whether a given level of anxiety (arousal) was detrimental or beneficial to performance.

In view of the distinctions that have already been made between the terms anxiety, activation, and arousal, it is perhaps not surprising that this approach has been extensively criticised in recent years from a number of standpoints (Hockey and Hamilton, 1983; Jones and Hardy, 1989; Krane, 1992; Neiss, 1988b). A central feature of these criticisms is the notion of an unitary arousal construct which is linearly related to anxiety in a positive fashion. Different theoreticians have attempted to overcome this problem in different ways which will be elaborated upon in the following subsections.

Individualised zones of optimal functioning

A central tenet of Hanin's (1980, 1986) individualised zones of optimal functioning (IZOFs) approach is that each performer has his or her own optimal pre-performance anxiety zone within which performance will be optimal. Conversely, if the performer's anxiety level lies outside this zone, then performance will be impaired (see Figure 6.1). The characteristic feature of individualised zones of optimal functioning is that individual differences in optimal anxiety levels cannot be predicted from task characteristics or the performer's level of experience. Rather, Hanin (1986) has argued that IZOFs can be determined either by direct repeated measurement of anxiety and subsequent performance, or by retrospective recall of anxiety levels prior to peak performances.

There is some evidence to support the claim that optimal anxiety levels can be determined by retrospective recall (Hanin, 1986; Raglin and Morgan, 1988). Furthermore, several researchers have also found that IZOFs do

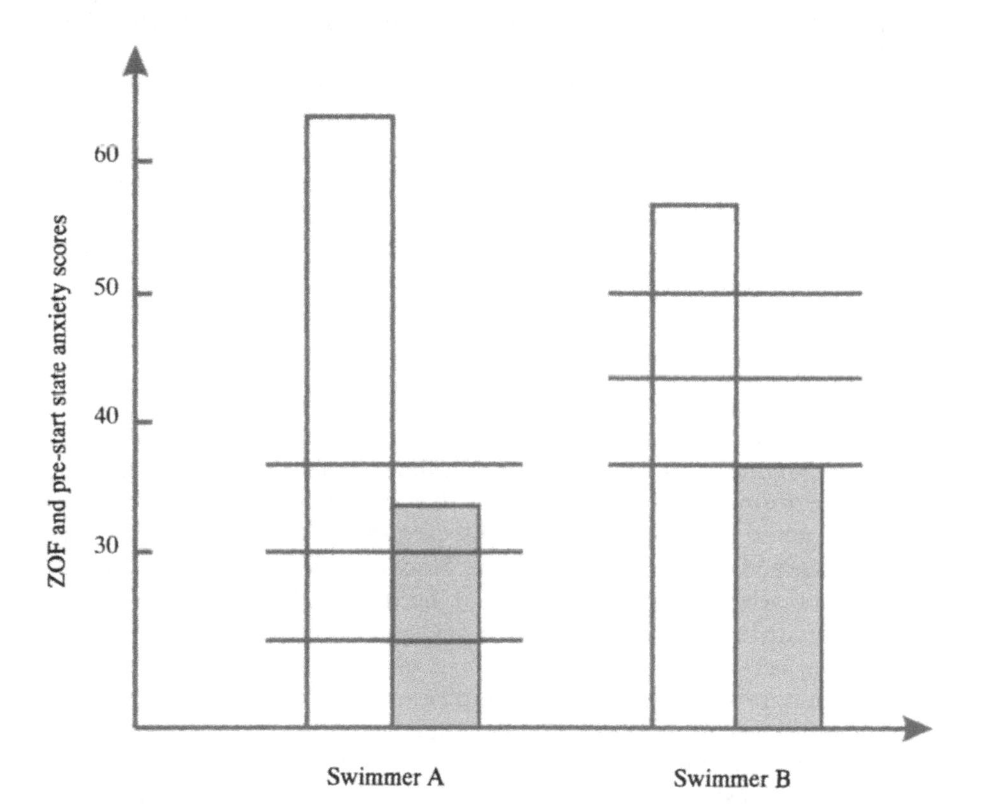

Figure 6.1: Two zones of optimal functioning, one with the performer in the zone and one with the performer out (modified from Hanin, 1986 with permission)

significantly predict performance (for a review, see Gould and Tuffey, 1996); while Turner and Raglin (1991) have shown that IZOFs predict performance significantly better than group determined zones based on an inverted-U hypothesis. Finally, following a call by Gould and Udry (1994) for sports performance researchers to examine a wider variety of arousal-related emotions in order to better understand the appropriate recipes of emotions that may be necessary for optimal performance, a recent innovation in the IZOF literature has been the extension of IZOFs to emotions other than anxiety (Hanin and Syrjä, 1995a, b; Prapavessis and Grove, 1991).

Despite their obvious practical significance for practising sport psychologists, individualised zones of optimal functioning appear to be somewhat barren ground at a theoretical level for two reasons. First, Hanin's original model utilised a unidimensional conceptualisation of anxiety, although subsequent research has considered IZOFs based on a multidimensional conceptualisation of anxiety (Dennis *et al.*, 1993; Gould *et al.*, 1993e; Krane, 1993; Scallen, 1993). Second, and much more serious, as Gould and Tuffey (1996) have indicated, individualised zones of optimal functioning is essentially an individual difference "theory" without any individual difference variables! In particular, it makes no attempt to identify factors that determine individual differences in IZOFs, or to explain *how* IZOFs affect performance. Gould and Tuffey (1996) do highlight attentional mechanisms (see Chapter 7) and muscular tension/co-ordination (see Chapters 5 and 7) changes as possible explanations of how IZOFs might affect performance; but even they are somewhat at a loss when it comes to explaining why zones of optimal functioning are individual.

Multidimensional anxiety theory

Following researchers in clinical psychology, psychophysiology, and test anxiety (Davidson and Schwartz, 1976; Lacey, 1967; Morris *et al.*, 1981), Martens *et al.* (1990b) proposed a multidimensional theory of anxiety and sports performance which predicted that cognitive and somatic anxiety were triggered by different antecedents (see earlier section), and influenced performance via different mechanisms. Since cognitive anxiety is principally concerned with the consequences of failure, multidimensional anxiety theory predicts that it should have a negative linear relationship with performance, because it is hypothesised to use up some of the performer's information-processing resources. Empirical support for this negative linear relationship has been obtained by Burton (1988) using collegiate swimmers. Somatic anxiety, on the other hand, is hypothesised to have an inverted-U shaped relationship with performance, presumably because it is associated with changes in (physiological) arousal; although it should be noted that Martens and associates do not actually offer any reason for this relationship.

Empirical support for an inverted-U shaped relationship between somatic anxiety and performance has also been obtained using pistol shooters (Gould *et al.*, 1987), and swimmers (Burton, 1988). However, several other studies have failed to find strong relationships between the CSAI-2 subcomponents and competitive sports performance, or have found relationships which run counter to multidimensional anxiety theory's predictions (for reviews, see Jones, 1995b; Krane, 1992; Martens *et al.*, 1990a; Parfitt *et al.*, 1990). A number of reasons may exist for these inconsistencies, including: the use of poor performance measures; failure to control for individual differences in ability, response sensitivity, and anxiety tolerance; and failure to consider subjects' interpretations of the meaning of their anxiety symptoms. In order to control for individual differences in ability and response sensitivity, Gould *et al.* (1987) and Burton (1988) standardised all scores within subjects prior to performing their main analyses; that is to say, they expressed subjects' raw anxiety and performance scores as a proportion of their normal (mean) score. However, Raglin (1992) has argued strongly that this procedure is invalid essentially because in order to test for an inverted-U shaped relationship, one must be sure that high anxiety scores are genuinely high, and not just intermediate; but standardising the data within subjects has the effect of removing all absolute reference points from the data. Consequently, a high standardised anxiety score only implies that anxiety is higher than it *usually* is for that subject. There is some truth in Raglin's claim that the analytical methods used by Burton (1988) and Gould *et al.* (1987) assume that mean levels of anxiety are the same as moderate anxiety levels, and high levels are genuinely high. However, the importance of this criticism is vastly overstated by Raglin (1992). If false, such an assumption would be expected to reduce the likelihood of obtaining the predicted relationships with performance (because of increased error variance), not increase it. Consequently, such confounding cannot be argued to have caused the *significant* results which were obtained by Burton (1988) and Gould *et al.* (1987). It could only explain nonsignificant results.

As has already been mentioned in Chapter 3, Martens *et al.* (1990a) also identified self-confidence as a third factor, independent of cognitive and somatic anxiety during their construction of the CSAI-2. According to multidimensional anxiety theory, self-confidence should have a positive linear relationship with performance, essentially because it is (incorrectly—see Chapter 3) regarded as the opposite of cognitive anxiety. Nevertheless, support has been found for the prediction of a positive linear relationship between self-confidence and swimming performance by Burton (1988), but not by Gould *et al.* (1987), who found a *negative* linear relationship between self-confidence and shooting performance.

The most obvious implications of multidimensional anxiety theory for elite performance are that elite performers will perform better the less cognitively anxious and more self-confident they are. Since the theory also proposes that the primary determinant of cognitive anxiety is concern about the consequences of failure, this suggests that coaches and sport psychologists might consider de-emphasising the importance of major competitions in order to reduce the personal significance of failure to the performer. It is fairly clear that there is not much point telling an Olympic finalist that his performance is not really that important. However, in the authors' experience, coaches, loved ones, and even sport psychologists, often over-emphasise the importance of events in quite subtle ways; for example, by "fussing" unnecessarily over a performer, by asking how excited the performer is ("You ought to be"), or by being overtly anxious themselves.

Multidimensional anxiety theory also predicts that athletes will perform best at intermediate levels of somatic anxiety. However, the theory proposes that somatic anxiety is a conditioned response to the competitive environment. Consequently, it is difficult to see how the somatic anxiety response might be optimised at an intermediate level by experience, because one would expect such a response to increasingly habituate with repeated exposure to the unconditioned stimulus (i.e. competitive environment). This line of reasoning seems to suggest that elite performers might be expected to peak earlier, rather than later in their careers, which does not usually appear to be the case. Of course, sport psychologists and coaches might also adopt stress management strategies to reduce cognitive anxiety and optimise somatic anxiety. Such strategies are discussed in more detail later in the chapter.

Catastrophe models of anxiety and performance

Dissatisfaction with the inverted-U hypothesis and multidimensional anxiety theory led Hardy and associates to propose a cusp catastrophe model of anxiety and performance, which attempted to clarify the relationship between cognitive anxiety, physiological arousal, and performance (Fazey and Hardy, 1988; Hardy, 1990). Features of this model include the fact that it incorporates physiological arousal, rather than somatic anxiety, as a predictor variable; and that it attempts to model the *interactive* effects of cognitive anxiety and physiological arousal upon performance, rather than simply describe their *separate* effects. Hardy and associates' use of physiological arousal in preference to somatic anxiety was based upon the argument that, theoretically, physiological arousal could exert an influence upon performance via two different mechanisms (Hardy, 1990; Hardy and Parfitt, 1991; Hardy *et al.*, 1994). It could cause a direct effect upon performance by changing the performer's activation state, and therefore the availability of certain resources to the performer (cf. Hockey and Hamilton, 1983; Humphreys and Revelle, 1984; Parfitt *et al.*, 1990). For example, Parfitt *et al.*

(1995) have shown that high levels of anxiety-induced physiological arousal are associated with enhanced anaerobic power, presumably because of neuro-endocrine changes associated with the "fight–flight" response.

Alternatively, physiological arousal could influence performance indirectly via performers' positive or negative interpretations of their perceived physiological symptoms (cf. Schachter, 1964). According to the cusp catastrophe model (see Figure 6.2), these interpretations will be influenced by performers' levels of cognitive anxiety. The cusp catastrophe model therefore allows the possibility that physiological arousal may influence performance either directly or indirectly. The use of somatic anxiety, on the other hand, could only allow indirect effects upon performance.

A detailed discussion of the cusp catastrophe model is beyond the scope of this chapter. However, such discussions can be found in Hardy (1990) and Hardy (1996). In essence, *the model predicts that increases in cognitive anxiety will have a beneficial effect upon performance at low levels of physiological arousal, but a detrimental effect upon performance at high levels of physiological arousal* (see the left and right edges of Figure 6.2). Another prediction of the model is that at low levels of cognitive anxiety, changes in physiological arousal should have relatively small effects upon performance possibly in the form

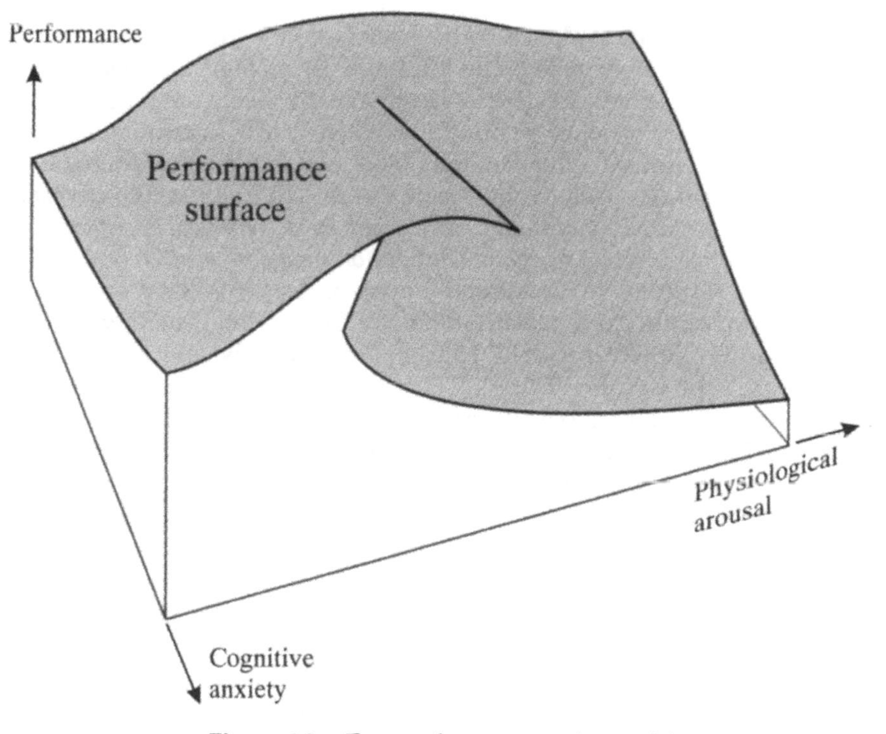

Figure 6.2: Two surface catastrophe model

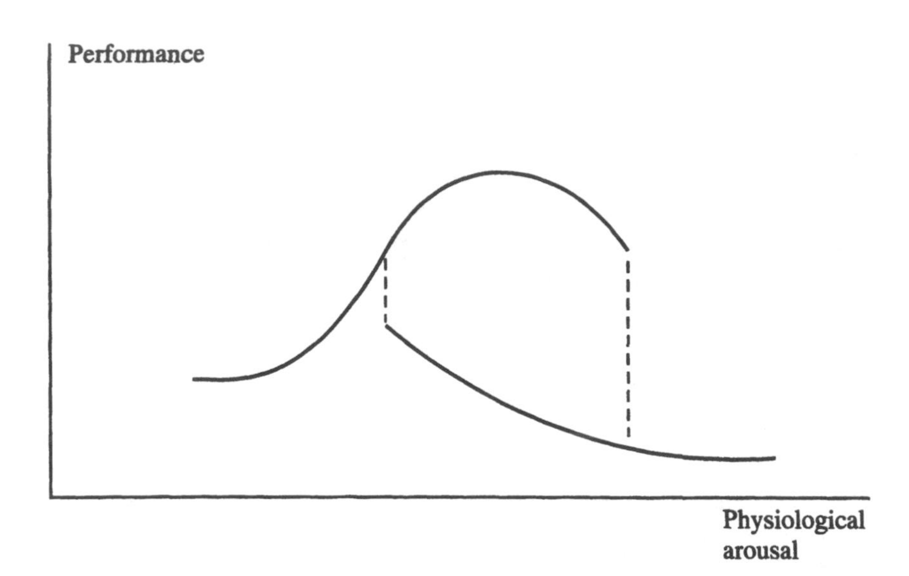

Figure 6.3: Hysteresis

of an inverted-U shape as shown by the back face of Figure 6.2. However, at high levels of cognitive anxiety, the effects of physiological arousal can be either positive or negative relative to baseline performance, depending upon exactly how high physiological arousal is. Furthermore, continual increases in physiological arousal will eventually lead to a sudden and dramatic decline in performance (see the front face of Figure 6.2). *Once such a performance decrement has occurred, it can only be reversed by a considerable reduction in physiological arousal beyond the point where the original decrement in performance occurred* (see Figure 6.3). The limited empirical tests that have so far been performed upon the cusp catastrophe model have been generally (but not unequivocally) supportive of it (Hardy, 1996a; Hardy and Parfitt, 1991; Hardy *et al.*, 1994; Krane, 1990).

An important addition to the basic cusp catastrophe model was the introduction of higher order factors which were hypothesised to moderate the effects of cognitive anxiety and physiological arousal upon performance (Hardy, 1990). One such higher order model, called a *butterfly catastrophe* has been proposed by Hardy (1990). This model hypothesises that self-confidence has the effect of swinging the front part of the behaviour surface shown in Figure 6.1 to the right, thereby increasing the probability that cognitively anxious performers will be able to tolerate higher levels of physiological arousal before experiencing a decrement in performance. Hardy (1996a) offers some evidence that the butterfly catastrophe model may provide a rather more complete description of the relationship between anxiety and performance than the cusp catastrophe model. Furthermore, Hardy (1996a) also shows that self-confidence can account for a significant proportion of the variance in performance, over and above the variance accounted for by cognitive anxiety and physiological arousal. This finding is important because it confirms the suggestion that has already been made in this book, and elsewhere, that cognitive anxiety and self-confidence are independent constructs (cf. Burrows *et al.*, 1977; Hardy, 1990; Hardy and Whitehead, 1984; Thayer, 1978). The finding also suggests that self-confidence may be one of the most powerful qualities that elite performers possess, certainly more powerful than anxiety and arousal management skills.

There are a number of implications of the catastrophe models of anxiety and performance which are rather at odds with multidimensional anxiety theory. First, the catastrophe models suggest that elite performers may actually use high levels of cognitive anxiety to enhance performance provided they can control the physiological arousal which accompanies it. There is some anecdotal evidence which supports this prediction. For example, in a qualitative study of stress in elite performers, Jones and Hardy (1990a) reported that former world champion javelin thrower, Steve Backley, estimated that the stress of competition improved his performance by at least 10 per cent, and said "I never think of stress as a negative thing . . . I think that as soon as you admit to stress being a negative factor then it will be" (p. 251). Similarly, world champion trampolinist, Sue Challis, stated that "When I'm prepared, it (the stress) is positive, and when I'm not prepared it's negative" (p. 250).

Second, Hardy's (1996a) findings suggest that self-confidence is relatively independent of cognitive anxiety, but may protect against its effects upon performance. These findings have been replicated in Hardy *et al.* (1996).Third, in the studies that have so far yielded the clearest support for the catastrophe model (Hardy and Parfitt, 1991; Hardy *et al.*, 1994), physiological arousal has been manipulated by means of exercise and operationalised as heart rate. Under these circumstances, the physiological arousal that has been measured may be more a reflection of the effort that the performers were required to invest in the task than a reflection of their anxiety level. If this were proved to be the case, then another implication of the model would be that elite performers may be able to tolerate higher levels of effort than non-elite performers.

Finally, a number of authors have suggested that the perception of control may be a crucial variable in determining when performers will disengage from the task and suffer performance decrements (Carver and Scheier, 1988; Gould *et al.*, 1992a, b, 1993a; Hardy and Jones, 1990; Jones, 1995b). There is also anecdotal evidence in support of this position. For example, trampolinist Sue Challis reported that it was important to have confidence in one's ability to cope with and control the stress of competition; whilst track athlete David Hemery stated that his performance "very much depended on having the stress of competition under control" (p. 251). However, in the context of catastrophe models, an important prediction is that when performance does decline, it should decline suddenly and dramatically (Fazey and Hardy, 1988). Furthermore, once this has happened, performers should experience considerable difficulty in reinstating optimal (peak) performance (Hardy, 1990). This prediction again seems to fit the personal experiences of the authors as sport psychology consultants, and quite strong empirical evidence also now exists to support it (Hardy and Parfitt, 1991; Hardy *et al.*, 1994). In conclusion, despite their complexity, many aspects of the catastrophe models of anxiety and performance are heuristically appealing. However, considerably more empirical support would be needed before one could consider rejecting multidimensional anxiety theory in favour of them.

Interpretation of anxiety states

Despite arguments to the contrary by Raglin (1992), the multidimensional conceptualisation of anxiety that is favoured by the majority of researchers has undoubtedly enhanced our understanding of the anxiety–performance relationship. Nevertheless, it has been argued that current measurement devices are based on a limited conceptualisation of the anxiety response which considers only the intensity of performers' symptoms, and ignores other potentially important variables; for example, the frequency of occurrence of anxiety symptoms and the interpretation that performers place upon them (Jones, 1991, 1995b; Swain and Jones, 1993). This situation may have arisen because the majority of researchers seem to view anxiety (particularly cognitive anxiety) as a negative construct that is *always* detrimental to performance. However, a number of avenues of research suggest that this assumption may not be a valid one. For example, Apter's (1982) reversal theory predicts that performers may interpret the same physiological state as either anxiety or excitement depending upon which of two "metamotivational" states they are in. In telic states, performers have a strong goal orientation and experience high physiological arousal as anxiety; but in paratelic states, performers are absorbed in their current behaviour and experience high levels of physiological arousal as excitement. Furthermore, according to the theory, performers may quickly "flip" from a telic state to a paratelic state and vice versa, thereby changing their interpretation of their felt arousal (for more detail, see Kerr, 1990). Similarly, in the context of catastrophe models of anxiety and performance, Hardy (1990) has suggested that performers' interpretations of their physiological state may be fundamental in determining whether their performance lies on the upper or lower performance surface.

To date, only a limited amount of research has considered the possibility that the influence of anxiety upon sports performance may be mediated by performers' interpretations of their anxiety symptoms. Mahoney and Avener (1977) explored the differences between successful and unsuccessful Olympic trialists for the United States Gymnastics Team. They reported that

> *verbal interviews suggested that the more successful athletes tended to "use" their anxiety as a stimulant to better performance. The less successful gymnasts seemed to arouse themselves into near-panic states by self-verbalizations and images which belied self-doubts and impending tragedies.* (Mahoney and Avener, 1977, p. 140)

Following on from this work, the notion of "directional interpretation" of anxiety was introduced into the sport psychology literature by Jones and associates (Jones, 1991; Jones and Swain, 1992). This notion refers to how sports performers label the cognitive and physiological symptoms they experience on a debilitative–facilitative continuum. Support for the distinction between *intensity* and *direction* of anxiety symptoms has been provided by several recent empirical studies. Jones *et al.*'s (1993) study of gymnasts performing in a beam competition showed no significant differences between high and low performance groups on cognitive and somatic anxiety intensity scores, or on somatic anxiety direction scores. However, the high performance group reported their cognitive anxiety symptoms to be more facilitative and less debilitative to performance than the low performance group. Jones *et al.* (1994) found no significant differences in cognitive or somatic anxiety intensity scores between elite and non-elite swimmers prior to an important race; but the elite swimmers interpreted both anxiety states as being more facilitative to performance than the non-elite swimmers. A later study of cricketers by Jones and Swain (1995) showed that elite performers have a predisposition to interpret their anxiety symptoms as being facilitative. Finally, Swain and Jones (1996) compared the relative contributions of the intensity and direction dimensions of cognitive and somatic anxiety to the prediction of basketball performance. Their results showed that direction was a better predictor of performance than intensity for both components of anxiety.

Two further points are perhaps worth noting. First, parallel arguments to those that have been presented here regarding the interpretation of anxiety symptoms have been presented in the test anxiety literature (Alpert and Haber, 1960; Carver and Scheier, 1988; Wine, 1980). Carver and Scheier's (1988) work is particularly interesting. They proposed that anxiety would be facilitative provided that the individual's expectations regarding coping and goal attainment remained favourable; however, when expectations became unfavourable, anxiety would become debilitative. Jones (1995b) adapted

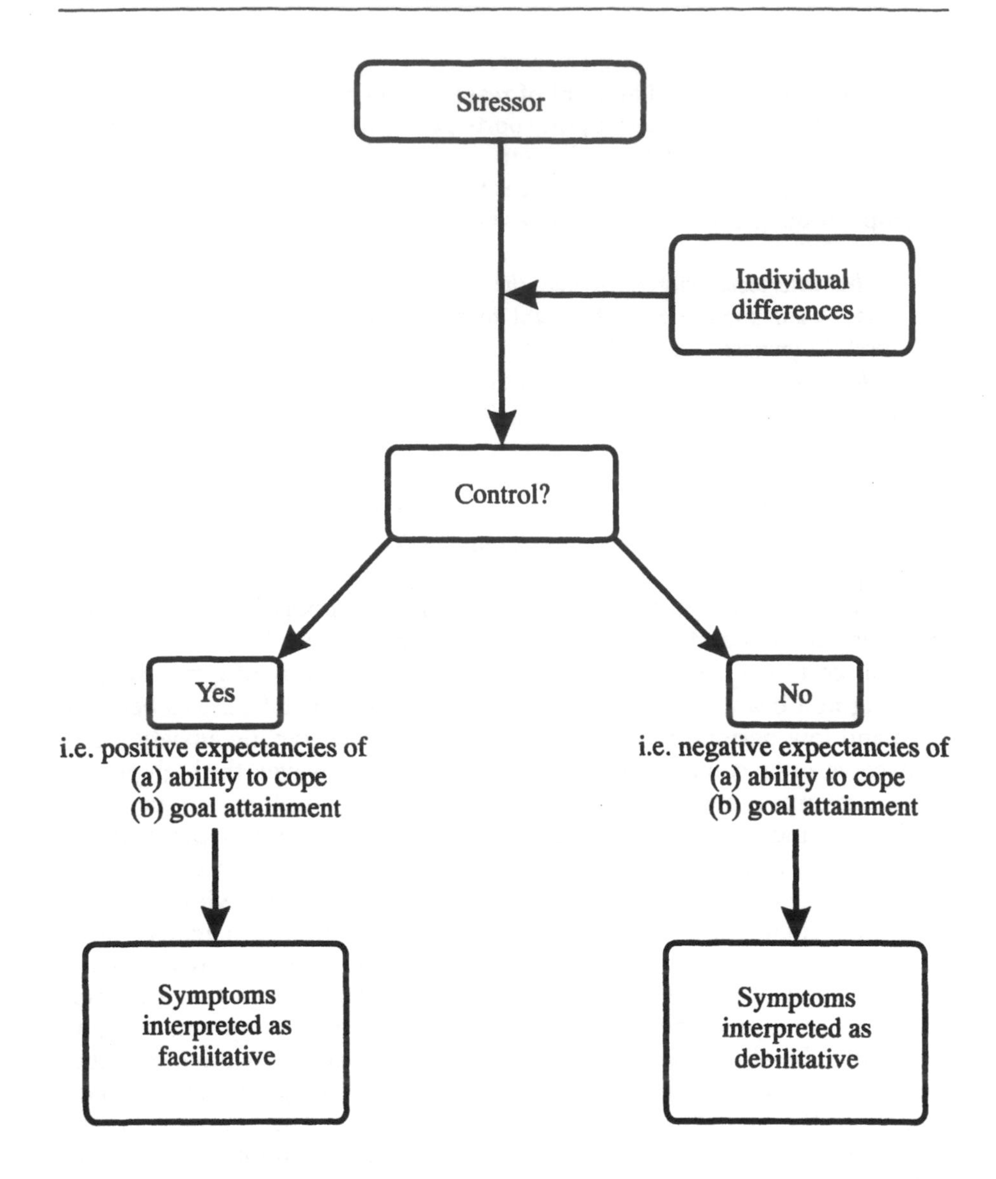

Figure 6.4: A model of facilitative and debilitative competitive anxiety (modified from Jones, 1995 with permission)

and modified Carver and Scheier's (1988) work to propose a model of debilitative and facilitative competitive anxiety (see Figure 6.4). In this model, control is broadly conceptualised as the performer's cognitive appraisal of the degree of control that he or she is able to exert over the environment and self. Some preliminary support for the predictions of this model has been provided in a study of swimmers by Jones and Hanton (1996).

Secondly, it has been proposed that self-confidence (or self-efficacy) plays some role in determining the interpretation that performers place upon their anxiety symptoms, and therefore the effect of anxiety upon performance (Hardy, 1990; Hardy and Jones, 1990; Jones, 1995b). Furthermore, there is some evidence to support this position; Jones *et al.* (1993) found that self-confidence intensity correlated more strongly with performers' directional interpretations of their cognitive and somatic anxiety symptoms than with the intensity of these symptoms.

Finally, Jones and associates' notion of "cognitive intrusions" has thrown further light on pre-competition affective states (Jones, 1991, 1995b; Parfitt *et al.*, 1990; Swain and Jones, 1993). One of the predictions of multidimensional anxiety theory is that cognitive anxiety should normally remain fairly stable during the pre-competition period, whilst somatic anxiety should become elevated just prior to competition. Furthermore, previous research (Jones and Cale, 1989; Martens *et al.*, 1990a; Parfitt and Hardy, 1987; Ussher and Hardy, 1986) had generally confirmed this prediction, although individual difference variables had also been shown to play a role in such patterning (Jones *et al.*, 1991; Krane and Williams, 1987; Swain and Jones, 1992). However, Jones (1991) argued that the notion that cognitive anxiety should be at the same level (say) one week before a competition as it was one hour before merely referred to the intensity of cognitive anxiety symptoms experienced on the two occasions, and was unlikely to represent the true cognitive state. Consequently, Jones and associates introduced the notion of "frequency" of competition-related cognitive intrusions in an attempt to gain further understanding of pre-competitive affective states. Frequency was operationalised within this context as the proportion of time which cognitions about the competition occupied the individual's thoughts. Using a sample of track and field athletes, Swain and Jones (1993) demonstrated that, although the intensity of cognitive anxiety symptoms remained relatively stable throughout the pre-competition period, the frequency with which the athletes experienced these symptoms increased progressively during that period. Swain and Jones concluded that a cognitive state in which worries about the upcoming event are only intruding for 5 per cent of the time is very different from one in which they are recurring 90 per cent of the time. Thus, the intensity-alone approach which has characterised the literature was again shown to represent a very limited perspective of the anxiety–performance relationship.

Ideal performance states

A rather different way in which research into the anxiety–performance relationship has been extended has been to examine the relationship between a broader range of emotions and performance. Although this approach is not strictly about stress or anxiety, it is included in this chapter because several anxiety–performance researchers have called for a broader range of emotions than just anxiety to be examined (e.g. Gould and Udry, 1994; Hanin, in press; Jones, 1996b; Prapavessis and Grove, 1991). The Profile of Mood States (McNair *et al.*, 1971) has been the most commonly used measure of emotional states for this purpose. Early research by Morgan and associates led to the development of the Mental Health Model of performance (Morgan, 1985). This predicts that ideal performance states are characterised by high levels of vigour, and low levels of tension, depression, anger, fatigue and confusion—the so-called *iceberg profile*. Thus, performance will be impaired to the extent that an athlete's pre-performance profile differs from this ideal (see Figure 4.5).

Despite evidence in support of the Mental Health Model (Morgan, 1985; Morgan *et al.*, 1988), there is strong prospective evidence which runs counter to the predictions of the model (Cockerill *et al.*, 1991; Frazier, 1988). For example, Cockerill *et al.* (1991) found that elevated tension and anger, but reduced depression, were associated with high levels of performance in club cross-country runners. Furthermore, a recent review by Renger (1993), and a meta analysis by Rowley *et al.* (1995), of the North American literature on iceberg profiles both concluded that the Profile of Mood States was of limited use in differentiating between successful and unsuccessful athletes. However, a second review by Terry (1995), which included a broader range of studies, identified a number of factors which appeared to account for the conclusions of Renger (1993) and Rowley *et al.* (1995). Terry's review also demonstrated that the Profile of Mood States was capable of discriminating between successful and non-successful elite performers, provided the sample was sufficiently homogeneous with regard to ability and sport. Perhaps the safest conclusion to draw from all this is that the utility of the Profile of Mood States for measuring ideal performance states is as yet unproven. It is also worth noting that the Profile of Mood States was not in fact developed with sport populations in mind. Consequently, it is at least possible that it does not even tap the moods and emotions which are most relevant to sport.

Summary

This section has examined different approaches to modelling and explaining the relationship between anxiety and performance. Research on individualised zones of optimal functioning proposes that each athlete has an anxiety zone within which performance will be optimal, and outside of which performance will be impaired. Empirical studies which have explored IZOFs suggest that such an individualised approach may account for more variance in performance than non-individualised approaches, although IZOFs make no predictions about how these individual differences come about. Multidimensional anxiety theory predicts that the effects of cognitive anxiety will always be negative; whilst the catastrophe models predict that cognitive anxiety will exert a positive effect upon performance when physiological arousal is low and a negative effect upon performance when physiological arousal is high. This may be because cognitively anxious performers who have low levels of physiological arousal interpret their anxiety symptoms positively, whilst cognitively anxious performers who have high levels of physiological arousal interpret their anxiety symptoms negatively. Regardless of this, there is good evidence to suggest that when athletes (for whatever reasons) interpret their anxiety symptoms negatively they perform badly. It has also been suggested that the perception of control may be a crucial variable here, but the empirical evidence in support of this contention is as yet very limited. Finally, research which has examined the prediction of performance from mood profiles has found little support for the so-called iceberg profiles of elite performers.

FACTORS INFLUENCING ANXIETY RESPONSES

Anxiety and experience

Very little quantitative or prospective research has been conducted on genuinely elite performers. However, Fenz and Epstein (1967) examined the physiological arousal responses of novice and expert sky divers prior to jumping from their aircraft. Interestingly, they found little difference in the maximum physiological arousal levels obtained by the two groups, but significant differences in the temporal patterning of their responses. Specifically, expert sky divers experienced their peak levels of physiological arousal well in advance of their jump, so that their physiological arousal was already declining as they approached the jump zone. In contrast, the physiological arousal levels of novice sky divers were relatively low during the early stages of the flight, but became progressively higher as the jump zone got nearer. A similar finding was obtained for self-reported anxiety by Mahoney and Avener (1977), using elite gymnasts competing for a place in the US Olympic team as subjects.

More recently, a number of qualitative studies have been conducted in an attempt to unearth some of the unique information which elite performers may possess about stress and performance. This research has clearly identified that the control of stress and anxiety is a very salient factor in elite performers' abilities to produce peak performances at really important competitions (Gould *et al.*, 1992a, b, 1993; Jones and Hardy, 1990a; Orlick and Partington, 1988). Strategies that elite performers have reported using to help them control their anxiety include: having (and sticking to) a strategic plan or performance routine; thought control strategies (e.g. dissociation, cognitive restructuring, positive thinking); emotional control strategies (e.g. imagery, physical relaxation, breathing control); and task-focusing strategies (e.g. narrow focus, process oriented goals, mental rehearsal of the performance routine). Furthermore, differences in the use of coping strategies have been reported between successful and less successful elite performers (see for example Gould *et al.*, 1992a, b; Orlick and Partington, 1988). However, Gould, *et al.* (1993a) reported that their *most important finding in terms of differences between Olympic medal winning and non-medal winning wrestlers was the degree to which the medal winning wrestlers* ***automatically*** *used coping strategies.*

Trait anxiety

According to Spielberger's (1966) original conceptualisations of trait and state anxiety, highly trait anxious performers should respond to stressful situations by demonstrating high levels of state anxiety, and studies have consistently confirmed this prediction with both univariate and multidimensional measures of state anxiety (Martens *et al.*, 1990b; Spielberger *et al.*, 1970). Furthermore, according to multidimensional anxiety theory, the impact of competitive trait anxiety upon performance is totally mediated by performers' state anxiety responses; that is, trait anxiety's only influence upon performance is via changes in state anxiety, as shown in Figure 6.5.

However, evidence from mainstream cognitive psychology (see Eysenck, 1992 for a review) suggests that this is probably *not* true. For example, several researchers (Broadbent and Broadbent, 1988; MacLeod, 1990; MacLeod and Mathews, 1988) have shown that attentional selectivity is determined by an interaction between trait and state anxiety which is such that highly trait anxious subjects who are state anxious selectively attend *towards* threat-related information, whilst low trait anxious subjects who are state anxious show an attentional *bias* away from such information. To the extent that perceptual attention is involved in competitive performance, one might therefore expect that low trait anxious performers would find high state anxiety facilitative, whilst high trait anxious performers would find it debilitative. This prediction is also consistent with the cusp catastrophe model of anxiety and performance; since high trait anxious performers show large elevations in physiological arousal when they are state anxious, and are therefore more prone to catastrophic decrements in performance than low trait anxious performers.

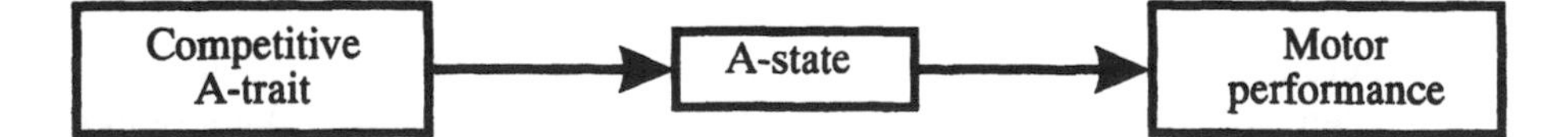

Figure 6.5: Relationship between competitive trait anxiety and motor performance as mediated by state anxiety (modified from Martens *et al.*, 1990b, with permission)

Stress management strategies

From the research literature that has been reviewed in this chapter and the preceding chapter on Arousal and Activation, a functional model of appraisal, arousal, activation, anxiety, and performance can be proposed (see Figure 6.6). According to this model, different tasks require performers to "fine tune" qualitatively different multidimensional activation states (Hockey and Hamilton, 1983; Parfitt *et al.*, 1990; see Chapter 5), which may be either enhanced or disrupted by cognitive anxiety and physiological arousal.

Most preparation and coping strategies employed by elite performers represent relatively crude and rather global unidimensional attempts to modify the current activation state of the organism either directly, or indirectly, via anxiety or physiological arousal. Add to this individual differences in the ease with which performers may achieve certain specific activation states and one clearly has a very complex problem. In consultancy work, sport psychologists are frequently concerned with questions about which strategy will be the most effective in different situations. However, the above line of reasoning would seem to suggest that a more reasonable question would be: why should any of these strategies work at all? One plausible answer to both these questions is that any given preparation strategy will work only to the extent that it helps the performer to establish a more appropriate activation state for the task at hand. Thus, "psych-up" interventions like getting mad, and other "fight–flight"-based strategies, may help some performers to generate the activation state that they need to perform strength or power tasks that are relatively simple in nature or extremely well learned (see, for example, Gould *et al.*, 1980; Murphy *et al.*, 1988; Cockerill *et al.*, 1991; Parfitt *et al.*, 1990; Weinberg *et al.*, 1980). Similarly,

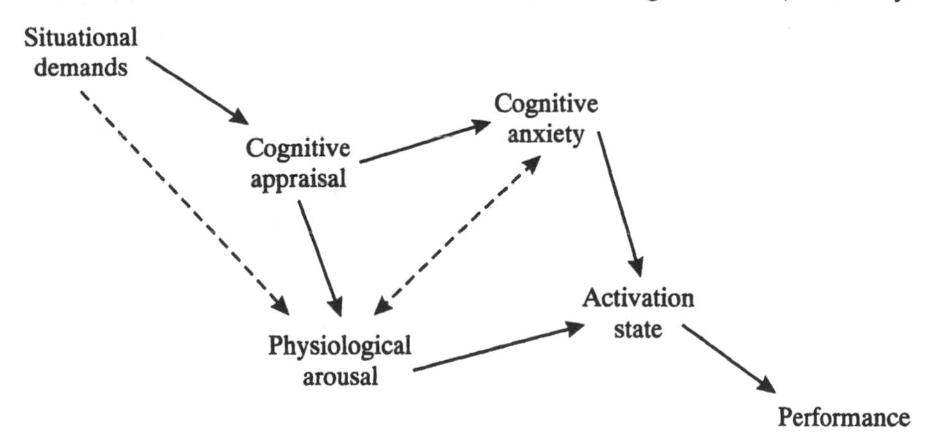

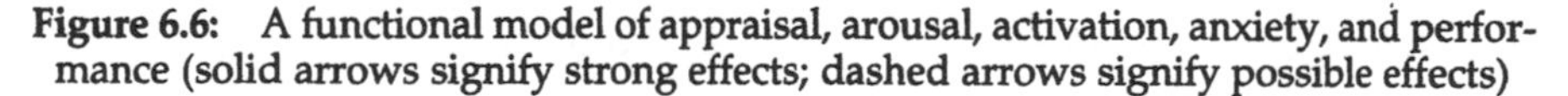

Figure 6.6: A functional model of appraisal, arousal, activation, anxiety, and performance (solid arrows signify strong effects; dashed arrows signify possible effects)

global physical relaxation strategies may help some performers to establish a more appropriate activation state for fine motor control tasks like shooting or golf putting by reducing the general level of tension (noise) in the musculature (Greenspan and Feltz, 1989; Murphy and Woolfolk, 1987; Weinberg and Hunt, 1976). However, *since most sports skills appear to require more than just a single quality for their optimal performance, it seems unlikely that peak performance on such tasks will ever be achieved by the application of any single psychological strategy* (cf. Gould and Udry, 1994; Shelton and Mahoney, 1978).

During the last fifteen to twenty years, several multimodal stress management programmes have been devised or adapted for sport; notably Meichenbaum's (1975) stress inoculation training, Smith's (1980) cognitive–affective stress management training, and Suinn's (1972b) visuo-motor behaviour rehearsal. Typically, these programmes combine self-talk, imagery, and relaxation skills according to some guiding principles that are then applied by the therapist. Although stress inoculation training and stress management training were originally devised in clinical settings, all three programmes have been successfully used in sport settings (for reviews, see Burton, 1990; Mace, 1990). However, Burton (1990) and others have argued that rather than teaching performers how to use specific stress management programmes, sport psychology consultants should teach the constituent skills which underlie such programmes. Such a position is entirely in keeping with the multi-systems approach that has been proposed in the current review, since it would allow athletes to tailor their preparation strategies to suit both their own individual needs and those of the tasks that they have to perform. A number of psychological skills have been implicated by the literature that has been reviewed in this chapter. However, it has been argued in Chapter 2 and elsewhere (e.g. Vealey, 1988) that at least four of these are fundamental in the sense that they appear to underlie many others; these four are goal-setting, imagery, relaxation, and self-talk (cf. Hardy and Jones, 1994a; Vealey, 1988). Since these skills have already been considered in some detail in Chapter 2, they will only be briefly discussed here.

Excessive goal difficulty may be a major source of anxiety for performers (Jones *et al.*, 1990) and also a primary reason for them disengaging from the task when they are anxious (Carver and Scheier, 1988; Eysenck, 1982). Process-oriented goals provide an obvious way of helping performers to focus on priority sources of information and key aspects of performance—either technical or emotional (Kingston and Hardy, 1994a, b; Orlick and Partington, 1988). Furthermore, qualitative studies of elite performers confirm such a view (Gould *et al.*, 1992a, b, 1993; Jones & Hardy, 1990a; Orlick & Partington, 1988):

> *I could say that I want to win the Gold Medal at the Olympics in Barcelona, but it doesn't really hold for me in that it's not a very strong sort of*

feeling that I really desire . . . I do want to be Olympic Champion, but I'll never use that as a goal psychologically . . . I would never use it as a goal to improve my performance, only something technical. . . . (Former World Champion javelin thrower, Steve Backley; Jones and Hardy, 1990a, pp. 260–261)

Process-oriented goals also form the basis of most pre-performance and performance routines (cf. Boutcher, 1990; Kingston and Hardy, 1994b; Orlick, 1986).

As has already been indicated in Chapter 5, it can be argued on both theoretical and empirical grounds that the successful mental rehearsal of a given task should provide a most efficient means of establishing an appropriate activation pattern prior to performance. Mastery imagery (see Chapter 2) should also provide some positive feedback to the performer, thereby reducing anxiety about the task to be performed (Gaudry, 1977; Vadocz and Hall, in press) and enhancing self-efficacy (Bandura, 1977; Moritz *et al.*, 1996). Finally, imagery is often cited as a means of cognitively restructuring failures (see, for example, Gauron, 1984; Syer and Connolly, 1984). Although, as the following example shows, there is considerable anecdotal evidence to support such applications of imagery, there does not as yet appear to be a substantial empirical database on these emotional uses of imagery in sport (for exceptions, see Kavanagh and Hausfeld, 1986; Lee, 1990).

I was on the track watching Jeff Vanderstock who was the expected winner of the Games. He did a start out of the blocks and I felt my throat constrict and recognised that my mind was on him, and I knew that I could not control how fast he ran and that I had to come back inside myself. I left my shoes and spikes on the side and used the in-field to simulate going back to my very early training days where I had been in the situation of running on very firm sand at the low water's edge. I just ran down the field imagining the feeling that I had at that stage, with the sun on my back, feeling the warmth, the power, the strength, the fluidity of flow, and recalling this one day when I had run on the beach. I had no idea how far it was . . . I just kept running and running, lifting up faster and faster, and there didn't seem to be any fatigue. It was just an unbelievable flowing feeling that went on and on over hundreds of yards. Eventually, I slowed down and jogged back. It was enough to come back into my senses, of what it felt like to be strong and flowing . . . it took my awareness back inside. By the time I had done that I was back inside me and Jeff Vanderstock could do his own thing. . . . (David Hemery prior to his World Record and Olympic Gold Medal winning 400 metres hurdles run at the Mexico Olympics in 1968; Jones and Hardy, 1990a, pp. 262–263)

In the context of Figure 6.6, relaxation is probably best viewed as a global strategy that helps the performer to "hold onto", or regain, emotional control thereby providing a known "starting position" from which to establish an appropriate activation pattern (cf. Burton, 1990; Hardy and Fazey, 1986; Nideffer, 1986). For example, Jones and Hardy (1990a) reported that Great Britain field hockey captain, Mary Nevill, used relaxation prior to stick-stopping on penalty corners, when there is a lot of pressure on her:

> *... It would just be a moment to physically relax, and also I think I just need a quiet moment to prepare myself for a very important event. If I miss that stop we could lose a goal because you have quite a fair chance of scoring off a penalty corner.* (Jones and Hardy, 1990a, p. 263)

Similarly, Olympic gymnast James May reported that he used a meditative-based relaxation strategy "if I have to stand around and wait for the judges and I feel a rush of nervousness that's too much" (Jones and Hardy, 1990a, p. 261).

Relaxation is implicated by multidimensional anxiety theory (Martens *et al.*, 1990a), and the catastrophe models (Hardy, 1996b) as a necessary part of any crisis intervention designed to help a performer regain the "upper performance surface" once a catastrophic decrement in performance has occurred. Furthermore, it is also indirectly implicated by a number of cognitive theories which have proposed impairments to working memory under conditions of high physiological arousal (e.g. Easterbrook, 1959; Humphreys and Revelle, 1984; Parfitt *et al.*, 1990; Sanders, 1983; see Chapter 5).

The ability to cognitively appraise one's circumstances in a positive way and maintain a problem-focused attitude prior to and during performance has been a recurring theme in the literature that has been reviewed in this chapter (e.g. Gould *et al.*, 1992a, b, 1993a; Jones, 1995b; Jones and Hardy, 1990a; Mahoney and Avener, 1977). Furthermore, it is thought likely that positive self-talk plays an important role in the maintenance of such attitudes and in cognitive restructuring skills (see Chapter 2). Cognitive restructuring clearly has an important role to play in helping performers to (re-)establish a positive interpretation of their anxiety symptoms, particularly following a mistake or when they are under pressure. Thus, in the context of Figure 6.6, cognitive restructuring is principally concerned with cognitive appraisal; whilst self-talk may exert an influence via cognitive appraisal, cognitive anxiety, or physiological arousal.

One might be tempted to imagine that elite performers do not make mistakes or have doubts, but this seems unlikely:

> *I was thinking "This is it ... we've never won the team championship. We've always threatened to do it ... this guy who's coaching us is one of*

> *the guys who threatened to do it but never did". Foxy was saying "Is God going to give me five clean runs?" . . . I remember thinking that it was a big weight to carry. . . .* (Alan Edge prior to his final run as "anchor man" in Great Britain's Gold Medal winning canoe slalom team in the 1979 World Championships; Jones and Hardy, 1990a, p. 257)

Rather, it seems more likely that elite performers have such good cognitive restructuring skills that they apply them *automatically* as soon as they start to interpret things negatively (Gould *et al.*, 1993a). This restructuring might use verbal affirmation statements (cf. Rotella *et al.*, 1980), visual imagery (see the earlier quotation from David Hemery), or a combination of both (cf. Meichenbaum, 1975; Smith, 1980):

> *If I miss a stickstop (from a penalty corner) then I can put that behind me until the next one. I might have this negative flash through my mind that I missed the last one, but I would immediately think of an image of positively stopping it.* (Mary Nevill, captain of Great Britain's field hockey team which won a Bronze Medal in the 1992 Olympic Games; Jones and Hardy, 1990a, p. 273)

Mood enhancement strategies

Although research on the Mental Health Model has found little evidence for the stability of iceberg profiles in elite performers (see earlier review), there is still a considerable body of evidence which suggests that (different) optimal mood states might exist for different tasks (cf. Cockerill *et al.*, 1991; Gould *et al.*, 1980; Kerr, 1990; Murphy *et al.*, 1988; Weinberg *et al.*, 1980).

Other evidence relating to the importance of mood enhancement strategies stems from research conducted in animal psychology (Gray, 1975, 1982, 1985). Gray's work suggests that anxiety has an inhibiting effect upon normal behaviour, and therefore upon performance. It is plausible that a distinguishing characteristic of elite performers is an ability not to inhibit their normal behaviour when under pressure. Consider, for example, the following comments from two tennis stars, Bjorn Borg and Charlie Pasarell, on the ways in which great players cope with the pressure of big points:

> *Against most players, whenever I need only one more point to win the set or to break serve, I can hit the ball fairly shallow because most players will not go for a winner off that shallow shot. They'll tighten up a little, hit the shot safer and give me a chance to win the point on the passing shot. But Connors doesn't play safe, he just hits out.* (Bjorn Borg in Tarshis, 1977, p. 3)

> *I can think of dozens of players that nobody has ever heard about who can hit the ball as well and as hard as anybody on the tour but just can't get it together in a match situation. The reason that guys like Laver, Newcombe and Connors are champions is that they always do their best on big points in key situations. Most players, on a big point, will play it safe, let the other guy make the error. But the other players aren't afraid to gamble. They'll choke too, every now and then, but usually they're going to put the pressure on you.* (Charlie Pasarell in Tarshis, 1977, p. 53)

Gray (1975, 1982, 1985) and others have produced extensive evidence which suggests that other emotions, such as excitement, frustration, and anger, may induce much more active behaviour. On the assumption that these arguments are true for humans, it is plausible that changes in mood from anxiety to other more active moods, such as excitement, frustration, or anger, might well facilitate the performance of anxious performers (cf. Cockerill *et al.*, 1991; Gould *et al.*, 1980; Kerr, 1990; Murphy *et al.*, 1988; Weinberg *et al.*, 1980).

Summary

Research on very experienced and elite performers suggests that they may get just as anxious prior to competition as their less elite counterparts. However, this research also suggests that elite performers: tend to reach their anxiety peak some time before the competition; tend to automatically utilise coping strategies; tend to have their anxiety symptoms under control by the time they are due to perform; and are more likely to interpret their anxiety symptoms positively than their non-elite counterparts.

The functional model that was presented in Figure 6.6 suggests that stress management and coping strategies will be effective only to the extent that they help the performer to generate an appropriate activation state. Given the variety and complexity of tasks that have to be performed in sports, it seems likely that performers must be capable of generating a wide variety of activation states. The multimodal strategies that have therefore been developed typically utilise at least four basic techniques: goal-setting, imagery, relaxation, and self-talk. Finally, research from various branches of psychology suggests that one way that anxiety may exert an influence upon performance is by inhibiting normal behaviour. This research also suggests that other moods, such as excitement, frustration, and anger, might encourage much more active behaviour which might well facilitate the performance of anxious athletes on at least some tasks. Consequently, mood enhancement strategies may well be a valuable tool for sport psychologists to possess.

IMPLICATIONS FOR RESEARCH

Conceptual issues

Previous research in the area of stress and performance has been greatly impeded by the considerable ambiguity that has surrounded the use of certain key terms. Consequently, future researchers should take great care to clarify exactly how they are using key terms such as stress, arousal, activation, and anxiety.

Antecedents of stress and anxiety

Although recent work on the antecedents of multidimensional anxiety represents a considerable advance in our understanding of the most likely causes of anxiety, there is still an urgent need to refine the approaches that have been used. For example, the vast majority of antecedents that have been considered are situational variables. However, very little is known about how these situational variables interact with personality variables such as goal orientations and perceptions of personal competence. There is also an urgent need to identify some of the specific antecedents of somatic anxiety.

Qualitative research that has recently been conducted on elite populations has started to unearth some of the organisational and occupational stressors which appear to have an influence on the performance of elite athletes. This is a much under-researched area, which could have a very powerful impact upon elite performers and international sport. So little research has been conducted that it is not even known how much of the variance in performance at international competitions can be accounted for by organisational factors. However, the present authors suspect that it will be a considerable proportion.

Competitive state anxiety and performance

Much of the literature that was reviewed in this section tends to polarise the multidimensional anxiety theory versus catastrophe models debate. Key issues in this debate which still need to be convincingly resolved include: the nature of cognitive anxiety effects upon performance (in particular, whether and when cognitive anxiety exerts a beneficial effect); the precise form that performance decrements take, when they do occur (i.e. are they catastrophic?); the extent to which recovery is possible once a performance decrement has occurred; the relative importance of physiological arousal and somatic anxiety; and whether cognitive anxiety and physiological arousal/somatic anxiety exert interactive or additive effects upon performance. Furthermore, given the volume of research which demonstrates a role for the directional interpretation of anxiety symptoms, any satisfactory explanation of anxiety–performance effects really ought to incorporate directional interpretations into its framework. One possibility, which is suggested by converging lines of research, is that the interpretation of anxiety symptoms and perceptions of control are intervening variables which mediate the interactive effects of cognitive anxiety and physiological arousal upon performance that are predicted by the catastrophe model. More precisely, it is possible that cognitively anxious performers interpret their physiological arousal symptoms negatively, and consequently perceive that they are no longer in control. This loss of control then leads to performance decrements via a decrease in self-confidence and motivation to succeed. This possibility is worthy of further investigation because it suggests that one reason why previous anxiety–performance research has accounted for only a relatively small proportion of the variance in performance is because the key variables were not being measured!

Other approaches to the study of stress and performance which are worthy of further research include individualised zones of optimal functioning and reversal theory. Individualised zones of optimal functioning do not appear to possess much potential for *explaining* anxiety effects; but they could be a very useful tool for the initial exploration of a broader range of stress-related emotions in an attempt to identify appropriate "recipes of emotions" for different sports (Gould and Udry, 1994). Reversal theory is heuristically appealing and appears to possess much potential for explaining anxiety effects upon metamotivational states (Kerr, 1990), but only a very limited amount of empirical research has been performed which links reversals to performance (e.g. Raedeke and Stein, 1994).

Factors influencing anxiety responses

It is still not entirely clear exactly what range of coping strategies is required for different sports. Indeed, there is health-related research (cf. Ingledew *et al.*, 1996) which suggests that people use the strategies they have "to hand" to deal with stress, and that more or less "any old strategy" will do, so long as it is not avoidance. Whilst it would be foolish to even consider generalising from health-related research to elite performance, the question of which, if any, coping strategies are *required* for elite performance remains an interesting one. Related to this issue is the suggestion that a distinguishing characteristic of elite performers is that they have learned their coping strategies so well that they use them automatically. This suggestion was derived from qualitative studies; however, the interview techniques which were used in these studies essentially require performers to use explicit (verbalise) knowledge to describe procedures that are certainly automatic and may well have been implicitly learned. Whilst it is well known that experts do possess more explicit knowledge about their skill than non-experts (see, for example, Williams and Davids, 1995), it is also well known that the link between verbal memory and automatic processes is not a strong one (Davids and Myers, 1990). Consequently, the use of interview techniques may well be problematic in this context (Brewer *et al.*, 1991), and further research using different methodologies is clearly desirable.

Finally, with regard to coping strategies, there is an urgent need to better understand the mechanisms and processes which underlie even the basic techniques which have been discussed in this chapter. For example, how do process, performance, and outcome goals, exert their respective influences upon the stress–performance relationship? How does imagery exert an influence upon motivation and affective states? On what basis should one select relaxation strategies? How does self-talk (a declarative strategy) exert an influence upon the motor performance of experts who are supposedly using automatic processes to support their performance?

The functional model which was presented in Figure 6.6 is a synthesis of the arguments that have been presented in this and the previous chapter. It is worthy of further investigation, either in part or in whole, using psychophysiological techniques in conjunction with other social psychological and biochemical techniques. A good starting point would be to explore the influence of emotional and mood manipulations upon the psychophysiological activation state and subsequent motor performance of skilled performers. Psychophysiological measures might include biochemical, as well as cardiovascular and electrocortical, parameters; whilst performance might be much more sensitively measured using biomechanical analysis to identify any changes in technique resulting from the intervention (cf. Weinberg, 1978; Weinberg and Hunt, 1976).

IMPLICATIONS FOR BEST PRACTICE

Antecedents of stress and anxiety

The situational variables which dominated the research reviewed in this section help to define the coach's role in the psychological preparation of elite performers. Factors which had a major influence upon performers' stress and anxiety included: attitudes towards previous performances; the external (performing) environment; the performance goals set; readiness and performance problems; competition organisation and officiating problems; interpersonal and management problems within the team; poor facilities; and financial and time pressures. A very substantial number of these variables are clearly open to influence by the coach. In particular, encouraging performers to have attainable goals, and ensuring that they are sufficiently well prepared to perceive that they can achieve these goals, is likely to have a major impact on athletes' pre-performance affective states. However, perhaps more than anything else, this section highlights the need for the coach, the performer, and the sport psychologist to design a preparation programme that "controls the controllables"; that is to say, all those factors over which the performer could reasonably be expected to exert some influence. One strategy that is used, particularly with team sports, by some sport psychologists is to have the squad play "what if . . . ?" games in which the psychologist asks the squad to decide what they would do to deal with different emergencies. For example, what if a key player is taken ill immediately before a competition? Or the transport to take the team to the competition venue does not arrive? Or the team goes a goal down after one minute? Imagination is the only constraint here. Another approach is to have performers generate a list of possible problems which could stop them from achieving their goals, and then help them to work out ways of dealing with each problem. However, whatever approach is used, it is important to encourage performers to practise and mentally rehearse their preparation and performance plans, so that they become automatic responses (see Gould *et al.*, 1993a; Jones and Hardy, 1990a).

Competitive state anxiety and performance

Considering the amount of research that has been conducted in this area, we know surprisingly little about the relationship between anxiety and performance. However, research on individualised zones of optimal functioning, together with research which has used intra-individualised measures of anxiety and performance, suggests that there are very large individual differences in the way that performers respond to stress. Moreover, there seems no reason to believe that such individual differences do not exist in elite performers.

Although the multidimensional anxiety theory versus catastrophe models issue is far from resolved, it is the contention of the present authors that there is sufficient evidence in favour of both positive and negative anxiety effects to conclude that cognitive anxiety is likely to be beneficial to performance so long as it is positively interpreted and physiological arousal is not too high. These beneficial effects may be largest in tasks which require high effort and place small skill demands upon the performer. However, if high levels of cognitive anxiety are accompanied by high levels of physiological arousal and are negatively interpreted, then performance is highly likely to be disrupted. Furthermore, when such performance decrements occur, they are likely to be large, sudden, and difficult to remove. One strategy that might enable performers who have "gone over the top" to regain their upper performance surface (see the catastrophe models) would be to have them physically relax (to move back along the physiological arousal axis), cognitively restructure (to regain the upper performance surface), and then re-activate (to regain the highest point on the performance surface).

The research that has been reported on self-confidence has shown that self-confidence exerts an influence upon performance over and above that exerted by cognitive anxiety and the associated physiological arousal. This research also suggests that self-confidence may in some way protect athletes against any debilitative performance effects associated with anxiety, possibly by influencing the directional interpretation that they place upon their anxiety symptoms.

The clearest implications of all this are that:

- Coaches and sport psychologists should use "psyching-up" strategies with caution; some performers could easily get "psyched-out" by such strategies, and recovery is difficult once they are psyched-out.
- Performers need good stress management strategies that include techniques to separately reduce cognitive anxiety and physiological arousal.
- Performers need good self-talk and cognitive restructuring skills.
- Performers need to have good re-activation strategies (e.g. mental rehearsal).
- Coaches, performers, and sport psychologists should do everything within their power to ensure that performers have complete confidence in their preparation.

Factors influencing anxiety responses

Research on the effects of experience upon anxiety responses indicated that early recognition and control of anxiety symptoms was associated with superior performance in elite athletes. Conversely, the research which was reviewed on trait anxiety suggested that elite performers would be at a considerable disadvantage if they were highly trait anxious because of their attentional bias towards threatening information. However, two additional points should be borne in mind here. First, the trait anxiety research in question was not conducted on elite sports performers; and it is possible that elite performers' extensive experience enables them to overcome the attentional bias effects that are associated with high trait anxiety. Second, it is also possible that the availability of appropriate coping responses (e.g. emotional and attention control skills—see Chapter 7) would enable highly trait anxious elite performers to use their attentional bias as an "early warning system" to help get their anxiety symptoms under control prior to entering the performance arena. Other research reviewed in this section suggests that performers need a wide range of coping strategies which have been overlearned to such an extent that they can be automatically invoked (see also

Chapter 7). The coping strategies that were identified included relaxation, self-talk, and imagery skills; but also included goal-setting skills in order to ensure that important outcome goals did not themselves become a source of stress and distraction.

SUMMARY

This chapter has viewed competitive state anxiety as a multidimensional construct. It has presented evidence that some antecedents exert a common effect upon more than one dimension of anxiety, whilst others appear to have different effects upon the different dimensions. Several models and theories of competitive state anxiety and performance were discussed. Unfortunately, no one model or theory as yet appears to be capable of accounting for a very large proportion of the variance in performance. Consequently, it was suggested that in future researchers might explore the effects of a wider range of emotions upon performance. A number of factors that might influence anxiety responses were also considered. It was concluded that, since coping strategies will only be effective to the extent that they help performers to generate an appropriate activation state, flexible multimodal intervention strategies are much more likely to be effective than rigid or unimodal strategies.

7

CONCENTRATION AND ATTENTION CONTROL

CONTENTS

INTRODUCTION

Perhaps the most appropriate way of demonstrating the importance of concentration in top level sport performance is to examine the consequences of lapses in concentration. Patmore (1986), for example, related the tale in which:

> *American (golfer) Billy Casper, after a disappointing showing in the French Open in 1978, confessed that he was . . . sick of all his missed chances; every round he loses concentration for a spell, and doesn't know how to cure it.* (p. 84)

Weinberg (1988) provided further evidence of performance impairment as a function of not being able to concentrate in the case of tennis player, Rod Laver:

> *Staying interested in a match is a lot harder than many people think. Throughout my career, I've always had trouble in the early rounds of a tournament mainly because it was hard for me to psychologically get up until I got to the quarters or the semis. What happened a lot of times is that I would fall behind early, maybe even lose the first couple of sets in a five-set match and then begin to concentrate. Still it wasn't something I could control from the start.* (p. 61)

These examples illustrate two points: firstly, loss of concentration impairs performance; and secondly, maintaining concentration can be a problem for sports performers.

Concentration is about focusing the mind upon one source of information, often to the exclusion of others. However, this does not quite complete the picture since it is important to consider precisely what the mind is focusing upon. Consider the example of a winger during a rugby match. The winger may be concentrating extremely well, but on the planes flying overhead instead of events occurring on the field of play. Even if the winger's concentration is on some aspect of the current match, it may still be inappropriate if it is focused upon a dropped pass from a few minutes earlier, or on how big his opposite number is. Thus, the *focus of attention* is crucial in determining whether an athlete's concentration is appropriate or not.

The research which has been conducted to examine differences between successful and less successful athletes demonstrates that attentional control is an important differentiating factor (Gould *et al.*, 1981; Highlen and Bennett, 1979, 1983; Mahoney *et al.*, 1987; Orlick and Partington, 1988). These studies generally show that successful athletes are less likely to become distracted by irrelevant stimuli and they maintain a more task-oriented attentional focus as opposed to focusing upon outcome or worries (Williams and Krane, 1993).

Boutcher (1990) has argued that findings from psychophysiological studies provide a further valuable insight into attentional states in elite and non-elite performers prior to, and during, performance. Pre-event cardiac patterns, for example, generally show a deceleration in heart rate just prior to performance (e.g. Lacey and Lacey, 1970; Landers *et al.*, 1980; Stern, 1976). This tends to be more pronounced in elite as opposed to non-elite performers, as evidenced by studies on parachute jumpers (Fenz, 1975), archers (Wang and Landers, 1986) and golfers (Boutcher and Zinsser, 1990). Attentional states have also been examined through the medium of EEG activity. Hatfield *et al.* (1984), for example, investigated left- and right-brain EEG activity in a sample of elite shooters whilst shooting and whilst performing a series of mental tasks. The findings suggested that progressive electrocortical lateralization occurred during shooting towards right hemispheric dominance just before the trigger pull. Hatfield *et al.* proposed that these elite shooters may possess such a high degree of attentional focus that they can effectively reduce the conscious mental activities of the left hemisphere, thus preventing distraction during the crucial moments of performance. However, Collins *et al.* (1990) later found only partial support for these findings in a sample of karate performers, although the different physical nature of the two tasks may be an important factor.

Equating patterns of heart rate and EEG with the nature of cognitive activity is clearly tenuous, but the above findings do suggest that elite performers in self-paced sports do practise some form of attentional control. Strategies for gaining and maintaining attentional focus will be addressed in greater detail later in this chapter. However, the next section will examine issues emanating from various cognitive theories of attention which are pertinent to understanding attention control in elite athletes.

THEORETICAL ASPECTS OF ATTENTION

Attention and its role in human performance has been the subject of debate and examination for a considerable number of years. As long ago as 1890, William James offered this often cited description of attention:

> *Everyone knows what attention is. It is taking possession by the mind, in clear and vivid form, of one out of what seems several simultaneously possible objects or trains of thought. Focalization, concentration of consciousness are its essence. It implies withdrawal from some things in order to deal effectively with others.*

Despite James' assertion that "everyone knows what attention is", Eysenck (1988) remained unconvinced: "the term 'attention' is one of the most notoriously vague theoretical constructs in psychology" (p. 9). Indeed, there has been a considerable amount of theoretical disagreement as to precisely how attention functions. James' description essentially refers to a selectivity of information processing, and this has been the focus of major theoretical thrusts in the development of knowledge of attention over the years.

Unfortunately, theories of attention relating specifically to sports performance are relatively underdeveloped so that empirical work has been hindered by the lack of theoretical models (Boutcher, 1992). Thus, the most appropriate place to start the following discussion is to look towards the general cognitive psychology literature, and examine the issues of focused versus divided attention, single versus multiple resources, and controlled versus automatic processes (Eysenck, 1984). These issues are helpful in gaining an understanding of how attention might function in elite as opposed to less successful athletes. Individual differences in attention in terms of width and direction (Nideffer, 1976) will then be considered as this approach has been extensively employed within the sport psychology literature. Finally, a preliminary integrated model of attention and sports performance (Boutcher, 1992) will be considered.

Focused versus divided attention

The basic distinction between focused and divided attention is derived from studies which have presented subjects with two or more concurrent stimuli and asked them to either "focus" on only one of them, or to "divide" their attention by attending to all of them (Eysenck, 1984). Focused attention is clearly important in closed skill sports such as golf where, because of the relatively stable environment and the self-paced nature of the performance, attention needs to be focused on a relatively small number of cues. In more open, externally paced sports, such as soccer or basketball, the player in possession of the ball may have to divide her attention by attending to visual information in terms of the relative positions of team-mates and opposition players, as well as to auditory stimuli in terms of verbal information conveyed by team-mates.

The notion of *focused attention* implies active selectivity in deciding which stimuli to attend to. Thus, the basketball player performing a free throw must attend to the basket and filter out irrelevant stimuli such as noise from the crowd. Effective performance in such a situation therefore requires certain stimuli to be attenuated or ignored. Several models have been developed over the years to explain how this might be achieved (e.g. Broadbent, 1958; Deutsch and Deutsch, 1963; Norman, 1969; Treisman, 1964). Although these models differ on the precise mechanisms via which this process occurs, they all hypothesise the existence of a bottleneck or selective filter in a limited capacity information processing channel. These theories propose that prior to reaching the filter, stimuli can be processed in a parallel fashion that does not require attention. Once the filter is reached, however, only one stimulus at a time is processed through the filter, so that information processing from then on is sequential, requiring attention in the single channel (Schmidt, 1982).

A rather different approach to examining focused attention has been to investigate the role of motivational variables on the breadth of the perceptual field which is attended to (Easterbrook, 1959). The basic assumption in Easterbrook's proposals is that heightened arousal, cognitive anxiety, and somatic anxiety all have comparable effects upon cue utilisation (see Chapters 5 and 6). The hypothesis simply states that an individual's breadth of perceptual attention narrows as his or her level of arousal increases. Thus, increases in arousal from low to moderate levels are accompanied by an increase in perceptual selectivity whereby irrelevant task cues are eliminated and performance improves. As arousal level continues to increase beyond the optimum, breadth of attention continues to decrease, causing a "tunnelling" effect, so that relevant cues are also eliminated, resulting in a deterioration in performance. In this context, therefore, arousal progressively reduces the range of environmental events considered by the cognitive system, producing a monotonic increase in the selectivity of attention.

At an intuitive level, Easterbrook's hypothesis does not appear to be very helpful in analysing the situation of the basketball free throw shooter referred to earlier. In this situation, there are, in relative terms, very few relevant cues to attend to so that this task could, according to the basic tenets of Easterbrook's hypothesis, be performed successfully at a relatively high level of arousal. However, it would appear that most basketball players actively attempt to compose themselves via arousal-reducing strategies in such situations (Predebon and Docker, 1992; Southard and Miracle, 1993). Furthermore, Eysenck (1984) has questioned the assumed automaticity of the attentional narrowing that accompanies increases in arousal by suggesting that any such narrowing may well be an active coping response. In other words, when the information-processing demands are too great for the available processing capacity, individuals make a strategic decision to restrict attention to a small proportion of the information available as a way of coping with the situation. Wine (1980) has also proposed that arousal and anxiety affect attentional focus, but not by reducing the attentional field. The assumption underlying Wine's proposals is the existence of an inflexible, limited capacity attention resource. Anxiety is hypothesised to use up some of this capacity so that the amount of attention which can be devoted to performance is reduced. The effects of anxiety on attention are addressed in greater detail in the following section.

Divided attention has been most commonly examined via dual-task experimental paradigms, with decrements in performance being attributed to attentional demands exceeding the capability of a single, fixed capacity attention resource such as that assumed by the theories mentioned above.

However, the notion of a single resource does not sit comfortably alongside findings which have demonstrated that two relatively complex tasks can be performed simultaneously and without any apparent interference effects (e.g. Allport *et al.*, 1972; Shaffer, 1975; Spelke *et al.*, 1976). Kahneman's (1973) explanation of this phenomenon was that attention is flexible in that its capacity changes as task requirements change. He proposed that parallel processing could occur in all stages provided that maximum capacity was not exceeded. Thus, as the complexity of two simultaneously performed tasks increases, so too does the attention capacity made available, and performance decrements will only occur when the capacity is exhausted. An alternative explanation has been to propose the existence of multiple resources as opposed to a single resource (e.g. McCleod, 1977; Navon and Gopher, 1979; Wickens, 1980). Each resource is hypothesised to have its own capacity and to deal with certain types of information. Thus, there may be separate pools of resources for attending to information derived from visual, auditory, kinaesthetic, and other types of stimuli. This provides a plausible explanation for why two dissimilar tasks such as driving and talking, reading and listening to music, can be performed simultaneously without impairment to either. It would also explain why a basketball player focusing upon the basket might be distracted by the movements of players around the key since information from both sources would be competing for a single resource which deals with visual information. However, it would not explain why a basketball player performing a free throw and focusing upon the basket (visual information) might be distracted by noise from the crowd (auditory information) since these two stimuli should, in theory, demand resources from two separate pools of attention.

Controlled and automatic processing

A crucial factor to consider in the debate outlined above, particularly within the context of elite performers, is that of practice (Eysenck, 1984). Eysenck argued that there are three reasons why practice might facilitate the concurrent performance of two tasks:

> *In the first place, subjects may develop new strategies for performing each of the tasks so as to minimise any task interference. Secondly, the demands that a task makes on attentional or other central resources may be reduced as a function of practice. Thirdly, while a task may initially require the use of several specific processing resources, practice may permit a more economical mode of functioning that relies on fewer such specific resources.* (p. 63)

The inevitable extension of these proposals is that some processing activities become automatic as a function of practice and, hence, skill level.

Thus, it is often argued that highly skilled performances are achieved effortlessly and without any need for attention (cf. Csikszentmihalyi, 1975; Jackson, S.A., 1992); indeed, it has been argued that attaining automaticity in routine acts is the goal in any mastery situation (Logan, 1988, 1990; Singer *et al.*, 1993). The traditional approach in this area has been to distinguish between controlled and automatic processes (Schneider *et al.*, 1984; Schneider and Shiffrin, 1977; Shiffrin and Schneider, 1977). *Controlled processes* require attention, are limited in capacity, and can be used flexibly; *automatic processes*, on the other hand, do not require attention, are of unlimited capacity, but are difficult to modify once learned. The empirical evidence which supports the existence of these two types of processes suggests that automatic processes operate in a parallel fashion and are thus more rapid than controlled processes, but have the disadvantage of being relatively inflexible. Therefore, they are of little use when the nature of the task alters and a modified response is required. Controlled processes are more flexible, but they operate more slowly due to the serial nature in which information is processed (Eysenck, 1982). According to cognitive psychologists, during the initial stages of learning, the performer makes extensive use of closed-loop control which will be attention-demanding in the controlled sense. Later in learning, when the performer becomes highly skilled, the mode of control used will tend to be more open-loop so that attentional demands from performing the task are relatively small (Eysenck, 1984; Reason, 1979). This leaves some spare attentional capacity and also some potential dangers. This capacity may be devoted to task-irrelevant information, such as noise in the crowd, which may actually distract the performer. Alternatively, the performer may devote too much controlled attention to the specific details of performing the task, thus disrupting the automatised activities (Keele, 1973; Langer and Imber, 1979). Such dangers are explored later in this chapter. For the moment, it is important to emphasise a limitation of this traditional view of open-loop control in later stages of learning. The implication is that elite performers do not monitor and respond to feedback during performance; this is, quite simply, unrealistic!

More recent motor control research has been dominated by the apparent paradox that exists between cognitive and ecological models of action (see, for example, Harvey, 1988; Schmidt, 1988; Whiting *et al.*, 1992). Basically, extreme ecological psychologists have argued that movement is controlled by direct links between perception and action systems without any involvement of cognition (Reed, 1982; Turvey and Kugler, 1984). More moderate ecological psychologists (Whiting *et al.*, 1992) have not gone so far as to deny the existence of cognition, but have simply attempted to explain as much as possible without recourse to cognition. However, a number of researchers have proposed hierarchical (or, to be more precise, heterarchical) models of control in which higher level perception and action schema direct the work of lower level operators, without necessarily having any conscious awareness of the operations performed by these lower level action systems (Annett, 1991; Neisser, 1976; Rummelhart and McClelland, 1986). Thus, elite performers may first "weigh up" the alternatives that are available in any given situation and then set conscious goals about what needs to be done. However, having done this, they trust their motor system to "get on with the job", and simply monitor progress to ensure that no major adjustments to the "game plan" are necessary. Minor alterations and adjustments are made at a lower level in the system without any conscious awareness on the part of the performer.

One consequence of such heterarchical models is that because elite performers are operating at an automatic level which does not involve conscious awareness, they may not in fact be able to verbally report exactly how they do things. This is, of course, the distinction between procedural knowledge (e.g. knowing how to hit a golf ball perfectly) and declarative knowledge (e.g. being able to describe the characteristics of a perfect golf swing). Unfortunately, a detailed discussion of this issue is beyond the scope of this book. The interested reader is referred to Anderson (1982), and Eysenck and Keane (1990) for further information.

Attentional style

The discussion of divided attention earlier in this chapter considered how it might be possible for individuals to attend concurrently to more than one relevant stimulus. One aspect of this process which was not considered was the performer's ability to switch attention from one stimulus to another. This is particularly important in open skill sports in which the athlete is bombarded with a large amount of information which is continually changing. Take the example of the soccer player in possession of the ball. The player must be able to switch very quickly between attending to the ball and attending to the surrounding visual display in terms of movements of the opposition and team-mates.

The work of Nideffer (1976) on attentional style has proved quite useful at a heuristic level in understanding the attentional demands on sports performers in such situations. Nideffer proposed that attentional style varies along two dimensions: width, ranging from broad (focusing on a wide range of cues) to narrow (focusing on a limited range of cues); and direction, ranging from internal (focusing on one's own thoughts and feelings) to external (focusing on objects and events outside the body). Figure 7.1 depicts these two continua and the four different classifications of attentional focus. It also provides some examples of activities which might be thought to fall into each type of attentional style. Although this classification of different types of sport is helpful, it is important to remember that it is only the primary focus and does not represent the switches of focus which are required in most sports. This necessary "switching" is aptly illustrated in Hemery's (1986) description of the attentional requirements of running a 400-metre hurdles race:

> *. . . the hurdler's primary focus of attention is in Quadrant III, narrow–external, because the focus and primary concentration is on the coming hurdle. However, at different instants focus is in each of the other quadrants. For example, in Quadrant I, the broad–internal focus is constantly reviewing the stride lengths required to reach the next hurdle in the proper position for a rapid, balanced clearance. There is also assessment of the effect the wind, track conditions and pace is having on the stride pattern for clearing the next hurdle. Also one has to see whether the pace is sufficient to maintain good position against the other competitors. In Quadrant II, the broad–external focus is assessing where one is in relation to all the other competitors in the race. In Quadrant IV, the narrow–internal focus is on personal race judgement and effort distribution. At any one moment in time any of these factors could be critical.* (pp. 122–123)

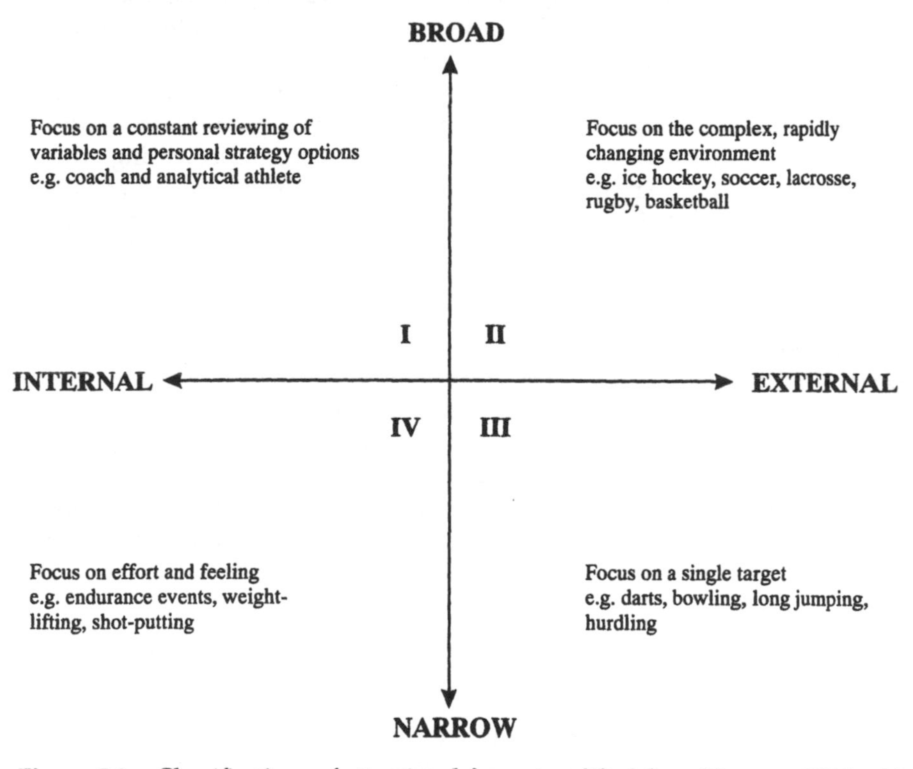

Figure 7.1: Classifications of attentional focus (modified from Hemery, 1986 with permission)

These represent considerable demands on the hurdler's cognitive system, in terms of both the quantity of information which must be continually monitored and the rapid switches from one attentional style to another.

In addition to identifying these different types of attentional style, Nideffer (1976) proposed that individuals differ in their ability to use the various styles. He therefore developed a measure of attentional style, the test of attentional and interpersonal style (TAIS) which was designed to assess this individual difference variable. However, research in sport psychology which has used the TAIS has generally failed to provide convincing evidence of its construct and predictive validity. For example, Van Schoyk and Grasha's (1981) and Albrecht and Feltz's (1987) findings showed that sport-specific measures of attentional style were more valid and reliable than the TAIS. Both of these studies, along with several others (e.g. Dewey *et al.*, 1989; Ford and Summers, 1992; Summers *et al.*, 1991) have also raised questions about the factor structure of Nideffer's model, although Nideffer's (1990) counterargument is that such evidence stems from the misuse of factor analysis.

Boutcher (1992) has raised questions over the validity of assessing attention via questionnaire. The major issue concerns whether attention can be accurately described through self-analysis and language, since the automatic aspect of attention is hypothesised to operate without conscious monitoring (Schneider *et al.*, 1984). Thus, there appears to be a paradox in requiring performers to assess non-conscious attentional states, representing what is basically procedural knowledge, through what is effectively the conscious processing of declarative knowledge. In an earlier criticism, Landers (1985) was quite damning in his assessment of the worth of the TAIS in sport psychology research, advocating less reliance on questionnaire measures and greater emphasis on physiological and behavioural measures of attention in sport. Several studies, as described earlier in this chapter, have been carried out to examine what are supposedly physiological concomitants of attention in sport (e.g. Boutcher and Zinsser, 1990; Hatfield *et al.*, 1984, 1987; Landers *et al.*, 1980; see Boutcher, 1990 for a review). Herein lies a problem, however, since the psychophysiological approach has its own equally limiting weakness in that the evidence that heart rate deceleration, for example, reflects attentional processes is far from conclusive. Behavioural measures of perception (e.g. Allard *et al.*, 1980; Allard and Starkes, 1980), on the other hand, have proved rather more encouraging.

At a conceptual level, Nideffer's approach tends to be too vague, lacking the specificity required to have strong predictive validity. For example, it is too general and simplistic to propose that a midfield soccer player in possession of the ball requires a broad external focus to scan the visual field before deciding upon an appropriate team-mate to pass to. Such a broad external focus might include distracting movements of individuals in the crowd, as well as movements of team-mates and opposition players. Thus, the attentional style approach may actually be too parsimonious in attempting to explain the attentional demands placed upon sports performers. However, despite the criticisms levelled at both the conceptual basis and the assessment of attentional style, the notion continues to attract attention and may be worth pursuing and refining as a means of understanding the attentional demands of different sports. Of particular interest is how elite performers are able to switch rapidly from one style to another, and how they have developed this attentional flexibility.

A preliminary integrated model of attention and sports performance

In response to the lack of a sport-specific theoretical underpinning in this area, and drawing upon theories and findings from the domains of information processing, social psychology, and psychophysiology, Boutcher (1992) has proposed an integrated model of the relationship between attention and sports performance (see Figure 7.2). The model incorporates individual differences, environmental influences, and changes in the performer's arousal level, and assumes that attention can be assessed via a variety of means. The model predicts that enduring dispositions (e.g. trait anxiety), demands of the activity (e.g. fine versus gross skills), and environmental factors (e.g. audience size) will determine the level of physiological arousal. During

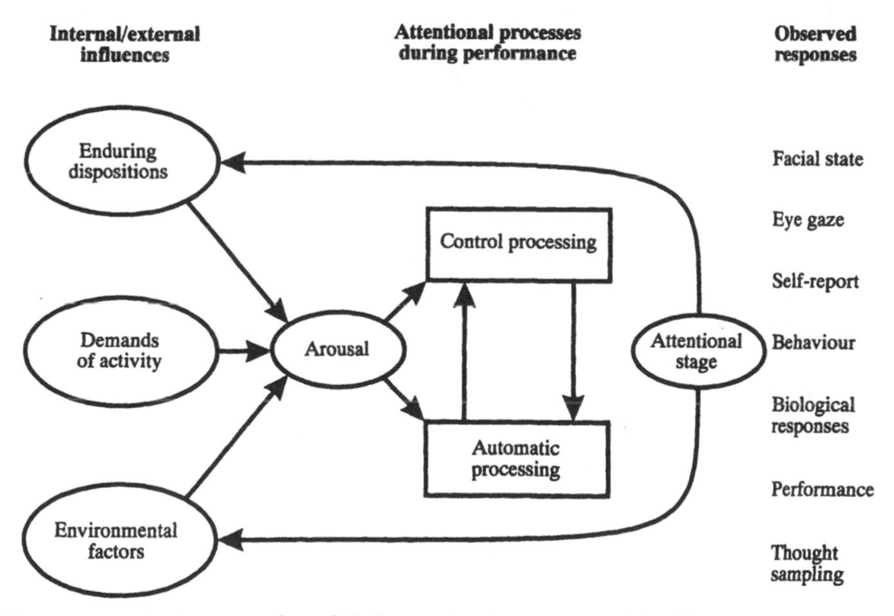

Figure 7.2: An integrated model of attention in sport (modified from Boutcher, 1992 with permission)

performance of the task, this arousal is channelled into either controlled processing, automatic processing, or a combination of the two, depending on the nature of the task. According to the model, optimal attentional states are achieved when the performer has achieved an exact balance between controlled and automatic processing necessary for that particular task. The feedback loops in the model allow for interaction between the various factors and for attention to be influenced both during and after performance. The model also incorporates possible measures of controlled and automatic processing, with self-report and thought sampling measures being more appropriate for assessing controlled processing. Measures such as facial state, eye gaze, and psychophysiological variables are proposed as being more appropriate for assessing attention during performance. This model is largely speculative and is almost certainly too vague and simplistic in its current form. However, it does offer a promising starting point for future research into attentional states and their relationships with sports performance. Implications of the model for attention control training are discussed later in this chapter.

Summary

Theories and models of attention relating specifically to sports performance are relatively under-developed. Nideffer's (1976) notion of attentional style and Boutcher's (1992) preliminary model of attention and sports performance both lack the specificity and detail required to make any significant impact on current knowledge. Approaches emanating from the mainstream psychology literature currently offer the greatest potential for understanding attention processes in elite athletes. However, these too have their limitations. There are clearly many questions related to focused and divided attention, for example, which remain unanswered. The notion of controlled and automatic attention seems to offer a plausible explanation of how elite performers are able to function effectively and successfully in environments in which they are faced with a considerable amount of potentially distracting information. However, little is known about the role of cognition in such functioning. The way forward would appear to be to adopt a moderate ecological approach and to examine the extent of the involvement of cognition and direct perception–action links in the control of highly skilled movement. The examination of heterarchical models of control may serve such a function.

ATTENTION AND ANXIETY

One of the major threats to controlling attention in sport is the increased anxiety and arousal that is often associated with top level competition. The relationship between arousal and attention has already been discussed in Chapter 5. The enormous influence that anxiety can have on attention is illustrated in the following quote from Orlick and Partington's (1988) account of an interview with an Olympic diver:

> *I was most aware of my nervousness . . . I tried to focus on my dives but was easily distracted by others around me, the competition, the crowd, the cameras, et cetera. It was difficult for me to focus or stay in control. I was agitated the whole time I was out there.* (p. 128)

Approaches to explaining the relationship between anxiety and attention within the sport psychology literature have mainly relied on traditional perspectives such as Easterbrook's (1959) cue utilisation theory and Wine's (1980) limited capacity explanation; these theories have already been considered earlier in this chapter and in previous chapters and will not be re-visited here. Numerous other approaches have been employed within the mainstream psychology literature to examine direct effects of anxiety upon performance, and also upon attentional processes which support performance. Some of these approaches are briefly considered below.

Multidimensional activation states

Several studies have now utilised Hockey and Hamilton's (1983) broad band approach (see Chapter 5) to examine the effects of different anxiety components upon a number of subcomponents of sports performance. The most reliable findings so far obtained suggest that cognitive anxiety enhances the speed at which simple information can be transferred through the system (Parfitt and Hardy, 1994; Parfitt *et al.*, 1990). Conversely, physiological arousal, or the associated somatic anxiety, reduces working memory, and therefore the ability to make decisions (Jones and Cale, 1989; Parfitt and Hardy, 1993). Finally, Eysenck (1988, 1992) has presented evidence which suggests that highly anxious performers may differ from non-anxious performers with respect to four other aspects of information processing: they are predisposed to process threatening, rather than neutral, or task-relevant, stimuli; they have less effective working memory available to handle complex cognitive tasks; they are hyperdistractable; and they exhibit greater attentional narrowing than low anxiety performers. The most obvious implication of these findings is that elite performers may be better able to control the negative influences of competitive state anxiety on attention, while still making full use of any positive influences (see Chapters 5 and 6).

Effects of anxiety upon automaticity

Although empirical evidence directly demonstrating the existence of heterarchical systems of control is scarce, they do possess considerable intuitive appeal, and also offer the possibility that the cognitive and physiological components of anxiety may affect the system in different ways. For example, it is possible that physiological arousal effects, such as increased muscle tension, influence the operation of the lower levels of the system via effector mechanisms (cf. Weinberg, 1978; Weinberg and Hunt, 1976). Conversely, recent research by Masters (1992) and Hardy *et al.* (in press) suggests the possibility that (cognitive) anxiety may exert its influence upon motor performance by leading the performer to use higher level cognitive mechanisms in an attempt to consciously control lower level automatic operations.

Put more crudely, performers who are anxious may waste valuable resources trying to tell themselves what to do, instead of simply trusting themselves to get on with a job of doing it. This has been referred to in the popular applied sport psychology literature as "paralysis by analysis". For example, an elite golfer who has perfected a suitable swing will hope to repeatedly perform it automatically, without consciously attending to any specific details of the process of swinging. She may not even want to "think" about the swing at all, but may want instead to focus all of her attention upon the ball or perhaps some relaxation strategy. In this way, the golfer is attempting to avoid interfering with the automatic nature of the swing. This fits in neatly with athletes' reports of their experiences during peak performances, which include automatic, effortless flow without really thinking about the performance (Ravizza, 1977; Williams and Krane, 1993). Strategies for achieving such a state have been popularised within the sport psychology literature through the "inner game" approach (Gallwey, 1974) and some mental training programmes (e.g. Syer and Connolly, 1984; Unestahl, 1983). These approaches are underpinned by the manner in which, some researchers have argued, the two hemispheres of the brain operate. In very crude terms, the left brain has been argued to be the seat of analytical thinking whilst the right brain has been argued to perform more intuitive, automatic processes (Blakeslee, 1980). Since peak performance is associated with lack of analysis and effortless, automatic concentration (cf. Csikszentmihalyi, 1975; Jackson, 1992), performers are urged to learn strategies whereby they can achieve right hemispheric dominance during performance. Whilst these proposals are appealing at an intuitive level, they present a very simplified, and possibly inaccurate, picture of a large area of neurophysiological literature which is extremely complex and offers only weak support for the notion of hemispheric specialisation (Beaumont, 1983; Collins *et al.*, 1990; Harris, 1988).

Processing efficiency theory

Perhaps more than any other researcher, Eysenck (1982, 1984, 1988, 1992) has generated plausible creative ideas and theories regarding the processes which might underlie the effects of anxiety upon performance. One of these theories incorporates an interesting combination of cognitive and motivational variables, and is particularly pertinent to understanding attentional processes. Following Wine (1971) and others, Eysenck (1982, 1992) argued that cognitive anxiety reduced the effective working capacity available to performers by wasting resources on worry, self-concern, and other task-irrelevant activities. However, he also argued that because anxious performers have a greater discrepancy between their current aspirations and their perceived ability, they invest more effort in the task, provided that they perceive themselves to have at least a moderate chance of success (cf. Erez and Zidon, 1984; Locke and Latham, 1985). Consequently, performance effectiveness may be maintained (or even enhanced), but at a reduced efficiency and an increased energetical cost to processing efficiency. Furthermore, this increased energetical cost may be reflected in increased physiological arousal and somatic anxiety (Frankenhaeuser and Johansson, 1976). Eventually, of course, the cost will become too great, the performer will give up, and performance will break down—essentially because, as Revelle and Michaels (1976) observed, "the tough get going when the going gets tough", but "wise men do not beat their heads against brick walls". Carver and Scheier (1988) also proposed a similar, but less detailed, model in which performers' confidence about achieving their goals determines whether they persist at, or disengage from, the task (see Chapter 6).

Although processing efficiency theory is not easy to test directly, Eysenck and Calvo (1992) have reviewed an impressive body of literature which supports it, and predictions of the cusp catastrophe model of anxiety and performance.

Mood congruent recall

Another possible explanation of anxiety effects upon performance is that they are simply an example of mood congruent recall (Barnard and Teasdale, 1991; Eysenck and Keane, 1990). Generally, performers appear to enjoy learning new skills, and do so in a relatively supportive environment; however, they are then expected to demonstrate their skill in a stressful environment where they are quite likely to be highly anxious. According to mood congruent recall, performance in such environments should be depressed because the performer's mood at recall does not match his or her mood at learning. A discussion of the theoretical explanations of mood congruent recall is beyond the scope of this chapter. For detailed discussions, the interested reader is referred to Barnard and Teasdale (1991), Gilligan and Bower (1984), and Tulving (1983).

Studies of mood congruent recall have generally used either laboratory-based mood inductions, or naturally occurring moods such as happiness and depression (for a brief review, see Eysenck and Keane, 1990). However, one study by Godden and Baddeley (1975) examined subjects' recall of lists of words which had been learned either on land or 6 m (20 ft) under water. Subjects who learned on land recalled more words on land than under water, whilst subjects who learned under water recalled more words under water than on land. Although Godden and Baddeley did not measure the anxiety levels of their subjects, their results are at least consistent with the suggestion that material which has to be recalled under conditions of high anxiety may be best learned in the same conditions. There are clearly extremely important ethical and practical considerations that would have to be considered before any recommendations could be made based on this finding. However, if such an interpretation of Godden and Baddeley's findings were confirmed it could radically alter current thinking regarding the "ideal" coaching environment for elite performers.

Summary

The relationship between anxiety and attention is a complex one, and one is forced to look beyond past and current research in sport psychology to begin to comprehend the "nature of the beast". The "beast" can clearly be examined from a number of different perspectives, including information processing, attentional resources, selective attentional biases, mood congruence, etc. This is an under-researched area in sport psychology where researchers have tended to rely on over-simplistic explanations in the form of, for example, Easterbrook's (1959) cue utilisation theory or Wine's (1971) theory of reduced processing capacity. Whilst not necessarily being inaccurate, such approaches to a great extent lack the specificity and detail required for further understanding. Sport psychology researchers need to progress beyond simplistic explanations of what are very complex phenomena, and begin to explore the relationship between attention and anxiety from some of the different perspectives outlined in this section.

STRATEGIES FOR ENHANCING CONCENTRATION AND ATTENTION CONTROL

Given the relatively under-developed theoretical framework in the attention-sports performance domain, it is not surprising that there is a paucity of experimental research which has examined the efficacy of attention control strategies. Even the work which has emanated from Nideffer's

(1976) original proposals on attentional style is devoid of firm recommendations for strategies and techniques that can be employed to enhance performers' ability to switch in and out of the various styles (see Nideffer, 1993). Consequently, the content of this section is heavily dependent on three sources: firstly, athletes' published accounts of strategies and techniques used for attention control; secondly, published accounts of researchers' observations and surveys of elite performers; and thirdly, the strategies and techniques advocated in mental training packages as methods of developing attention control. Whilst the rationales which have been presented for the majority of the techniques discussed below are largely intuitive, an attempt will be made to encompass them within the theoretical framework addressed in the previous sections.

Simulation training

The competitive environment clearly includes numerous factors which are not present to the same degree, or even at all, in the training environment. Physical factors such as the presence of the opposition, perhaps a noisy and restless crowd and an official during competitive events, undoubtedly produce a very different environment from training. Even if a competition venue is the actual site of the normal training venue, the psychological environment will be very different in the two types of situation. Levels of perceived stress, anxiety, confidence, and motivation are all likely to differ in such situations. All of these factors are also, of course, potential distractions to the athlete and so may impair performance. The ability to remain focused and not be distracted in such an environment is clearly crucial. One technique which is used by many sports performers to enhance their attention control in highly pressured and potentially distracting situations is that of simulation training.

Orlick and Partington's (1988) reports of Olympic athletes emphasised the importance they attributed to simulation training as part of their preparation:

> *the best athletes made extensive use of simulation training. They approached training runs, routines, plays, or scrimmages in practice as if they were at the competition, often wearing what they would wear and preparing like they would prepare.* (p. 114)

Jones and Hardy's (1990a) reports of interviews with named elite athletes also demonstrate very clearly the valuable contribution of simulation training in enhancing attention control skills. Indeed, simulation training was a high priority for all of the athletes interviewed. This training took two forms; physical practice in the presence of simulated competition stressors and mental rehearsal of the actual competitive event.

Looking firstly at the methods of physical practice used by Jones and Hardy's subjects, Alan Edge (former Olympic kayaker) reported using simulation training as often as he could. This involved not only simulation of the moves which would probably be encountered on a course, but also where on the course they would come. For example, he would simulate a particularly hard move that might come late in a course by paddling very hard for five minutes and then going straight into the move. Olympic javelin thrower, Steve Backley, stated that he sometimes structured his training in such a way as to put himself under the same sort of pressure encountered on the qualifying day of a major competition:

> *I'd have three throws to get over 75 or 76 metres and put the mark out and actually go through the process of trying to simulate the pressure. If I've got a minor club competition, I'll slip in a "qualifying round" the day before to create the physical fatigue the day after and also the mental stress.* (Jones and Hardy, 1990a, p. 270)

Former World Champion trampolinist, Sue Challis, regarded herself as being very good at simulating competitive conditions in training:

> *I actually do the routine in training and imagine that I've got one chance. I present to the judges and make it as near to the competition as possible. I often get quite uptight if I don't get it right, but if it's good it really boosts my confidence.* (Jones and Hardy, 1990a, p. 271)

Jones (1993) has recently reported a psychological intervention with an elite racket sport player in which simulation training formed a major component. The player presented herself with a problem of losing concentration when she had what she perceived to be a bad call against her by the referee. Following training in a meditation-based relaxation technique, she then practised using this technique in practice matches in which a referee was primed to give bad calls against her. This helped to reinforce the use of the technique in such a situation which was then transferred successfully to the competitive environment.

Mental rehearsal was also identified as an important technique for developing attention control by the athletes interviewed by Jones and Hardy (1990a). Steve Backley, for example, said that he often used it to simulate the stress of competition by imagining that he was

> *in the last round of a major competition losing and with only one throw left . . . Imagining myself in that position and succeeding made me feel stronger.* (Jones and Hardy, 1990a, p. 270)

David Hemery, Olympic 400 metre hurdles Gold Medal winner in 1968, mentally rehearsed a large number of variations prior to his Gold Medal winning race in an attempt to ensure that nothing would distract him:

> *he reported regularly mentally rehearsing "every lane and condition that I could conceivably think of: drawn in lane one, having people hare off, but maintaining my control; drawn in the outside lane and not being able to see (the other runners) and still having sufficient confidence in my going for world record pace, so if I couldn't see anyone I would still go for it, not letting them determine my aim.* (Jones and Hardy, 1990a; p.269)

The theoretical rationale for using simulation training as part of an athlete's preparation for competition is a very strong one at a cognitive–behavioural level. However, the rationale for simulation training is also very persuasive at a cognitive level. The works of Hockey and Hamilton (1983), Humphreys and Revelle (1984), and Sanders (1983) (see Chapters 5 and 6; Jones, 1990; Jones and Hardy, 1989) all suggest that stress effects are situation-specific, so that different stressors have different effects upon attention and performance. This suggests that competitive anxiety, fatigue, pain, "bad calls", etc. may all have different effects, so that it is appropriate to simulate as many different conditions as possible, both internal and external, in order to fully prepare the athlete. In addition, the available literature on mood congruent recall (Barnard and Teasdale, 1991; Eysenck and Keane, 1990) provides further evidence of the importance of simulation training.

Competition plans, performance routines, and process-oriented goals

The findings of Orlick and Partington (1988) clearly indicate the importance of competition plans for elite athletes. The best athletes in their study have well-established and well-practised pre-performance plans in the form of routinised behaviours which help them to prepare for performance. As was indicated in Chapter 5, the precise means by which pre-performance plans affect performance are not known. However, Boutcher (1990) has proposed that attentional control is likely to be one of these means, and it is worth recalling that the focus of pre-performance routines is in the process of performing not the outcome (see Chapter 5).

The best athletes in Orlick and Partington's (1988) study also had very clear and detailed plans of action for events during performance which, in the vast majority of cases, were designed to facilitate attentional focus on the process of performance as opposed to factors over which they had no direct control, such as other competitors and final outcome. This strategy is aptly described in the following quote from an Olympic pairs kayaker interviewed in Orlick and Partington's (1988) study:

> *My focus was very concentrated throughout the race. We have a start plan, and in it I concentrate* only *on the first few strokes . . . Then I concentrate on the next little bit of the race . . . Then it's getting to the end, we have to really push. Almost every 3 seconds or so towards the end I'd have to say, "Relax", and I'd let my shoulders and my head relax, and I'd think about putting on the power, and then I'd feel the tension creeping up again so I'd think about relaxing again, then power, then relax. . . .* (p. 116)

Jones and Hardy's (1990a) report of their interview with kayaker, Alan Edge, similarly highlights the importance of carefully thought-out competition plans:

> *Alan always had a very detailed race plan with clearly defined process-oriented goals about how he wanted to paddle each section of the course. Because this plan included subgoals about what to do if he made any mistakes, it was theoretically possible for him to stick to the plan regardless of anything that happened during a run . . . Alan attached a great deal of significance to having this sort of plan, and used it to help him focus his attention and feel in control.* (p. 269)

David Hemery's (Olympic hurdler) competition plan had as its cornerstone an internal focus of attention upon his body so as to monitor his process-oriented goals for the race:

> *I focused on the feeling that generated the pace. I couldn't tell you how it was . . . a percentage of effort was how it came . . . it had to do with how much effort you were going to put into each section of the race . . . going down the back straight at 80 percent, but then accelerating the legs and running wide because I hadn't learned to hurdle off the other leg sufficiently well, and I had to put in two extra strides so I revved higher round the bend intentionally . . . and took a foot off every stride.* (Jones and Hardy, 1990a, p. 269)

The findings from Jones and Hardy (1990a), and Orlick and Partington (1988), indicate that elite athletes often use very detailed plans which specify how they can achieve the performance goals they set for themselves. These competition plans usually have process-oriented goals as their central feature. Little empirical research has been conducted to examine the influence of process-oriented goals, but several researchers have suggested that such goals should enhance attentional focus (cf. Beggs, 1990; Boutcher,

1990; Hardy and Nelson, 1988), and Kingston and Hardy (1994a) have recently provided empirical support for these proposals in a sample of golfers.

When viewed in the context of automaticity of skilled performance, the use of process-oriented goals to help elite performers focus their attention on important aspects of performance presents what, at first sight, may appear to be a paradox. The resolution of this apparent paradox requires some subtlety. First, process-oriented goals need not necessarily be problem-focused, but may, instead, be emotion-focused; for example, a golfer might have a goal of ensuring that she is relaxed prior to putting. Second, process-oriented goals require performers to reward themselves for successfully completing the process, not the outcome, and may therefore reduce the pressure which makes performers want to try to consciously control their performance. Third, the process goals that are used may be so well programmed into the performer's sub-conscious that they do not normally operate at a conscious level. Fourth, holistic process-oriented goals may not encourage lapses into conscious control because conscious control can only be exerted over parts of a movement (Anderson, 1982; Eysenck and Keane, 1990). In conclusion, the automatic processing versus process-oriented goals paradox can be resolved by a consideration of the appropriateness of specific process-oriented goals for the performer in question. Nevertheless, the extent to which elite performers actually use process-oriented goals remains an open question.

Overlearning of skills

A further feature to emerge from Jones and Hardy's (1990a) interviews was the emphasis placed on overlearning of skills as an aid to concentration in competitive situations. The general consensus amongst the athletes was that the skill they were required to reproduce in competition had to be overlearned to the extent that, no matter what situations or doubts arose, they would still be able to perform despite them. For example, Sue Challis (former World Champion trampolinist) stated:

> *I like to do what I'm going to do in competition over and over again . . . I like to have done the whole routine many times so I know that, whatever happens, I can do it.* (Jones and Hardy, 1990a, p. 272)

Whilst no empirical research has directly addressed the question of how much overlearning is required to achieve such a state, it seems likely to be a very considerable amount from the anecdotal evidence which emerged from the interviews in Jones and Hardy's (1990a) study. On the other hand, there is, of course, a substantial empirical literature which indicates the value of overlearning in general terms (cf. Eysenck, 1982; Hockey and Hamilton, 1983; Humphreys and Revelle, 1984; Parfitt *et al.*, 1990).

One explanation of overlearning as an aid to concentration relates to the notion that practice facilitates the concurrent performance of more than one task (Eysenck, 1984). Overlearning may enable the athlete to establish automatic attention processes (Schneider and Shiffrin, 1977; Shiffrin and Schneider, 1977) which are supposedly of unlimited capacity and operate more rapidly than controlled processes. It should also be emphasised, however, that automatic processing is relatively inflexible so that athletes could encounter problems in situations which are novel. This provides a further argument, of course, for varied practice during simulation training in which the skills are overlearned in as many different situations as possible so that automatic processing is not disrupted during competition.

One final comment is worthwhile in the context of overlearning and automaticity. In just the same way that physical skills need to be overlearned in order to be performed automatically, so Gould *et al.* (1993a) have presented evidence that the automaticity of psychological skills and strategies is also a distinguishing characteristic of truly elite performers.

Attentional training programme

Boutcher (1992) has proposed an attentional training programme based upon his integrated model of attention and sports performance (see earlier section in this chapter). The programme comprises three phases: assessment of the performer's attentional strengths and weaknesses; basic attentional training; and advanced attentional training. The first phase involves a multifaceted approach to assessing attentional skills via a combination of some or all of a number of techniques, including questionnaires, interviews, thought sampling, observational analysis, performance tests, and psychophysiological measurements. Specific measures include sport-specific versions of the TAIS (e.g. Albrecht and Feltz, 1987; Van Schoyck and Grasha, 1981), the Stroop test (Stroop, 1935), concentration grid tests (e.g. Harris and Harris, 1984), facial/eye states, and EEG and cardiac patterns.

Boutcher proposed that the basic attention training phase could be structured around a variety of laboratory tasks, such as the Stroop and concentration grids. The use of biofeedback could also help the performer to acquire basic control over variables such as heart rate, respiration, and attentional focus. The advanced attentional training phase is more sport-specific and is aimed at the development of effective pre-performance routines which enable the performer to direct "competition-generated arousal into automatic processing of the task at hand while suppressing analytical processing" (Boutcher, 1992, p.262). Boutcher proposed that the most efficient attentional style is one in which the performer thinks of "nothing" so that skills can be performed reflexively. Such a state is described in Newman's (1992) account of an interview with international soccer goalkeeper, Tony Meola:

> *When I'm really concentrating, I would say it's almost like I'm playing unconscious.* (p. 95)

Research has shown that individuals can suppress cortical activity by learning to enhance alpha waves and also that they can self-regulate EEG activity (Bauer, 1976; Elder *et al.*, 1985; Jackson and Eberly, 1982). Whilst it must be emphasised that reduced cortical activity does not necessarily imply increased concentration, sport-specific EEG biofeedback is advocated by Boutcher as an effective means of teaching performers how to acquire such states. Although not mentioned by Boutcher, meditation-based relaxation techniques have also been shown to enhance concentration in sports performers (Jones, 1993).

Boutcher's (1990) programme is speculative and unsubstantiated by empirical evidence. Nevertheless, it does present some interesting ideas. However, there is an inherent danger that the extensive use of laboratory tasks and non-sport-specific content in the early stages of the programme could cause adherence problems in some performers. Furthermore, the extent to which such laboratory strategies will transfer to the sport environment remains questionable.

Training for trust

The notion of *trust* as a psychological skill in which athletes release conscious control over movements, thus inducing automaticity in movement execution, has recently been proposed by Moore and Stevenson (1991, 1994). They identified trust as representing a performance goal which depends upon three fundamental psychological skills: concentration, confidence, and composure (see Figure 7.3). *Concentration* refers to what athletes focus on (e.g. self-statements, mistakes, sensory cues) and is proposed to be a primary determinant of *confidence,* which refers to the athletes' belief that they have the specific abilities necessary to execute the sport skill. Moore and Stevenson then proposed that high confidence is expressed by *composure,* reflected by a quiet and relaxed mind prior to skill execution.

Moore and Stevenson (1994) suggested a three-phase training programme comprising education, skills training and competition simulation phases. The emphasis during the education phase is on gaining the athlete's commitment to train for trust. In the second phase, the goals of the concentration training activities are twofold: "(a) to develop a reference point so that athletes know when they are connected to, and trusting in, skill execution, and (b) to identify when and how trust breaks down in terms of the specific

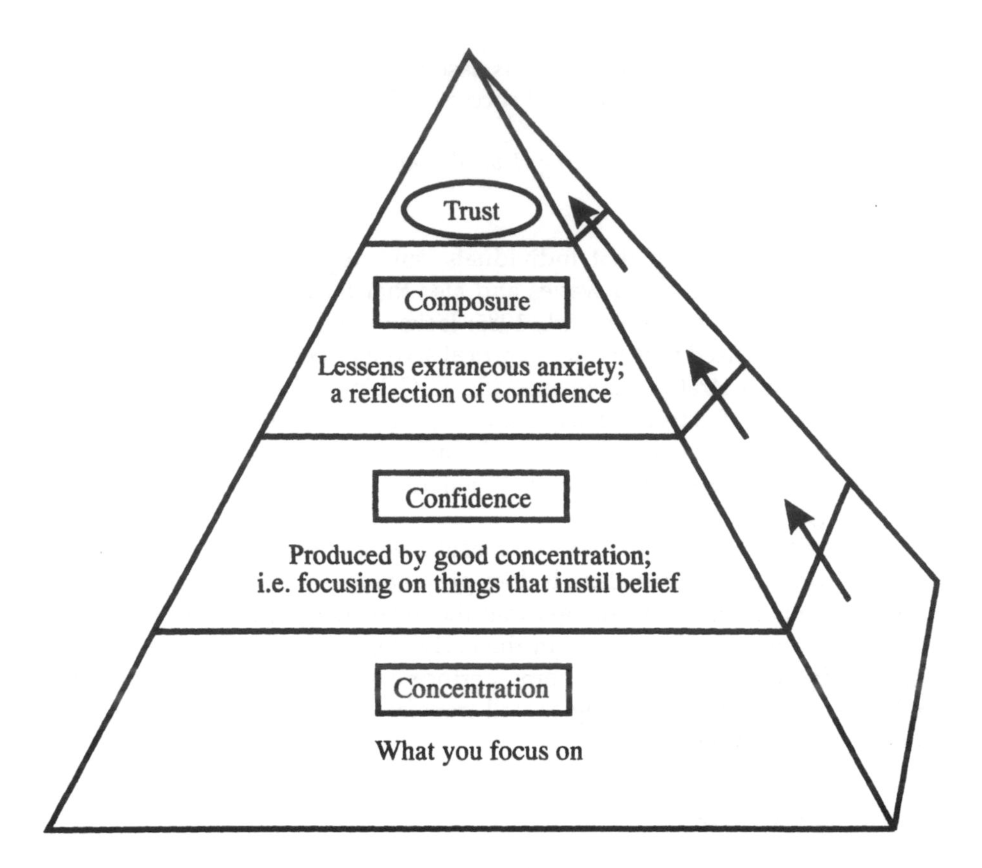

Figure 7.3: Fundamental psychological skill components of trust (modified from Moore and Stevenson, 1994 with permission)

skill and situation" (Moore and Stevenson, 1994; p. 7). Three types of drills are advocated for developing reference points for trust. Firstly, "feel" drills involve athletes attending to the kinaesthetic feel of specific movements, either through actual physical practice or imagery. Secondly, "quiet" drills involve athletes identifying distractions and practising refocusing. Thirdly, "connect" drills require athletes to attend to present moment sensations during skill performance in order to enhance sensory awareness. Similar strategies have also been proposed by Syer and Connolly (1984).

The final phase comprises structured competitive simulations in which the psychological skills acquired in phase two are monitored and evaluated. Monitoring sheets and the use of video are advocated at this stage. Athletes performing self-paced skills are encouraged to develop an execution routine prior to executing the skill. This routine moves through three stages: analysis ("check it out"), comprising recognising the situation at hand and then reviewing a plan of action; feel ("click it in"), involving accessing the correct motor programme; and trust ("let it go"), which involves the initiation of movement by clearing the mind and releasing conscious effort.

This approach can be criticised on a number of grounds. Not least, it is conceptually weak and fails to take into account conceptual advances in both attention and confidence in recent years, and also the recent work of ecological psychologists. Secondly, the "performance" goals referred to by the authors are actually process-oriented goals. Third, it is not at all clear how the proposed training should enhance trust.

Associative versus dissociative attentional strategies

Associative versus dissociative attentional strategies were identified as a cognitive style dimension which distinguished elite from non-elite marathon runners (Morgan and Pollock, 1977). Specifically, elite runners were generally found to use associative strategies whereby their direction of attention was internalised towards the body's feedback signals, whilst non-elite runners tended to use dissociative strategies in which attention was externalised. However, Schomer's (1986) more rigorous investigation of elite and non-elite marathon runners showed that, regardless of the runner's status, increased running pace was accompanied by a predominantly associative cognitive strategy. It is likely, of course, that runners, whether elite or non-elite, do not use solely one or the other type of strategy, but a combination of the two. In any case, research findings have suggested that associative strategies are not always superior (Gill and Strom, 1985; Pennebaker and Lightner, 1980; Weinberg *et al.*, 1984). Gill (1986) has attempted to explain these inconsistencies. She proposed that dissociative strategies might enhance performance in endurance tasks where maintaining performance is the primary goal via reduced perception of pain and fatigue. Gill went on to argue that associative strategies are beneficial in achieving specific time or position goals when monitoring bodily sensations is an important part of pacing oneself.

The notion of athletes adopting dissociative strategies is very different from ideas discussed earlier in which the major concern is to remain focused on task-relevant cues. Dissociative strategies, on the contrary, involve a conscious effort to direct attention towards what may be task-irrelevant cues. Clearly, the application of this form of attentional control is at best limited to those sports which are relatively low in terms of skill complexity and which involve intense physical fatigue and pain.

Summary

One of the clear conclusions that can be drawn from the content of this section is that there are a wide variety of techniques and strategies used by elite athletes as a means of enhancing their attentional control. Often, they appear to use a combination of techniques, in which process-oriented goals, imagery, and relaxation appear to be particularly prominent.

Several of the strategies discussed in this section have emphasised the importance of automaticity in elite sports performance. However, recent empirical work has illustrated the prominence of process-oriented goals in enhancing attention, thus highlighting the importance of conscious control. This apparent paradox has been addressed by Kingston and Hardy (1994b) who argued that the two perspectives are not necessarily contradictory so long as the process goals are "holistic" in nature. For example, a golfer might focus during her swing on "smooth", "slow" or "tempo". This does not involve focusing upon component parts of the skill of swinging a golf club, but rather on a generalised, holistic process-oriented goal. Kingston and Hardy (1994b) also suggested that since such routines themselves become automated with practice, so they help performers to get into a state of automatic processing prior to performing. Further support for the efficacy of such holistic process-oriented goals has been provided by Swain and Jones (1995) in a single-subject design study of basketball players.

IMPLICATIONS FOR RESEARCH

There is still much to unearth at both a conceptual and an empirical level in the area of attention in sport. The whole area is relatively underdeveloped and in need of concerted efforts. Studying and understanding how elite athletes, in particular, are able to control their attention appears to offer an important step forward.

Theoretical aspects of attention

There are essentially two options open to researchers working in this area. The first is to empirically examine and refine approaches currently available within the sport domain. Nideffer's (1976) attentional style approach could prove useful if refined at both the conceptual and measurement levels. Boutcher's (1992) model is interesting and in its very earliest stages of development; it would require substantial empirical investigation, and possibly considerable refinement before it could be used to guide training and interventions. The second option is to employ approaches available in the mainstream psychology literature, but which have received little attention in the sport domain. Generally speaking, these theories take such a strong cognitive position that they virtually ignore the motoric demands of sports skills. They therefore need to be empirically tested within the sport psychology domain, and modified as appropriate.

The available literature emphasises a crucial role for automaticity in elite performance. The notion of automaticity needs to be much better understood. The traditional distinction between controlled and automatic processing is an appealing one, but the heterarchical models of control approach seems to offer the greatest potential for developing an understanding of automaticity and the role that cognition may or may not play in elite performance. Psychophysiological studies may have an important part to play in this context. Such studies may help to determine the details which are currently lacking about why elite performers are better at controlling attention than their non-elite counterparts. But before psychophysiologists are able to do this, they will need to present much stronger evidence regarding the precise relationships between the variables measured and various attentional constructs.

Attention and anxiety

There is a need to progress beyond explanations of the relationship between attention and anxiety which are oversimplistic. Approaches discussed from the mainstream psychology literature emphasise that this is a complex relationship which can be examined from a number of different perspectives. Such approaches could be employed to address an important question in the context of understanding elite performance, namely: is attention in elite athletes less affected than in non-elite athletes because they are better at controlling anxiety, or because they are better at controlling attention?

Strategies for enhancing concentration and attention control

This area is characterised by a paucity of quality research examining the effects of the various strategies discussed earlier in this chapter upon attention control. Consequently, empirical investigations of the efficacy of such strategies are urgently required. In particular, relatively little is known about the processes that underlie the benefits of many of the strategies and techniques. For example, simulation training appears to be an important technique employed by elite athletes; but precisely how does simulation training aid attention control? Furthermore, a number of the strategies discussed use a combination of techniques, such as imagery and meditative relaxation. What are the relative contributions of these specific techniques to enhancing attention control? And how do they influence it?

The discussion on strategies for enhancing attention control also identified what, at first sight, appeared to be a paradox. On the one hand, the consistent aim of these strategies is to induce automaticity in the form of performing without conscious control. On the other hand, the use of process-oriented goals emerged as a prominent technique employed by many elite athletes. This finding requires further empirical investigation into possible links, and processes which might underlie such links, between automaticity and process goals which are holistic in nature.

IMPLICATIONS FOR BEST PRACTICE

The empirical literature which demonstrates that elite athletes are better at controlling attention than their non-elite counterparts (e.g. Orlick and Partington, 1988) has not been particularly helpful in identifying how these differences occur. This section examines some of the approaches to attention discussed in this chapter to tease out some possible pointers to furthering understanding and implications for best practice.

Theoretical aspects of attention

A number of implications are evident from the various theoretical aspects of attention discussed earlier in the chapter. It appears that elite athletes are good at *focusing* their attention in those sports or tasks in which there are relatively few relevant cues. Elite athletes are also good at *dividing* their attention among relevant cues in those situations where there may be many relevant and simultaneously occurring cues. It could be inferred from Nideffer's (1976) classification of attentional style that elite athletes are very efficient at switching quickly between the various types of attentional focus as required by the demands of the situation. Boutcher's (1992) integrated model of attention in sport proposes that elite sports performers are able to achieve an appropriate balance between controlled and automatic processing necessary for particular tasks. However, the overwhelming implication appears to be the need to develop automaticity during performance in order to achieve peak performance. Perhaps, the really great athletes are those who can consistently achieve such states.

Attention and anxiety

The empirical literature which has compared elite and non-elite athletes has consistently shown that elite athletes interpret their anxiety states more positively than non-elite athletes (e.g. Jones *et al.*, 1994; Mahoney and Avener, 1977; Orlick and Partington, 1988). This implies that anxiety may not have the same impact on attention in elite athletes as it will in non-elite athletes. However, to assume that athletes can enhance their attention by merely devoting their efforts directly towards controlling their anxiety would be too simplistic. Indeed, some elite athletes appear to prefer to devote their efforts to employing attention control strategies which may have an indirect effect on anxiety. For example, 400 m hurdler, David Hemery, reported using such a strategy prior to his Olympic Gold Medal winning run:

> *I was on the practice track watching Jeff Vanderstock who was the expected winner of the (1968 Olympic) Games. He did a start out of the blocks and I felt my throat constrict and recognised that my mind was on him, and I knew that I could not control how fast he ran and that I had to come back inside myself. I left my shoes and spikes on the side and used the in-field to simulate going back to my very early training days where I had been in the situation of running on very firm sand at the low water's edge. I just ran down the field imagining the feeling that I had at that stage, with the sun on my back, feeling the warmth, the power, the strength, the fluidity of flow, and recalling this one day when I had run on the beach. I had no idea how far it was . . . I just kept running and running, lifting up faster and faster, and there didn't seem to be any fatigue. It was just an unbelievable flowing feeling that went on and on and on over hundreds of yards. Eventually I slowed down and jogged back. It was enough to come back into my senses, of what it felt to be strong and flowing . . . it took my awareness back inside. By the time I had done that I was back inside me and Jeff Vanderstock could do his own thing.* (Jones and Hardy, 1990a, pp. 262–263)

The crucial implication to emerge from the earlier discussion on attention and anxiety is that anxiety should not be permitted to interfere with automaticity. Non-elite athletes are more likely than elite ones to waste valuable resources in trying to consciously control movement. Eysenck's (1982, 1992) processing efficiency theory suggests that performance effectiveness can still be maintained in such circumstances, since investing greater effort can compensate for anxiety effects. However, this occurs at a cost to processing efficiency which increases the likelihood of impaired performance. Eysenck's theory has several other implications for elite performance. Firstly, elite performers could maintain their performance under pressure because they retain their attentional resources better than other performers by not worrying as much about the consequences of failure. Secondly, elite performers could have so much technical expertise that they can still perform their skills even though they have depleted attentional resources due to worry. Thirdly, elite performers may manage to avoid performance catastrophes by being able to maintain their confidence even in the face of large goal discrepancies. Fourthly, elite performers may have the motivation to sustain very high levels of effort.

Finally, the literature on mood congruent recall (Barnard and Teasdale, 1991; Eysenck and Keane, 1990) has important implications for athletes at both ends of the skill continuum. If skills are to be eventually performed in a highly pressured environment, then the implication is that they will be performed most effectively if they have been learned and then practised in a similar environment. For ethical reasons, this implication needs to be treated with caution, particularly in sports where athletes are required to perform potentially dangerous manoeuvres.

Strategies for enhancing concentration and attention control

The major factor to emerge from the section on strategies for concentration and attention control is that there are numerous strategies and techniques, together with various combinations of them, that are employed by elite performers. One of the most prominent strategies to emerge was simulation training, which involves not only physical practice but also mental rehearsal. The competition environment needs to be simulated as closely as possible, so that performers can experience and become accustomed to the external conditions and accompanying emotions. Elite athletes appear to feel that this aspect of training is very important.

Elite athletes also have very well-developed competition plans and performance routines which often incorporate process-oriented goals during skill execution. However, the available literature suggests that such goals should be holistic in nature in order to avoid interfering with automaticity (Kingston and Hardy, 1994b; Swain and Jones, 1995). Indeed, such goals could actually enhance automaticity (Kingston and Hardy, 1994b). It is also important that athletes strive to develop a similar level of automaticity in their use of psychological skills (Gould *et al.*, 1993a).

Overlearning is a prominent strategy employed by elite athletes. This may not only aid automaticity but also enhance confidence and reduce worry, thereby decreasing threats to attention control. Finally, although anecdotal accounts from elite performers used in this chapter do not offer any evidence of biofeedback being used in attentional focus training, this technique is prominent in Boutcher's (1992) model. It could be particularly valuable in acquiring basic control over physiological responses likely to influence attentional focus.

SUMMARY

This chapter has examined theories and models of attention emanating from the mainstream and sport psychology literatures, including: the issues surrounding focused versus divided attention; controlled and automatic processing; and attentional style. Particular emphasis was placed on the relationship between attention and anxiety. In this respect, several different perspectives on attention have been examined, including information processing, attentional resources, selective attentional biases, and mood congruence. Strategies for enhancing concentration and attention control were then identified and discussed. Finally, implications for research and best practice have been proposed.

8

COPING WITH ADVERSITY

CONTENTS

Much of this chapter is based on a 1994 keynote address entitled "Coping with stress: sport psychological research, theory and practice" given by the third author at the Association for the Avancememt of Applied Psychology conference, Lake Tahoe, Nevada. The authors would like to thank Mark Anshel for his help in identifying reference materials for the chapter, and for his helpful comments on an earlier draft of the chapter.

INTRODUCTION

> *When it comes to choking, the bottom line is that everyone does it. The question isn't whether you choke or not, but how—when you do choke—you are going to handle it . . . Choking is a big part of every sport, and a part of being a champion is being able to cope with it better than everyone else. (John McEnroe, in Goffi, 1984, pp. 61–62)*

This quote from tennis great John McEnroe nicely demonstrates that elite athletes, regardless of their levels of ability, must learn to cope with stress and adversity. For example, given the definition of stress discussed in Chapters 5 and 6 (a state in which some demand is placed upon an individual, who is then required to react in some way to that demand), it is not uncommon for elite athletes to have to deal with high levels of stress regarding such factors as physical injury, performance slumps, career transitions, time management, and their own and others' extremely high expectations (Gould *et al.*, 1993d; Scanlan *et al.*, 1991). In its simplest form, coping is the way elite athletes attempt to deal with these types of demands.

McEnroe's quote also reflects why psychologists in general, and sport psychologists in particular, are interested in understanding coping better. There is great interest in coping because not everyone succumbs to long-term stress (Folkman, 1992). Hence, this point is consistent with McEnroe's belief that, while all athletes experience stress and choke at times, champions are those elite performers who cope better than their less successful counterparts. Sport psychology consultants also want to learn more about coping so that they may more effectively prepare elite athletes to deal with adversity and stress.

Given the practical importance of coping to the psychological preparation of elite athletes, it is surprising that until very recently little attention was paid to coping as a sport psychological construct in its own right. Instead, if it was examined at all, it was studied as a secondary variable thought to influence the relationship between other variables of interest such as anxiety and concentration. For instance, Hanson *et al.* (1992) examined coping as one of several variables thought to influence the relationship between life stress and athletic injuries, with primary emphasis on predictors of injuries. Few investigators have examined coping in and of itself.

This chapter is designed to review the research literature on coping in sport, with particular emphasis placed on coping in elite athletes and how it may influence their performance. The chapter has six purposes. First, it is designed to increase awareness of the need for sport psychology researchers and consultants to better understand coping as a central variable affecting performance in elite athletes. Second, coping research and theory from mainstream psychology will be summarised to provide a backdrop for the emerging sport psychology coping research. Third, sport psychology coping research will be reviewed and discussed. Fourth, to further facilitate understanding of the coping process, an integrated working model of coping will be forwarded and explained. Fifth, future research directions for sport psychology coping research will be offered. And, sixth, practical implications for helping elite athletes cope more effectively with adversity will be identified.

GENERAL PSYCHOLOGY COPING RESEARCH AND THEORY

Although coping has only recently been studied in sport psychology, it has been a topic of considerable interest in the general psychology literature for the last 20 years. In fact, there is a vast, almost unwieldy, literature on coping in psychology and its various subfields. Consequently, only key conceptual points, themes, and conclusions will be discussed. In particular, definitions of coping, coping characteristics, coping categories, coping assessments, unresolved methodological and conceptual issues, and general conclusions derived from mainstream psychological research will be examined.

Defining coping

Over the years, psychologists have defined coping in a number of different ways. In fact, it has been viewed as both a behavioural action ("I exercised more in an effort to cope with the stress") and as an end result ("I coped with the pressure and made the free throw to win the game"). This is problematic because "anything and everything" becomes some aspect of coping. In an effort to sort through this definitional confusion, various definitional perspectives have evolved. These include: the animal-behavioural perspective; the psychoanalytic–ego perspective; the trait/dispositional perspective; and the transactional-process perspective (Folkman, 1992; Stone *et al.*, 1992).

The animal-behaviour perspective views coping as the degree of some stressor that an organism can tolerate (e.g. the animal coped with 20 volts of electric shock), placing little emphasis on the coping process and cognitions (Houston, 1987). For these reasons it is seldom utilised today.

The psychoanalytic perspective defines coping as unconscious defences that allow the organism to manage instinct, affect, and stress (Folkman, 1992). For instance, altruism, sublimation, and humour are considered mature forms of coping that allow the individual to deal with stress. Unfortunately, the psychoanalytic model has a number of problems, including: its sole focus on the individual; little consideration of the situation; only minor attention being paid to the problem solving functions of coping; and measurement difficulties (Folkman, 1992).

The trait/dispositional perspective views coping as a personality trait that allows an individual to deal with stress more or less effectively (e.g. an individual is a "stress monitor" or a "stress blunter"). Unfortunately, this model is plagued by many of the problems that have haunted sport personality research in general (see Vealey, 1992 for an extensive review). Hence, while it has some proponents, today it is not the dominant definitional perspective.

The dominant model for defining coping today utilises the transactional-process perspective. According to this view, coping is "a process of constantly changing cognitive and behavioural efforts to manage specific external and/or internal demands or conflicts appraised as taxing or exceeding one's resources" (Lazarus and Folkman, 1984, p. 141). One of the advantages of this view is its process orientation in that it views coping as a dynamic sequence of steps involving both cognitive and behavioural efforts to manage stress. This is important because almost all contemporary anxiety theorists view stress as a process as opposed to a static state. In addition, a wide range of responses (from situational assessments to emotion management efforts) are included in this model. Not only are personal factors seen as important in this view, but considerable emphasis is placed on understanding the situation or context in which coping takes place. Finally, no reference is made to coping outcomes, so coping includes all attempts to manage stress regardless of their effectiveness.

Given the advantages of the transactional-process view of coping and the fact that process views of stress are widely accepted in psychology and sport psychology, this is the definitional perspective that will guide this chapter. However, it is important to recognise that while dominant, this view is not universally accepted.

Primary appraisal, secondary appraisal, and coping

Like cognitive models of stress, the coping process begins with an individual's appraisal of the person-environment demands placed upon him or her. Furthermore, Lazarus and Folkman (1984) indicate that stress appraisals typically focus on harm/loss, threat, and challenge, and consist of two types: primary appraisal and secondary appraisal.

Primary appraisal consists of an evaluation of the situation to determine if the demands are likely to be stressful. In essence, the individual asks "what is at stake (for me) in this encounter?" (Folkman, 1992). Secondary appraisal focuses on judgements relative to the status and stability of resources available for dealing with stress and likely outcomes. Essentially, the person asks "what can I do (about the stressor)?" (Folkman, 1992).

Together, primary and secondary appraisal determine the quality and intensity of the stress one perceives, which in turn, influence coping. Moreover, because the stress process is continually changing, so too is the coping process. Coping shifts occur, then, because of constant stress appraisal and reappraisal, so that, as Folkman (1992, p. 30) has indicated, "coping changes as an encounter unfolds and from encounter to encounter". In summary, to understand coping, both primary and secondary appraisal must be considered. In addition, because of the ever-changing nature of stress, coping must be viewed as a constantly changing process.

Categories of coping responses

One major difficulty that coping researchers have faced is the fact that there are virtually hundreds of specific coping behaviours that can be exhibited in response to stressful situations. Moreover, because specific coping behaviours vary widely across individuals even in response to the same stressor, coping theorists and researchers have tried to derive broader categories of coping behaviours (Carpenter, 1992). In so doing, Cox and Ferguson (1991) have indicated that it has been assumed that a small number of general groupings or taxonomy categories will be functional in terms of increasing knowledge of coping.

The two most widely accepted coping categories are problem-focused and emotion-focused coping (Folkman and Lazarus, 1980). Problem-focused coping involves efforts to alter or manage the problem that is causing the stress for the individual involved. It includes such specific behaviours as information gathering, goal-setting, employing time management skills, problem solving, and adhering to an injury rehabilitation programme. Emotion-focused coping involves regulating the emotional responses that result from the problem that causes stress for the individual. It includes such specific behaviours as meditation, relaxation, and cognitive efforts to change the meaning (but not the actual problem or environment) of the situation. Folkman and Lazarus (1980) theorise that problem-focused coping is relied upon more when situations are amenable to change, and emotion-focused coping is relied upon more when situations are not amenable to change.

In addition to problem- and emotion-focused coping categorisations, other coping categories have been suggested. Endler and Parker (1990), for example, have proposed a three-factor classification which includes task-oriented coping, emotion-oriented coping, and avoidance coping. Task-oriented coping is akin to problem-focused coping and emotion-oriented coping is similar to emotion-focused coping, so the real contribution of this model is the addition of avoidance coping. For these researchers, avoidance coping involves efforts to physically or mentally disengage from the stressful situation. It is predicted that avoidance coping would be more effective for short-term stress where the consequences would go away or change at a later time, while non-avoidance would be more effective for dealing with long-term stress because the consequences would not necessarily dissipate by themselves.

Lastly, based on the work of Billings and Moos (1984), Cox and Ferguson (1991) have suggested that, in addition to problem-focused, emotion-focused and avoidance coping, an appraisal–reappraisal coping category be included. As the name suggests, this category involves efforts to appraise or reappraise the stressful problem or situation one faces. For example, appraisal–reappraisal focused coping includes logical analysis such as searching for the causes of an event, and cognitive redefinition such as acceptance and social comparison (Cox and Ferguson, 1991). Hence, coping behaviours in this category are thought to influence the amount of stress one perceives.

In summary, then, coping researchers and theorists have searched for categories of coping responses in the hope of relating these categories to important variables in the coping process. Only the most popular categories were briefly described here; numerous other coping categorisations have been proposed.

Coping dispositions

One area of some disagreement in the coping literature relates to the existence of coping styles which remain relatively constant across time and situations. Some investigators (Cox and Ferguson, 1991; Folkman, 1992; Lazarus and Folkman, 1984) argue that coping dispositions are not predictive of how individuals actually cope in naturally occurring stressful situations, while others (Carver *et al.*, 1989; Krohne, 1988) feel that coping styles are useful predictors of coping behaviour. However, a closer examination of the arguments offered by those endorsing these differing positions shows that the two positions may not be as divergent as they at first appear. Folkman (1992), for instance, feels that there are some stable aspects of the coping process which need to be identified by coping researchers. Similarly, Krohne (1988) feels that a major problem with taking a traditional trait orientation to coping is that both situational factors and stable coping dispositions need to be considered in predicting coping behaviour. This has led researchers such as Bouffard and Crocker (1992) to adopt a state-trait interaction model of coping where stable coping dispositions are examined in the light of specific situational influences.

While the debate about the usefulness of coping dispositions has not been settled, adopting a state-trait interaction approach appears to be the most productive strategy at this time. This conclusion is further supported when the predictive efficacy of state-trait anxiety models is considered, together with the recent work of Bouffard and Crocker (1992). Studying 30 individuals with physical disabilities (e.g. brain injury), these investigators asked subjects to complete Carver *et al.*'s (1989) COPE inventory on three separate occasions over a six-month period. On each occasion, subjects were asked to complete the inventory with respect to the most physically challenging activity which they had faced during the last week. Generalizability theory (Shavelson and Webb, 1991) was used to determine the consistency of use of coping strategies. Results revealed that, while at times personal styles and on a few occasions situations predicted coping, by far the biggest proportion of the variance was accounted for by person × situation interactions (over 50 per cent in most cases). Hence, it would appear that coping can best be understood by taking into account both the situation and the individual's coping disposition.

Coping assessments

The first major attempt to measure coping came when Folkman and Lazarus (1980; 1988) developed their Ways of Coping Checklist (WCC) and later revised and modified it. The WCC has been among the most popular assessments of coping strategies. The WCC measures an individual's efforts to cope with a particular stressful event. Hence, it is not a trait-like measure, but a situation-specific assessment. The original WCC was a 68-item yes–no checklist, while the later revised version is a 66-item multidimensional likert-type scale. Both versions tap a variety of behavioural and cognitive coping strategies, although the revised version is now the more popular measure. Stone *et al.* (1992) have indicated that the WCC represented a significant development in coping assessment and had a major impact on the field. However, while recognising the contribution this assessment has made to research on coping, these authors also indicate that it is not without its problems and that more attention must be given to the further development of coping assessment instruments.

Due to concerns like those voiced by Stone *et al.* (1992), other measures of coping have been developed. For example, Carver *et al.* (1989) developed an instrument called the COPE which assesses 13 conceptually distinct classes of coping strategies. Unlike the WCC which assesses situation-specific coping strategies, the COPE measures coping dispositions or preferred styles that are assumed to remain relatively fixed across time and situations. In addition, a direction set for state coping assessments (directions where subjects are asked to complete the COPE relative to a specific stressful event in their lives versus in general) is also included. Similarly, Endler and Parker (1990) developed the Multidimensional Coping Inventory (MCI), which assesses three coping styles: task-oriented coping; problem-oriented coping; and avoidance coping.

The previous measures of coping have all attempted to measure coping strategies that could cut across situations. However, a number of investigators have also sought to develop situation-specific measures of coping. Endler *et al.* (1996), for instance, have developed the Coping with Health and Injury Problems (CHIP) scale which assesses four major categories of coping (instrumental, distractive, palliative, negative emotion) specific to that setting. Similarly, Madden *et al.* (1989) and Crocker (1992) both revised the WCC to make it a sport-specific measure. However, the Madden, Kirkby and McDonald measure needs to be viewed with caution since only scant psychometric properties were published on it, while Crocker (1992) concluded that his revision of the WCC had serious psychometric problems because of a large number of items switching scales as compared to the original WCC.

Finally, Smith *et al.* (1995) recently developed a multidimensional measure of sport-specific coping, the Athletic Coping Skills Inventory-28 (ACSI-28). This instrument yields a total personal coping resource score as well as seven sport-specific subscales which include coping with adversity, peaking under pressure, goal-setting/mental preparation, concentration, freedom from worry, confidence and achievement motivation, and coachability. While initial research revealed that the scale appears to have strong psychometric properties, conceptually it seems to go beyond traditional coping strategies by looking at more general psychological coping resources (e.g. coping with adversity), as well as global psychological skills (e.g. concentration, mental preparation).

In summary, a number of coping assessment instruments presently exist and investigators can choose from dispositional or situationally based measures, as well as context-specific or noncontext-tied general measures of coping. While coping assessment improvements have definitely been made, problems still remain and further improvements in measurement and measurement validation are needed.

Coping efforts and outcomes

It is important to recognise that it is not sufficient to merely describe coping and develop coping strategy assessments; researchers must determine how coping influences stress and stress-related outcomes in individuals (Folkman, 1992). Unfortunately, assessing coping effectiveness is not as easy as one might at first think.

The first decision one must consider in examining coping effectiveness is which dependent variable(s) to use. One approach is to identify important outcomes (e.g. athletic performance, satisfaction, affect) and to assess whether the use of particular coping strategies is associated with improvements in these outcome variables. However, this approach is not free from problems (Folkman, 1992). For example, given the short-term, acute nature of most coping research (where subjects are assessed only once at a brief point in the stress coping process) outcome measures used in studies must be relatively quickly affected by coping. Because these episodic studies are over in such a short period of time, long-term outcome effects often appear non-existent, when they may simply be undetected. Similarly, the same coping strategy may simultaneously affect some outcome variables in a positive manner and others negatively. For example, in a qualitative coping study conducted by Gould *et al.* (1993b) a national champion figure skater with a history of alcoholism in her family ingested a shot of whisky before performing in order to calm her nerves. While this positively affected her performance, it eventually had negative effects on a second outcome measure—her health. It is also important that outcome measures be relevant to the subject and the situation at hand. For example, if an elite ski racer is coping with the return to competition after a serious knee injury, race finish may not be an appropriate outcome measure for the athlete. Regaining confidence that he or she can turn at race speed and ski aggressively may be a much more appropriate measure. Finally, Carpenter (1992) has indicated that, because coping is embedded within a stress process that is constantly updated via complex feedback loops, it is often difficult to determine if causal relationships exist between stress, coping, and stress-coping outcomes.

A second approach to examining coping efforts and effectiveness is not to look at coping outcomes, *per se,* but the quality of the coping exhibited. Folkman (1992) has indicated that this is important because some stressors are so powerful (e.g. a terminal disease) that an individual may cope effectively (lessen stress while alive), but may not be able to change the final outcome of the stressful setting (e.g. death). The main way the quality of coping has been examined is through the goodness-of-fit notion where coping quality is judged based on two fits: (1) the fit between reality and appraisal; and (2) the fit between appraisal and coping (Lazarus and Folkman, 1984). While there are many aspects to the goodness-of-fit notion, its basic predictions are that: (1) problem-focused coping strategies will be most effective in situations where the individual has personal control over important elements of the stressful encounter (e.g. he or she can do something about what is causing the stress); and (2) emotion-focused coping strategies will be most appropriate in stressful encounters where the individual has little control over the situation and the recurrence of stress. In such cases, since little can be done about changing the source of the stress, the individual should focus on managing his or her emotional reaction to it.

Unfortunately, the goodness-of-fit notion is difficult to test and reviewers are in disagreement over its utility with some seeing it in a positive light (e.g. Folkman *et al.*, 1991) and others judging it less favourably (e.g., Cox and

Ferguson, 1991; Dewe *et al.*, 1993). Hence, further tests using improved designs are needed to judge its utility.

Given these two views of coping efforts and outcomes, the best approach is to follow the advice of Folkman (1992) and utilise both in examining coping effectiveness. In that way, the strengths of the two approaches can be maximised and limitations offset.

Explanations for coping effectiveness

Carpenter (1992) has indicated that it is extremely important for coping researchers to pursue explanations of how coping strategies influence stress and, in turn, stress-related outcomes. He further suggests that this may occur through any number of mechanisms. In particular, he suggests that coping may: (1) counteract the effects of stress by causing improved outcomes; (2) act as a stress buffer; and (3) lower stress levels. Moreover, within the stress process, coping may influence stress by reducing the demands placed on, and perceived by, the individual, increasing resources to deal with demands, altering stress-related appraisals, and helping to minimise stress responses.

It is unfortunate that little research has been conducted to determine the likelihood and power of these mechanisms. Thus, this is a fruitful area for future coping research.

Unresolved conceptual and methodological issues in coping research

Psychologists are only now learning how to study coping and an established conceptual and methodological paradigm has not been fully identified (Perlin, 1991). Hence, there are a number of conceptual and methodological issues that those interested in better understanding coping must be aware of. Some of these issues will now be addressed.

First, coping must be studied simultaneously with stress (Perlin, 1991). This is because a "stressful encounter is a dynamic unfolding process, not a static unitary event" (Folkman and Lazarus, 1985, p. 167). Hence, it cannot be assumed that identifying single coping strategies and linking them to single stress sources at one particular time will be effective. Coping must be examined relative to ongoing stress appraisal and reappraisal (Endler *et al.*, 1993), in light of primary stressors causing secondary stressors, how different coping strategies may be related to these stressors (Perlin, 1991), and in a fashion that considers reciprocal causation between stressors and coping strategies. For this reason structural equation modelling techniques may be particularly useful in studying the transactional stress and coping process (Endler *et al.*, 1993).

A second unresolved issue in coping research focuses on the extent to which coping is situationally determined versus a stable disposition. For this reason, researchers must continue to examine individual differences in coping strategy use. The percent of variance explained by stable coping dispositions, specific situations, and the interaction of dispositions and situations must be better understood. Thus, coping researchers must adopt an interactional orientation to the study of coping.

Third, while it is important to determine and study stable coping dispositions, personality measures which are thought to influence stress and coping must also be examined (Carver *et al.*, 1989). Hardiness, locus of control, and optimism might be especially good candidates in this regard (Scheier *et al.*, 1986; Solcova and Tomanek, 1995).

Finally, our understanding of coping and how it changes over time is, for the most part, unexplored. Longitudinal studies are needed so that latent effects of coping can be examined (Perlin, 1991; Stone *et al.*, 1992). Such an approach would also allow investigators to determine how coping influences, and is influenced by, primary and secondary appraisal. Additionally, longitudinal assessments would allow researchers to determine if the nature of coping differs for given stages of the stress process (Folkman and Lazarus, 1985).

Summary

This brief overview of the general psychology research on coping leads to several major conclusions. First, coping is a complex ever-changing process and cannot be conceptualised in simple, univariate, linear, and stagnate terms. Indeed, as Folkman (1992, p. 46) has indicated, "coping is a complex phenomena [sic]. Coping research is no less so." Researchers, then, must recognise the complex, ongoing nature of coping, and design investigations that consider this complexity.

Efforts to show that coping is purely dispositional have not proved successful (Udry, 1995). While coping dispositions have been shown to exist, they must be considered in light of the specific context in which coping occurs. Examining the interaction of coping dispositions and specific stressors and situations seems especially fruitful.

While the distinction between problem- and emotion-focused coping was a major development in the field, these two categorisations alone may be too simplistic (Carver *et al.*, 1989; Endler *et al.*, 1993). Other coping categorisations such as avoidance and appraisal-reappraisal must be considered.

Two approaches exist to judging coping effectiveness: looking at coping outcomes, and assessing the quality of coping through goodness-of-fit notions. When looking at outcomes, multiple measures which are relevant to the subject should be examined over time. Goodness-of-fit tests require a detailed understanding of the coping context. At this point it time, it is advisable to examine both of these approaches simultaneously.

Finally, while coping research has great potential for helping psychologists better understand stress and derive better ways to alleviate and manage it, it should not be viewed as a panacea. Certain kinds of life experiences may be particularly resistant to individual coping efforts (Perlin, 1991).

SPORT PSYCHOLOGY COPING RESEARCH

Coping as a primary variable

Compared to the general psychology literature there is a paucity of sport psychology coping research. In fact, prior to the late 1980s there were almost no articles published on the topic. In the last five to eight years, however, increased interest in coping has occurred and research studies have begun to appear in the literature.

Before beginning the review of this literature, it is important to note that, because the focus of this chapter is on examining coping as a psychological construct in its own right, we will focus primary attention on those studies which have examined the coping process and assessed coping in a broad and comprehensive fashion. Those studies looking at coping as a single or as one of a number of possible moderator variables will not be featured here. In addition, the general literature on stress management training (the bulk of which actually represents a form of emotion-focused coping) reviewed in Chapter 6 will not be re-discussed.

Sport psychology coping studies

One of the first studies to examine coping in sport was conducted in Germany by Krohne and Hindel (1988). In this investigation, 36 top table-tennis players were administered a variety of anxiety assessments to examine the relations between general and sport specific trait anxiety, self-regulatory techniques, emotional reactions to stress situations, coping dispositions, and athletic performance. Avoidant coping dispositions (reflected by the tendency to avoid threat-relevant information) versus vigilant coping dispositions (reflected by the tendency to focus attention on threat-relevant information) were assessed. Discriminant function analysis results revealed that players who won more than 13 matches at a regional championship could be distinguished from their less successful counterparts who won 12 or less matches by a specific combination of anxiety and coping dispositions. These included intensity of cognitive anxiety reactions, the use of vigilant coping in threat situations, and frequency of avoidant coping. In particular,

Krohne and Hindel (1988) found "that general as well as sport-specific coping strategies, which were only marginally associated with anxiety reactions in low stress situations, turned out to be good predictors of success under stress" (p. 232). The authors concluded that successful top table-tennis players reduce threat and anxiety in stressful situations by using avoidant as opposed to vigilant coping, and by exhibiting less worry during competition.

The Krohne and Hindel (1988) investigation was important because it showed that coping strategies influence athletic performance in top athletes. In addition, it studied coping and stress simultaneously, and demonstrated that these variables interact.

Unfortunately, no follow-up investigations were conducted to Krohne and Hindel's study. However, a number of investigators (Crocker, 1992; Grove and Prapavessis, 1995a, b; Madden *et al.*, 1989; Madden *et al.*, 1990) have used sport-specific versions of the WCC to study coping.

In the first of these studies, Madden *et al.* (1989) administered a sport-specific ways of coping checklist to 12 male and 9 female Australian middle distance runners who were asked to indicate how they coped when experiencing a personal slump in performance. Results revealed that seeking social support, problem-focused coping, and increased effort and resolve were the most used strategies. It was also found that the runner's age was correlated with use of problem-focused coping, with older athletes more often using these strategies. Finally, significant positive correlations were found between the number of injuries a runner experienced, and general emotionality and wishful thinking coping. Severity of injury was also associated with denial coping.

In a follow-up study, Madden *et al.* (1990) used the same coping assessment instrument to measure reactions to performance slumps in 133 basketball players. A measure of stressful situations in basketball was also administered and subjects were subdivided into low, medium, and high stress groups. Results revealed that subjects reporting high stress more often used increased effort and resolve, problem-focused coping, social support seeking, and wishful thinking. Hence, the more stress subjects experienced the more they employed these coping strategies.

Although the Madden *et al.* (1989) and Madden *et al.* (1990) studies are interesting, they must be viewed with some caution for several reasons. First, in-depth psychometric properties and methodological procedures on the development of the sport-specific WCC were not reported. Second, the "slump" situations to which subjects reacted were not well delineated or standardised and, in fact, in the first study may have reflected injuries in some cases. Third, in the first study, the sample was very small and only scant statistical information was provided. Fourth, much of the evidence is correlational, not causal. Finally, conclusions from this sort of self-report retrospective study need to be treated with considerable caution because of factors such as demand characteristics and negative affectivity.

Grove and Prapavessis (1995a) followed up on the work of Madden and his associates by examining coping with performance slumps in 142 high performance Australian baseball players. In a related study (Grove and Prapavessis, 1995b), these researchers had established scale reliability and conducted a factor analysis on a sport-specific version of the WCC. Correlational results from the baseball study revealed that emotion-focused coping was positively related to perceived frequency of batting slumps and slump-related stress. Problem-focused coping was not found to be related to batting slumps. However, problem-focused coping was associated with batting self-efficacy in such a way that players with high self-efficacy reported using more problem-focused coping. The authors concluded that efforts to increase batting self-efficacy may also promote problem-focused (adaptive) coping when an athlete faces a batting slump.

Finally, Grove and Prapavessis (1995b) looked at slumps in athletic performance using their sport-specific WCC. In particular, these investigators examined how athletes coped with performance slumps, as well as self-handicapping, a self-protective attributional strategy where one proactively increases responsibility for success and lessens personal responsibility for failure by making external attributions (excuses). In one of the studies reported, 141 female athletes representing a variety of sports served as subjects and completed the WCC for sport, as well as a measure of self-handicapping. Comparison of how high versus low self-handicappers coped with slumps revealed that high self-handicappers more often used the emotion-focused strategies of detachment/avoidance and wishful thinking, and less often used the task-focused strategies of cognitive problem solving and positive emphasis. These results were generally consistent with a previously reported study using 65 male athletes (published in the same article) where Endler and Parker's (1990) Coping Inventory for Stressful Situations was used. Based on the findings, the authors imply that when experiencing a slump athletes with strong self-handicapping tendencies are likely to adopt unproductive coping strategies such as disengagement and fantasy. They may also avoid the use of cognitive problem solving (e.g. task-focused mental preparation strategies) and positive emphasis coping. Those with undesirable self-handicapping tendencies, then, may benefit from being taught more productive coping strategies for use when they are experiencing declines in performance.

In one of the most methodologically sound ways of coping studies conducted to date, Crocker (1992) examined how competitive athletes cope with stress. Male and female athletes (N = 237) representing a variety of sports completed a 68-item modified version of the WCC. Findings revealed that the athletes used a wide variety of coping strategies. Furthermore, factor analysis showed that the coping strategies could be classified into eight separate dimensions: active coping; problem-focused coping; seeking social support; positive reappraisal; self-control; wishful thinking; self-blame; and detachment. Based on his findings, Crocker (1992) suggested that active coping and problem-focused coping are highly adaptive strategies which athletes in slumps should utilise to alter the environmental circumstances that contribute to their stress. Wishful thinking and detachment, however, if continued over time, could be maladaptive. As previously mentioned, Crocker also identified major problems with the psychometric properties of the WCC and adaptations to it—most notably a lack of internal factor consistency. He concluded that the fact that an exploratory factor analysis needs to be performed each time the WCC is used is a very limiting factor, and improved instruments must be developed.

Taking a different tack, Gould *et al.* (1993a, b) utilised in-depth qualitative interviews to examine the coping strategies used by US Olympic wrestlers and US national champion figure skaters. In the first study, all 20 members of the 1988 US Olympic wrestling team were interviewed and asked about how they tried to cope with the adversity associated with unforeseen events and negative aspects of expectations at the Seoul Olympics. Content analysis of the findings revealed that the wrestlers employed four major categories of coping. The largest category was thought-control strategies, cited by 80 per cent of the wrestlers, and made up of subcategories dealing with blocking distractions, perspective taking, positive thinking, coping thoughts, and prayer. For example, one wrestler talked about blocking distractions in the following way:

> *I focus on having tunnel vision . . . I eliminate anything that's going to interfere with me. I don't have any side doors, I guess, for anyone to come into. I make sure that nothing interferes with me.* (Gould *et al.*, 1993a, p. 88)

Similarly, another wrestler described how he used perspective taking to cope when he said:

> *A lot of times I just think about what other people have to deal with. You know, handicapped men or starving men or something like that and just kind of put it into the total perspective. Knowing that, hey, I am doing pretty good over here.* (Gould *et al.*, 1993a, p. 88)

A second general category, task-focused strategies, emerged and included narrow, more immediate focus, and concentrating on goals. This category was cited by 40 per cent of the participants. Examples of task focus strategies included:

> *I just stayed positive and focused on putting it behind me and not thinking about it [the loss] anymore . . . and then just started thinking about the next match; and I just tried to focus on my individual, I do best when I prepared myself and know what I need to do individually . . . You just try to focus on your matches.* (Gould *et al.*, 1993a, p. 89)

The final two general categories of coping were behavioural-based strategies (consisting of such subcategories as changing or controlling one's environment, and following a set routine), and emotional control strategies (consisting of arousal control and visualisation strategies). Each of these were cited by 40 per cent of the wrestlers.

In accordance with the notions of Folkman and Lazarus (1985) and Compas (1987), it was concluded that the coping efforts of these athletes reflected an ever-changing complex process involving multiple strategies, often used simultaneously and in combination with one another.

In addition to identifying the coping strategies used by the wrestlers, comparisons of strategy use were made between medal- and non-medal-winning wrestlers, but no differences were found to emerge. Interestingly, however, the more successful wrestlers seemed to have their strategies so well learned that they were automated. As one highly successful Olympic wrestler said:

> *Something I've always practiced is to never let anything interfere with what I'm trying to accomplish at a particular tournament. So what I try to do is if something is trying to bother me, it's an automatic effect for me to completely empty my mind and concentrate on the event coming up . . . My coping strategy is just to completely eliminate it from my mind, and I guess I'm blessed to be able to do that.* (Gould *et al.*, 1993, p. 90)

It was suggested that the idea of having coping skills "automatised" might be particularly important for athletes to develop, since coping must often be accomplished in short time periods in sports competitions. This issue is clearly worthy of further study.

In the second study, Gould *et al.* (1993b) interviewed 17 current or former US national champion figure skaters for the purpose of identifying and describing the coping strategies they employed, and to examine the relationship between the use of these coping strategies and particular sources of stress. Categories of coping strategies identified by at least 40 per cent of the skaters included:

- rational thinking and self-talk (testing/accepting/dealing with the reality of the situation, self-referenced focus, taking a rational perspective of oneself and skating);

- positive focus and orientation (positive thinking and self-talk, positive belief in one's ability, programme and goals, negative to positive self-appraisal);
- social support (assistance from sport/clinical psychologist, support from coach, support from family and friends, unconditional love and support);
- time management and prioritisation (making time for personal interests and growth, time utilisation, day-to-day goal focus);
- precompetitive mental preparation and anxiety management (mental practice and reflections, narrow focus, precompetitive ritual, physical relaxation strategies, acknowledging and dealing with nervousness);
- training hard and smartly (hard-work ethic, taking responsibility for and keeping an open attitude towards one's training);
- isolation and deflection (not letting troublesome things get to me, avoiding and screening the media); and
- ignoring the stressor (ignoring at the appropriate time, ignoring).

An example of a quote that was classified as a self-referenced rational thinking and self-talk coping strategy was:

> *Then I decided after our defeat that there was so much negativism going on, as far as judges and this and that and negative comments and I felt, "listen, if I want to skate, I have to skate, I have to do it for myself. I'm not out here to do it for anyone else or for the USA I am here to do it for myself. I've worked this hard'" I kind of got angry about it and I think that's where my views changed.* (Gould *et al.*, 1993b, p. 456)

Similarly, a skater spoke about taking time for himself (a time management and prioritisation coping dimension subcategory) when he indicated:

> *I used to zip out of town every weekend just to get away. I would go to a friend's house. I'd say, "I'm out of here for the weekend. I can't deal with this [skating] anymore." That really helped a lot.* (Gould *et al.*, 1993b, p. 458)

Another skater spoke about prioritising time in the following manner:

> *You have to learn how to say no sometimes. You have to get your priorities straight, and I feel that it's something that every new champion does not learn until they have been through it for a season.* (Gould *et al.*, 1993b, p. 458)

Finally, a skater discussed a mental preparation and anxiety management strategy as follows:

> *I did a lot of visualization. A lot of that . . . It's a coping strategy. It felt like you did more run-throughs. You went through the program perfectly, more times. So, it gave you a sense of security and understanding about what was to take place and how it was supposed to go. It just gives you a calmer, more serene way.* (Gould *et al.*, 1993b, p. 458)

A number of sources of stress were also identified by the skaters. For example, the psychological demands placed upon the skaters' resources, relationship issues, etc. Furthermore, when the relationship between coping strategies and these specific sources of stress was examined, it was found that while some coping strategies were related to several sources of stress, in general, different coping strategies were used to deal with different stress sources. For instance, skaters experiencing sources of stress involving relationship issues usually used positive focus and orientation, social support, striving for a positive working relationship with partner, isolation and deflection, and rational thinking and self-talk as coping strategies; while skaters experiencing excessive psychological demands usually used precompetitive mental preparation and anxiety management, positive focus orientation, and training hard and smartly as coping strategies.

Based on these findings, it was concluded that the skaters did not employ one or two "simple" coping strategies. Rather, as was the case in the previous study of Olympic wrestlers, the skaters employed a variety of strategies which differed depending on the source of stress. This clearly supports Lazarus and Folkman's (1984) transaction model of coping. It was also interesting to note that both problem and emotion-focused coping strategies were used, as well as adaptive (e.g. social support, rational thinking, and self-talk) and maladaptive (e.g. alcohol consumption, bulimic behaviours) strategies. Finally, based on the findings of both the skating and wrestling studies, it was concluded that Carver *et al.*'s (1989) COPE subscales reflect the coping categories which emerged through these content analyses better than the subscales of other coping inventories. Hence, at this point, the COPE inventory may be the best quantitative instrument to assess coping in the sport context.

Finch (1994) used the COPE instrument to examine the coping–performance relationship in 148 collegiate female softball players. The results revealed that the athletes used a variety of coping strategies to deal with the stress experienced during the season that they were assessed. Higher subject competitive anxiety was found to be positively related to maladaptive and emotion-focused coping, and negatively related to adaptive and problem focused coping. Coping was found to be significantly related to performance, but only accounted for a small percentage of the variance (from 3 to 6 per cent). In particular, the maladaptive coping strategy of mental disengagement was associated with poorer batting performance, while a maladaptive strategy of denial was associated with poorer fielding performance. Based on a self-report rating of how easy it was to use coping strategies, more effective copers were also found to be significantly more likely to have automated coping strategies. It is important to note here, however, that while maladaptive strategies were associated with poorer performance, the adaptive/maladaptive coping strategy distinction in this and other studies is conceptually a thorny issue. This results from the fact that maladaptive strategies are determined by their effects on certain outcome variables (e.g. the effect of drinking alcohol on health), and because of this may in one situation be seen as adaptive and in another situation be seen as maladaptive. This makes the adaptive/maladaptive distinction somewhat fluid and dependent on the particular context of coping.

In another study examining the coping–performance relationship, Smith and Christensen (1995) administered the ACSI-28 to 104 minor league baseball players. The results revealed that the psychological skills measured by the ACSI (especially confidence and achievement motivation) were significantly related to hitting and pitching performance, as well as survival in professional baseball 2 and 3 years after the assessments were made. In addition to the total scale score, the authors noted that the confidence and achievement motivation subscales were also the most consistently related to batting and fielding efficacy. In the Year 2 follow-up analysis, the survivors (those who were asked to stay with the baseball club versus those who were "cut") reported *lower* perceived ability to cope with adversity subscale scores. The authors explained this unexpected finding as a possible attempt at positive impression management by the nonsurviving athletes. Hence, while these results are encouraging in that they show a significant coping–performance link, they must be viewed with caution because of the likelihood that some subjects responded in a socially desirable manner. In addition, the ACSI-28 may not be a very pure measure of coping strategies, since it also measures other psychological resources related to coping such as confidence and achievement motivation.

In a series of experimental studies Anshel and his associates (Anshel, 1990; Anshel *et al.*, 1993; Anshel *et al.*, 1990) examined whether an educational-intervention programme, also called COPE, was effective in helping athletes deal with stress and improve performance. The programme focuses on a number of psychological techniques such as relaxation and attentional focusing to help athletes learn how to control stress. The aims of the programme are to help the athlete control emotions (C), organise input (O), plan responses (P), and execute skills (E) in an efficient and effective manner. Hence, it is similar to the multimodal stress management programmes discussed in Chapter 6. Like those programmes, initial research (Anshel, 1990; Anshel *et al.*, 1993; Anshel *et al.*, 1990) examining the COPE intervention model has been promising. However, more research with larger samples is needed.

Although the focus of this review has been on studies which have examined coping as a primary (as opposed to a moderator) variable, Smith *et al.*'s (1990a) investigation of coping as a moderator variable is important because it demonstrates the importance of examining coping in relation to the complex stress process. In particular, the focus of Smith *et al.*'s (1990a) investigation was psychological factors associated with the incidence of athletic injuries in 250 male and 201 female high school athletes. More specifically, this well-controlled, prospective study examined the relationship between life stress, social support, coping skills, and athletic injuries. Of particular interest was the finding that no relationship was found between life stress, social support, coping skills and athletic injuries, when all the subjects were examined. However, when an "at risk" subpopulation, comprising athletes with low social support and low coping skills, was examined, a significant relationship emerged between life stress and injuries. This suggests that coping skills are likely to exert interactive rather than simply additive effects upon outcome variables, and may not affect outcome variables in all subjects. Consequently, certain groups of subjects may be more important to study than others; for example, those who have coping skills deficits, or deficits in other stress-related resources. The findings also demonstrate the complexity of the coping process, and the importance of researchers examining the complex interactions that occur between stress and coping factors.

Summary

Although sport psychology research on coping is only just beginning to develop, some patterns have already emerged in the findings. First, the sport psychology research to date demonstrates that coping is a complex, multidimensional process. Multiple strategies are used by athletes, often in combination with one another. Second, a wide variety of different strategies are used by athletes. These include both problem- and emotion-focused coping strategies, and adaptive and maladaptive ones. The finding that elite athletes use maladaptive strategies is important because, based on their performance capabilities, it has often been erroneously assumed that elite performers do not have difficulty in coping with stress. Third, Gould *et al.* (1993b) found that different coping strategies were used to deal with different sources of stress. Fourth, research has shown that a significant relationship exists between increased anxiety and increased coping efforts, although the causal nature of this relationship remains to be demonstrated. Fifth, there is some evidence to show that coping efforts are associated with variations in athlete performance. Sixth, some studies have shown that having coping strategies so well learned that they can be executed in an automatic fashion is associated with superior performance. Seventh, research suggests that some athletes may use maladaptive coping strategies when experiencing slumps. Finally, the work of Anshel and his colleagues supports the stress management research reviewed in Chapter 6 by showing that athletes can be taught to cope more effectively with stress.

A WORKING MODEL OF COPING IN SPORT

Because of the diverse and complex nature of coping, it is difficult to obtain a complete understanding of it. Hence, it can be hard to derive implications for best practice and to plan future research. One way to form a more comprehensive understanding of coping is to try to integrate the conceptual and empirical research on coping into a model. We have developed such a stress-coping model. The coping aspects of the model are actually an adaptation of a coping model developed by Folkman *et al.* (1991), while the stress aspects of the model are an adaptation of McGrath's (1970) model of stress. In addition, both the general and sport psychology coping literature reviewed in this chapter have also influenced the model's development.

For ease of explanation the model will be presented in two parts; Part 1 focuses on stress-appraisal and Part 2 focuses on coping. After discussing the two parts separately, they will be integrated to produce the total model.

Part 1: Stress appraisal

Figure 8.1 depicts Part 1 of the model. An inspection of Box A of this figure shows that the stress-appraisal process begins with some physical or psychological environmental demand being placed on the athlete (e.g. an athlete must swim a career-best time to qualify for the Olympic team). However, whether or not environmental demands are perceived as stressful depends on how the athlete appraises the situation (Box B). Moreover, in accordance with the ideas of Folkman and Lazarus (1985), appraisal is made relative to threat, harm/loss, and challenge, and takes two forms: primary appraisal and secondary appraisal. Often when threat or harm is perceived by an athlete, global stress results (Circle C.1). However, Folkman *et al.* (1991) emphasised that, in helping individuals to cope better, it is important to identify exactly what is causing the stress (Box C.2). Furthermore, in accordance with the goodness-of-fit notion, it is also important to identify whether the individual athlete can have any influence on the source of stress; i.e. whether it is controllable or uncontrollable (Level C.3). Following appraisal, the psychophysiological state will reflect varying levels of cognitive and somatic arousal and activation (Box D). Finally, stress appraisal is influenced by a variety of personality and motivational factors such as trait anxiety, optimism, self-confidence, and self-esteem (Box E).

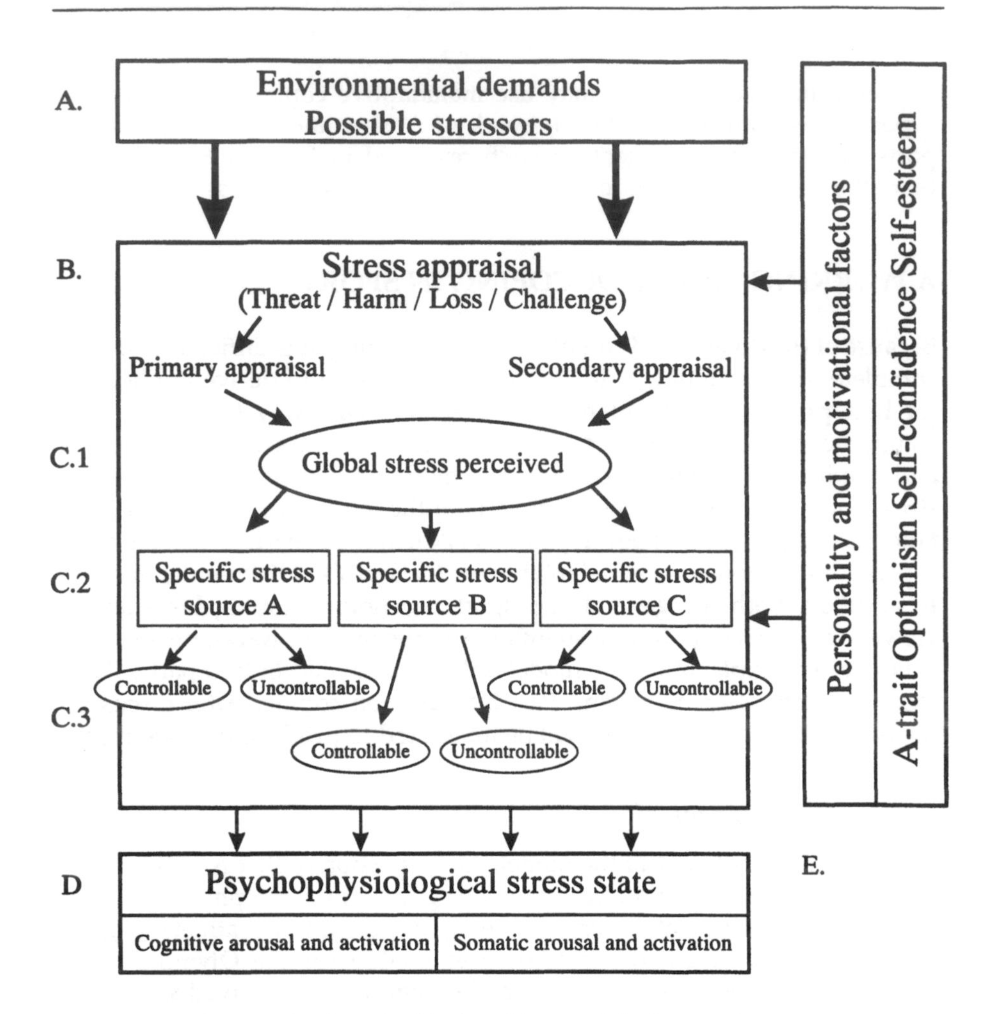

Figure 8.1: Part 1 of the working model of coping in sport

Part 2: Coping

If a psychophysiological stress state is perceived by the athlete as a result of the appraisal process, coping or attempts to effectively deal with the perceived stress are initiated (see Box A, Figure 8.2). While specific coping behaviours or strategies (Box C) may directly influence coping outcomes such as performance or health (Box E), these behaviours can also be classified into various coping behaviour categories such as emotion-focused coping, problem-focused coping, avoidance coping, and appraisal/reappraisal coping (Circle B). Circle D contains the coping–situation match which focuses upon the adaptive or maladaptive nature of specific coping resources, and whether goodness-of-fit exists between the specific coping

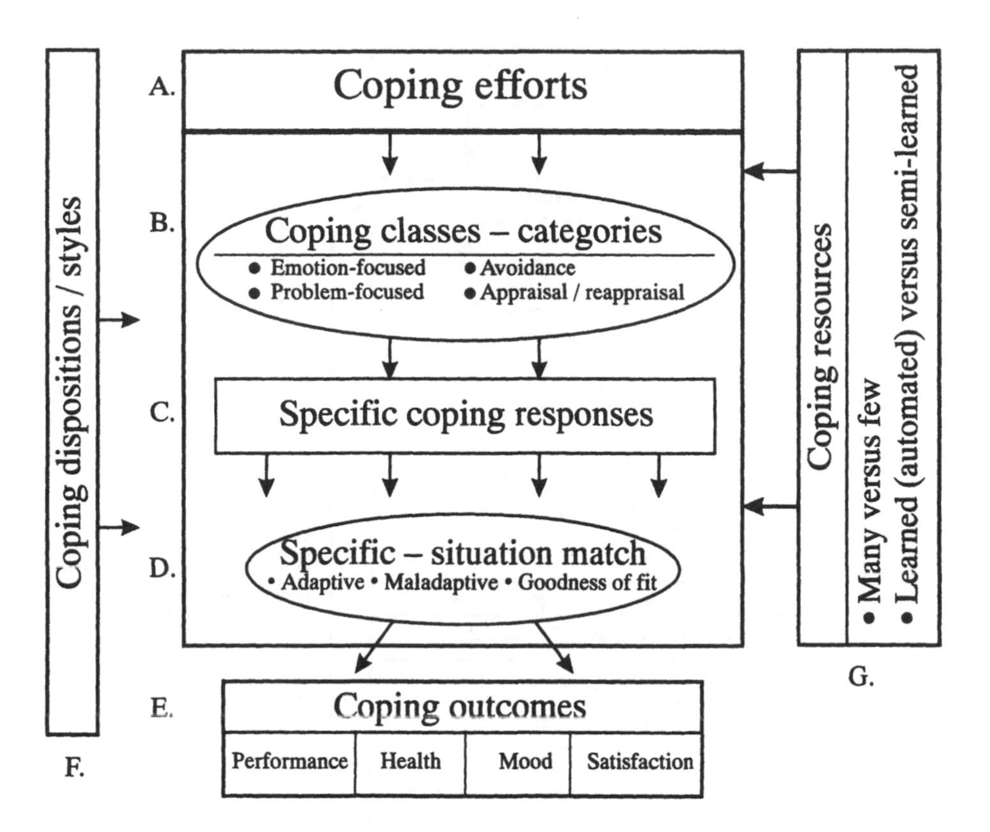

Figure 8.2: Part 2 of the working model of coping in sport

behaviours used and the specific stressors identified in Part 1 of the model. For example, coping with the stress which resulted from a disagreement with a coach by ignoring the situation when in fact it needed to be dealt with immediately, would be considered maladaptive. Similarly, using a problem-focused coping behaviour in a situation which cannot be changed would be a poor fit in goodness-of-fit terms. The specific coping behaviour and situation match will in turn have an influence on coping outcomes such as performance, mood, and satisfaction (see Box E).

Lastly, coping efforts are influenced by each individual athlete's coping dispositions or preferred styles of coping (Box F), and the coping resources the athlete has at his or her disposal (e.g. social support sources), as well as how well learned or automated specific coping responses are (Box G).

The integrated model of coping

Figure 8.3 integrates Parts 1 and 2 of the model into the full model. Given the previous explanations of Parts 1 and 2, only three additional comments need

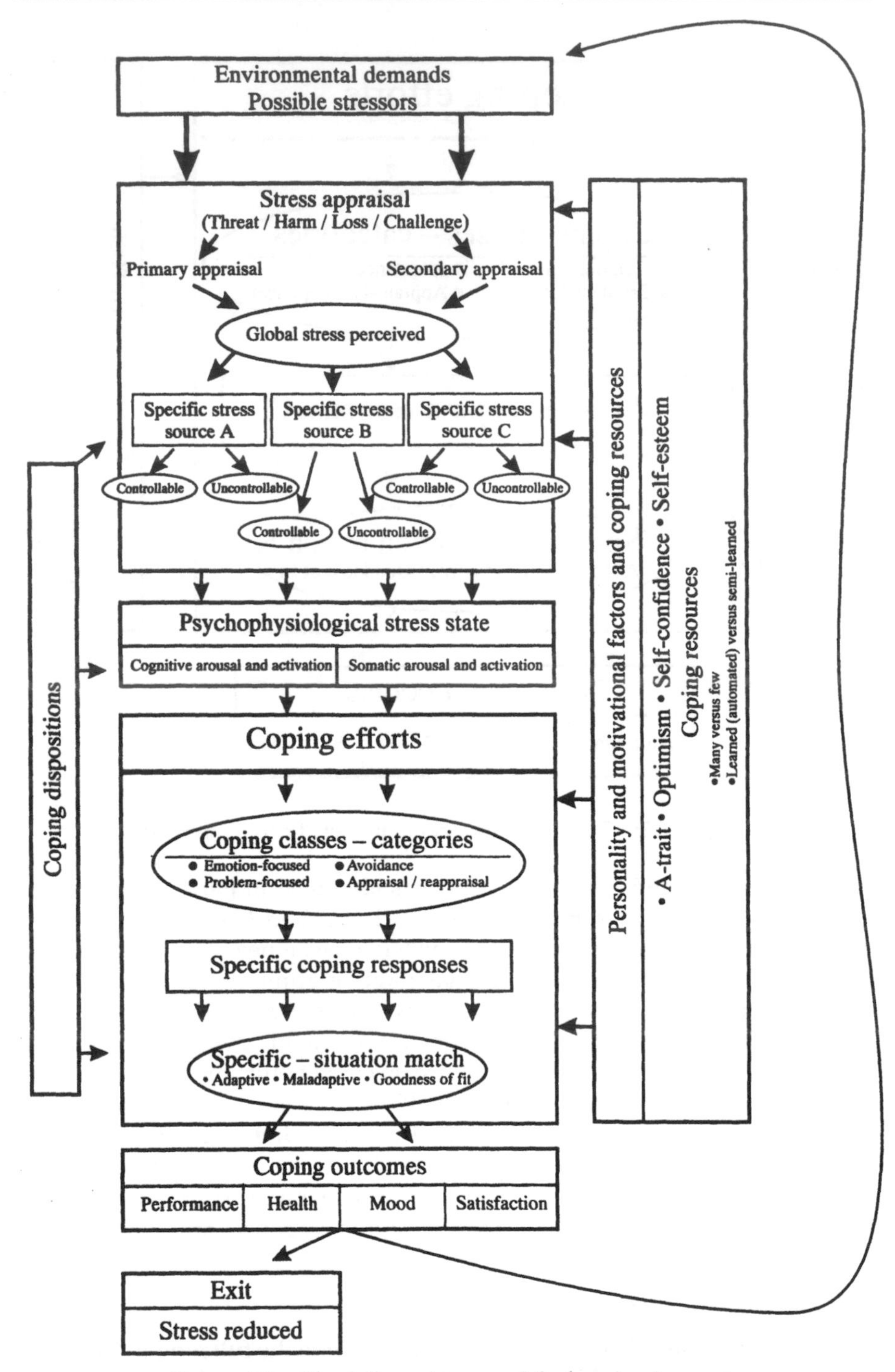

Figure 8.3: The full working model of coping in sport

to be made. First, at the bottom of the model an exit box exists. This represents what happens when a coping effort is successful and reduces stress. Stress is no longer appraised and coping efforts are no longer needed. An arrow from the bottom of the model also leads back to the environmental demand box at the top of the model. This arrow represents the closed-loop nature of the model and shows how the model will continue in a circular fashion until the stress is alleviated, or perhaps in some cases the frustration of not being able to cope becomes an additional source of stress.

Second, the large box to the right of the model integrates personality, motivational, and coping resource factors (which were presented in separate boxes in Figures 8.1 and 8.2). These factors were integrated into one box here because they would appear to influence both stress appraisal and coping efforts. Finally, while only one feedback loop is shown in the model (for simplicity reasons) it is likely that a number of the model's components would reciprocally influence each other leading to multiple feedback loops.

Summary

To help integrate the diverse and complex literature on coping with adversity, a working model of coping has been presented. The stress appraisal part of the model focused on: the primary and secondary appraisal of environmental demand; the perception of global stress; the controllability of the source of stress; and the resulting psychophysiological stress state comprising cognitive and somatic arousal and activation. Personality and motivational factors such as trait anxiety, optimism, and self-esteem were also identified as potential influences on all aspects of the appraisal process. The coping part of the model reflects the response to a stress appraisal, and focuses on general coping categories and classes (e.g. problem- versus emotion-focused coping), specific coping responses, and the coping by situation match. All these factors in turn affect various coping outcomes. Moreover, coping efforts are also influenced by coping dispositions and resources. Finally, the model functions in a circular fashion whereby coping outcomes feed back into stress appraisals of the environmental demand.

IMPLICATIONS FOR FUTURE RESEARCH

Because coping is such a new area of research for sport psychologists there are many questions needing further study. In fact, there are more areas needing study than can be addressed in the space available here. However, we will address what we think are the most important questions in need of further study. Then, several important methodological concerns that future researchers must address in order to answer these questions will be discussed.

The most important questions for future research

Seven of the most important coping research questions for future research are:

(1) What are the psychological characteristics of those athletes who effectively cope with major setbacks?
(2) What are the major factors influencing coping?
(3) Do coping dispositions exist and, if so, what effect do they have on stress appraisal, coping behaviours, and coping outcomes?
(4) What is the relationship between coping behaviours and coping outcomes?
(5) How does coping influence stress and athletic outcome variables?
(6) How are coping behaviours, resources, and dispositions developed?
(7) Can coping skills be taught?

Each of these questions will be briefly discussed below.

One of the most important topics for future coping researchers to examine is the distinguishing characteristics of those athletes who cope most effectively with stress. Since Folkman (1992) has indicated that not everyone succumbs to the adverse effects of stress, this topic can be best addressed by comparing individuals who cope more effectively with major setbacks in sport (such as season-ending injuries, or major performance failures) against individuals who cope less effectively with such events. Important sub-issues relating to this general question include an examination of whether, compared with less effective copers, more effective ones (a) use different coping strategies; (b) employ a larger number of strategies; (c) are more flexible (versus rigid) in their use of coping strategies; (d) use more adaptive (versus maladaptive) strategies; and (e) have their strategies better learned or automated. For time and cost efficiency reasons, retrospective designs may at first be a productive way to examine these issues. However, after key variables have been identified, prospective designs where causal links between variables can be established, such as that employed by Smith *et al.* (1990a), will be needed.

Related to this general question is a finding from health-related coping research. Ingledew *et al.* (1996) found that hospital workers who were stressed about the imminent closure of the hospital, generally used any strategies that they had "to hand" to deal with their stress, and that these strategies were all equally effective, so long as they were not avoidance strategies. While it would be foolish to even consider generalising from health-related research to elite performance, the question of which, if any, *particular* coping strategies are required for elite performance remains an interesting one.

A second important area for future coping research focuses on identifying the major factors which influence coping efforts. For example, are the coping strategies used by elite athletes influenced by personality dispositions such as trait anxiety, optimism, hardiness, and perceptions of control? The initial sport psychology coping research which has examined self-handicapping (Grove and Prapavessis, 1995b) and trait anxiety (Finch, 1994) provides some evidence that personality factors play an important role in coping (cf. also Carpenter, 1992). Moreover, this type of research will be important in determining whether certain types of individuals are predisposed to using certain classes of coping strategies (e.g., adaptive-maladaptive; problem-focused versus emotion-focused; approach-avoidance, etc.).

One area of controversy in the general psychology coping literature is whether coping dispositions exist. Hence, an important area of further study for sport psychology coping researchers is the study of coping dispositions. Two questions seem paramount in this area. First, can stable coping dispositions or styles be identified in elite athletes? And, second, if these dispositions are found to exist, do they have an influence on stress appraisal, coping behaviours, and coping outcome variables?

A bottom line for most elite athletes and coaches is performance improvement and success. An important issue needing further study, then, is the relationship between coping behaviours and coping outcomes, especially athletic performance. Sub-issues falling under this general question include: determining whether classes of coping behaviours are related to coping outcomes; testing the goodness-of-fit hypothesis; assessing whether automaticity of coping responses is related to athletic performance; and, examining whether athletes who have more coping behaviours at their disposal experience more positive outcomes. The examination of possible interactions amongst the variables identified in these sub-issues is also important.

If coping theory and research is to advance, explanations for coping must be sought. For example, does coping lower stress or buffer its effects? Unfortunately, little research has been conducted on this type of question. For this reason, future researchers need to design investigations that explain how and why coping behaviours influence stress and coping outcomes. Testing the efficacy of Carpenter's (1992) theoretical contentions would be a good starting point: that is, does coping buffer stress, counteract stress effects by improving outcomes, directly remove stress and therefore reduce its impact, and/or affect stress appraisal?

The sixth area of coping that future research might focus upon is the development of coping behaviours, resources, and dispositions in elite athletes. The best way to do this would be through longitudinal studies that examine elite athletes across their careers, tracking their coping resources from the junior through the senior elite levels.

Finally, one of the most important issues to be addressed is the extent to which coping skills can be taught to athletes. Intervention studies are urgently needed and both nomothetic and idiographic case study methods would be useful approaches to employ in examining this topic. Sub-issues related to this general question include: does teaching athletes to anticipate potential stressors that they may face at a major competition (and appropriate coping strategies) lead to reduced stress and more effective coping? is it more effective to develop multiple, or single coping, strategies? and, can athletes be taught goodness-of-fit notions?

Methodological issues of concern

Investigators interested in conducting future sport psychology coping research must be cognisant of several methodological issues of concern. The first of these focuses on the need for better coping assessment instruments. Crocker (1992) has identified serious problems with the stability of the WCC and its sport-specific versions. For example, in factor analysing a sport-specific version of the WCC, Grove and Prapavessis (1995b) found a six-factor structure, while Madden *et al.* (1989) reported an eight-factor structure. Crocker (1992) concluded that an exploratory factor analysis is needed whenever the WCC is used. Because it has good psychometric properties, both dispositional and state-like directional options, and matches most of the elite athlete coping strategies derived in the Gould *et al.* (1993a, b) studies, the COPE instrument may be one of the better quantitative measures to use at this time. However, it should be noted that while this inventory has generally good psychometric properties, Finch (1994) found that several of the smallest factors combined together in her study, and an examination of Carver *et al.*'s (1989) original psychometrics for the scale showed that the decision to label these as separate factors was made on rather weak statistical grounds. For this reason, the COPE factor structure should also be checked initially.

In addition to using the COPE, it would be useful to compare general coping measures like the COPE with situation-specific assessments. For instance, those studying coping with athletic injuries might want to examine how inventories like the COPE correlate with Endler *et al.*'s (1993) CHIP scale. If high correlations result from such comparisons, there would be no need to develop sport-specific measures. However, if only moderate or poor correlations result, it might prove useful to develop sport-specific coping measures and determine if they are better predictors of coping in athletic injury situations.

It would be a mistake to only assess coping via quantitative instruments; qualitative assessments should continue to be used as well. These assessments may prove especially useful when examining questions such as how coping behaviours develop, or when conducting individual athlete coping case studies. In addition, it may be particularly useful to combine qualitative and quantitative measures. For instance, the goodness-of-fit notion has proved particularly hard to test with quantitative measures as it is often difficult to identify enough information about the context of a stressor to determine whether it is controllable or not. Using qualitative interviews to assess specific stressors and controllability, and quantitative assessments to measure coping strategies, might prove to be a more productive approach to examining this issue.

A second methodological issue which is related to coping assessment is the need to develop reliable and valid ways of measuring the degree to which coping skills are well learned or automatised. This is especially important since the notion of automating coping strategies arose out of retrospective qualitative studies that required performers to use declarative knowledge to describe procedural phenomena; that is to say, the athletes had to verbalise about how they did things which were automatic. Such methodologies have serious limitations when used in this context (Brewer *et al.*, 1991), so that further research into this phenomenon using alternative methods is clearly desirable. Not only would such measures facilitate sport psychology coping research, but a need exists to examine the issue in the general psychology coping literature since it has not yet been examined in that more general context.

A third important methodological concern facing coping researchers is the need to move from episodic, "one off" assessments to more process-oriented, longitudinal assessments. This is important because coping is thought to be a constantly changing process, which cannot be accurately reflected by a single "snapshot" taken at one point in time. Time series designs where multiple assessments of coping and stress are taken must be employed. Case studies tracking athletes' stress, coping, and performance efforts over an extended period of time may also be helpful.

Finally, in a related coping process issue, it is important that coping researchers move to more sophisticated statistical analyses that can examine the complex stress-coping relationship. For example, structural equation modelling is well-suited to the examination of the stress coping process and might be employed more often than it has been in the past.

Summary

The most important coping questions in need of study have been identified. In addition, methodological issues of concern were discussed. These included the need to: develop better coping instruments; develop reliable and valid ways of measuring the degree to which coping skills are well learned or automatised; move from episodic, "one off" assessments to more process-oriented, longitudinal assessments; and, employ more sophisticated statistical techniques that are better suited to examining the complex stress coping process.

IMPLICATIONS FOR BEST PRACTICE

The literature that has been reviewed on coping offers a number of implications for guiding best practice. First, both sport and general psychology coping research has clearly shown that coping is a complex process. Hence, it is most unlikely that any single kind of coping will be appropriate for all situations (McCrae, 1984). What is interesting, however, is that when working with elite athletes who are experiencing stress problems many sport psychology consultants almost automatically prescribe traditional stress management techniques such as progressive relaxation. While research discussed in this book has clearly demonstrated that these techniques can be effective in managing stress, they are predominantly emotion-focused in their orientation. As Carpenter (1992) has indicated, such blanket prescriptions leave other potentially effective stress management avenues (such as the diverse array of problem-focused coping techniques that have been discussed in this chapter) unexplored. For this reason, teaching a relatively broad spectrum of coping strategies to athletes to use in different situations, and for different sources of stress, may be a better option.

Given the above, it is also important for sport psychology consultants and coaches to understand the integrated stress coping model presented in this chapter, and to consider it when assisting elite athletes who experience problems in coping with adversity. In accordance with the work of Folkman *et al.* (1991), the first implication that comes from the model is the need to identify the specific source(s) of stress involved in the appraisal process. Identifying the specific causes of stress is especially important when problem-focused coping strategies are the most appropriate response in the situation.

In addition to identifying the specific sources of stress involved, our model suggests that it is important for the consultant to determine if the stress source is controllable or uncontrollable. If the athlete has little control over the stress source then emotion-focused coping strategies (e.g. centring, or relaxation techniques to manage stress) may be most appropriate. However, if the athlete can potentially change or influence the stressor (e.g. reduce time management concerns by learning to prioritise tasks and better manage time), then problem-focused coping responses may be a more productive alternative.

A third implication coming from the model deals with the importance of evaluating the effectiveness of coping efforts by looking at multiple coping outcome variables. Hence, while performance is certainly a "bottom line" for most elite athletes, satisfaction, health, and mood states are all important outcomes as well, since these factors can have profound effects on motivation, training, and psychological well-being. Evaluation also needs to take place relative to the coping response–situation match. Consultants and coaches need to determine if the strategies employed are potentially maladaptive in the long term, and if they are appropriate given the situational causes of stress.

Finally, the model emphasises the importance of considering coping dispositions, coping resources, and personality and motivational factors which may influence the coping process. For example, the initial sport psychology research by Grove and Prapavessis (1995b) and Finch (1994) showed that athletes with high self-handicapping orientations and high trait anxiety have a tendency to use maladaptive coping strategies more often. Similarly, Cox and Ferguson (1991) have emphasised the important roles that hardiness and internal locus of control may play in the coping process, while Scheier *et al.* (1986) have emphasised the importance of optimism in this same process. Consequently, as Krohne (1988) has concluded, effective coping should integrate cognitive appraisals, situational assessments, coping dispositions, and personality considerations.

In addition to the implications derived directly from the model, there are a number of other things that coaches and consultants can do to facilitate coping in elite athletes. These include: facilitating awareness of the need for coping; teaching coping strategies to athletes; helping athletes learn when to cope; eliminating coping myths; and beginning coping training early. Each of these will be briefly discussed below.

One important role that sport psychology consultants can play is to increase athlete awareness of the need for coping with stress at major competitions. While at first sight this may not seem to be necessary, Gould *et al.* (1993a) found that world-class wrestlers experienced a number of unforeseen events (e.g. perceived bad calls from referees, travel problems) that influenced them during their Olympic experience. Interestingly, the wrestlers had experienced all these events before but did not expect them to occur at "their" Olympics. This suggests that by discussing possible unforeseen stressful events (e.g. dealing with the media) and developing appropriate coping strategies for dealing with such potential stressors, athletes will be better prepared to cope. Indeed, while this approach has yet to be examined empirically, the authors have had good success with it in their consultancy work with elite athletes involved in a variety of sports.

Not only do elite athletes need to understand the need for coping, but they must identify effective coping strategies for dealing with stressful situations. One alarming finding in the Gould *et al.* (1993b) national champion skating study was the that some athletes were occasionally unable to identify strategies to cope with certain stressors. Sport psychology consultants may help in this regard. In fact, one strategy that we have found effective is to hold group discussions with athletes about stress and coping (e.g. how to deal with the stress of living up to the expectations of others; how to deal with the stress caused by having to maintain a low body weight and a certain appearance in sports like gymnastics and figure skating). In these meetings athletes share their concerns and possible coping strategies with one another, and can learn a great deal from each other. It should be noted, however, that this approach is most effective when the elite athletes involved are not in direct competition with one another; for example, retiring athletes talking with junior competitors.

When teaching coping strategies to athletes, it is also important that coaches and consultants ensure that the athletes do not merely model specific coping strategies used by other, more successful, competitors. Of course, athletes can learn from other athletes, but they must also individualise strategies by trying them out on themselves in order to further evaluate, revise, and refine them as appropriate. The research by Gould *et al.* (1993a) and Finch (1994) clearly suggests that athletes should learn coping skills so well that they become automated if they are to employ them successfully in competition. It has been our experience, however, that this rarely happens. Efforts must constantly be made to incorporate coping strategies into actual performance situations and practise them repeatedly.

As well as learning how to cope, athletes need to learn when to employ certain coping strategies. Athletes must select the right coping strategy for the situation. For example, in the Gould *et al.* (1993b) skating study, it was apparent that a number of athletes reported "ignoring" as a coping strategy. In studying individual cases, it became clear that some athletes used an "ignoring" strategy appropriately since they needed to perform in a short period of time and could not do anything about the stressor they faced. Others used an "ignoring" strategy inappropriately—ignoring the fact that they needed to deal with an uncomfortable situation which could be changed and controlled until it was too late to deal with the problem at hand (e.g. discussing communication differences with a partner or coach). Athletes must learn, then, when it is most effective to use particular coping strategies.

Sport psychology consultants and coaches can also play an important role in eliminating coping myths. For example, some elite athletes feel that they must "go it alone" when dealing with stress. However, increasing evidence has been shown for the use of social support as a coping strategy (Cohen and Wills, 1985). Consequently, athletes must be helped to feel that it is not a sign of weakness to seek social support; whether it be emotional, informational, or tangible social support (Hardy, C.J. and Crace, 1991). As will be discussed in Chapter 11, the sport psychology consultant must work to create an environment of trust where athletes feel comfortable in bringing concerns to them.

Finally, while the primary focus of this book is on elite athletes, it must not be forgotten that coping skills take time to develop and to reach automated levels. For example, Madden *et al.* (1989) concluded that older middle distance runners used problem-focused coping more often than their younger counterparts because they had been able to develop them over a longer period of time. Part of the psychology of preparing elite athletes, then, is to implement programmes where developing junior athletes learn how and when to use coping strategies. Moreover, Orlick and McCaffrey (1991) have identified a number of stress management coping strategies that are developmentally appropriate and can be taught to younger child athletes.

Summary

While sport psychology coping research is only now emerging, a number of implications already exist for guiding best practice. These include: (1) recognising that coping is a complex process, so that it is unlikely that any single coping strategy will be effective in all situations; (2) developing a broad spectrum of coping strategies for elite athletes; (3) evaluating coping effectiveness by looking at multiple coping outcomes; (4) considering coping dispositions, coping resources, and personality and motivational factors which may influence the coping process; (5) recognising and eliminating maladaptive coping strategies; (6) increasing athlete awareness of the need for coping at major competitions by discussing possible unforeseen events and ways to cope with them; (7) individualising coping strategies; (8) encouraging the elimination of coping myths; (9) facilitating the "automatic execution" of coping strategies by ensuring that they are well learned; and, (10) implementing programmes to develop effective coping strategies in pre-elite and junior elite athletes. Consultants and coaches should therefore build these implications into their mental skills training programmes for elite athletes.

SUMMARY

In this chapter, research and theory on coping with adversity and stress was examined. Coping was viewed as a complex process involving primary and secondary appraisal to generate stress, which is then dealt with by the individual using specific coping strategies. These specific coping strategies can be classified into more general coping categories which are thought to be related to a variety of coping outcomes such as performance, mood, and satisfaction. Various means of assessing coping strategies were discussed, and the controversy surrounding the existence of coping dispositions was examined. The importance of examining both coping outcomes and efforts via goodness-of-fit was discussed, as well as possible explanations for how coping influences stress and performance. Unresolved conceptual and methodological issues in coping research were also discussed.

An examination of the emerging sport psychology coping literature revealed that: coping is a complex, multidimensional process; a wide variety of coping strategies are used by athletes, including both problem- and emotion-focused coping strategies, and both adaptive and maladaptive ones; increased anxiety is associated with increased coping efforts; different coping strategies are used to deal with different sources of stress; coping efforts are associated with variations in athlete performance; having coping strategies so well learned that they can be executed in an automatic fashion is associated with superior performance; some athletes use maladaptive coping strategies when experiencing slumps; and, athletes may need quite a long time to learn how to cope with adversity and stress. A working model of coping was presented which integrated both the general and the sport psychology coping literatures. The chapter concluded by identifying future directions for research, and the implications for best practice of the material reviewed.

PART III

IMPLICATIONS AND FUTURE DIRECTIONS

9

A UNIFYING MODEL OF PSYCHOLOGICAL PREPARATION FOR PEAK ATHLETIC PERFORMANCE

CONTENTS

INTRODUCTION

The previous eight chapters in this text have focused on summarising the latest research and theory on the most important topics involved in the psychological preparation of elite sport performers. A problem facing those reading a text like this, and sport psychology in general, is that as readers we are limited in our information processing capabilities. For this reason we cannot address all the factors involved in the psychology of the elite athlete simultaneously. Hence, as has been the case in this text, we examine the field by looking at separate components such as self-confidence, motivation, and concentration. However, elite athletes are not simple, unidimensional beings—they are multivariate and complex, so that all the psychological factors discussed in this text, and more, are operating simultaneously. In addition, elite athletes do not live in a vacuum; they function within a highly complex social and organisational environment which exerts major influences on them and their performances. For these reasons, it is helpful to incorporate the topics and variables that have been discussed in the separate chapters of this book into a unifying model of psychological preparation for peak performance, so that the relationships between them and the social–organisational environment can be understood.

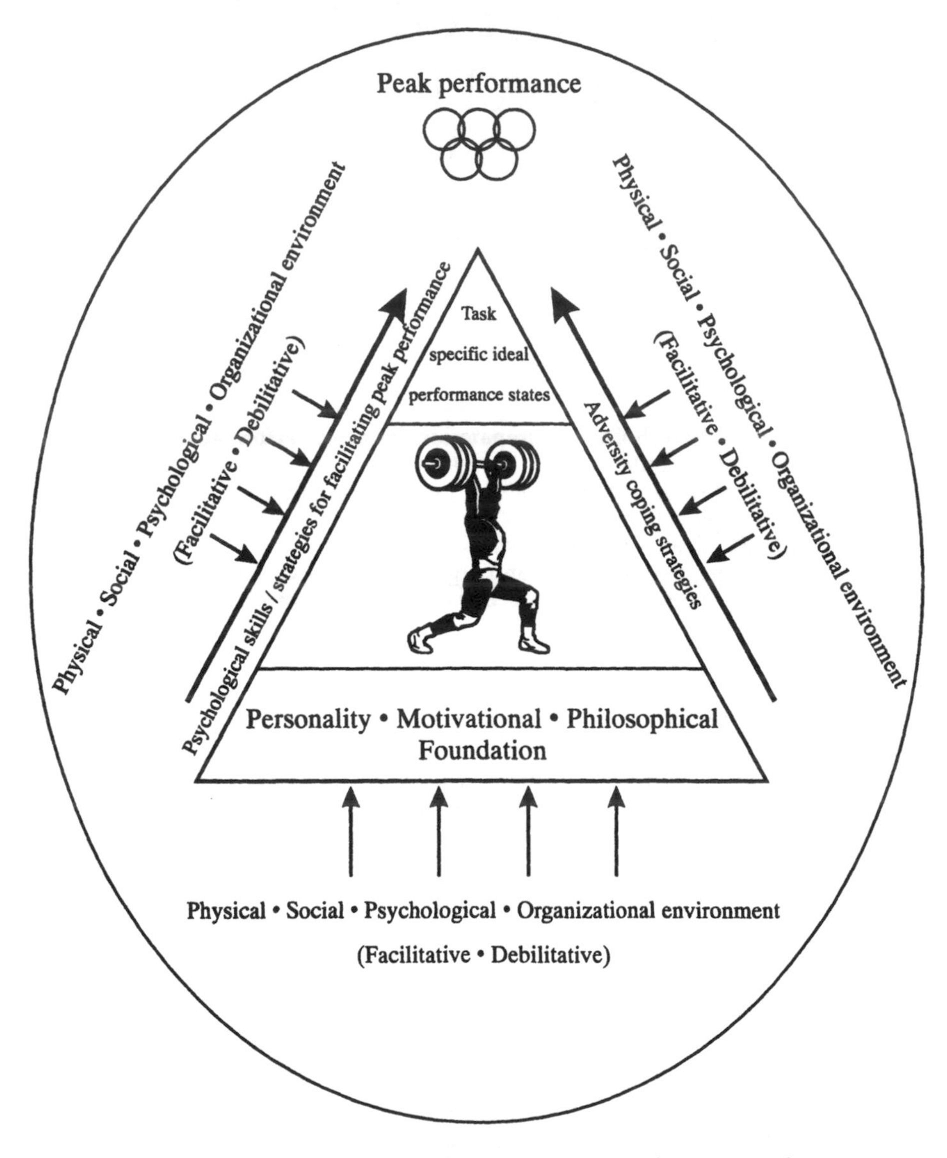

Figure 9.1: A model of psychological preparation for peak performance

A UNIFYING MODEL OF PSYCHOLOGICAL PREPARATION FOR PEAK PERFORMANCE

Figure 9.1 depicts a model of psychological preparation for peak performance which was originally proposed by Gould and Damarjian (in press), and has been further developed here. This model consists of five major components. These are: (1) the base of the model contains fundamental foundation attributes, including such factors as personality dispositions and motivational orientations; (2) the left side of the model depicts the psychological skills and strategies that can be used to help performers achieve ideal performance states; (3) the right side of the triangle model contains the adversity coping strategies that elite performers use to deal with negative stressors such as injury, interpersonal conflict, financial problems, and organisational stress; (4) the top of the triangle shows the task-specific ideal performance state that leads to peak performance (symbolised by the Olympic rings) in elite athletes; and (5) the area contained in the circle surrounding the triangle is the physical, social, psychological, and organisational environment in which the elite athlete trains and performs. Each component of the model, and the specific variables that are contained within it, are discussed in more detail below.

Fundamental attributes

This component of the model includes the personality characteristics, motivational orientations, values, and philosophical beliefs of the athlete. Specific variables identified in the chapters of this book that would be included in this component are trait confidence, goal orientations, trait anxiety, attentional style, and individual difference variables which influence arousal and activation (See Figure 9.2). These factors are important because they influence everything the performer does which in turn, either directly or indirectly, influences the degree to which the athlete achieves the desired task-specific ideal performance state. For example, an elite athlete's level of trait anxiety would influence his or her cognitive and somatic state anxiety which, in turn, would influence his or her arousal and activation state.

This element of the peak performance model is extremely important, but it is also very difficult to work with because of the difficulty in modifying personality and motivational dispositions once they are established. However, this is one reason that those interested in elite performance should also be interested in and informed by youth sport research. Children's sport research has identified: the important role that perceived competence plays in motivation and achievement (Weiss and Chaumeton, 1992); how positive coaching practices facilitate the development of positive self-esteem, reduce trait anxiety, and lower dropout rates (Barnett *et al.*, 1992; Smith and Smoll,

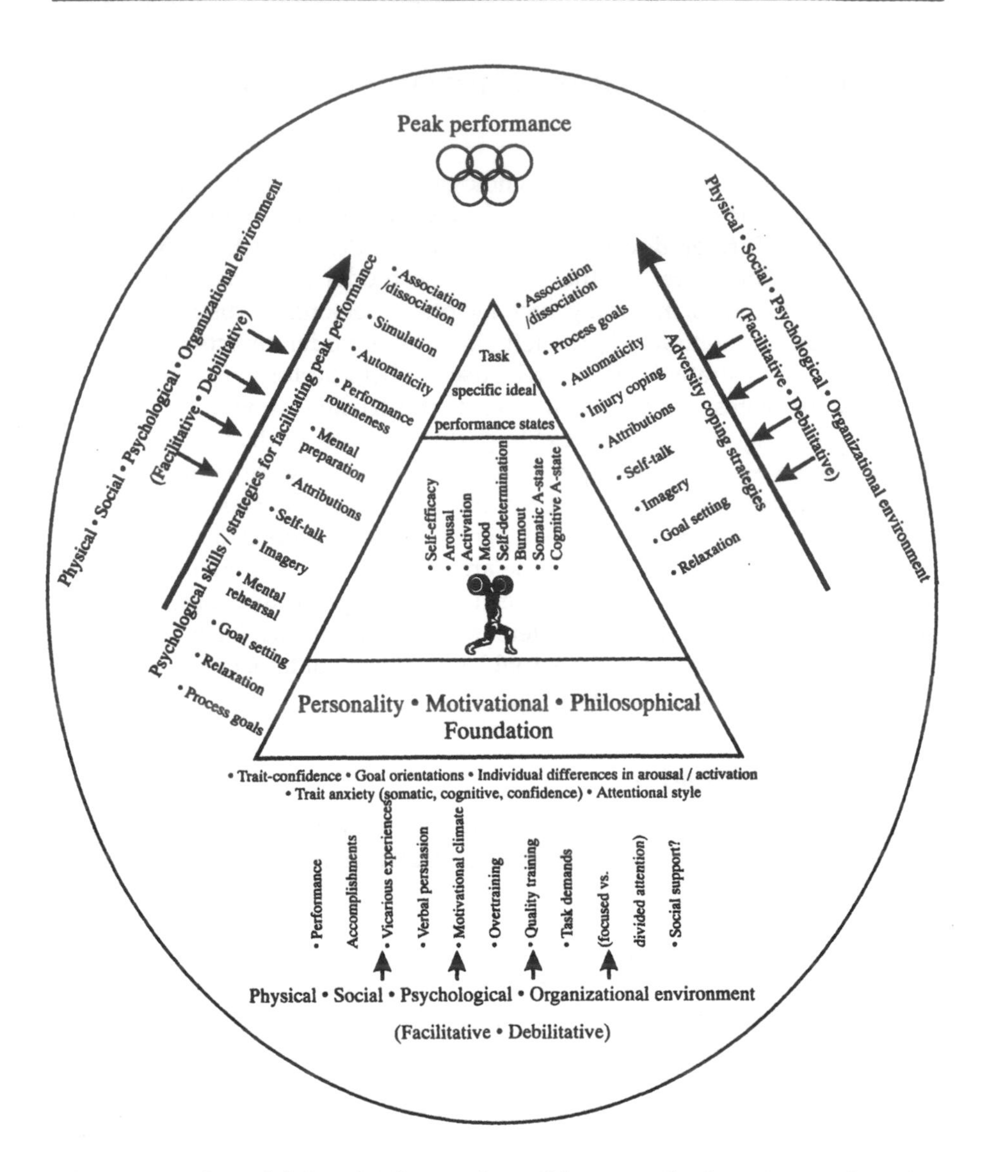

Figure 9.2: A model showing how trait confidence, goal orientations, trait anxiety, attentional style and individual difference variables influence arousal and activation

1995); how goal orientations influence achievement behaviour (Duda, 1993); what makes sports stressful for young athletes and how high levels of stress can be reduced (see Gould, 1993b).

While it is much easier to develop positive psychological attributes through effective coaching practices when performers are young, this does not imply that there is nothing that can be done in this area for seasoned adult competitors. For example, when asked to consult with elite performers who are experiencing performance difficulties, highly respected North American mental training consultant Ken Ravizza spends considerable time having them discuss "why" they participate in their sport and what "meaning" it has for them. In his opinion (and in the opinion of the authors) athletes perform much better when they are not questioning the reasons for their involvement and its meaningfulness to them (Ravizza, 1988). The discussion is therefore designed to help them resolve any questions that they may have in this area. In a similar vein, Orlick (1986) begins his mental training efforts by having athletes consider their long-term goals for sport participation, including a discussion of their dreams and overall aspirations. Finally, it must be recognised that meaningfulness differs greatly across athletes. Some may have their lives in total order with clear sport and non-sport goals and objectives. Others, like former diving great Greg Louganis (Louganis and Marcus, 1995) or former baseball great Mickey Mantle, may have a life outside sport which is totally chaotic, so that sport can serve as a refuge or safe haven for them. Still others may be in a process of transition, where their once clear sport and life objectives are being questioned as they face retirement from sport (Danish *et al.*, 1995; Murphy, 1995).

Given the importance of the above philosophical value and direction issues, it is ironic that these factors have been given almost no attention by sport psychology researchers. While these issues would be difficult to study because they are hard to quantify and examine using traditional positivistic methods and nomothetic research designs, the emergence of idiographic case study and qualitative methods, which are discussed in Chapter 10, provides investigators with the necessary tools to address these issues.

Lastly, seasoned athletes may change or learn to deal more effectively with their motivational orientations and personality characteristics. For instance, elite athletes who are very outcome oriented and focus primarily upon winning may learn that thinking about the outcome of a competition close to, or during, performance often interferes with the achievement of their objective. Hence, they may learn not to focus on winning before or during competitions. Similarly, it has been found recently that perfectionism is associated with sport burnout in elite junior tennis players (Gould *et al.*, 1995b), but it is the authors' experience that many of the most effective world class athletes are perfectionist in their orientations. However, they have learned to deal with their perfectionist tendencies in a positive manner, allowing these tendencies to facilitate, as opposed to inhibit, their development.

In addition to the specific future research recommendations that will be forwarded in Chapter 10, researchers interested in examining factors in this component of the model might do well to think more holistically, moving beyond the study of those traditional, isolated, personality factors that may be associated with peak athletic performance. For instance, to our knowledge "meaningfulness" of involvement represents a broad heuristic construct which has not been examined in the sport psychology literature. Similarly, the roles that "optimism", "hardiness", and "perceived control" might play as core foundation attributes need to be examined.

Finally, both researchers and consultants should remember that psychological factors rarely operate in isolation in elite performers. Rather, they are influenced by athletes' foundational mental skills (e.g. an athlete's state cognitive anxiety will be influenced by his or her trait confidence and anxiety). Hence, this component of the model must be kept in mind when any other components of the unifying model are being examined.

Psychological skills and strategies for peak performance

Over the last decade the predominant focus of psychological research into elite performance has been on examining the psychological skills and strategies that athletes can use to achieve peak performance. Hence, in the various chapters of this text, advances in research on process goals and goal-setting, relaxation strategies, imagery and mental rehearsal, self-talk, attributions, mental preparation strategies, pre-performance and performance routines, the automatisation of routines, simulation training, and association/dissociation strategies have all been discussed (see Figure 9.2). In essence, the goal of this research has been to identify psychological skills and strategies that (elite) performers can employ to increase their probability of creating an ideal performance state, which is why these factors are all contained in this component of the model.

For example, it was shown in Chapter 2 that research over the last decade has emphasised the importance of focusing on process or performance, as opposed to outcome, goals during competition (Burton, 1992; Duda, 1993; Gould, 1993a; Kingston and Hardy, 1994b; Orlick and Partington, 1988). The logic behind this recommendation is that process and performance goals are more flexible and under the performer's control than outcome goals, as they are not so dependent on other competitors. Because of this, outcome goals often create anxiety and interrupt psychological functioning (Burton, 1992). An excellent example of focusing on process goals in competition was given by Olympic gold medal skier Tommy Moe. When asked by the media prior to his gold medal performance whether he was thinking about winning (an outcome goal), Moe indicated that he certainly wanted to win, but had found in the past that when he thinks about winning while racing he tightens up and does not perform well. He skis at his best when he focuses on "letting his outside ski run" and keeping his "hands out in front" of himself—clear process goals.

The above is not to imply that elite performers do not hold outcome goals. Most have these types of goals and find them very salient. However, in the heat of competition they do not focus on these outcome goals—only on what they can control, their performance and process objectives.

This example, then, shows that to consistently perform well elite athletes must prepare themselves psychologically by employing psychology of peak performance strategies like the ones identified in Figure 9.2. In a very practical sense, athletes need to "set the table" for success by psychologically readying themselves in certain identifiable ways that are uniquely customised to their sport, context, and personality.

Adversity coping strategies

By focusing their attention on peak performance skills and strategies, sport psychology researchers and consultants have implicitly assumed that this is all that is needed for peak performance to occur. However, recent elite performer research discussed in Chapter 8 clearly shows that elite athletes must deal with all types of stressors, ranging from injury and travel demands to their own and others' expectations for them to live up to previous performance standards. Hence, elite performers need not only to possess psychological skills and strategies which will facilitate an ideal performance state, they also need to develop coping strategies which will enable them to deal with the various types of adversity that could prevent ideal performance states from occurring, or interrupt them once they are in place. Our coping with adversity component of the model, then, includes the factors of emotion-focused coping, problem-focused coping, cognitive restructuring, avoidance, relaxation techniques, goal-setting, imagery, self-talk, attributional patterns, process goals, and associative/dissociative strategies (see Figure 9.2). Interestingly, some of these coping strategies utilise the same skills and techniques that are used to facilitate peak performance. However, the way in which they are used may differ markedly.

Task-specific ideal performance state

Recent research discussed in Chapter 6 has shown that athletes perform best when they achieve an ideal performance state. This has been referred to as flow by Csikszentmihalyi (1975), the recipe of emotions needed for best performance by Gould and Udry (1994), or the zone of optimal functioning by Hanin (1980). As has been indicated in Chapters 5 and 6, this ideal state is most likely not some unidimensional arousal zone, but rather a complex multivariate recipe of cognitions, emotions, and associated physiological parameters that lead to peak performance. The precise mixture and levels of these cognitions and emotions needed for ideal performance are most likely individual and task specific (cf. Gould and Udry, 1994). However, the research that has been reviewed in the previous chapters of this book identifies some common elements, such as self-efficacy, arousal, activation, mood, self-determination, and cognitive and somatic state anxiety, which are highly likely to be included in this recipe. In addition, athlete burnout would also have a direct effect on this state. For these reasons, this component of the model contains these factors (see Figure 9.2).

It is important for researchers and practitioners to remember this component of the model when focusing on other components. For example, one may be studying, or using, one of the relaxation techniques discussed in Chapter 2 (e.g. progressive muscular relaxation) as a psychology of peak performance preparation or a coping with adversity strategy component. However, having an athlete relax without knowing how relaxed (both physically and cognitively) he or she needs to be to achieve an ideal performance state can do more harm than good. Similarly, while the notion of an ideal performance state is both empirically and experientially well grounded, no one has studied how such states develop and whether they change over time (see Gould and Tuffey, 1996, for a more detailed discussion). It would seem logical to suggest that such states might be influenced by many of the factors listed under the fundamental foundation skills component of the model. For example, do athletes who vary in their trait anxiety or confidence have different zones of optimal functioning? Important questions like this await further investigation, but are unlikely to be examined unless the specific variables within each component of the model are seen from a broader perspective.

Physical, social, psychological, and organisational environment

While the focus of this book is on the psychology of the elite athlete, it would be a mistake to forget that elite performers compete and train in a physical, social, psychological, and organisational environment that can have both facilitative and debilitative effects upon the achievement of ideal performance states. For example, through evaluations of their long-term consulting efforts with British gymnasts, Hardy and Parfitt (1994) have shown that the addition of a new coach can have a major impact on the psychological preparation of elite performers. Similarly, Gould and his colleagues (Gould *et al.*, 1991, 1993b) have identified a number of organisational stressors such as national governing body politics, bad officiating, lack of finances, and family problems that cause stress in elite athletes. For this reason, those working in long-term consulting roles must monitor these environmental influences and, if needed, try to help performers change them.

Although this component was not the primary focus of this text, its importance cannot be denied and general implications derived from it will be further discussed in Chapter 11. In addition, factors such as performance accomplishments, quality training, vicarious experiences, verbal persuasion, motivation climate, overtraining, task demands, and social support that have been discussed in the previous chapters are classified as belonging to this component (see Figure 9.2). These factors, and their influence on other components of the model, must be better understood before a more complete understanding of psychological preparation for peak performance can be attained.

USING THE UNIFYING MODEL TO GUIDE PRACTICE AND FUTURE RESEARCH

A common mistake made in mental skills training is to focus sole attention on one isolated psychological strategy without an understanding of how this strategy fits into an athlete's psychological whole. Therefore, to effectively study, or help performers to achieve, athletic excellence, sport psychologists must not only understand and consider specific techniques, but also athletes' psychological foundation attributes, their peak performance skills, their adversity coping strategies, and their ideal performance states.

To help in this regard, it is highly recommended that the pyramid model of peak performance which has been presented in this chapter be considered. For example, psychological consultants who are helping athletes to prepare mentally for peak performance should examine the personality and psychological make-up of each athlete and help him or her to identify the ideal performance state needed for peak performance. Components of the intervention programme should also focus upon developing specific personal characteristics or orientations which are deemed to be important in the athlete's current sport and context. In addition, the programme should identify the most important psychology of peak performance skills to be taught and which strategies will be most useful for coping with adversity. In the authors' opinions, mental skills training programmes which address psychological factors at the base and on the two sides of this pyramid will have the greatest probability of helping athletes consistently enhance performance and achieve success.

When using the model, it is important to recognise that specific psychological variables may be contained in several components of the model. For instance, setting certain types of goals (e.g. process and performance goals) may be both a peak performance and a coping strategy. Similarly, progressive muscle relaxation could be used to help a performer achieve an ideal performance state, or as a coping strategy to reduce anxiety. A key, then, in using the model is to recognise that variables may have several functions and contribute to achieving and maintaining peak performance in several different ways.

As has been demonstrated several times in this book, components of the unifying model interact. For example, coping efforts are influenced by athletes' self-handicapping personality characteristics, whilst personality disposition of goal orientation influences the selection of specific goals when athletes are mentally preparing for a performance. By thinking in terms of the general model, then, sport psychologists are able to better conceptualise and identify these interactions.

Finally, although the unifying model is the authors' best attempt to present a simple yet effective framework for conceptualising the many findings and variables discussed in this text, it is in no way offered as the only such model. In fact, what may be more important than adopting any one unifying model is the need for individual researchers and consultants to develop their own (possibly unique) models that allow them to view the field from a more unified, holistic perspective. The development of such models would provide a broad integrative perspective that would facilitate both research and practice in elite performance.

SUMMARY

This chapter has presented a unifying model of psychological preparation for peak performance that organised the many variables discussed throughout the text into one framework. Hence, separate components have been conceptualised within a holistic framework for understanding elite athlete peak performance. The model demonstrates that peak performance strategies are a necessary, but not a sufficient, condition for ideal performance. Foundational attributes, adversity coping strategies, task and individual specific ideal performance states, and the physical, social, psychological, and organisational environment must also be considered and addressed. It has been emphasised that the development and adoption of such models will enable sport psychologists to have a broader and more holistic perspective on the field, as well as facilitate efforts to conduct future research and enhance professional practice.

10

FUTURE RESEARCH DIRECTIONS

CONTENTS

INTRODUCTION

In this chapter, we will focus on future research directions for advancing knowledge on psychological preparation for peak athletic performance. The chapter will certainly be of interest to those who are researchers in the area, or are graduate students hoping to undertake research. However, the authors would contend that practitioners should also read it, because this book has repeatedly demonstrated that peak performance research has a number of important implications for guiding practice. However, not all research is equal—some studies are better than others and all investigations have strengths and limitations. Hence, to be an informed consumer, a practitioner must have an adequate understanding of both research outcomes and research methodology.

Consultants and researchers must also recognise the importance of establishing a research base for professional accountability reasons. Some authors (e.g. Dishman, 1983; Morgan, 1988) have strongly criticised applied sport psychology consultancy work because of a lack of research demonstrating the effectiveness of elite athlete interventions. Others, who support consultancy work (e.g. Silva, 1989; Smith, R.E., 1989; Weinberg, 1989b), have emphasised the importance of demonstrating intervention effectiveness as a means of protecting athletes from fraudulent, or well-meaning but inept, individuals working in the field. Still further others (e.g. Kroll, 1971) have argued that a research base and a structured body of knowledge are important criteria for any profession. For all these reasons, applied research into performance enhancement is important. However, another reason for conducting performance enhancement research is to uncover new knowledge that can be used to assist elite athletes in reaching their goals. While scientific study is certainly not the only way to discover new knowledge, it is an important one that cannot be ignored if our profession is to advance.

This chapter has five purposes. First, the most important psychological preparation for peak performance research questions in need of study will be identified, rated in importance and difficulty. Second, the utility of various methods for conducting peak performance research will be examined. Third, examples of how different methodological approaches can be used to answer critical questions in the area will be discussed. Fourth, characteristics of previously conducted "significant" studies will be addressed in an effort to further assist investigators in designing powerful research studies. And, fifth, the psychology of conducting research that takes knowledge in our field to the "next level" will be examined by discussing such issues as theoretical and methodological tolerance, investigator risk taking, and conducting studies that make the best use of an investigator's strengths while minimising his or her limitations.

CRITICAL QUESTIONS FOR FUTURE RESEARCH

Table 10.1 contains a list of the research questions identified as being most in need of study in Chapters 2 to 8 of this book. These questions are summarised and rated in terms of both their importance and their difficulty. We have included these ratings because we expect researchers at various stages of development to read this text (e.g., from graduate students just beginning

Table 10.1: Priority questions for future research, importance ratings and difficulty ratings. Both importance and difficulty are rated on a three-point scale, with 1 = most importance/difficulty, 2 = intermediate importance/difficulty, and 3 = least importance/difficulty

Research question	Importance	Difficulty
Basic psychological techniques		
(1) To what extent do different relaxation techniques affect performance on different sports skills? What are the processes that underlie these effects? To what extent does the matching hypothesis hold?	3	3
(2) What are the processes underlying goal-setting effects in sport? Under what circumstances are goals dysfunctional, and what are the personal and situational antecedents of such dysfunctional effects?	1	2
(3) What are the processes underlying imagery effects? How can imagery be used optimally to enhance motivational, attentional, emotional, and performance effects? Under what circumstances should elite performers be encouraged to use different imagery perspectives?	1	1
(4) What is the nature of the self-talk that successful elite athletes use? How does this self-talk exert its influence upon motivation, attention, emotion, and performance?	2	2
Self-confidence		
(1) Exactly how do trait self-confidence, goal orientations, and situational factors interact to affect state self-confidence and subjective outcomes?	2	3
(2) To what extent can coaches' and team-mates' modelling of efficacy behaviours influence self-efficacy? Furthermore, should coaches try to verbally persuade low self-efficacy performers that they can perform the physical actions required, or the cognitive restructuring actions required, to modify their own self-efficacy?	2	3
(3) In comparison to their non-elite counterparts, do elite performers maintain a higher commitment to difficult goals, increase their persistence when goals are not achieved, show greater resistance to setbacks (e.g. injury), and attribute failure more to unstable internal factors as opposed to external or stable factors? Furthermore, are these effects mediated by self-efficacy and/or intrinsic motivation?	2	3
(4) Exactly how and when does collective efficacy exert an influence upon performance? In particular, which variables moderate and mediate the collective efficacy–performance relationship?	2	2
(5) How independent are self-confidence and cognitive anxiety? Furthermore, do they exert additive or interactive effects upon performance? What are the processes underlying these effects?	2	2
(6) Is the self-confidence–performance relationship mediated by changes in the perception of control?	1	2

Table 10.1: *(continued)*

Research question	Importance	Difficulty
Motivation		
(1) To what extent are elite performers extrinsically and intrinsically motivated? In particular, what are the goal orientation profiles of elite performers? How might these profiles be developed in (young) performers? Does the development of such motivational profiles impact upon the moral development of performers?	2	3
(2) How, when, and in what ways do elite performers make use of outcome-, performance- and process-oriented goals? In particular, do they use process-oriented goals to enhance the quality of their training, to develop strategies for performing complex tasks, and to reduce goal-related stress?	1	1
(3) Exactly what are the relative contributions of intuitive and reflective appraisal to the attributional process? Does intuitive appraisal affect only emotional reactions, or does it also affect efficacy expectations?	3	2
(4) Is it the stability or the controllability of attributions which is the primary determinant of subsequent efficacy expectations?	2	3
(5) Do elite performers have characteristic attributional styles for success and failure? In particular, do they typically make internal, unstable, and controllable attributions for failure?	2	3
(6) What is the (possibly cyclical) relationship which exists between goal perspectives, performance, rewards, attributions, self-competence, and (intrinsic) motivation in elite performers and do these change over time?	1	1
(7) To what extent is social disempowerment responsible for burnout in elite, and potentially elite, performers? What are the roles of commitment, investment, and satisfaction in burnout?	2	2
(8) To what extent are cognitive appraisals and emotional reactions influential in rehabilitation from injury? What are the implications of such influences for intervention?	2	2
Arousal and activation		
(1) What are the primary sub-components of performance (activation states) for different sports skills?	3	2
(2) How can activation states be measured psychophysiologically? Exactly how are they influenced by such strategies as imagery, self-talk, pre-performance routines, goal-setting, biofeedback, and emotional arousal inductions?	2	1

Table 10.1: *(continued)*

Research question	Importance	Difficulty
(3) What are the effects of emotional and mood manipulations upon the phasic and tonic psychophysiological states and subsequent motor performance of high level performers?	2	2
(4) Can ideal recipes of emotion be identified which promote appropriate activation states for different sports skills? What are the specific ingredients for these recipes, and the relative "mixtures" required?	1	2
(5) Should elite performers vary their competition routines when they are performing at different times of day or in different time zones?	2	3
Stress, anxiety and performance		
(1) How do the situational antecedents of state anxiety interact with personality variables to affect the different subcomponents of anxiety?	3	3
(2) How serious a problem is organisational stress in international sport, and what are the major organisational factors that affect elite performance in different sports?	1	2
(3) Under what circumstances (if any) does cognitive anxiety exert a positive influence upon performance?	1	2
(4) Do cognitive anxiety and physiological arousal (or somatic anxiety) exert interactive or additive effects upon performance?	2	2
(5) What is the precise nature of stress-related performance decrements when they do occur, and to what extent is peak performance recoverable once such a decrement has occurred?	1	1
(6) Does self-confidence protect against negative anxiety effects by influencing performers' directional interpretation of their anxiety symptoms?	1	2
(7) To what extent do perceptions of demand (effort) and perceptions of control mediate or moderate the anxiety performance relationship?	2	2
Concentration and attention control		
(1) Does state anxiety mediate, or moderate, the effects of trait anxiety upon perceptual selectivity and performance?	3	3
(2) Do elite performers show any attentional bias when they are anxious?	2	3
(3) How flexible is the attentional style of elite performers in different sports?	2	3
(4) To what extent do elite performers utilise both consciously controlled and automatically controlled attentional processes during peak performance?	1	1

Table 10.1: *(continued)*

Research question	Importance	Difficulty
(5) Does cognitive anxiety primarily affect conscious processes and does physiological arousal primarily affect lower level automatic processes?	1	1
(6) To what extent do anxious performers attempt to consciously control automatic processes?	2	2
(7) Under what circumstances do anxious performers invest more effort in performance?	2	2
(8) At what stage during the acquisition of a new skill should stress be introduced?	2	2
(9) How do elite performers use process-oriented goals without lapsing into conscious control?	2	2
(10) How much overlearning is enough for any given task? How is the optimal amount of overlearning influenced by individual difference variables?	3	3
(11) How can attentional control strategies be developed more effectively?	1	1
(12) How can the construct of trust be more rigorously defined in a way that takes account of what we know about anxiety and perceptual attention?	3	3
(13) Exactly what role do trust and self-confidence play in stress-induced lapses into conscious processing?	2	2
Coping with adversity		
(1) What are the psychological characteristics of those who have coped effectively with major setbacks? Do these individuals use different strategies to non-copers? Do they have more strategies? Are their strategies more automated?	1	3
(2) To what extent do personality and dispositional factors influence coping efforts?	3	3
(3) Do coping dispositions exist? If so, what effect do they have on stress, coping behaviours, and coping outcomes?	3	3
(4) What is the relationship between coping behaviours and coping outcomes? Are different classes of coping behaviour differentially related to coping outcomes? Does the goodness-of-fit hypothesis work? Is the use of multiple coping resources related to coping outcome?	1	2
(5) What are the processes underlying the effects of coping upon athletic outcome variables?	2	1
(6) How are coping behaviours, resources, and dispositions developed?	2	2
(7) How are coping strategies best taught? Is it helpful to teach athletes to expect unexpected stressors? Is it more effective to teach multiple coping strategies? Can athletes be taught the goodness-of-fit hypothesis?	1	2

the research process to widely published and seasoned investigators). We thought it would be helpful to the readership, then, if all the questions were rated in terms of their potential impact and how difficult they might be to test. It should be noted, however, that all the questions listed were originally identified because of their importance. Hence, there are no unimportant questions on the list so that the importance ratings reflect only importance relative to the other questions in the list. Furthermore, we would always recommend that investigators select a topic that truly interests them, regardless of its importance rating.

In terms of the difficulty ratings, inexperienced investigators and especially student investigators would be well advised to select questions with lower ratings. We know that students and less experienced investigators can conduct quality research, so this suggestion is not made in an effort to limit capabilities, but only as a guide for the inexperienced investigator who often lacks the time and resources required to answer the more difficult rated questions on the list. Hence, the selection of a topic within the researcher's capabilities will increase the probability of better research being conducted and knowledge being truly advanced.

The above is not to suggest that there is any stigma associated with an experienced investigator selecting a question with a low difficulty rating. Indeed, factors such as time demands, equipment, resource availability, and research assistance are as relevant to experienced researchers as they are to graduate students. It is better to be successful in addressing a lower difficulty rated question than to address a higher rated one unsuccessfully.

Summary

The critical research questions from the previous chapters of this book which are most in need of further study were identified. These questions were also rated in terms of their importance to the area and the difficulty of conducting research which more meaningfully addresses them. It was emphasised that investigators should select topics that they are truly interested in examining. Additionally, they need to select questions within their research capabilities given the time, research experience, and resource constraints that operate upon them.

METHODOLOGICAL CONSIDERATIONS

Those who regularly attend conferences in sport psychology can attest to the considerable debate that has taken place in recent years as to the most appropriate methodologies and methodological paradigms needed in sport psychology research. The merits of qualitative versus quantitative approaches, what constitutes methodological rigour, idiographic versus nomothetic research designs, internal and external validity trade-off, and direct versus indirect levels of measurement are issues that have all surfaced in these debates. We will now briefly discuss the issues being debated in each of these areas. Then, following this discussion, we will examine the question of which of these scientific approaches is best for guiding elite athlete psychological preparation for peak performance research.

The quantitative versus qualitative research debate

In the last five years a substantial increase has occurred in the amount of qualitative research being conducted in sport psychology. Accompanying this increased interest has been a debate about the utility of qualitative research, as well as the utility of the positivistic paradigms which have guided scientific sport psychology research in the past. Before discussing this debate, however, each type of research must be defined.

Quantitative research focuses on studying a selected sample from some larger population for the purposes of producing factual, reliable, and objective data which can be generalised to the larger population (Steckler *et al.*, 1992). In quantitative research, the general method used to study the physical sciences is adopted and a high value is placed on deriving causal relationships via the use of experimental and quasi-experimental designs. In addition, researchers following this approach strive to be unbiased and to distance themselves from the data in the hope of making it more objective. Quantitative research derives its name from the emphasis that is placed on collecting objective numerical data and using inferential statistics to test significant relationships between variables of interest.

Qualitative sport psychology research has adopted traditional ethnographic and anthropological non-numerical approaches to study. Hence, techniques such as participation observation, interviews, life histories, and analysis of historical records are used in an effort to better understand the experiences of individuals and groups, together with the corresponding psychological processes involved in sport. The goal is to obtain rich, in-depth, and detailed information from an "insider's" view—one that stresses the perspective of the participant (subject) and strives to understand the context or situation in which the experience takes place. Unlike their quantitative counterparts, qualitative investigators do not try to distance themselves from the data, but instead immerse themselves in the groups or participants being studied. Qualitative research derives its name from its emphasis on non-numerical data.

The above provides a succinct explanation of how qualitative and quantitative research is viewed in contemporary sport psychology. However, our definitions are plagued by one problem: we have defined each type of research by using both a description of the methods used (quantitative–qualitative), and the two major philosophical paradigms (positivistic–naturalistic) most frequently used to justify each method. However, although the positivistic paradigm is most often associated with quantitative methods and the naturalistic paradigm is most often associated with qualitative research, this does not necessarily have to be the case. For example, one could perform a qualitative study (in-depth interviews) within a positivistic paradigm (e.g. counting the number of content themes emitted by a participant and then turning the qualitative data into numbers by employing statistical analyses in the hope of generalising the significant findings to some population). Hence, a brief discussion of each philosophical paradigm is also in order.

Kuhn (1962) defined a scientific paradigm as a school of thought relative to the nature of knowledge and how one goes about studying the world. In particular, a paradigm involves a series of assumptions about the nature of reality, knowledge, and truth which often influences a scientist in subtle, even subconscious, ways. For example, a positivistic scientist should discount important insightful comments made by subjects because they are not part of the objective numerical evidence collected in an experiment. Similarly, one's paradigm may influence the types of data viewed as valid for inclusion in a review of the literature. For instance, a naturalistic researcher might ignore traditional scientific knowledge because of the low value that it places on the situational context of subjects' experiences. A paradigm, then, can formally and informally influence how a scientist views the world and in turn how science is conducted.

Table 10.2: Positivistic versus naturalistic paradigm axiom comparison (modified from Lincoln and Guba, 1985 with permission)

Axioms about	Positivistic paradigm	Naturalistic paradigm
The nature of reality	Reality is single, tangible, and fragmentable.	Realities are multiple, constructed, and holistic.
The relationship of knower to the known.	Knower and known are independent, a dualism.	Knower and known are interactive, inseparable.
The possibility of generalisation.	Time- and context-free generalisations (nomothetic statements) are possible.	Only time- and context-bound working hypotheses (idiographic statements) are possible.
The possibility of causal linkages.	There are real causes, temporally precedent to, or simultaneous with, their effects.	All entities are in a state of mutual simultaneous shaping, so that it is impossible to distinguish causes from effects.
The role of values.	Inquiry is value free.	Inquiry is value-bound.

The positivistic paradigm is "a family of philosophies characterised by an extreme positive evaluation of science (as traditionally thought of in the physical sciences) and the scientific method" (Reese, 1980). As indicated by Lincoln and Guba (1985), and presented in Table 10.2, this view assumes that reality can be studied by reducing it to smaller parts (reductionism), that the knower and subject are independent, that generalisations are possible, that causal relationships can be identified, and that scientific inquiry is value free. In contrast, an inspection of this table shows that those who adhere to the tenets of the naturalistic paradigm assume that realities are holistic, created, and multiple, that the knower and subject are interconnected, that generalisations cannot be made (only working hypotheses), that causal relationships cannot be determined, and that inquiry is not value free, but value bound. These two paradigms, then, are guided by very different basic assumptions.

The debate in sport psychology about the appropriateness of the positivistic versus naturalistic paradigms can be traced to two articles by Martens (1979; 1987). In the first article, Martens (1979) urged investigators to move out of the laboratory and into the field, and in so doing sacrifice some internal validity for much more external validity. The second article (Martens, 1987) was focused much more on paradigmatic assumptions—calling for an abandonment of the positivistic paradigm and the development of a more heuristic naturalistic-type paradigm. In this article, Martens indicated that as he developed as a scientist he had come to severely question many positivistic assumptions, especially objectivity and reductionism.

While we concur with many of Martens' (1987) epistemological concerns with positivism we also see problems with blindly accepting the axioms of the naturalistic paradigm. For instance, if realities can only be understood in a holistic nature, how can scientists as limited processors of information understand realities? Similarly, given this assumption, how can one justify conducting a qualitative study in sport psychology that is not interdisciplinary and holistic in nature? We also disagree that it is impossible to distinguish causes and effects—some things cause others to occur in this world. However, we also hold that not all events are causal, as some events are random acts.

The above certainly shows how complex epistemological debates about the axioms of science can be and how unlikely it is that one paradigm will eventually be judged correct and the other refuted (although we feel that discussing these issues from time to time is of paramount importance to the development of all scientists). In fact, Patton (1990) contends that:

> *there aren't just two paradigm dictated choices. All kinds of variations, combinations, and adaptations are available for creative and practical situational responsiveness . . . The issue then becomes not whether one has*

uniformly adhered to prescribed canons of either logical positivism or phenomenology [naturalistic inquiry] but whether one has made sensible methods decisions given the purpose of inquiry, the questions being investigated, and the resources available. (p. 39)

The key for Patton (1990), then, is to make responsible methodological choices. We concur wholeheartedly! At times it is best to use a qualitative method, and at other times a quantitative approach. Because both methods have strengths and limitations, sometimes it may also be advisable to combine the two approaches.

Figure 10.1 depicts a simple but effective way in which Steckler *et al.* (1992) have indicated that quantitative and qualitative research methods can be combined. First, qualitative measures could be used to help develop a quantitative instrument that allows one to study a phenomenon of interest. For example, Gill *et al.* (1983) conducted qualitative interviews with youth sport participants for the purpose of identifying motives for sport participation and then used these open-ended responses as the basis for developing a psychometrically sound quantitative instrument to measure sport participation motivation.

A second way these methods might be combined would be to use qualitative methods to help explain quantitative findings. For instance, in an effort to learn why swimmers discontinued involvement Gould *et al.* (1982) conducted a survey study using Gill *et al.*'s (1983) participation motivation questionnaire, but also supplemented their primarily quantitative findings with interview data from the swimmers. Although they found that some of these athletes rated injuries as a major motive for discontinuing involvement, the qualitative data revealed that the injuries were not career-ending, but served as a socially acceptable reason for discontinuing. This fact would not have emerged without the supplementary qualitative interviews being conducted.

Further inspection of Figure 10.1 reveals that quantitative data can be used to supplement primarily a qualitative study. Jackson (1994), for example, interviewed elite athletes in an effort to better understand and record in detail their flow experiences in sport. However, she supplemented her findings via the use of Privette's (1984) peak experience scale.

Finally, quantitative and qualitative methods can be used as equal partners in an investigation. For example, Gould *et al.* (1995a, b) recently investigated burnout in elite junior tennis players. Phase 1 of the project compared players who burned out with players who did not burn out on a variety of personality, motivation, and demographic measures. Discriminant function analysis was then used to identify a number of important significant differences. In Phase 2 of the project, in-depth interviews were conducted with the 10 players from Phase 1 who evidenced the most burnout. Results from this phase allowed the investigators to better understand each player's

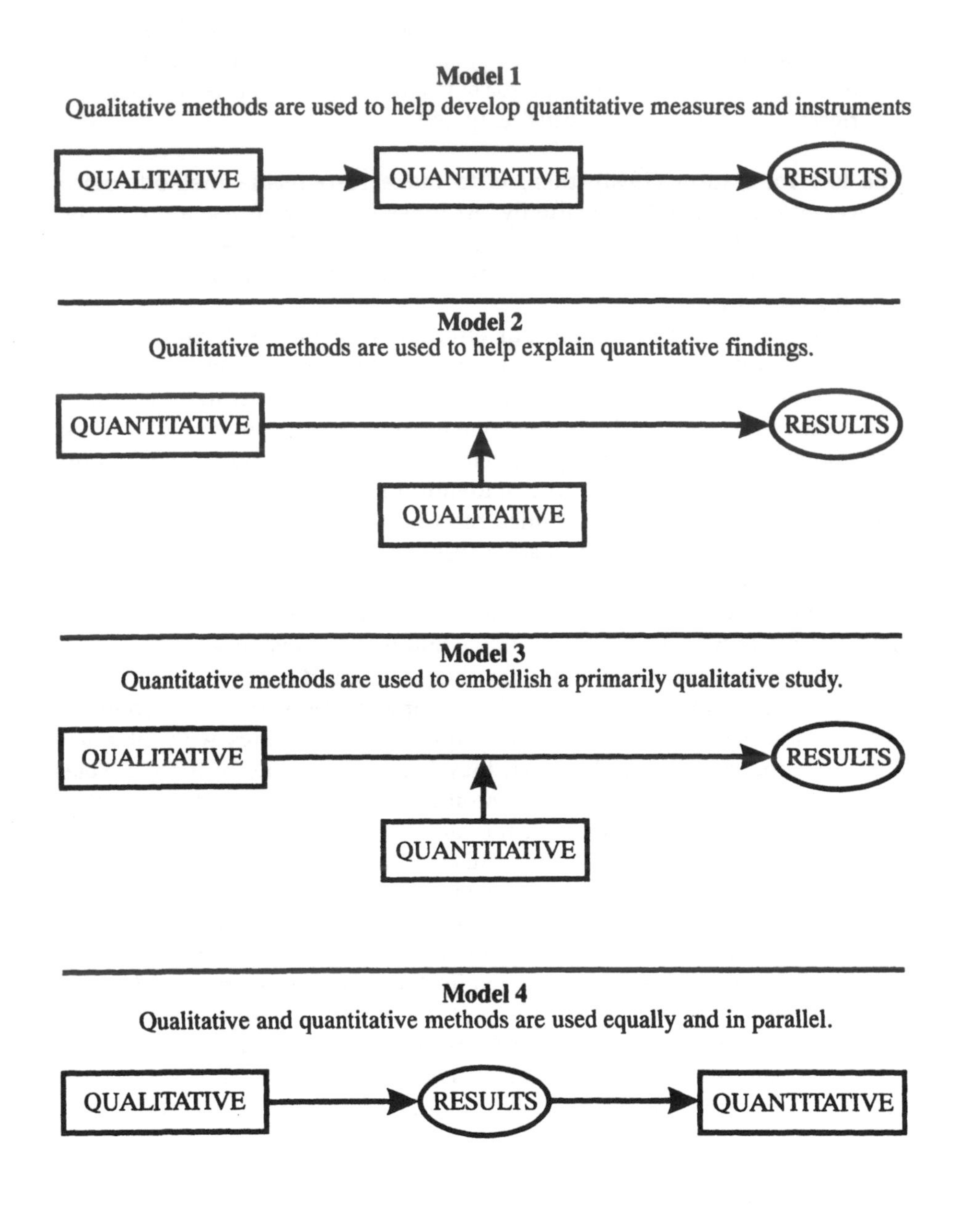

Figure 10.1: Possible ways to integrate qualitative and quantitative methods (modified from Steckler *et al.*, 1992 with permission)

burnout experience, and identify variables of potential importance in the burnout process that had been previously unidentified in the literature. Thus, because the two methods were combined as equal partners in the project, more was learned than if each method had been used alone.

Of course, it is not always advisable to combine qualitative and quantitative methods. Some questions are best answered using quantitative methods and others qualitative, but as these examples show there are times when combining them is most useful.

Methodological rigour in qualitative research

Unfortunately, while clear criteria for judging methodological rigor in quantitative research have evolved over the years, criteria for judging the rigor of qualitative research have only recently begun to emerge. Lincoln and Guba (1985), for instance, indicate that qualitative research should be judged as to its "trustworthiness", or how an investigator persuades other scientists (including himself or herself) that the findings of an inquiry are worthy of attention. A number of criteria for establishing trustworthiness have been identified and they are summarised in Table 10.3. These include establishing: credibility (the qualitative equivalent of internal validity) through such techniques as prolonged engagement, peer debriefing, and negative case analysis; transferability (equivalent to external validity) via such things as "thick" description and making a database available to the reader; dependability (similar to reliability) through techniques such as stepwise replication and inquiry audits; and conceivability (the qualitative equivalent to

Table 10.3: Criteria for trustworthiness in qualitative research (modified from Lincoln and Guba, 1985 with permission)

Credibility (internal validity)	Prolonged engagement Persistent observation Triangulation Peer debriefing Negative case analysis Referential adequacy Member checking
Transferability (external validity)	Provide thick description Database for reader to judge transferability
Dependability (reliability)	Achieve credibility Multiple methods Stepwise replication Inquiry audit
Conceivability (objectivity)	Inquiry audit Audit trail

objectivity) through such things as inquiry audits and audit trails. Those conducting qualitative research must have an understanding of these criteria for trustworthiness and build them into their research designs.

Because the criteria for judging methodological rigor in qualitative research are not as well known as the criteria for judging rigor in quantitative research, the authors felt that it might be useful at this juncture to discuss and evaluate a qualitative research project in some depth. The investigation to be discussed was briefly examined in *Chapter 5* and alluded to earlier in this chapter. It focused on burnout in elite junior tennis players (Gould *et al.*, 1995a, b).

The overall goal of the project was to better understand burnout in junior tennis; that is, to understand why players who have been highly motivated in the past, withdraw psychologically, physically, and/or emotionally from their sport. As previously indicated, the study was conducted in two phases. Phase 1 involved a statistical comparison of nomothetic survey results collected from a national sample of burned out junior players (as defined by US Tennis Regional Directors) and a comparative group of players of similar age, sex, and experience who had not burned out. This phase will not be further discussed here because our focus is on examining this study in the light of criteria for judging methodological rigor in qualitative research.

The second, qualitative, phase of the study involved in-depth interviews with 10 of the 30 burned-out players from Phase 1. These individuals had scored highest on the burnout and perfectionism measures collected in the first phase. Content analyses of the interview transcripts of the ten players revealed two major categories of burnout symptoms: (1) "mental" symptoms which included staying motivated, lacking motivation/energy, negative feeling–affect, feelings of isolation, concentration problems, and highs and lows; and (2) "physical" symptoms which included having injuries, illness, or lacking energy. Categories of themes cited for burning out included: physical concerns (e.g. being sick, not satisfied with play); logistical concerns (e.g. time demands, travel concerns); social/interpersonal concerns (e.g. dissatisfaction with social life, negative parental influence); and the largest category—psychological concerns (e.g. unfulfilled/unrealistic expectations, pressure). Recommendations for preventing burnout were also identified. What was important about these findings was that contrary to the investigators' beliefs going into the study, burnout was found to be much more psychologically (as opposed to physically) driven. The varied reasons these young athletes gave for leaving tennis were identified in a very specific fashion, providing rich holistic data that highlighted consistent patterns across individuals while at the same time reflecting clear individual differences.

As previously mentioned, this study is a good example of combining quantitative and qualitative methods as equal partners in a research project.

Quantitative methods were deemed most appropriate in Phase 1 because one of the investigative team's goals was generalisation—to derive conclusions that would apply to players across the United States and not be specific to players from a particular geographic region. It was also felt that a number of psychometrically sound instruments were available to measure many of the variables of interest. In Phase 2, the investigators were hoping to identify a number of previously unidentified personal and situational variables affecting burnout, unrestrained by current theory and measurement instruments. Because this was one of the first burnout studies conducted with athletes the researchers also wanted to obtain in-depth information on the players' experiences with particular emphasis on profiling psychological characteristics as well as describing the situational considerations that were associated with burning out.

To collect the data for Phase 2, telephone interviews were conducted by the same investigator who was trained extensively in qualitative research methodology as outlined by Patton (1990) and Lincoln and Guba (1985). The interviewer was well versed in sport psychology and had an extensive athletic background including time spent playing competitive junior tennis. Each participant was asked to respond to an identical sequence of questions from a structured interview guide. The athletes were asked the interview questions in the same manner with predetermined probing questions asked as needed during the interview. The probes were determined *a priori* as an attempt to minimise interviewer bias by ensuring that all follow-up questions were similar. This semi-structured format was chosen as it facilitated comparison across participants while still allowing for flexibility in individual responses. The interviews lasted from 50 to 90 min, were tape recorded, and were later transcribed verbatim.

A hierarchical content analysis, as recommended by Patton (1990) and successfully adapted to sport by Scanlan *et al.* (1989), Gould *et al.* (1992a, b), and Gould *et al.* (1993c, d), was used to analyse the interview findings. Specifically, the following six step data analysis procedure was utilised.

(1) All ten tape recorded interviews were transcribed verbatim resulting in 214 pages of single-spaced text.
(2) The three investigators, each of whom had a background in qualitative research methodology, read and re-read all ten transcripts to become completely familiar with each participant. The investigators also listened to each taped interview to gain additional insight that the printed word cannot provide such as tone of voice, pauses, and the use of sarcasm.
(3) Idiographic profiles consisting of two to three page summaries of each athlete's burnout experience were independently developed by three of the investigators. Each profile was then discussed extensively by the three investigators until consensus was reached and a single profile

developed. This allowed the investigators to contextualise specific findings relative to the players' "whole" burnout experience.

(4) In addition to the idiographic profiles, each investigator independently identified raw data themes that seemed to characterise each participant's responses within each section of the interview. Raw data themes were defined as quotes or paraphrased quotes that captured a distinct idea or concept provided by the athlete. After each investigator had independently identified raw data themes for a given participant, they met to discuss the identified themes and to come to a consensus. Triangular consensus had to be reached for each raw data theme to be used in analysis. Any disagreement necessitated a review of the transcript to settle the dispute. This validation process resulted in a list of agreed upon data themes from all ten subjects for each section of the interview.

(5) Using the raw data themes developed in Step 4, an inductive analysis was conducted to identify common themes or patterns of greater generality. Higher level themes were labelled "first-order themes", "second-order themes" and "third-order themes", in order of increasing generality. The highest level, therefore, represented common themes of the greatest generality, meaning that no links could be uncovered among these themes. As with the idiographic profiles and raw data theme generation, triangular consensus had to be reached on all identified higher order themes.

(6) Lastly, after all higher order themes had been identified, the investigators reviewed the emergent patterns to ensure that the descriptors made intuitive sense and could be easily understood. The raw data themes comprising each higher-order theme were re-read to check that they fitted coherently into the broader category. Again, consensus had to be reached.

Keeping the method and data analysis procedures in mind, it is instructive to evaluate Phase 2 of the study by employing the criteria for trustworthiness contained in Table 10.3. A summary evaluation of this study in light of these criteria is contained in Table 10.4. An inspection of this table reveals that credibility was achieved in three ways. First, by method triangulation (consistency across findings were found between the quantitative (Phase 1) and qualitative (Phase 2) results and via investigator triangulation (the three investigators had to agree on all three themes identified). Second, the investigators also conducted negative case analyses by constantly examining individuals and themes which did not seem to follow the general patterns of the group. Finally, referential adequacy (or ways of recording data so others could check its accuracy) was achieved by tape recording and transcribing all interviews. Credibility could have been improved further by prolonged engagement (interviewing the players a

Table 10.4: Summary evaluation on qualitative method criteria met in a burnout in junior tennis investigation (modified from Gould *et al.*, 1995a with permission)

Credibility criteria
Prlonged engagement—*not achieved*
Persistent observation—*not achieved*
Triangulation—*achieved (via method and evaluators)*
Peer debriefing—*not achieved*
Negative case analysis—*achieved*
Referential adequacy—*achieved (via tape recorded and transcribed interviews)*
Member checking—*not achieved*

Transferability criteria
Provide thick description—*achieved*
Database for reader to judge transferability—*achieved*

Dependability criteria
Achieve credibility—*achieved*
Multiple methods—*achieved*
Stepwise replication—*achieved*
Inquiry audit—*not achieved*

Conceivability criteria
Inquiry audit—*not achieved*
Audit trail—*achieved*

number of times), persistent observation (actually observing players in practices and games), peer debriefing (having an independent investigator consult with us regarding methodological and data analysis during the course of the investigation), and via member checking (having the participants read their results to ensure that interpretations were correct).

Transferability was achieved in the investigation by providing thick description (detailed quotes from the players) in write-ups, as well as through idiographic profiles which convey each player's story. In addition, this thick description provided a database for the reader to judge transferability.

Dependability criteria were met by demonstrating competence in three ways. First, the interviewer and investigators were well trained in qualitative research, and methodological and data analysis procedures were described in depth. Second, multiple methods were employed (quantitative and qualitative). And, third, stepwise replication was achieved by interviewing ten players and noting consistent patterns across them. A weakness of the study was that the investigators did not conduct an inquiry audit by having an independent researcher trained in qualitative research come in for several weeks to study the methods and procedures used, and the results obtained.

Lastly, conceivability was achieved via an audit trail. That is, detailed records are available regarding the data and data analysis procedures in case others who question our findings would like to inspect them. The previously mentioned failure to conduct an inquiry audit was a weakness not only in terms of dependability but also in terms of conceivability.

Table 10.4, then, reports the degree of methodological rigour achieved in this investigation by meeting trustworthiness criteria. In so doing, however, we do not want to imply that the particular method and data analysis procedures employed in this study are the only acceptable way to collect qualitative data. In fact, there are many other appropriate methodological procedures and data analyses that could, and should, be used. Yet, all these methods and data analysis choices should be evaluated relative to the trustworthiness criteria described above.

Returning to our example, an inspection of Table 10.4 also shows the weaknesses of this study and how it could be improved. However, it is important to note that perfect studies are seldom, if ever, conducted (from a qualitative or quantitative perspective), and that all investigations will have strengths and limitations. Hence, while one should strive to achieve all the trustworthiness criteria mentioned in Table 10.4, it will seldom be possible to do so.

The idiographic–nomothetic design struggle

Although not as hotly debated as the quantitative–qualitative research issue, some concerns have been voiced over the appropriateness of idiographic versus nomothetic designs in sport psychology research (Dunn, 1994; Martens, 1987; Smith, 1989). The nomothetic approach focuses on studying groups of individuals and drawing conclusions (generalities) about populations. It has been the dominant approach used, and tends to be deductive, trait-oriented, norm referenced, and focused on between subject variations (Smith, 1989). The idiographic approach focuses on the in-depth study of a single individual. It is inductive, tends to focus on discrete behaviours, is criterion referenced, and focuses on within subject variation (Smith, 1989). In the past idiographic research has been conducted less often than nomothetic in sport psychology.

As was the case with the quantitative–qualitative debate, arguing that one approach is better than the other is moot. Both approaches have advantages. Nomothetic research allows us to determine what psychological characteristics and strategies are dominant across a group of individuals, while the idiographic approach reveals how variables may change within an individual or be uniquely used by him or her. Dunn (1994) has also recently demonstrated how idiographic and nomothetic approaches can be combined where an idiographic investigation serves as a means of assessing whether nomothetic principles apply to individual athletes; while Smith (1988) and Bryan (1987) have identified a number of methodological advances that make idiographic research more powerful.

Internal versus external validity concerns

Sport psychology researchers differ in their opinions of the weight that should be placed on internal versus external validity in designing their studies. Martens (1979; 1987), for example, argued that sport psychologists have focused too much attention on internal validity concerns at the expense of external validity. In fact, he urged researchers to "take off their smocks" and get out of the laboratory, "put on their jocks" and move into the field to study their questions in externally valid situations. In response, Landers (1983) warned against a mass move away from internally valid laboratory research, citing the importance of such research in allowing investigators to develop sport psychology theory through the process of strong inference (Platt, 1964).

A primary reason for the internal–external validity debate stems from the fact that internal and external validity are negatively correlated to each other. For instance, the more a researcher stresses internal validity the more likely he or she will be to initiate experimental controls which change the nature of the elite sport setting. Similarly, the more sport psychologists attempt to study elite athletes in actual performance situations, the less control they will have over that situation and the key variables within it.

One solution to this problem is to strive for a balance between internal and external validity concerns. At times, in order to appropriately answer some questions more internal validity will be needed at the expense of some external validity. At other times and with other questions, more external validity will be needed at the expense of internal validity. In the end, the individual investigator must strike her or his own balance between internal and external validity emphasis, relative to the purposes of the investigation at hand and the currently available evidence.

Direct versus indirect measurement concerns

Although not usually discussed in the sport psychology literature, most conference goers have witnessed individual debates or heard comments concerning the appropriate level of measurement that should be used in our research. Some scientists argue that we will only make major advances in knowledge if direct measures of psychological and psychophysiological processes such as EMG and brain wave activity are made. Others feel that these measures have little meaning because they are too far removed from actual behaviour, and instead focus their attention on information processing assessments, or actual athlete behaviours. Like the other issues discussed elsewhere in this section there is no simple answer to the appropriateness of direct versus indirect measurement in sport psychology. The individual investigator needs to determine what types of measure are best suited for the problem under study. Moreover, investigators develop certain measurement competencies which would certainly influence such a decision. Yet, it is our contention that both direct and indirect measures are needed in our field of enquiry, and that knowledge will be gained in the most efficacious manner if all levels of elite athlete psychological functioning are tapped. Level of measurement dogmatism will only retard the growth of knowledge in the area.

Reconciling methodological debates

As can be seen there is no shortage of methodological debates in sport psychological research. Allegiance to a single method is certainly not the answer, as this type of methodological dogmatism does not recognise either the fact that every method has both its strengths and weaknesses, or the fact that one "perfect" approach for advancing knowledge does not exist. A more fruitful track is to recognise that both quantitative and qualitative investigations, idiographic and nomothetic methods, studies that vary in their internal and external validity, and investigations using both indirect and direct measures are needed.

A practical way to help make the appropriate methodological decisions along these lines is to spend considerable time thinking about which method choices are best suited to the question being studied. In addition, it is often helpful to think of how the factors depicted in Figure 10.2 play off against one another in an investigation. For instance, the more one stresses causality in a study's design (for example, by using laboratory tasks to facilitate experimental manipulation and control) the less likely it will be that one's findings will generalise to real-life settings. Similarly, the more objectivity is stressed in the measurement of key variables the less likely it is that one will be able to detect the subtle changes in those variables which characterise real-life relationships; hence, once again one's findings may not be generalisable to the real world. For example, psychophysiological research is potentially highly objective, but the precise interpretation of psychophysiological data in terms of psychological constructs remains problematic. However, if

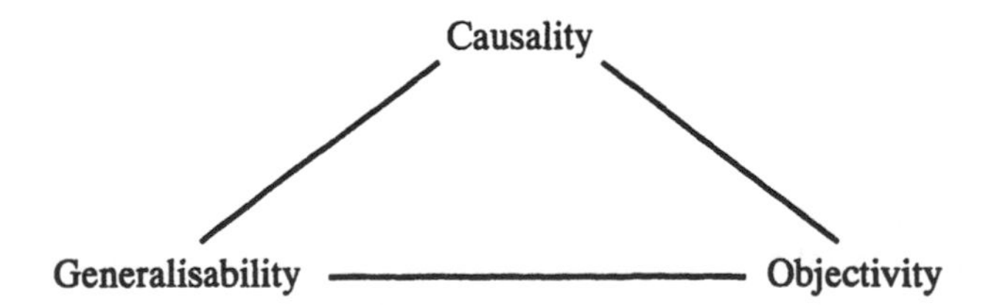

Figure 10.2: The causality, generalisability, and objectivity triangle

all of this sounds like a good argument for rejecting all laboratory-based and true experimental work in favour of naturalistic methods (cf. Martens, 1987), it is worth bearing in mind that qualitative methods are only strong with respect to generalisability. They are extremely weak in terms of both causality and objectivity. Indeed, some naturalistic researchers even deny the existence of objectivity, although when taken to its logical conclusion such a naturalistic philosophy renders all attempts to gain knowledge about the nature of the world or people rather pointless, since everybody's understanding would be considered to be relevant only to themselves at that moment in time. The solution, then, is to arrive at the best possible balance between these three factors when designing a particular study, or to conduct a series of related studies focusing on the same basic question, but with each particular investigation demonstrating these three characteristics to differing degrees.

Summary

In this section qualitative and quantitative research methods were defined, together with positivistic and naturalistic research paradigms. While qualitative methods are most often associated with the naturalistic paradigm and quantitative with the positivistic, it was stressed that this does not have to be the case. Thus, it is best for investigators to distinguish between both methodologies and paradigms. It was also emphasised that researchers must recognise how their own paradigm choice can subtly bias their investigative efforts.

In line with the notion of Patton (1990), we argued strongly that no one method choice is always best. Rather, different methods have different strengths and weaknesses. Hence, different methods should be employed depending on the question being asked. Steckler *et al.*'s (1992) ways of combining qualitative and quantitative methods were also discussed.

Lincoln and Guba's (1985) criteria for evaluating "trustworthiness" or methodological rigour in qualitative research were presented. These included: credibility (the qualitative counterpart to internal validity); transferability (generalisability); dependability (reliability); and conceivability (objectivity). A recent qualitative research project was evaluated relative to these criteria.

The idiographic–nomothetic research design struggle was examined. While only a relatively small amount of idiographic sport psychology research has been conducted, it was concluded that both types of research design must be employed if knowledge is to advance in the future.

It was argued that a balance must be achieved between internal and external validity relative to the current state of knowledge in an area, the purpose of an investigator's study, and the phase of the research programme. Similarly, investigators should spend time thinking about the balance that they hope to achieve between causality, generalisability, and objectivity given the purpose of a particular study within the programme of research being conducted.

MATCHING METHODS WITH PROBLEMS

While Table 10.1 lists the most important questions for future research regarding the psychological preparation of elite athletes, once a question is selected from this listing, the investigator must determine which methodological approach should be used to examine the particular question of interest.

In making a method choice, it is important to remember a major theme of this chapter, that no one best method or research approach exists for all investigations. The suitability of a methodological approach is determined by the question posed and the goals of the investigator. The old adage "the problem determines the method" is certainly the message that we wish to convey.

A second major and related theme of this chapter is that while the problem determines the range of method choices available, investigators should *consider using multiple methods both within and across investigations* because of the strengths and limitations associated with different methods. Thus, different methods and designs can be combined within the same investigation. Alternatively, an investigator may want to employ a range of methods, varying from a quantitative nomothetic to a qualitative idiographic approach, across a series of studies on a particular topic.

Lastly, it goes without saying that a proper methodological choice for the question being posed does little good if the study is not carried out in a rigorous fashion. There is a need for methodological rigour regardless of the method choice.

At this juncture, it may be helpful to see how different methods and designs can be used to examine several of the questions listed in Table 10.1. Question 4 of Basic Psychological Techniques asks "what is the nature of the self-talk that elite athletes use and how does this self-talk exert its influence on motivation, attention, emotion, and performance?" This question could be examined using both quantitative and qualitative approaches. For example, using a qualitative approach, in-depth interviews could be conducted with outstanding athletes to determine the nature of their self-talk. The researcher could ask the athletes to describe their self-talk in a variety of situations (e.g. winning, losing, practice, competition), possibly asking them to use imagery or look at videos of themselves in these situations to help recall what they were thinking. Another option might involve having athletes wear microcassette tape-recorders and "think aloud" as they engage in practice or in competition (e.g. a marathon runner could describe her thoughts prior to, during, and after an actual race). Raw data themes could be extracted from the data obtained and content analysed to determine categories of self-talk. If a series of probing questions were asked relative to "how" various self-statements influenced performance, the investigator would also be able to derive possible explanations of how self-talk influenced performance (e.g. motivation, attention).

Because the above study would be high in generalisability, but low in objectivity and causality, it might be in order to follow it up with quantitatively based field studies. For example, a group of swimmers might receive a two-week self-talk training programme. Then, in both training and a special competition (organised by the researcher), the swimmers would employ specific kinds of self-talk strategies; for example, positive versus negative self-statements; energising/motivating versus technical/tactical self-statements. The researcher could determine the effect of the different strategies on standardised performance in the same event using appropriate between or within subjects statistics. Questionnaires asking the subjects to rate their levels of motivation, attentional focus, and emotions during the practices and competitions could also be administered so that the statistical relationships between uses of particular self-talk techniques and changes in motivation, attention, and emotions could be determined.

Finally, investigators interested in the above issues might explore them in one individual over time (a season) or in groups of subjects in a relatively short time period (one practice or event). Hence, different combinations of qualitative–quantitative and idiographic–nomothetic designs might be employed.

The second part of this question (how does self-talk exert its influence on motivation, attention, emotion and performance?) also lends itself to the use of direct process measures. Using a task such as golf putting, experienced golfers could be taught to use various self-talk strategies (e.g. positive versus negative) prior to putting. The effects of these strategies on activation, attentional processing, and muscle tension could be determined using measures of EEG and EMG.

The previous question is fairly global and open to a number of varied method and design choices. Question 6 of the Self-confidence section of Table 10.1 asks "Is the self-confidence–performance relationship mediated by changes in the perception of control?", and is much more limiting in terms of design choices. Direct process measures would not be very relevant in examining this question. Similarly, other than for initially exploring the relationship between self-confidence and perceptions of control, qualitative methods would not be that instructive either. A correlational field study using path analysis or structural equation modelling to link changes in athletes' perceptions of control and self-confidence over time might be especially useful, particularly in light of the fact that fairly good measures of self-confidence and perceptions of control exist. This would allow for a good balance between objectivity, causality, and generalisability. It is perhaps worth noting at this stage that, despite the fact that one is trying to establish a causative relationship between these variables, it is not possible to use a true experimental design to answer this question because *two sequential* effects are hypothesised. True experiments can only examine main effects and interactions; they should not really be used to examine sequential effects.

Finally, Question 6 of the Coping with Adversity section of Table 10.1 asks "how are coping behaviours, resources, and dispositions developed?" Given the nature of this question laboratory studies, or direct measures, would not be appropriate. An investigator would most likely conduct some type of qualitative or quantitative field study. From a qualitative perspective, it might be useful to interview elite performers and determine what coping behaviours and resources they use. Then both the athletes and those who have known them very well and followed their careers closely (e.g. coaches, parents, significant others, spouses) could be asked a series of questions relating to the development of these behaviours and resources. Identifying developmental patterns in these variables would be the focus of the interviews, together with the development of an instrument to assess factors that influence the development of coping.

Given that a number of coping disposition measures have been developed, a second phase might combine both quantitative and qualitative methods. Several hundred pre-elite athletes could complete a coping disposition measure such as the COPE on a semi-annual basis together with a survey of how coping dispositions are developed (based on the previous qualitative phase of the project). Changes in coping dispositions over time could then be associated with the results of the survey in a nomothetic research design. It might also be useful to follow a small number of individuals over time in an idiographic fashion by conducting a series of qualitative interviews aimed at better understanding changes associated with COPE scores.

Summary

Examples of different methods and designs that could be used to examine several critical future research questions, as well as questions previously identified in this book, were discussed. The examples given are not complete, nor are the approaches identified the only approaches that could be taken in order to study these issues. Nevertheless, the examples clearly demonstrate how the use of a number of different methodological approaches (quantitative–qualitative; direct–indirect assessments; idiographic–nomothetic; laboratory–

field) could greatly enhance our understanding of the psychological preparation of elite performers. Similarly, because of the strengths and limitations of each approach, the use of varied methods both within studies and within lines of systematic research would enable a good balance to be struck between objectivity, causality, and generalisability.

CHARACTERISTICS OF SIGNIFICANT STUDIES

A knowledge of methodological considerations will clearly facilitate the design of future performance enhancement studies. However, future research could also be enhanced by an analysis of the characteristics of previous studies which have had a major impact on the field. Looking back over the chapters of this book, and the reviews of literature contained within them, three characteristics of significant studies emerge most frequently. These are: (1) asking important questions; (2) conducting studies which are part of a line of systematic research; and (3) striving for, developing, and being guided by theory. Each of these characteristics will now be briefly examined.

Asking important questions

The importance of asking a high impact question has been repeatedly emphasised throughout this manuscript, and the questions listed in Table 10.1 should be especially helpful in this regard. However, considerable thought should still be given not only to identifying specific subquestions falling under these more global queries, but also to the best settings for operationalising and testing these questions. Significant studies ask questions which have high impact from a theoretical and/or a practical perspective, so time spent thinking about one's question and its importance is a very good investment when conducting performance enhancement research that counts.

Systematic lines of research

The research discussed in this book has repeatedly demonstrated that we have learned most about the psychological preparation of elite athletes for peak performance from systematic lines of research, not isolated studies. It is critical, then, that investigators plan systematic lines of research aimed at answering important questions. Similarly, it is important for investigators to determine how their particular research programme fits into the larger line of research being conducted in an area. This is not to say that we simply mimic previous research methods, strategies, and conceptual approaches—these should always be critically analysed and advanced, or radically changed if need be. We must constantly strive to design each new study to help us take the area to the "next" level of knowledge.

Theoretically based research

Finally, many of the most significant studies tend to be theoretical in their orientations, integrate theory with their findings, or attempt to develop grounded theory. This does not imply that they are not of practical significance, only that the investigators conducting them strive to go beyond specific findings and data patterns to develop explanations that help us better understand the psychology of peak performance. In addition, it does not imply that all studies were tests of specific theories—only that they had as a major goal the development of theory, whether it be an advanced theory test or an initial attempt to develop possible theoretical explanations. The adage that "nothing is more practical than a good theory" remains a guiding principle for those conducting significant psychological preparation for peak performance research.

Summary

Some of the characteristics of previous elite athlete sport psychology studies which have had a major impact on the field were discussed. These included: asking questions of theoretical and/or practical importance; conducting studies which are parts of systematic lines of research; and, striving for theoretical explanations whether this be testing a specific theory, integrating theory into one's study, or attempting to develop a new theory. Future investigators are encouraged to incorporate these characteristics into their own research.

THE PSYCHOLOGY OF ADVANCING KNOWLEDGE

Like other areas in higher education, today more than ever before there is external pressure for scholars in sport psychology to conduct research, publish their studies in respected journals, and obtain external funding for their work. While this has certainly increased the amount of research conducted in our field and helped to motivate investigators to find funding for their research, it has also resulted in problems. In particular, these external pressures may have caused some investigators to try to "pump out studies", focusing more on the total quantity of studies they conduct and less on the contribution these studies make to advancing knowledge. For example, because investigators are pressured to publish a large number of studies there appears to be a tendency to examine only "safe" questions that will lead to a publication, but are limited in scope and do not challenge existing scientific beliefs. Similarly, in order to produce more articles there also appears to be a tendency for projects to be chopped up into small and less meaningful parts. Lastly, these pressures may have caused many investigators to be so busy collecting data that they fail to spend enough quiet time thinking about the most critical questions in need of study, the best methods for answering those questions, and how their work will help to take the field to the next level of knowledge.

Given these concerns (all of which have been felt at times by the authors in conducting their own research), it is important that the psychology of advancing knowledge in the area of psychological preparation for peak performance be discussed. Specifically, four key areas need to be addressed. These are: (1) turning out papers versus conducting research which makes a meaningful contribution to knowledge; (2) the importance of theoretical and methodological tolerance; (3) risk taking in research; and (4) using one's scientific strengths to maximise research payoffs. Each of these issues will now be examined.

Turning out versus conducting meaningful research

The pressures on today's researchers make it easy to fall into the trap of working diligently at turning out one study, and then immediately turning to the next, and then the next, and so on. While most of these studies contribute in some way to the body of knowledge in sport psychology, they do not maximise their contribution. In essence, we creep forward at a very slow pace with each study adding a small part to the total knowledge pool.

It is our view that this "creep" strategy is not the best approach to advancing knowledge in applied sport psychology. Our own experience has taught us that our best research has come after considerable thought and planning. So, the first step in the psychology of advancing performance enhancement research is for investigators to slow down, step off the research treadmill, and "think" about the field at large, the most important issues needing study, which research questions will contribute most to knowledge development, and their own ability to conduct that research. While pressures to publish and produce in today's research environment cannot be ignored, we must ensure that we do not fall into the trap of being a research machine, cloning one study after the next without taking time to reflect on their significance and meaning. We must continually take the time to ask how our next study will contribute to the field and whether it will maximise knowledge gain.

Theoretical and methodological tolerance

For the field to advance at a faster rate it is also important for investigators to develop theoretical and methodological tolerance. Too often, researchers have closed their minds to alternative or new theoretical views without really studying them because of their own extremely strong views regarding some conflicting position. It would be naive for us to suggest that theorists will not argue varying theoretical positions—indeed, *critical analysis and discussion is normal and very healthy for the development of scientific thought*. However, investigators must be aware of their theoretical biases and not blindly discourage alternative views just because they do differ from their own. Instead, the development of alternative theoretical views should be encouraged because if they are not better explanations than existing perspectives, then they will not be supported by research. This may not tell us more about a phenomenon, but it will eliminate false explanations which should not be further pursued. Moreover, at times new or alternative views will evolve into more powerful and appropriate explanations. Finally, developing alternative views provides investigators with the opportunity to test multiple theories in single investigations and, in so doing, provide "critical" tests of competing explanations.

Tolerance is needed not only in terms of theoretical perspectives, but also regarding methodological approaches. As previously stated, different problems require different methods and levels of measurement and, often, multiple methodologies and measures will allow the strengths and weaknesses of different studies to complement one another. This does not imply that every investigator must be an expert at all approaches, methods, measures, and designs. In this day and age, that is not possible. However, regardless of one's methodological and measurement perspectives, other approaches should be appreciated and encouraged. Alternatively, joint research projects which combine the talents and unique methodological perspectives and training of different investigators could be utilised very productively.

Risk taking in research

Although seldom discussed in research methods texts, doing state-of-the-art research which helps the field "leap", as opposed to "creep", forward requires some risk taking on the part of the individual investigator. It is much easier to conduct research on questions for which we can anticipate what answers will be derived, with existing theories to guide us, with methods we have used in the past, and in areas where we have a great deal of experience. Going "where no one has gone before" involves much more uncertainty and more investigator discomfort.

Vealey (1994) has recently discussed this issue by applying the ideas of Bauer (1992) to the field of sport psychology. In particular, she emphasises that most contemporary sport psychology research falls into the "known–

unknown" classification where researchers pursue novel findings, but not results which are so novel that they conflict with the dominant school of thought. Vealey (1994) emphasises, however, that more "unknown–unknown" research is needed where novel findings are pursued without being restricted by conventional thinking, paradigms, and schools of thought (although the investigator should certainly be aware of these). Perhaps the work of Terry Orlick, cited throughout this book, best reflects "unknown–unknown" sport psychological performance enhancement research. The strengths of his work lie in creativity and, although the methodology is often less rigorous than might be desired, the creativity of the questions posed often bears considerable scholarly fruit. We agree with Vealey, then, and feel that more emphasis needs to be placed on "unknown–unknown" research in our field. That said, it must be mentioned that less experienced researchers (e.g. assistant professors, lecturers, graduate students) have to realise that it is (wrongly) much easier for a senior scholar to challenge existing scholarly conventions than someone in their position. For this reason, some caution is needed in "unknown–unknown" question selection when one is beginning a career in the field. "Unknown–unknown–creative" questions can still be pursued, but how far one can successfully push conventional thought is more limited for less experienced scholars. Senior scholars, however, have a professional responsibility to actively pursue "unknown–unknown" research.

Using one's scientific strengths to maximise research payoff

A final consideration in the psychology of conducting research that maximises knowledge advancement is the importance of the scientist in learning how to recognise her or his own strengths and limitations. Good researchers will always work to improve their scientific weaknesses, but they should also recognise how their strengths can best be utilised. The first author, for example, has a doctorate in pure mathematics and hence has been able to develop complex modelling procedures for testing anxiety–performance catastrophe relationships. It would not be productive or successful for the third author to attempt to pursue such an endeavour (although he should certainly strive to understand it). As compared to the lead author, the third author has a much more extensive history of conducting qualitative research. For this reason, it plays to his strength to ask critical questions where this methodology can be used either by itself or to supplement traditional quantitative data analysis procedures.

Given the above, the advantage of each investigator conducting research which maximises his strengths as an investigator is important. More important, however, are planned research collaborations between the two investigators where the strengths of each (sophisticated quantitative and qualitative analyses) will be maximised and the limitations offset. Other investigators are encouraged to pursue similar projects.

Summary

It has been argued that while more research on the psychological preparation of elite athlete performance is being conducted than ever before, the external pressures which act upon researchers have caused some problems that interfere with the advancement of knowledge in the area. Investigators must not fall into the trap of turning out research without spending enough time thinking about critical issues. Critical issues that must be contemplated include: maximising the payoff of one's research by: ensuring that meaningful questions are being asked; developing theoretical and methodological tolerance; taking appropriate risks with regard to the research questions asked and the methods used; investigating more "unknown–unknown" issues in the area; and conducting research that maximises one's research strengths or involves collaboration with others who have complementary strengths.

SUMMARY

This chapter has been designed to identify future directions for research into psychological preparation for elite sports performance. Critical questions identified throughout the book and in need of further study were summarised and rated in terms of their importance and difficulty. Four important methodological concerns were also discussed: the quantitative–qualitative research debate; the idiographic–nomothetic design struggle; external versus internal validity trade-offs and choices; and direct versus indirect levels of measurement. It was argued that no one methodological choice regarding these issues is best. Rather, different questions and investigator goals will require different methodological approaches and, often, multiple methods will need to be employed to adequately study a topic. Characteristics of previous "significant" or high impact investigations were identified. These included asking important questions, conducting studies which fit within a line of systematic research, and using and striving for theory development. Finally, the psychology of advancing knowledge in this area was discussed. It was argued that greater emphasis needed to be placed on: conducting well thought out and meaningful research (versus "pumping out" study after study); increasing theoretical and methodological tolerance; increasing investigator risk-taking; and investigators using their research strengths to maximise research knowledge payoff. It is our hope that by employing these principles, research knowledge about the psychological preparation of elite performers will develop more efficiently and rapidly than it has to date.

11

IMPLICATIONS FOR GUIDING PRACTICE

CONTENTS

INTRODUCTION

The first eight chapters of this book focused on summarising the latest research and theory on the most important topics involved in the psychological preparation of elite sport performers. The practical implications of this research were identified within each chapter. The present chapter will also focus on those practical implications by drawing together the most important guidelines obtained from both within and across the previous chapter topics. The chapter will go beyond the previously delineated consulting guidelines, however, by showing how best to consult and develop psychological skills to facilitate peak performance in elite athletes. In so doing, critical elements of the consultancy process will be identified and discussed, including programme guidelines, and the characterising features of effective and ineffective consultancy.

While this chapter will be of most interest to those who desire to be, or are already, involved in psychological consultancy work with elite athletes, it is also important for those whose interest may be primarily research-focused. Sport psychology is an applied field and researchers will be in a better position to design the most meaningful elite athlete research if they understand the context in which psychological consultancy takes place. In that way, the most conceptually sound and externally valid research can be conducted.

Table 11.1: Practical guidelines for peak performance

Basic techniques: relaxation

1. Elite performers must learn both mental and physical relaxation techniques.
2. Relaxation techniques that can be used both before and during actual performance must be emphasised and developed. Because articles and books on how to learn relaxation techniques do not do this, consultants must learn to adapt generic relaxation techniques for use with specific athletes in actual competitive conditions.
3. It may be best to tailor relaxation techniques to the specific type of anxiety (e.g. cognitive, somatic) experienced by the athlete. In cases where both types of anxiety are experienced or the type of anxiety experienced cannot be specifically identified it may be best to use techniques that involve both physical and mental relaxation.

Basic techniques: goal-setting

1. Specific, difficult, but realistic goals (as perceived by the athlete) should be set.
2. When setting goals, the specific behaviours targeted should be within the performer's control.
3. Both long- and short-term goals should be set by athletes.
4. Elite performers should be encouraged to set outcome-, performance- and process-oriented goals.

Basic techniques: mental rehearsal

1. Mental rehearsal and imagery are very effective techniques, but are not replacements for physical practice. Therefore, these techniques must be planned, integrated into, and used in conjunction with physical practice.
2. Both stimulus and response propositions should be incorporated into athletes' imagery scripts.
3. Sport psychology consultants and athletes should experiment with different imagery perspectives for different tasks and different situations.

Basic techniques: self-talk

1. Elite athletes should be instructed in the use of positive self-talk and cognitive restructuring techniques.

Self-confidence

1. Efficacy expectations will not predict performance when necessary skills and incentives are not present. Hence, elite athletes must be physically trained and technically prepared if high efficacy is to be maintained and play a role in enhancing performance.
2. Not only do elite athletes need high general confidence, but specific efficacy expectations must be developed for all important subcomponents of task performance.
3. Collective or team efficacy is more than the sum of individual athlete efficacy. Thus, specific strategies for developing group or team efficacy must be implemented.
4. Collective or team efficacy best predicts performance in highly cohesive units. Hence, team cohesion is important to develop in elite sport groups.
5. In anxiety provoking situations, elite athletes must develop strategies for both reducing anxiety and enhancing confidence, allowing the athlete to maintain a feeling of control in such situations.

Table 11.1: *(continued)*

6. Male and female athletes differ in their antecedents of confidence. Hence, male athletes should focus on both perceived readiness and superior ability relative to opponents, while females should focus on their physical and mental readiness and thoughts about a good personal performance.
7. Past performance accomplishments are a major source of efficacy for elite athletes. In this regard, efficacy can best be enhanced by employing good goal-setting procedures (see Basic Techniques Implications) and a combination of long- and short-term, performance, process, and outcome goals.
8. Successfully coping with hard physical training can also be a major source of athlete efficacy, so it is important for coaches not only to train athletes hard but remind them to be confident because of such hard training.
9. Elite coaches should model confidence and more often emphasise the daily use of imagery to help athletes enhance confidence. Also, they can have a powerful influence on athlete efficacy through encouragement and verbal persuasion.
10. Elite athletes should maintain their high confidence through positive self-talk and cognitive restructuring.
11. Elite athletes should not only be able to manipulate their arousal levels, but they should also be able to view high levels of arousal as a positive sign of readiness and not as a negative state.

Motivation

1. High levels of intrinsic and extrinsic motivation are necessary for elite performance.
2. High levels of motivation are developed and sustained by positive feedback about competence. Good goal-setting and self-reward strategies in athletes and a positive coaching environment are the best ways to enhance these perceptions of competence.
3. High levels of motivation are developed and sustained by enhancing athletes' perceptions of self-determination. This can be best accomplished by allowing athletes to have choice and input into their training and competitive environments, as well as into the direction of their careers.
4. Elite athletes have strong ego, and strong task, goal orientations. Immediately before competition, process goals are most salient and should be emphasised; at this point in time, athletes should therefore be encouraged to use their performance and outcome goals *only* as a stimulus to focus their attention more strongly on their process goals.
5. Elite performers with a strong ego orientation and low perceived competence (for whatever reason) are most likely to experience motivational difficulties and should be monitored carefully.
6. To facilitate quality training and enhance motivation, process-oriented goals should be emphasised in practice environments (not just competitions).
7. Elite athletes should be encouraged to take responsibility for success and failure. In particular, they should be encouraged to make internal, controllable, and stable attributions for success and internal, controllable, and unstable attributions for failure. Attributing failure to poor strategy choice may be better than attributing it to lack of effort.
8. Attributional research implications are culturally bound and current findings may only apply to elite athletes in "Western" cultures.
9. Elite athletes need to possess good cognitive restructuring strategies to get out of "learned helplessness" spirals.

Table 11.1: *(continued)*

10. Active regeneration, stress management training, and social support are likely to help athletes avoid overstressing and burnout.
11. Elite performers most vulnerable to burnout have perfectionist tendencies, poor cognitive restructuring strategies, and little self-determination.
12. Goal-setting and attributional skills help prevent athlete burnout. In addition, coaches should structure the organisation of practice to empower performers, provide social support, and increase self-determination.
13. Training and lead-up to competitions prior to a major event should be planned in such a way that the athlete experiences performance success.

Arousal and activation

1. Imagery-based strategies appear to be a highly effective means of generating an appropriate activation state.
2. The development and adherence to pre-performance routines influence activation states in a positive manner.
3. The ability to generate appropriate activation states is an acquired skill and should be facilitated by sport psychology consultants and coaches.
4. Elite performers should modify mental preparation strategies in accordance with the time of day they will be performing.

Stress and anxiety

1. The coach plays an important role in helping determine the performer's perceived readiness for competition. In conjunction with their elite athletes, coaches should develop specific mental preparation and readiness strategies for each of their athletes.
2. Elite performers may demonstrate quite high levels of cognitive anxiety or somatic anxiety. However, high levels of both are likely to have catastrophic effects upon performance. Elite performers therefore need strategies for controlling both cognitive and somatic anxiety.
3. Ideal performance states are highly idiosyncratic and are unlikely to be a simple "iceberg" profile. Hence, coaches and consultants must help athletes identify their individual and task-specific ideal performance states and an appropriate recipe of emotions that helps to facilitate such a state.
4. Self-confidence appears to play an important role in determining the interpretation that performers place upon anxiety symptoms. For this reason, when assisting athletes with anxiety problems both anxiety management and confidence enhancement interventions will be needed.
5. Elite performers may maintain their performance under pressure by having exceptionally high levels of achievement motivation, by having exceptionally low levels of anxiety, or by overlearning skills to such an extent that they become sustained information tasks with a very small short-term memory component.
6. Simulation training is very important for elite performers—they should train under the physical, psychological, and social conditions under which they will have to perform.
7. It is unlikely that peak performance on more complicated sport tasks will ever be achieved by the application of any single psychological strategy; elite performers should be taught multimodal strategies.
8. Mental rehearsal of a given sport task should provide a most efficient means of establishing an appropriate activation pattern for peak performance. Thus, it is important to emphasise mental rehearsal.

Table 11.1: *(continued)*

9. Interpretation of anxiety and perceptions of control appear to be key factors in determining stress and anxiety effects upon performance. Increasing athletes' perceptions of control over their own performance and the performance situations that they face, and helping them to become accustomed to and comfortable with high levels of anxiety are therefore critical steps in helping them achieve outstanding performance.
10. Once a catastrophe occurs, the elite performer must substantially relax, restructure and then reactivate. Hence, elite performers need to develop both relaxation and reactivation strategies to use in the event of unexpected catastrophe situations.
11. Coaches and sport psychologists should consider the use of dual-task paradigms in training to enhance coping with excessive resource demands; for example, holding a conversation whilst performing.
12. Athletes should use process-oriented goals to direct attention where it is most needed; for example, a soccer defender might have the process-oriented goal of always marking at arm's length from his or her opponent.
13. Changes in mood from inhibiting moods (e.g. anxiety) to more active moods (e.g. determined) may facilitate the performance of anxious performers on some tasks. For this reason, elite performers should practise manipulating mood changes.

Concentration

1. Athletes should use mental rehearsal with simulation training (physical, technical, tactical, and psychological) to enhance concentration. For example, they might repeatedly rehearse every conceivable competition situation prior to competitions.
2. Elite performers may need to use both controlled and automated attentional capabilities. Hence, consultants and coaches should help elite performers to set process-oriented goals which do not interfere with automatic processing (e.g. holistic, as opposed to part, goals for well-learned skills).
3. Elite performers should train under dual-task paradigms.
4. Elite performers should incorporate imagery into competitive plans.
5. Pre-performance routines should be designed to control attention, cognitive anxiety and physiological arousal, and foster behavioural consistency.
6. Concentration may be enhanced by focusing on process-oriented goals.
7. Sport skills should be overlearned in as many different situations as possible. Simulation training is an excellent way to do this.
8. It is important for elite athletes to be taught to let things happen as opposed to trying to over-control performance and make things happen when they are anxious.
9. Attentional training should be incorporated into sport psychology consultancies.

Coping

1. Coping must be viewed as a complex process influenced by both performers' personalities and the situations in which they practise and compete. It is unlikely that single kinds of coping will be appropriate for all situations, or that any one form of coping will always be effective.

Table 11.1: *(continued)*

2. Coping strategies influence performance in elite athletes. For this reason, elite athletes should develop a broad spectrum of coping strategies which should include problem-focused, emotion-focused, restructuring, and avoidance strategies, as well as learning the most effective strategies for different situations.
3. It is incorrect to assume that elite performers do not have difficulty coping with stress or that, when they do cope, they will never employ maladaptive coping strategies.
4. When selecting effective coping strategies, it is important to isolate the specific source of stress involved and identify whether or not it is controllable.
5. Efforts must be made to identify and eliminate maladaptive coping strategies.
6. Athlete awareness of the need for coping with stress at major competitions should be developed by discussing unforeseen events that may possibly occur (e.g. dealing with the media) and identifying appropriate coping strategies for dealing with such potential stressors.
7. Efforts should be made to eliminate coping myths. Elite athletes should realise that "going it alone" is often not the best strategy. Rather, efforts should be made to seek out social support.
8. Coping strategies used in performance situations should be so well learned that they can be executed in an automatic fashion.
9. Coping strategies take time to develop and automate. Hence, programmes should be implemented to develop effective coping strategies in pre-elite and junior athletes.

PREPARATION FOR PEAK PERFORMANCE GUIDELINES

Table 11.1 contains a listing of the practical guidelines emanating from the research discussed, and variables addressed, in each of the chapters in this book. Over 60 implications have been identified and this speaks well for the research conducted in sport psychology. Certainly in such a young field, more questions remain unanswered than have been answered, but these guidelines clearly show that research can be used to guide practice and assist elite performers to achieve their goals.

While these guidelines were derived from specific topics discussed in each of the chapters in this book, it is interesting to note that some overlap exists between the topics identified. This reinforces the importance of integrating these topics (and, in turn, the subsequent guidelines) into the unifying model presented in Chapter 9. It also provides a means of identifying topics and guidelines which are particularly important for consultancy work.

It should not be surprising that goal-setting, relaxation, mental rehearsal–imagery, and self-talk were topics discussed in the implications sections of many of the chapters. After all, that is why these strategies were originally classified as basic techniques. They are vehicles which have important influences on most of the key variables discussed in this book. This not only reinforces the importance of these strategies, but also emphasises the importance of consultants and coaches being thoroughly schooled in their theory and application. For this reason, we recommend that consultants and coaches interested in enhancing elite athlete performance obtain an excellent grasp of these areas. Recommended readings include Burton's (1992) and Gould's (1993a) reviews of goal-setting, Murphy and Jowdy's (1992) and Vealey's (1993) reviews of mental rehearsal–imagery, Bunker *et al.*'s (1993) review of self-talk, and Gould and Udry's (1994) review of relaxation and arousal regulation strategies.

In addition to these four basic techniques, an inspection of Table 11.1 shows that simulation training is an extremely important vehicle for facilitating the achievement of ideal performance states during competition. While simulation training is often mentioned as an afterthought in many practical articles on psychological preparation for peak performance, this work demonstrates that it needs to be further studied and discussed in the literature. However, more information is needed as to how best to create and use simulations, how to incorporate them into other strategies such as imagery and goal-setting, and how, in turn, simulations may affect athlete efficacy, anxiety, activation, and perceptions of control. Until this further knowledge is developed, we can conclude only that coaches and consultants are encouraged to place more emphasis on simulations in their preparation of elite performers (cf. Jones and Hardy, 1990a; Orlick and Partington, 1988).

In terms of specific psychological attributes mentioned in Table 11.1, the role of self-efficacy or confidence becomes very apparent. It played a major role in motivation, stress and anxiety management, and attributions for success and failure. For this reason, coaches and consultants working with elite performers should place great importance on developing, maintaining, and protecting their athletes' self-confidence. They should also thoroughly understand the means by which self-confidence is developed and can be influenced.

In addition to self-efficacy, perceptions of control emerge in Table 11.1 as a potential major contributor to elite athlete psychological well-being, having a direct impact upon intrinsic motivation and burnout, and an indirect but possibly critical role in anxiety, stress management, and coping. Consultants and coaches, then, need to develop and nourish athletes' perceptions of control. This can be best accomplished by helping performers to develop good attributional, goal-setting, coping, and cognitive restructuring skills. Furthermore, given the likely relationship between self-confidence, self-determination, and perceptions of control, any autonomy-building strategies are also likely to produce beneficial effects upon performance. Simple autonomy building strategies include involving performers in important decision-making processes, and encouraging them to function independently when coaches are unable to work with them during their normal training.

Summary

This section has brought together the major implications of the previous chapters for the practising sport psychology consultant. In doing so, emphasis was placed on the important role played by the basic psychological skills of goal-setting, relaxation, imagery, and self-talk. The importance of helping elite performers to use simulation training, to develop high levels of self-confidence, and to maintain their perceptions of control was also highlighted.

PUTTING THE PSYCHOLOGY OF PEAK PERFORMANCE GUIDELINES INTO PRACTICE

Unfortunately, knowing the above guidelines and the scientific literature behind them is not enough to help elite athletes prepare psychologically for peak performance. Consultants and coaches must know how to package these guidelines into a psychological support programme. They must also realise that the nature of psychological support changes over time, and often becomes less directed and educationally oriented and more problem-focused, preventative, and organisationally involved with the passing of time (cf. Hardy and Parfitt, 1994). Finally, even with this knowledge, not everyone will be effective in assisting elite athletes. The consultant and/or coach must have the right personal characteristics and consultant skills to be able to effectively relate to athletes and teams. Given this state of affairs, three issues will now be discussed: (1) developing a psychological skills training programme; (2) going beyond psychological skills training to understand the complex and changing nature of consultancy; and (3) effective consultants and consultancy.

Developing a psychological skills training programme

Most consultants (Boutcher and Rotella, 1987; Thomas, 1990) feel that packaging psychological skills into some sort of assessment and training system is the best approach to use when working with individual athletes or teams. This usually involves a process that includes some sort of psychological skills assessment and evaluation (be it formal or informal), and athlete education about psychological skills together with exercises designed to develop, implement, and evaluate them. After reviewing the psychological skills training literature, and having observed and discussed the topic with a number of experienced practising sport psychologists, Thomas (1990) summarised what he had learned by formulating a seven-phase performance enhancement process in applied sport psychology. This model is depicted in Figure 11.1.

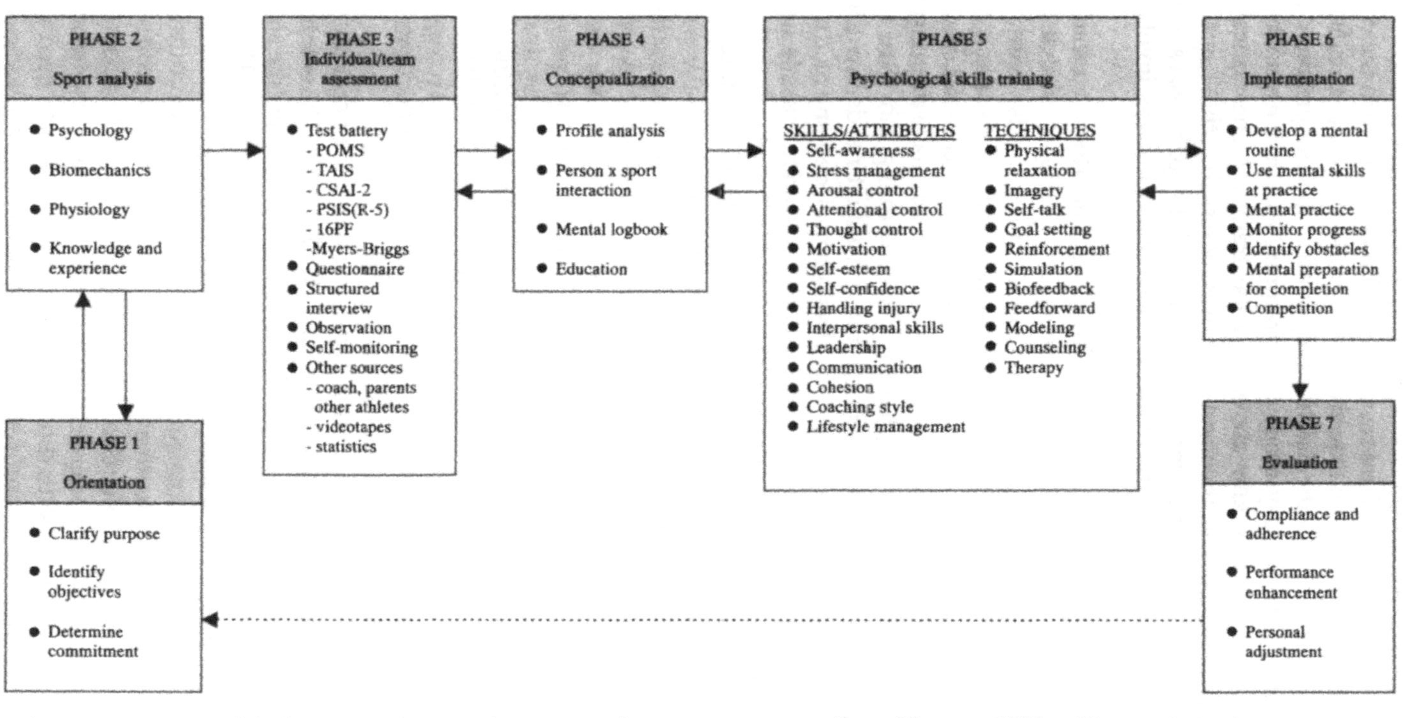

Figure 11.1: A model of a seven-phase performance enhancement process (from Thomas, 1990, with permission)

An inspection of this figure reveals that Phase 1 focuses on the consultant clarifying the purpose and objectives for working with a particular team or individual athlete. Do they desire help with a specific problem, or the development of a sport psychology programme? Are their expectations realistic and what do they know about mental training? These issues must be addressed. In addition, the consultant must assess the athlete's or the organisation's level of commitment to the mental training process, as well as his or her own level of commitment if the consultation process involves a long-term effort.

Phase 2 involves an analysis of the sport. This does not mean that the consultant has to have actual experience of participation in that sport (although this would most likely help), but he or she needs to learn about the sport. Reading books, attending clinics, watching videos, talking to experienced coaches and athletes, and observing actual practices and competitions are excellent ways to do this if one does not already have a thorough knowledge of the sport. But this phase involves learning more than the rules, language, and culture of the sport—the consultant needs some idea of the psychological, biomechanical, and physiological demands of the activity. This can often be obtained by reading coach education materials and talking to coaches or other sport scientists.

Individual and team assessment is the focus of Phase 3. It is in this phase that the consultant would want to obtain information on the performer's psychological strengths and limitations, as well as perceived problems in the psychological domain. As can be seen in the Phase 3 box, no one form of assessment is emphasised. Instead, consultants vary in their approaches. Some use structured psychological tests, others their own non-validated questionnaires, and still others individual-specific interviews and informal observations. The best method is probably the one the consultant and client feel most comfortable with, although inexperienced consultants should recognise that athletes do not usually respond well to extensive psychological testing unless they obtain highly specific and useful feedback from it (Hardy and Parfitt, 1994; Orlick and Partington, 1988).

One method of assessment that is gaining increased popularity is performance profiling (Butler, 1989; Butler and Hardy, 1992). The method involves helping the athlete to brainstorm those qualities which he or she considers to be most important for elite performance in his or her sport. The athlete then rates the relative importance of each quality, and rates his or her current status with respect to that quality. The athlete's coach can also rate the athlete on those qualities that have been identified. The scores are then transferred onto a profile sheet for visual inspection in order to identify major discrepancies between current and desired status, in order to facilitate goal-setting with respect to those qualities that are most in need of change. The advantage of this approach is that it results in psychological qualities generated from the athlete that he or she has rated as being important. Furthermore, because of the collaborative nature of the process the athlete and the coach can feel a good deal of ownership in the assessment which provides an excellent start to consultant–coach–athlete rapport and motivation. Further examples of the use of performance profiling are given in Butler *et al.* (1993) and Jones (1993).

The fourth phase, conceptualisation, is where the consultant takes what is learned from Phase 3 and considers it relative to Phase 5 (Actual Psychological Skills Training—discussed next). In essence, the consultant must determine which skills and attributes are most needed based on the information provided by the specific client and what the best techniques are to further develop those skills and attributes.

As indicated in Figure 11.1, Phase 5 focuses on psychological skills training and, in line with the work of Vealey (1988), depicts many of the skills and attributes that athletes or teams may want to further develop. Additionally, a variety of techniques which are of potential use are listed.

Implementation is the focus of Phase 6. Building from the previous five phases the consultant implements his or her intervention aimed at helping the athlete or team. Examples include developing a pre-performance routine, using mental practice prior to performance, and positively monitoring progress in order to enhance self-efficacy. A very important, and often neglected, part of this phase is to help the performer integrate any skills or strategies developed into his or her normal training and performance routines.

Some form of evaluation is the focus of Phase 7. For example, compliance and adherence to practising a relaxation strategy may be assessed. Similarly, performance improvements and personal adjustment may be monitored. It is important to note, however, that as in the initial assessment phase, effective consultants can vary widely in how formal or informal their evaluations are. Hence, this phase does not imply that some formal evaluation research must take place for a consultant to be effective. In fact, the evaluation often takes the form of a subjective and informal discussion with the performer and the coach.

Lastly, Thomas's model is closed-loop so that the evaluation phase feeds back into the sport analysis phase. Hence, evaluation would be directly related to the consultant's stated purpose and objectives.

The Thomas model is not the only one that has been offered to guide consultancy. Other models have been proposed; Murphy (1988) offered a model derived from that used in medical practice, Gipson *et al.* (1989) proposed an industrial–organisational based approach to practising sport psychology, and Butler and Hardy (1992) advanced one based on personal construct theory. While all these models have advantages and are important to consider, the Thomas model reflects the general approach emphasised by most of those writing in contemporary sport psychology. Hence, it was emphasised here.

Examination of the complex and changing nature of consultancy

While the Thomas (1990) model is extremely useful in overviewing the typical peak performance consulting process, it can be easily misinterpreted. First, some individuals read the model and assume that sport psychology consultants are simply hired to formally assess athletes or teams, prescribe what needs to be done psychologically, teach the athletes the skills needed to improve performance through group and individual meetings, and evaluate effectiveness. While consulting can occur in such a fashion, this is not usually the case. In fact, viewing a consultancy in this way overregiments, overstandardises, and oversimplifies the process. It also implies that consultants are the sport psychology experts who simply tell elite athletes what they need to know. In reality, the consulting process is a complex social interaction which actively involves athletes and coaches who usually have extensive sport psychology knowledge (although it may not be formalised in the terms that sport psychologists use). Indeed, in the authors' experience, the importance of working alongside and through the coach cannot be overemphasised. Consequently, the consultancy process is a much more collaborative and non-sequential effort than Thomas' model implies.

A second misinterpretation that can be made is that the consultancy process is a static one that does not change across time. In fact, the formal, sequential process depicted in Figure 11.1 may well occur at the start of a consultation, but over time the consulting process becomes much less structured, so that the consultant's role may well change quite dramatically. For example, in the first year of a programme a sport psychology consultant may follow the model fairly closely, identifying the athlete's psychological strengths and weaknesses, and then providing individual and group educational sessions where psychological skills are taught and practised. In later years, however, the consulting process may become much more problem-centred with fewer formal psychological skills training sessions and more one-on-one problem solving sessions where the consultant helps athletes or teams to use the psychological skills they have developed to solve specific problems. Similarly, athletes may "check in" (in a preventative medicine way) with the consultant when no major problems are evident, but in doing this they provide the consultant with the opportunity to help them deal with minor issues before they become full-fledged problems. Coaches may also use consultants in different ways as the programme evolves and trust is established. They may want the consultant to serve as a facilitator in team meetings where difficult issues must be discussed. The consultant may also act as a neutral, unbiased intermediary facilitating communication between the coaching staff and the athletes. Finally, a consultant often acts as a sounding board for the coach—providing social support and giving input as to the best way to prepare the team or individual athletes psychologically (cf. Hardy and Parfitt, 1994).

In summary, while the Thomas model provides an excellent overview of the early stages of the peak performance consultancy process, the overall consultancy process is much more complex and dynamic than the model depicts. It involves a complex collaborative effort between the consultant, the coaches, and the athletes, in which the consultant assumes different roles at different stages during the development of the programme.

Effective consultants and consultancy

To be most effective, sport psychology consultants must: understand the research-based principles identified in this chapter; have an understanding of how psychological factors interact to influence performance (either via the unifying model presented in Chapter 9, or through their own conceptualisations); and know how to implement a psychological skills training programme. However, having this knowledge does not guarantee that one will be effective. Still further personal characteristics and situational variables come into play. Orlick and Partington (1987), and Partington and Orlick (1987), for example, interviewed 75 Canadian Olympic athletes and 17 coaches who had worked with 21 sport psychology consultants for the purpose of determining effective versus less effective consulting practices. Results from these interviews revealed that the most "highly effective" consultants were:

- likeable and able to quickly establish rapport with athletes, showing care and interest in them;
- accessible;
- good listeners;
- very applied, concrete, and having useful practical suggestions to make;
- flexible, open and creative in their approaches;
- good at meeting individual athlete needs by providing person-specific suggestions and feedback;
- involved in long-term contacts with athletes and teams (from a minimum of nine months and in many cases as long as two to three years);
- involved in multiple contacts with the athletes and teams, conducting follow-ups to individual sessions; and,
- willing to accept low fees for their work.

Consultants who were evaluated as "least effective" were found to be characterised by the following:

- poor interpersonal skills (e.g. were perceived as "wimpy", or domineering);
- input that was not sport specific and/or applied enough;
- inflexibility in that they did not adapt to individual athlete needs;
- inappropriate on-site behaviour (e.g. crowded athlete during competition, interrupted athlete pre-performance routines with psychological assessments);
- bad timing (e.g. initial involvements were too close to competitions);
- not enough feedback;
- limited contact with individual athletes and teams;
- a "shrink" image where they interpreted everything athletes did as a personality problem; and,
- an "ivory-tower" research image resulting from imposing time-consuming psychological tests with little or no useful feedback provided.

These findings certainly emphasise the importance of consultants being "down-to-earth" individuals who are able to help athletes by providing individualised feedback through long-term involvements. They also reveal that effective consultants are hard working individuals who deeply care about the athletes and teams with whom they work. Finally, effective consultants have the ability to translate psychological principles and findings into concrete practical terms that athletes can understand.

Highly respected North American sport psychology consultant, Ken Ravizza, echoed some of the same themes as those found in the Orlick and Partington research, and introduced several new considerations when discussing his consulting experiences (Ravizza, 1988). In particular, he too emphasised the importance of not being perceived as a "shrink" by athletes, and of understanding the task-specific demands and terminology of the sport that one is involved with. This does not mean that clinical issues or problems do not arise with athletes or teams, nor that clinical psychologists are not needed as sport psychology consultants (indeed they are). Rather, it emphasises the importance of realising that the majority of issues in elite athlete psychological preparation are not clinical problems and, when clinical issues are evident, athletes react much better to clinicians who do not act in what the athlete sees as a stereotypical "shrink" manner.

In addition to further validating these points, Ravizza identified the importance of consultants understanding "organisational politics". He indicated that organisational politics are important because consultants are often retained or released on the basis of feedback from key individuals in an organisation (e.g. an athletic trainer) who may not on the surface be viewed as a key decision-maker. It is also important to learn who within the organisation, on the coaching staff and on the team, supports the use of sport psychology and who does not. Effective consultants, then, must become politically astute so they can understand and hopefully circumvent potential politically based problems. However, in the authors' experience, it is usually a grave mistake for consultants to become involved in organisational politics, so being politically astute certainly should not be interpreted as meaning being politically active.

In addition to these characteristics, based on over 40 years of combined consulting experience, and experience supervising and observing countless other new consultants, the authors have identified seven further characteristics of effective consultants. These are: (1) the confidence to make only a small number of suggestions when consulting; (2) being able to recognise that at times doing nothing is the best intervention; (3) anticipating adherence problems and taking steps to promote adherence; (4) having a total commitment to the process; (5) recognising that they are not right for every situation; (6) developing mutual trust and respect with coaches and athletes; and (7) realising that the nature of consultancy and the consultant's role changes over time. Each of these will be briefly discussed below.

Effective consultants have the confidence to focus on only a few skills or techniques that in their best judgement will help the elite athlete. They do not feel a need to try to show or tell the athlete everything they know; this is often a characteristic of inexperienced or ineffective consultants. Effective consultants also realise that elite athletes and coaches do not really care if there is not enough research to be totally confident that a technique or strategy will work. Effective consultants are not afraid to give their expert opinion and take responsibility if things do not work out.

Inexperienced and ineffective consultants at times fall into the trap of feeling that since they are serving as a consultant they must constantly give advice, motivate athletes, or psych teams up. In contrast, effective consultants have learned that if problems do not exist, then athletes do not want to be interfered with. Instead, they spend their time inconspicuously listening and observing. At competitions they make themselves available to the athletes, but are careful not to interrupt the athletes' mental preparation by offering unrequested advice or administering unwanted assessments.

Even with elite athletes, adherence to the systematic practice and use of mental skills training can be a problem (Bull, 1989; 1991). Hence, like effective coaches, effective consultants are not afraid of being made redundant by encouraging athletes to repeatedly practise skills they want to develop. They are also careful, however, not to force themselves on athletes, or try to force elite athletes to develop skills they are not interested in improving. Instead, they offer friendly reminders and assist coaches in organising the purposeful practice of these skills. They are also familiar with emerging research and theory on adherence which indicates that those athletes who do not adhere to psychological skills training are less motivated, feel that they have made more progress toward achieving their sport goals, do not view psychological skills development efforts as valuable, want more individualised programmes, feel that they do not have time in their busy schedule for mental skills practice, and may have disruptive home environments (Bull, 1991). Knowing these findings, consultants can make efforts to individualise programmes, work on skills that athletes perceive to be valuable, and discuss time management with athletes.

Those who have worked with highly successful elite athletes are usually impressed with the high levels of commitment these individuals espouse. Indeed, Orlick and Partington (1988) found that a total commitment to achieving excellence was a characteristic that distinguished more rather than less successful Olympians. It is not surprising, then, that elite athletes most respect sport psychology consultants who are as totally committed to their field as they are to their particular sport. Furthermore, this commitment cannot be faked. Sport psychology consultants must be intrinsically motivated and willing to endure the highs and lows of sport (e.g. sitting on the sideline in inclement weather, long bus rides and travel delays, disappointing losses) while demonstrating their own excellent psychological skills, just as the athletes do.

One difficult lesson effective consultants learn is that they are not always right for every consulting situation. At times, despite apparently doing everything "right" things do not work out. For example, the personality match between the consultant and coach or athletes may not "click". Or because of organisational politics and financial constraints, good programmes and effective consultants are dropped. Given the level of commitment it takes to be an effective consultant, programme cancellation or failure to be retained is often hard to cope with, but these setbacks come with the territory and must be understood. In such situations, it may be helpful and instructive to remind oneself that the frustration and disappointment that is experienced is similar to that felt by an athlete when he or she is cut or dropped by a coach or team selection committee. Consequently, effective consultants find it useful to employ many of the same coping strategies that they teach their athlete clients.

One of the most important characteristics of effective consultants is their ability to develop trust and respect with coaches and athletes. In many ways this is accomplished by demonstrating the characteristics discussed throughout this chapter. It is also important to recognise that elite athletes and coaches are often sceptical of new people because they are so often approached by individuals who only want to know them for their celebrity status or because they want something from them. Hence, even when proven consulting techniques for establishing rapport are used it takes time to develop trust, so effective sport psychology consultants must be patient. Coach and athlete trust is so important that effective consultants discuss, and then clearly specify, their roles to all parties involved (especially with regard to confidentiality and team selection). Most prefer not to become involved in player selection issues because of the difficulties it causes in maintaining athletes' trust. Last, but certainly not least, trust comes from being honest, and honesty is one of the most important characteristics of effective consultants. Given the importance of honesty and trust in effective consulting, consultants are well advised to become familiar with and adhere to the professional and ethical codes of practice that apply to them (e.g. AAASP, 1995; BASES, 1995).

Given the above characteristics it is not surprising that effective consultants realise that the nature of a consultancy changes over time. For example, initial contact may last up to a year and only involve formal presentations and educational sessions on standard psychological skills training. Later, the focus may shift to helping athletes solve individual problems, cope with stress, and anticipate potential problems. Finally, the consultant may become a trusted confidant of the coaching and administrative staff, advising them on many problems they face and helping them to structure the athletic environment so as to promote maximum mental preparation. An especially difficult dilemma faced by experienced consultants is realising that they could have a much more potent effect, but the organisation or athletes are not yet at a state of readiness to allow them to change the nature of the consultancy; for example, practices could be structured much better, but the coach does not yet trust the consultant enough for him or her to suggest practice changes. Similarly, it may be hard for a consultant who has worked with a team for a long time and knows what needs to be done to adjust to new coaching staff (where trust has to be built before the staff will consider the consultant's input). However, by knowing that the nature of consultancy changes over time, effective consultants realise that they must often wait until the time is right to move to the next level.

SUMMARY

Research on psychological preparation for peak performance does little good if it sits in our research journals and is not used by those involved in consulting elite athletes. However, to be of use this research needs to be translated into meaningful implications for guiding practice. This chapter focused on summarising and integrating the latest scientifically derived implications for practice identified in the previous chapters of this book. This was done in two ways. First, over 60 practical guidelines were presented, content analysed, and discussed. And, second, the means by which these guidelines can be put into practice were examined with regard to: Thomas' (1990) psychological skills training model; the need to go beyond psychological skills training by recognising the complex, multifaceted, and changing nature of consultancies; and the characteristics of effective and ineffective consultants. In closing, however, it is important to recognise that there is no one method of effective consultancy; rather, there are multiple ways to be effective as a peak performance consultant. To most effectively help elite athletes develop psychologically, consultants must integrate what has been presented here with their own personality and their understanding of their clients, together with the athletic context in which they operate.

EPILOGUE

This text has attempted to explicitly relate theory and research on the psychological preparation of elite performers to the best practice of applied sport psychology consultants working with such performers. In order to achieve this aim, the first part of the book reviewed the quantitative and qualitative research literatures on: the basic psychological skills of relaxation, goal-setting, imagery, and self-talk; self-confidence; motivation; arousal and activation; stress, anxiety, and performance; concentration and attention control; and coping with adversity. These reviews were integrated with quotations from elite athletes, and the applied consultancy experiences of the authors, in order to extract the implications for future research and best applied practice in the area. Following the reviews, a unifying model of psychological preparation for peak performance was presented to help the reader understand the relationships between the various factors that had been identified, and also to place those factors within their social–organisational context. This model showed how the attainment of task-specific ideal performance states was determined by the interaction of four primary components: foundation attributes, such as personality dispositions; the psychological skills and strategies used by elite performers to try to achieve ideal performance states; adversity coping strategies; the physical, social, psychological, and organisational environment in which elite performers train and perform.

The final two chapters of the book focused on the implications of the previous chapters for future research into the psychological preparation of elite performers, and best practice in applied consultancy work with such performers. Chapter 10 summarised over 50 research questions in urgent need of study, and rated these questions in terms of their relative importance and difficulty. It then critically appraised the qualitative and quantitative methods that might be used to address different questions, together with the philosophical positions and assumptions that underlie these methods. Finally, the chapter identified some of the characteristics of previous research studies that have had a major impact on the area, and made a plea for researchers to adopt a similar "leap", as opposed to "creep", strategy in their future research. Chapter 10 has summarised over 60 of the implications identified in previous chapters for best practice in applied consultancy work with elite performers. However, as well as identifying the implications for programme content, the chapter also discussed the actual process of consultancy work, and highlighted a number of personal qualities and characteristics that a consultant must possess if he or she wishes to be effective at this level.

For many reasons, this has not been an easy book for us to write and, to be quite honest, it is highly likely that none of us could have written it without the help and support of the other two. Sometimes, we were stopped by problems that could not be easily overcome. Once, after we had found a way to overcome one such obstacle, we asked ourselves why it was that we worked so well together. After much "navel contemplating", we all agreed that the reason was because we had such a strong commitment in both our research and our consultancy work to try to "take things to the next level". This, we decided, is what motivates, excites, and challenges us. Throughout this book, we have attempted to convey this same challenge to the reader. We imagine that this has not always been an easy book to read, but we hope that it will have motivated, excited, and challenged the reader to strive to take their own research and consultancy work "to the next level" also. We wish you every success in this quest, and as much satisfaction from your work in this area as we have had from our own.

REFERENCES

AAASP (1995) Ethical principles of A.A.A.S.P., *Association of the Advancement of Applied Sport Psychology Newsletter*, **10** (1), 15, 21.

Abramson, L.Y., Seligman, M.E.P., and Teasdale J.D. (1978) Learned helplessness in humans: critique and reformulation, *Journal of Abnormal Psychology*, **87**, 49–74.

Ahsen, A. (1972) *Eidetic Parents Test and Analysis*, Brandon House, New York.

Ahsen, A. (1984) ISM: The triple code model for imagery and psychophysiology, *Journal of Mental Imagery*, **8**, 15–42.

Ainscoe, M.W., and Hardy, L. (1987) Cognitive warm-up in a cyclical gymnastics skill, *International Journal of Sport Psychology*, **18**, 269–275.

Albrecht, R.A., and Feltz, D.L. (1987) Generality and specificity of attention related to competitive anxiety and sport performance, *Journal of Sport and Exercise Psychology*, **9**, 231–248.

Allard, F., and Starkes, J.L. (1980) Perception in sport: Volleyball, *Journal of Sport Psychology*, **2**, 22–33.

Allard, F., Graham, S., and Paarsalu, M.L. (1980) Perception in sport: Basketball, *Journal of Sport Psychology*, **2**, 14–21.

Allport, D.A., Antonis, B., and Reynolds, P. (1972) On the division of attention: A disproof of the single channel hypothesis, *Quarterly Journal of Experimental Psychology*, **24**, 225–235.

Alpert, R., and Haber, R.N. (1960) Anxiety in academic achievement situations, *Journal of Abnormal and Social Psychology*, **61**, 207–215.

Anderson, C.A., and Williams, J.M. (1988) A model of stress and athletic injury: prediction and prevention, *Journal of Sport and Exercise Psychology*, **10**, 721–786.

Anderson, D.C., Crowell, C.R., Doman, M., and Howard, G.S. (1988) Performance posting, goal setting, and activity-contingent praise as applied to a University hockey team, *Journal of Applied Psychology*, **73**, 87–95.

Anderson, J.R. (1982) Acquisition of cognitive skill, *Psychological Review*, **89**, 396–406.

Andre, J. C., and Means, J. R. (1986) Rate of imagery in mental practice: An experimental investigation, *Journal of Sport Psychology*, **8**, 124–128.

Annett, J. (1991) Skill acquisition. In J.E. Morrison (ed.), *Training for Performance: Principles of Applied Human Learning*, Wiley, Chichester.

Anshel, M.H. (1990) Toward a validation of a model for coping with acute stress in sport, *International Journal of Sport Psychology*, **21**, 58–83.

Anshel, M.H., Gregory, W.L., and Kaczmarek, M. (1990) Effectiveness of a stress training program in coping with criticisms in sport: A test of the COPE model, *Journal of Sport Behaviour*, **13**, 194–218.

Anshel, M.H., Brown, J.M., and Brown, D.F. (1993) Effectiveness of a program for coping with acute stress on motor performance, affect, and muscular tension, *Australian Journal of Science and Medicine in Sport*, **25**, 7–16.

Apter, M.J. (1982) *The Experience of Motivation: The Theory of Psychological Reversal*, Academic Press, London.

Averill, J.A. (1968) Grief: Its nature and significance, *Psychological Bulletin*, **70** (6), 721–748.

Baddeley, A.D., and Idzikowski, C. (1985) Anxiety, manual dexterity and performance, *Ergonomics*, **28**, 1475–1482.

Bakker, F.C., Whiting, H.T.A., and Van der Burg, H. (1990) *Sport Psychology: Concept and Applications*, Wiley, Chichester.

Bandura, A. (1977) Self-efficacy: Toward a unifying theory of behavioural change, *Psychological Review*, **84**, 191–215.

Bandura, A. (1982) Self-efficacy mechanism in human agency, *American Psychologist*, **377**, 122–147.

Bandura, A. (1986) *Social Foundations of Thought and Action: A Social Cognitive Theory*, Prentice-Hall, Englewood Cliffs, NJ.

Bandura, A. (1989) *Perceived Self-Efficacy in the Exercise of Personal Efficacy*. Coleman Griffith Memorial Lecture at the Annual Conference of the Association for the Advancement of Applied Sport Psychology, Seattle.

Bandura, A. (1990) Perceived self efficacy in the exercise of personal agency, *Journal of Applied Sport Psychology*, **2**, 128–163.

Bandura, A., and Adams, N.E. (1977) Analysis of self-efficacy theory of behavioural change, *Cognitive Therapy and Research*, **1**, 287–310.

Bandura, A., and Schunk, D.H. (1981) Cultivating competence self efficacy and intrinsic interests through proximal self motivation, *Journal of Personality and Social Psychology*, **41**, 586–598.

Bandura, A., and Simon, K.M. (1977) The role of proximal intentions in self regulation of refractory behaviour, *Cognitive Therapy and Research*, **1**, 177–193.

Bandura, A., Adams, N.E., and Beyer, J. (1977) Cognitive processes mediating behavioural change, *Journal of Personality and Social Psychology*, **35**, 129–139.

Barnard, P.J., and Teasdale, J.D. (1991) Interacting cognitive subsystems: A systematic approach to cognitive affective interaction and change, *Cognition and Emotion*, **5**, 1–39.

Barnett, M.L. (1977) Effects of two methods of goal-setting on learning a gross motor task, *Research Quarterly*, **48**, 19–23.

Barnett, M.L., and Stanicek, J.A. (1979) Effects of goal-setting on achievement in archery, *Research Quarterly*, **50**, 328–332.

Barnett, N.P., Smoll, F.L., and Smith, R.E. (1992) Effects of enhancing coach–athlete relationships on youth sport attrition, *The Sport Psychologist*, **6**, 111–127.

BASES (1995) *Code of Conduct*, British Association of Sport and Exercise Sciences, Leeds.

Bauer, H.H. (1992) *Scientific Literacy and the Myth of the Scientific Method*, University of Illinois Press, Urbana, IL.

Bauer, R.H. (1976) Short term memory: EEG alpha correlates and the effect of the increased alpha, *Behavioural Biology*, **17**, 425–433.

Beaumont, J.G. (1983) The EEG and task performance: A tutorial review. In A.W.K. Gallard and W.Ritter (eds), *Tutorials in ERP Research: Endogenous Components*, North Holland, London.

Beck, A.T. (1970) Cognitive therapy: Nature and relation to behavior therapy, *Behavior Therapy*, **1**, 184–200.

Beck, A.T. (1976) *Cognitive Therapy and Emotional Disorders*, International Universities Press, New York.

Beggs, W.D.A. (1990) Goal setting in sport. In J.G. Jones and L. Hardy (eds), *Stress and Performance*, Wiley, Chichester, pp. 135–170.

Bell, K.F. (1983) *Championship Thinking: The Athlete's Guide To Winning Performance In All Sports*, Prentice Hall, Englewood Cliffs, NJ.

Benson, H. (1976) *The Relaxation Response*, Avon, New York.
Benson, H., and Proctor, W. (1984) *Beyond the Relaxation Response*, Berkley, New York.
Berger, B.G. (1994) Coping with stress: The effectiveness of exercise and other techniques, *Quest*, 46, 100–119.
Biddle, S.J.H. (1993) Attribution research and sport psychology. In R.N. Singer, N. Murphey, L.K. Tennant (eds), *Handbook of Research of Sport Psychology*, MacMillan, New York, pp. 437–464.
Biddle, S.J.H., and Hill, A.B. (1988) Causal attributions and emotional reactions to outcomes in a sporting contest, *Personality and Individual Differences*, **9**, 213–223.
Billings, A.G., and Moos, R.H. (1984) Coping, stress, and social resources among adults with unipolar depression, *Journal of Personality and Social Psychology*, **46**, 877–891.
Blakeslee, T.R. (1980) *The Right Brain*, Doubleday, Garden City, NY.
Bogen, J.E. (1969) The other side of the brain. 1: Dysgraphia and dyscopia following cerebral commissurotomy, *Bulletin of the LA Neurological Society*, **34**, 73–105.
Bond, M.H. (1983) A proposal for cross cultural studies of attributions. In M. Hewstone (ed.), *Attribution Theory: Social and Functional Extensions*, Blackwell, Oxford, pp. 144–157.
Borkovec, T.D. (1978) Self-efficacy: Cause or reflection of behaviour change. In S. Rachman (ed.), *Advances in Behaviour Research and Therapy* (Volume 1), Pergamon Press, Oxford.
Bouffard, M., and Crocker, P.R.E. (1992) Coping by individuals with physical disabilities with perceived challenge in physical activity: Are people consistent? *Research Quarterly for Exercise and Sport*, **63**, 410–417.
Boutcher, S.H. (1990) The role of performance routines in sport. In J.G. Jones and L. Hardy (eds), *Stress and Performance in Sport*, Wiley, Chichester, pp. 231–245.
Boutcher, S.H. (1992) Attention and athletic performance: An integrated approach. In T.S. Horn (ed.), *Advances in Sport Psychology*, Human Kinetics, Champaign, IL, pp. 251–266.
Boutcher, S.H., and Crews, D.J. (1987) The effect of a preshot routine on a well-learned skill, *International Journal of Sport Psychology*, **18**, 30–39.
Boutcher, S.H., and Rotella, R.J. (1987) A psychological skills educational program for closed-skill performance enhancement, *The Sport Psychologist*, **1**, 200–207.
Boutcher, S.H., and Zinsser, N.W. (1990) Cardiac deceleration of elite and beginning golfers during putting, *Journal of Sport and Exercise Psychology*, **12**, 37–47.
Brawley, L.R. (1984) Attributions as social cognitions: Contemporary perspectives in sport. In W.F. Straub and J.M. Williams (eds), *Cognitive Social Psychology*, Sport Science Associates, Lansing, NY.
Brewer, B.W. (1994) Review and critique of models of psychological adjustments to athletic injury, *Journal of Applied Sport Psychology*, **6**, 87–100.
Brewer, B.W., Van Raalte, J.L., Linder, D.E., and Van Raalte, N.S. (1991) Peak performance and the perils of retrospective introspection, *Journal of Sport and Exercise Psychology*, **10**, 45–61.
Broadbent, D.E. (1958) *Perception and Communication*, Pergamon Press, London.
Broadbent, D.E. (1971) *Decision and Stress*, Academic Press, London.
Broadbent, D.E., and Broadbent, M. (1988) Anxiety and attentional bias: State and trait, *Cognition and Emotion*, **2**, 165–183.
Broadhurst, P.L. (1957) Emotionality and the Yerkes–Dodson law, *Journal of Experimental Psychology*, **54**, 345–352.
Brody, E.B., Hatfield, B.D., and Spalding, T.W. (1988) Generalization of self-efficacy to a continuum of stressors upon mastery of a high-risk sport skill, *Journal of Sport Psychology*, **10**, 32–34.

Bryan, A.J. (1987) Single-subject design evaluation of sport psychology interventions, *The Sport Psychologist*, **1**, 283–292.

Bull, S.J. (1989) Adherence to mental skills training: The need for systematic research. In C.K. Giam, K.K. Cook, and K.C. The (eds), *Proceedings 7th World Congress In Sport Psychology* Singapore: Singapore Sports Council/International Society of Sport Psychology, pp. 164–165.

Bull, S.J. (1991) Personal and situational influences on adherence to mental skills training, *Journal of Sport and Exercise Psychology*, **13**, 121–132.

Bunker, L., Williams, J.M., and Zinsser, N. (1993) Cognitive techniques for improving performance and self-confidence. In J.M. Williams (ed.), *Applied Sport Psychology: Personal Growth to Peak Performance*, Mayfield, Mountain View, CA, pp. 225–242.

Burrows, G.C., Cox, T., and Simpson, G.C. (1977) The measurement of stress in a sales training situation, *Journal of Occupational Psychology*, **50**, 45–51.

Burton, D. (1988) Do anxious swimmers swim slower? Re-examining the elusive anxiety–performance relationship, *Journal of Sport Psychology*, **10**, 45–61

Burton, D. (1989a) The impact of goal specificity and task complexity on basketball skill development, *The Sport Psychologist*, **3**, 35–47.

Burton, D. (1989b) Winning isn't everything: Examining the impact of performance goals on collegiate swimmers' cognitions and performance, *The Sport Psychologist*, **3**, 105–132.

Burton, D. (1990) Multimodal stress management in sport: Current status and future directions. In J.G. Jones and L. Hardy (eds), *Stress and Performance in Sport*, Wiley, Chichester, pp. 171–201.

Burton, D. (1992) The Jeckyl/Hyde nature of goals: Reconceptualising goal setting in sport. In T. Horn (ed.), *Advances in Sport Psychology*, Human Kinetics, Champaign, IL, pp. 267–297.

Burton, D. (1993) Goal setting in sport. In R.N. Singer, M. Murphey, and L.K. Tennant, *Handbook of Research in Sport Psychology*, MacMillan, New York, pp. 467–491.

Butler, R.J. (1989) Psychological preparation of Olympic boxers. In J. Kremer and W. Crawford (eds), *The Psychology of Sport: Theory and Practice*, British Psychological Association, Leicester, England, pp. 78–84.

Butler, R.J., and Hardy, L. (1992) The performance profile: Theory and application, *The Sport Psychologist*, **6**, 253–264.

Butler, R.J., Smith, M., and Irwin, I. (1993) The performance profile in practice, *Journal of Applied Sport Psychology*, **5**, 48–63.

Carpenter, B.N. (1992) Issues and advances in coping research. In B.N. Carpenter (ed.), *Personal coping: Theory, research, and application*, Praeger, Westport, Conn, pp. 1–14.

Carpenter, P.J., Scanlan, T.K., Simons, J.P., and Lobel, M. (1993) A test of the sport commitment model using structural equation modelling, *Journal of Sport and Exercise Psychology*, **15** (2), 119–133.

Carroll, S.J. (1986) Management by objectives: Three decades of research and experience. In S. L. Reynes and G. T. Milkovich (eds), *Current Issues in Human Resource Management*, Business Publications, Plano, TX, pp. 295–312.

Carver, C.S., and Scheier, M.F. (1982) Outcome expectancy, locus of attribution for expectancy, and self-directed attention as determinants of evaluations, and performance, *Journal of Experimental Social Psychology*, **18**, 184–200.

Carver, C.S., and Scheier, M.F. (1988) A control perspective on anxiety, *Anxiety Research*, **1**, 17–22.

Carver, C.S., Scheier, M.F., and Weintraub, J.K. (1989) Assessing coping strategies: A theoretically based approach, *Journal of Personality and Social Psychology*, **56**, 267–283.

Caudill, D., Weinberg, R., and Jackson, A. (1983) Psyching-up and track athletes: a preliminary investigation, *Journal of Sport Psychology*, **5**, 231–235.
Chartrand, J.M., Jowdy, D.P., and Danish, S.J. (1992) The Psychological Skills Inventory for Sports: Psychometric characteristics and applied implications, *Journal of Sport and Exercise Psychology*, **14**, 405–413.
Chase, M.A., Feltz, D.L., Tully, D.C., and Lirgg, C.D. (1994) Sources of collective and individual efficacy in sport, *Journal of Sport and Exercise Psychology*, **16** (supplement, S18).
Chelladurai, P. (1993) Leadership. In R.N. Singer, N. Murphy and L.K. Tennant (eds), *Handbook of Research in Sport Psychology*, Macmillan, New York, pp. 647–671.
Chernis, C. (1980) *Staff Burnout: Job Stress in the Human Services*, Sage Publishers, Beverly Hills, CA.
Chidester, J.S., and Grigsby, W.C. (1984) A meta-analysis of the goal-setting performance literature. In J. A. Pearce and R. B. Robinson (eds), *Academy of Management Proceedings*, Academy of Management, Ada, OH, pp. 202–206.
Coakley, J. (1992) Burnout among adolescent athletes: A personal failure or a social problem?, *Sociology of Sport Journal*, **9**, 271–285.
Cockerill, I.M., Nevill, A.M., and Lyons, N. (1991) Modeling mood states in athletic performance, *Journal of Sport Sciences*, **9**, 205–212.
Cohen, S., and Wills, T. (1985) Stress, social support and the buffering hypothesis, *Psychological Bulletin*, **98**, 310–357.
Collins, J. (1982) *Self-Efficacy and Ability in Achievement Behaviour*. Paper presented at the meeting of American Educational Research Association, New York.
Collins, D.J., Powell, G.E., and Davies, I. (1990) An electroencephalographic study of hemispheric processing pattern during Karate performance, *Journal of Sport and Exercise Psychology*, **12**, 37–47.
Collins, D.J., Powell, G.E., and Davies, I. (1991) Cerebral activity prior to motion task performance: An electroencephalographic study, *Journal of Sports Sciences*, **9**, 313–324.
Compas, B.E. (1987) Coping with stress during childhood and adolescence, *Psychological Bulletin*, **101**, 393–403.
Corbin, C.B. (1972) Mental Practice. In W. P. Morgan (ed.), *Ergogenic Aids and Muscular Performance*, Academic Press, New York, pp. 94–118.
Covington, M.V., and Omelich, C.L. (1979) Effort: The double edged sword in school achievement, *Journal of Educational Psychology*, **71**, 169–182.
Cox, T. (1978) *Stress*, Macmillan, London.
Cox, T., and Ferguson, E. (1991) Individual differences, stress and coping. In C.L. Cooper and R. Payne (eds), *Personality and Stress: Individual Differences in the Stress Process*, Wiley, Chichester, pp. 7–30.
Crews, D. (1989) *The Influence of Attentive States on Golf Putting as Indicated by Cardiac and Electrocortical Activity*. Unpublished doctoral dissertation, Arizona State University, Tempe.
Crews, D.J., and Boutcher, S.H. (1986) The effect of structured preshot behaviours on beginning golf performance, *Perceptual and Motor Skills*, **62**, 291–294.
Crews, D.J., and Boutcher, S.H. (1987) An observational analysis of professional female golfers during tournament play, *Journal of Sport Behaviour*, **9**, 51–58.
Crocker, P.R.E. (1992) Managing stress by competitive athletes: Ways of coping, *International Journal of Sport Psychology*, **23**, 161–175.
Crocker, P.R.E., Alderman, R.B., and Smith, F.M.R. (1988) Cognitive–affective stress management training with high performance youth volleyball players: Effects on affect, cognition, and performance, *Journal of Sport and Exercise Psychology*, **10**, 448–460.

Csikszentmihalyi, M. (1975) *Beyond Boredom and Anxiety*, Jossey-Bass, San Francisco, CA.

Cuthbert, B.N., Vrana, S.R., and Bradley, M.M. (1991) Imagery: Function and physiology, *Advances in Psychophysiology*, **4**, 1–42.

Cutrona, C.E., Russell, D., and Jones, R.D. (1984) Cross-situational consistency in causal attributions: Does attributional style exist?, *Journal of Personality and Social Psychology*, **47**, 1043–1058.

Dagrou, E., Gauvin, L., and Halliwell, W. (1991) La préparation mentale des athlètes ivoiriens: Pratiques courantes et perspectives de recherche (Mental preparation of Ivory Coast athletes: Current practice and research perspectives), *International Journal of Sport Psychology*, **22**, 15–34.

Dagrou, E., Gauvin, L., and Halliwell, W. (1992) Effets du langage positif, négatif, et neutre sur la performance motrice (Effects of positive, negative and neutral self-talk on motor performance), *Canadian Journal of Sport Sciences*, **17**, 145–147.

Dale, J., and Weinberg, R.S. (1990) Burnout in sport: A review and critique, *Journal of Applied Sport Psychology*, **2** (1), 67–83.

Danish, S.J., Petitpas, A., and Hale, B. (1995) Psychological interventions: A life development model. In S.M. Murphy (ed.), *Sport Psychology Interventions*, Human Kinetics, Champaign, IL, pp. 19–38.

Davids, K., and Myers, C. (1990) The role of tacit knowledge in human skill performance, *Journal of Human Movement Studies*, **19**, 273–288.

Davidson, R.J., and Schwartz, G.E. (1976) The psychobiological of relaxation and related states: A multiprocess theory. In D. Mostofsky (ed.), *Behavioural Control and Modification of Physiological Activity*, Prentice-Hall, Englewood Cliffs, NJ, pp. 399–442.

Deaux, K. (1984) From individual differences to social categories: Analysis of a decade's research on gender, *American Psychologist*, **39**, 105–116.

De Charms, R. (1968) *Personal Causation: The Internal Affective Determinants of Behaviour*, Academic Press, New York.

Deci, E.L., and Ryan, R.M. (1985) *Intrinsic Motivation and Self Determination in Human Behaviour*, Plenum Press, New York.

Deci, E.L., and Ryan, R.M. (1991) A motivational approach to self: Integration in personality. In R. Dienstbier (ed.), *Nebraska Symposium on Motivation: Vol. 38, Perspectives of Motivation*, University of Nebraska Press, Lincoln, NA, pp. 237–288.

Deci, E.L., Vallerand, R.J., Pelletier, L.G., and Ryan, R.M. (1991) Motivation and Education: The self determination perspective, *The Educational Psychologist*, **26**, 325–346.

Dennis, K.M., Bartsokas, T., Lewthwaite, R., and Palin, D. (1993) Relationship between CSAI-2 subscales and performance in youth athletics: The zone of optimal functioning, *Medicine and Science in Sports and Exercise*, **25**, Suppl., S155.

Deutsch, J.A., and Deutsch, D. (1963) Attention: Some theoretical considerations, *Psychological Review*, **70**, 80–90.

Dewe, P., Cox, T., and Ferguson, E. (1993) Individual strategies for coping with stress at work: A review, *Work and Stress*, **7**, 5–15.

Dewey, D., Brawley, L.R., and Allard, F. (1989) Do the TAIS attentional style scales predict how visual information is processed?, *Journal of Sport and Exercise Psychology*, **11**, 171–186.

Dillon, K.M., and Minchoff, B. (1985) Positive emotional states and enhancement of the immune system, *International Journal of Psychiatric Medicine*, **86**, 13–17.

Dishman, R.K. (1983) Identity crisis in North American sport psychology: Academics in professional issues, *Journal of Sport Psychology*, **5**, 123–134.

Doyle, L.A., Landers, D.M., and Feltz, D.L. (1980) *Psychological Skills for Elite and Subelite Shooters*. Paper presented at the North American Society for Psychology of Sport and Physical Activity. Boulder, CO.

Duda, J.L. (1988) The relationship between goal perspective, persistence and behavioural intensity among male and female recreational sport participants, *Leisure Sciences*, **10**, 93–106.

Duda, J.L. (1989a) The relationship between task and ego orientation and the perceived purpose of sport among male and female high school athletes, *Journal of Sport and Exercise Psychology*, **11**, 318–335.

Duda, J.L. (1989b) Goal perspectives, participation and persistence in sport, *International Journal of Sport Psychology*, **20**, 42–56.

Duda, J.L. (1992) Motivation in sport settings: A goal perspective approach. In G. Roberts (ed.), *Motivation in Sport and Exercise*, Human Kinetics, Champaign, IL, pp. 57–91.

Duda, J.L. (1993) Goals: A social cognitive approach to the study of achievement motivation in sport. In R.N. Singer, M. Murphey, and L.K. Tennant (eds), *Handbook of Research on Sport Psychology*, Macmillan, NY, pp. 421–436.

Duda, J.L., and Allison, M.T. (1989) The attributional theory of achievement motivation: Cross cultural considerations, *International Journal of Intercultural relations*, **13**, 37–55.

Duda, J.L., and Chi, L. (1989) *The effect of task- and ego-involving conditions on perceived competence and causal attributions in basketball*. Paper presented at the meeting of the Association for the Advancement of Applied Sport Psychology, University of Washington, Seattle.

Duda, J.L., Smart, A., and Tappe, M. (1989) Personal investment in the rehabilitation of athletic injuries, *Journal of Sport and Exercise Psychology*, **11**, 367–381.

Duda, J.L., Newton, M., and Chi, L. (1990) *The relationship of task and ego orientations and expectations of multidimensional state anxiety*. Paper presented at the annual North American Society for the Psychology of Sport and Physical Activity. University of Houston, TX.

Duda, J.L., Olson, L.K., and Templin, T. (1991) The relationship of task and ego orientation to sportsmanship attitudes and the perceived legitimacy of injurious acts, *Research Quarterly for Exercise and Sport*, **62**, 79–87.

Duffy, E. (1962) *Activation and Behaviour*, Wiley, New York.

Dunn, J.C.G. (1994) Toward the combined use of nomothetic and idiographic methodologies in sport psychology: An empirical example, *The Sport Psychologist*, **8**, 376–392.

Dweck, C.S. (1980) Learned helplessness in sport. In C. Nadeau, W. Halliwell, K. Newell and G. Roberts (eds), *Psychology of Motor Behaviour and Sport*, Human Kinetics, Champaign, IL, pp. 1–11.

Dweck, C.S., and Leggett, E.L. (1988) A social–cognitive approach to motivation and personality, *Psychological Review*, **95**, 56–273.

Earley, R.C., Connolly, T., and Ekegren, G. (1989) Goals, strategy development and task performance: Some limits on the efficacy of goal setting, *Journal of Applied Psychology*, **74**, 24–33.

Easterbrook, J.A. (1959) The effect of emotion on the utilisation and the organisation of behaviour, *Psychological Review*, **66**, 183–201.

Eklund, R.C., Gould, D., and Jackson, S.A. (1993) Psychological foundations of Olympic wrestling excellence: Reconciling individual differences and nomothetic characterization, *Journal of Applied Sport Psychology*, **5**, 35–47.

Elder, S.T., Grenier, C., Lansley, J., Martyn, S., Regenbogen, D., and Roundtree, G. (1985) Can subjects be trained to communicate through the use of EEG biofeedback? *Biofeedback and Self Regulation*, **10**, 88–89.

Ellis, A. (1962) *Reason and Emotion in Psychotherapy*, Lye Stuart, New York.
Ellis, A. (1970) *The Essence of Rational Psychotherapy: A Comprehensive Approach to Treatment*, Institute for Rational Living, New York.
Ellis, A. (1982) Self-direction in sport and life. In T. Orlick, J. Partington, and J. Salmela (eds), *Mental Training For Coaches And Athletes*, Coaching Association of Canada, Ottawa, Ontario, pp. 10–17.
Endler, N.S., and Parker, J.D.A. (1990) Multidimensional assessment of coping: A critical evaluation, *Journal of Personality and Social Psychology*, **58**, 844–854.
Endler, N.S., Parker, J.D.A., and Sumerfeldt, L.J. (1993) Coping with health problems: Conceptual and methodological issues, *Canadian Journal of Behavior Sciences*, **25**, 384–490.
Endler, N.S., Parker, J.D.A., and Summerfeldt, L.J. (1996) Coping with Health Problems: Developing a Reliable and Valid Multidimensional Scale. Manuscript submitted for publication.
Epstein, M.L. (1980) The relationships of mental imagery and mental practice to performance of a motor task, *Journal of Sport Psychology*, **2**, 211–220.
Erez, M., and Zidon, I. (1984) Effects of goal acceptance on the relationship of goal difficulty to performance, *Journal of Applied Psychology*, **69**, 69–78.
Evans, L., and Hardy, L. (1995) Sport injury and grief responses: A review, *Journal of Sport and Exercise Psychology*, **17**, 227–245.
Ewing, M.E. (1981) *Achievement motivation and sport behaviour of males and females*. Unpublished doctoral dissertation, University of Illinois, Urbana.
Eysenck, H.J. (1967) *The Biological Basis of Personality*, Thomas, Springfield.
Eysenck, H.J. (1978) Expectations as causal elements in behavioural change. In S. Rachman (ed.), *Advances in Behavioural Research and Therapy*, Pergamon, Oxford.
Eysenck, M.W. (1982) *Attention and Arousal: Cognition and Performance*, Springer, Berlin.
Eysenck, M.W. (1984) *A Handbook of Cognitive Psychology*, Lawrence Erlbaum, London.
Eysenck, M.W. (1986) Individual differences in anxiety, cognition and coping. In G.R.J. Hockey, A.W.K. Gaillard and M.G.H. Coles (eds), *Energetics and Human Information Processing*, Martinus Nijhoff, Dordrecht, The Netherlands.
Eysenck, M.W. (1988) Anxiety and attention, *Anxiety Research*, **1**, 9–15.
Eysenck, M.W. (1992) *Anxiety: The Cognitive Perspective*, Lawrence Erlbaum, Hove, England.
Eysenck, M.W., and Calvo, M.G. (1992) Anxiety and performance: the processing efficiency theory, *Cognition and Emotion*, **6**, 409–434.
Eysenck, M.W., and Keane, M.T. (1990) *Cognitive Psychology: A Students Handbook*, Lawrence Erlbaum, Hove, England.
Farber, B. (1983) *Stress and Burnout in Human Services Professions*, Pergamon Press, New York.
Fazey, J.A., and Hardy, L. (1988) *The Inverted-U Hypotheses: A Catastrophe for Sport Psychology*. British Association of Sport Sciences Monograph No. 1 National Coaching Foundation, Leeds.
Feltz, D.L. (1982) The effect of age and number of demonstrations on modelling of form and performance, *Research Quarterly for Exercise and Sport*, **53**, 291–296.
Feltz, D.L. (1983) *Gender Differences in Causal Elements of Bandura's Theory of Self-Efficacy on a High Avoidance Motor Task*. Paper presented at the North American Society for the Psychology of Sport and Physical Activity, Annual Meeting, East Lansing, MI.
Feltz, D.L. (1984) Self-efficacy as a cognitive mediator of athletic performance. In W.F. Straub (ed.), *Cognitive Sport Psychology*, Sport Science Associates, Lansing, NY, pp. 191–198.

Feltz, D.L. (1988a) Self-confidence and sports performance, *Exercise and Sport Science Reviews*, **16**, 423–457.

Feltz, D.L. (1988b) Gender differences in causal elements of self-efficacy on a high avoidance motor task. *Journal of Sport and Exercise Psychology*, **10**, 151–166.

Feltz, D.L. (1992) Understanding motivation: A self-efficacy perspective. In G. C. Roberts (ed.), *Motivation in Sport and Exercise*, Human Kinetics, Champaign, IL., pp. 93–105.

Feltz, D.L. (1994) Collective efficacy in sport. *Journal of Sport and Exercise Psychology*, **16** (supplement), 516.

Feltz, D.L., and Doyle, L.A. (1981) Improving self-confidence in athletic performance, *Motor Skills*, **5**, 89–96.

Feltz, D.L., and Landers, D.M. (1983) The effects of mental practice on motor skill learning and performance: A meta-analysis, *Journal of Sport Psychology*, **5**, 25–27.

Feltz, D.L., and Mugno, D. (1983) A replication of path analysis of the causal elements in Bandura's theory of self efficacy and the influence of autonomic perception. *Journal of Sport Psychology*, **5**, 263–277.

Feltz, D.L., and Riessinger, C.A. (1990) Effects of in vivo emotive imagery and performance feedback on self-efficacy and muscular endurance, *Journal of Sport and Exercise Psychology*, **12**, 132–143.

Feltz, D.L., and Weiss, M.R. (1982) Developing self-efficacy through sport, *Journal of Physical Education, Recreation and Dance*, **53**, 24–26, 36.

Feltz, D.L., Landers, D.M., and Raeder, V. (1979) Enhancing self-efficacy in high avoidance motor tasks: A comparison of modelling techniques, *Journal of Sport Psychology*, **1**, 112–122.

Feltz, D.L., Bandura, A., and Lirgg, C.D. (1989) Perceived collective efficacy in hockey. In D. Kendzierski (chair) *Self-Perceptions in Sport and Physical Activity: Self-Efficacy and Self-Image*. Symposium conducted at a meeting of the American Psychological Association, New Orleans.

Feltz, D.L., Lirgg, C.D., and Albrecht, R.R. (1992) Psychological implications of competitive running in elite young middle distance runners: A longitudinal analysis, *The Sport Psychologist*, **6**, 128–138.

Fender, L.K. (1989) Athlete Burnout: Potential for research and intervention strategies, *The Sport Psychologist*, **3**, 63–71.

Fenz, W.D. (1975) Coping mechanisms and performance under stress. In D.M. Landers, D.V. Harris and R.W. Christina (eds), *Psychology of Sport and Motor Behaviour*, Penn State HPER series, University Park, Pennsylvania.

Fenz, W.D., and Epstein, S. (1967) Gradients of physiological arousal in parachutists as a function of an approaching jump, *Psychosomatic Medicine*, **29**, 33–51.

Fenz, W.D., and Epstein, S. (1968) Specific and general inhibitory reactions associated with mastery of stress, *Journal of Experimental Psychology*, **77**, 52–56.

Feuerstein, M., Labbe, E.E., and Kuczmierczyk, A.R. (1986) *Health Psychology: A Psychobiological Perspective*, Plenum Press, New York.

Finch, L. (1994) *The Relationship Among Coping Strategies, Trait Anxiety, and Performance in Collegiate Softball Players*, Paper presented at the Association for the Advancement of Applied Sport Psychology Conference, Lake Tahoe, Nevada.

Fitts, D. M. (1962) Skill training. In R. Glasser (ed.), *Training Research and Education*, University of Pittsburgh Press, Pittsburgh, pp. 177–199.

Fitzgerald, L. (1988) Exercise and the immune system, *Immunology Today*, **9**, 337–339.

Fitzsimmons, P.A., Landers, D.M., Thomas, J.R., and van der Mars, H. (in press) Does self-efficacy predict performance in experienced weightlifters?, *Research Quarterly for Exercise and Sport*.

Fleishman, E.A., and Hempel, W.E. (1955) The relationship between abilities and improvement with practice in a visual discrimination-reaction task, *Journal of Experimental Psychology*, **49**, 301–312.

Folkman, S. (1992) Making the case for coping. In B.N. Carpenter (ed.), *Personal Coping: Theory, research and application*, Praeger, Westport, Conn., pp. 31–46.

Folkman, S., and Lazarus, S. (1980) An analysis of coping in a middle-aged community sample, *Journal of Health and Social Behavior*, **21**, 219–239.

Folkman, S., and Lazarus, R.S. (1985) If it changes it must be a process: A study of emotions and coping during three stages of a college examination, *Journal of Personality and Social Psychology*, **48**, 150–170.

Folkman, S., and Lazarus, R.S. (1988b) *Manual for the Ways of Coping Questionnaire*, Consulting Psychologists Press, Palo Alto, CA.

Folkman, S., Chesney, M., Mckusick, L., Ironson, G., Johnson, D.S., and Coates, T.J. (1991) Translating coping theory into practice. In J. Eckenrode (ed.), *The Social Context of Coping*, Plenum Press, New York, pp. 239–260.

Ford, S.K., and Summers, J.J. (1992) The factorial validity of the TAIS attentional style subscales, *Journal of Sport and Exercise Psychology*, **14**, 283–297.

Forsterling, F. (1988) *Attribution Theory in Clinical Psychology*, Wiley, Chichester.

Frankenhaeuser, M., and Johansson, G. (1976) Task demand as reflected in catecholamine excretion and heart rate, *Journal of Human Stress*, **2**, 15–23.

Frazier, S.E. (1988) Mood state profiles of chronic exercisers with differing abilities, *International Journal of Sport Psychology*, **19**, 65–71.

Freudenberger, H.J. (1980) *Burnout: How to Beat the High Cost of Success*, Bantam Books, New York.

Frierman, S., Weinberg, R.S., and Jackson, A. (1990) The relationship between goal proximity and specificity in bowling: A field experiment, *The Sport Psychologist*, **4**, 145–154.

Gallwey, W.T. (1974) *The Inner Game of Tennis*, Random House, New York.

Gannon, T., Landers, D., Kubitz, K., Salazar, W., and Petruzzello, S. (1992) An analysis of temporal electroencephalographic patterning prior to initiation of the arm curl, *Journal of Sport and Exercise Psychology*, **14**, 87–100.

Garland, H. (1983) Influence and ability, assigned goals and normative information on personal goals and performance: A challenge to the goal attainability assumption, *Journal of Applied Psychology*, **68**, 20–30.

Gaudry, E. (1977) Studies of the effects of experimentally induced experiences of success and failure. In C.D. Spielberger and I.G. Sarason (eds), *Stress and Anxiety Vol. 4*, Halstead, London.

Gauron, E.F. (1984) *Mental Training for Peak Performance*, Sports Science International, Lansing, NJ.

Gayton, W.F., Matthews, G.R., and Burchstead, G.N. (1986) An investigation of the validity of the physical self-efficacy in predicting marathon performance, *Perceptual and Motor Skills*, **63**, 752–754.

George, T.R. (1994) Self-confidence and baseball performance: A causal examination of self-efficacy theory, *Journal of Sport and Exercise Psychology*, **16**, 381–399.

Gill, D.L. (1986) *Psychological Dynamics of Sport*, Human Kinetics, Champaign, IL.

Gill, D.L. (1988) Gender differences in competitive orientation and sport participation, *International Journal of Sport Psychology*, **19**, 145–159.

Gill, D.L., and Deeter, T.E. (1988) Development of the Sport Orientation Questionnaire, *Research Quarterly for Sport and Exercise*, **59** (3), 191–202.

Gill, D.L., and Strom, E.H. (1985) The effect of attentional focus on performance of an endurance task, *International Journal of Sport Psychology*, **16**, 217–223.

Gill, D.L., Gross, J.B., and Huddleston, S. (1983) Participation motivation in youth sports, *International Journal of Sport Psychology*, **14**, 1–14.

Gilligan, C., and Bower (1984) Cognitive consequences of emotional arousal. In C. Izard, J. Kagan and R. Zajonc (eds), *Emotion, Cognitions and Behaviour*, Cambridge University Press, NY.

Gipson, M., McKenzie, T., and Lowe, S. (1989) The sport psychology program of the USA Women's National Volleyball Team, *The Sport Psychologist*, **3**, 330–339.

Godden, D.R., and Baddeley, A.D. (1975) Context-dependent memory in two natural environments: On land and under water, *British Journal of Psychology*, **66**, 325–331.

Goffi, C. (1984) *Tournament Tough*, Ebury Press, London.

Goleman, D.J. (1971) Meditation as meta-therapy: Hypotheses toward a proposed fifth state of consciousness, *Journal of Transpersonal Psychology*, **3**, 1–25.

Goss, S., Hall, C., Buckolz, E., and Fishburne, G. (1986) Imagery ability and the acquisition of retention of movements, *Memory and Cognition*, **14**, 469–477.

Goudas, M., Fox, K., Biddle, S., and Armstrong, N. (1992) Children's task and ego goal profiles in sport: Relationship with perceived competence, enjoyment and participation, *Journal of Sport Sciences*, **10** (6), 606–607.

Gould, D. (1993a) Goal setting for peak performance. In J. Williams (ed.), *Applied Sport Psychology: Personal Growth to Peak Performance* (2nd edn), Mayfield, Palo Alto, CA, pp. 158–169.

Gould, D. (1993b) Intensive sport participation and the prepubescent athlete: Competitive stress and burnout. In B.R. Cahill and A.J. Pearl (eds), *Intensive Sports Participation in Children's Sports*, Human Kinetics, Champaign, IL, pp. 19–38.

Gould, D., and Damarjian, N. (in press) Mental skills training in sport. In B.C. Elliot (ed.), *Applied Sport Science: Training in Sport. International Handbook of Sport Sciences – Vol. 3*, Wiley, Chichester.

Gould, D., and Petchlikoff, L. (1988) Participation motivation in young athletes. In F.L. Simon, R.A. Magill, M.J. Ash (eds), *Psychological Foundations of Sport*, Human Kinetics, Champaign, IL, pp. 359–370.

Gould, D., and Tuffey, S. 1996 Zones of optimal functioning research: A review and critique, *Anxiety, Stress and Coping: An International Journal*, **9**, 53–68.

Gould, D., and Udry, E. (1994) Psychological skills for enhancing performance: Arousal regulation strategies, *Medicine and Science in Sports and Exercise*, **26**, 478–485.

Gould, D., and Weinberg, R. (1985) Sources of worry in successful and less successful intercollegiate wrestlers, *Journal of Sport Behaviour*, **8**, 115–127.

Gould, D., and Weiss, M. (1981) Effect of model similarity and model self-talk on self-efficacy in muscular endurance, *Journal of Sport Psychology*, **3**, 17–19.

Gould, D., Weinberg, R., and Jackson, A. (1980) Mental preparation strategies, cognitions, and strength performance, *Journal of Sport Psychology*, **2**, 329–339.

Gould, D., Weiss, M.R., and Weinberg, R.S. (1981) Psychological characteristics of successful and non-successful Big Ten wrestlers, *Journal of Sport Psychology*, **3**, 69–81.

Gould, D., Feltz, D., Horn, T., and Weiss, M.R. (1982) Reasons for attrition in competitive youth swimming, *Journal of Sport Behaviour*, **5**, 155–165.

Gould, D., Horn, T., and Spreemann, J. (1983) Sources of stress in junior elite wrestlers, *Journal of Sport Psychology*, **5**, 159–171.

Gould, D., Petchlikoff, L., and Weinberg, R.S. (1984) Antecedents of, temporal changes in, and relationships between CSAI-2 subcomponents, *Journal of Sport Psychology*, **6**, 289–304.

Gould, D., Petchlikoff, L., Simons, J., and Vevera, M. (1987) Relationship between Competitive State Anxiety Inventory-2 subscale scores and pistol shooting performance, *Journal of Sport Psychology*, **9**, 33–42.

Gould, D., Hodge, K., Peterson, K., and Giannini, J. (1989) An exploratory examination of strategies used by elite coaches to enhance self-efficacy in athletes, *Journal of Sport and Exercise Psychology*, **11**, 128–140.

Gould, D., Eklund, R.C., and Jackson, S.A. (1991) *An In-depth Examination of Mental Factors and Preparation Techniques Associated with 1988 U.S. Olympic Team Wrestling Success*. Grant report to USA Wrestling.

Gould, D., Eklund, R.C., and Jackson, S.A. (1992a) 1988 U.S. Olympic wrestling excellence: I Mental preparation, precompetitive cognition and affect, *The Sport Psychologist*, **6**, 358–362.

Gould, D., Eklund, R.C., and Jackson, S.A. (1992b) 1988 U.S. Olympic wrestling excellence: II Thoughts and affect occurring during competition, *The Sport Psychologist*, **6**, 383–402.

Gould, D., Eklund, R.C., and Jackson, S.A. (1993a) Coping strategies used by U.S. Olympic wrestlers, *Research Quarterly for Exercise and Sport*, **64**, 83–93.

Gould, D., Finch, L.M., and Jackson, S.A. (1993b) Coping strategies used by national champion figure skaters, *Research Quarterly for Exercise and Sport*, **64**, 453–468.

Gould, D., Jackson, S.A., and Finch, L.M. (1993c) Life at the top. The experiences of U.S. national champion figure skaters, *The Sport Psychologist*, **7**, 354–374.

Gould, D., Jackson, S.A., and Finch, L.M. (1993d) Sources of stress in national champion figure skaters, *Journal of Sport and Exercise Psychology*, **15**, 134–159.

Gould, D., Tuffey, S., Hardy, L., and Lochbaum, M. (1993e) Multidimensional state anxiety and middle distance running performance: An exploratory examination of Hanin's (1980) Zone of Optimal Functioning Hypothesis, *Journal of Applied Sport Psychology*, **5**, 85–95.

Gould, D., Tuffey, S., Udry, E., and Loehr, J. (1995a) Burnout in junior elite tennis players: Qualitative content analysis and case studies. Manuscript submitted for publication.

Gould, D., Udry, E., Tuffey, S., and Loehr, J. (1995b) Burnout in junior elite tennis players: A quantitative psychological assessment. Manuscript submitted for publication.

Gray, J.A. (1975) *Elements of a Two-Process Theory of Learning*, Academic Press, London.

Gray, J.A. (1982) *The Neuropsychology of Anxiety*, Clarendon, Oxford.

Gray, J.A. (1985) A whole and its parts: Behaviour, the brain, cognition and emotion, *Bulletin of the British Psychological Society*, **38**, 99–112.

Greenspan, M., and Feltz, D. (1989) Psychological intervention with athletes in competitive situations, *The Sport Psychologist*, **3**, 219–236.

Griffin, N. S., and Keogh, J. F. (1982) A model for movement confidence. In J.A.S. Kelso and J. Clark (eds), *The Development for Movement Control and Coordination*, Wiley, New York, pp. 213–236.

Grove, J.R., and Pargman, D. (1986) Relationships between success and failure, attributions and performance expectancies in competitive settings. In L. Van der Velden and J.H. Humphrey (eds), *Psychology and Sociology in Sport. Current Selected Research I*, AMS Press, New York, pp. 85–95.

Grove, R.J., and Prapavessis, H. (1995a) Correlates of batting slumps in baseball. Manuscript submitted for publication.

Grove, R.J., and Prapavessis, H. (1995b) Self-handicapping tendencies and slump-related coping in sport. Manuscript submitted for publication.

Grove, J.R., Hanrahan, S.J., and MacInman, A. (1991) Success / failure, bias in attributions across involvement categories, *Personality and Social Psychology Bulletin*, **17**, 19–37.

Hackfort, D., and Schwenkmezger, P. (1993) Anxiety. In R.N. Singer, M. Murphey and L.K. Tennant (eds), *Handbook of Research on Sport Psychology*, MacMillan, New York, pp. 328–364.
Hackney, A.C., Pearman III, S.N., and Nowacki, J.M. (1990) Physiological profiles of overtrained and stale athletes: A review, *Journal of Applied Sport Psychology*, **2**, 21–33.
Hale, B.D. (1981) *The Effects Of Internal And External Imagery On Muscular And Ocular Concomitants*, Unpublished doctoral dissertation, Pennsylvania State University, University Park, PA.
Hale, B.D. (1982) The effects of internal and external imagery on muscular and ocular concomitants. *Journal of Sport Psychology*, **4**, 379–387.
Hall, C.R., and Schmidt, D. (1992) Cognition in motor learning: positive versus negative imagery. Paper presented at the International Workshop on Imagery and Motor Processes, Beaumont Hall, Leicester.
Hall, C. R., Rogers, W. M., and Buckolz, E. (1991) The effect of an imagery training program on imagery ability, imagery use and figure skating performance, *Journal of Applied Sport Psychology*, **3**, 109–125.
Hall, C.R., Mack, D., and Paivio, A. (1996) Imagery use by athletes, Manuscript submitted for publication.
Hall, E.G., and Byrne, A.T.J. (1988) Goal-setting in sport: Clarifying recent anomalies, *Journal of Sport and Exercise Psychology*, **10**, 184–198.
Hall, E.G., and Erffmeyer, E.S. (1983) The effect of visuomotor behaviour rehearsal with videotaped modelling on free throw accuracy of intercollegiate female basketball players, *Journal of Sport Psychology*, **5**, 343–346.
Hall, H.K. (1989) *A Social Cognitive Approach to Goal Setting: The Mediating Effects of Achievement Goals and Perceived Ability*. Unpublished dissertation, University of Illinois, Urbana-Champaign, IL.
Hall, H.K., and Byrne, A.T.J. (1988) Goal setting in sport: Clarifying recent anomalies, *Journal of Sport and Exercise Psychology*, **10**, 184–198.
Hall, H.K., Weinberg, R.S., and Jackson, A. (1987) Effects of goal specificity, goal difficulty, and information feedback on endurance performance, *Journal of Sport Psychology*, **9**, 43–54.
Hall, J.R. (1983) Hypnosis and the immune system: A review of the implications for cancer and the psychology of healing, *American Journal of Clinical Hypnosis*, **25**, 95–103.
Hanin, Y.L. (1980) A study of anxiety in sport. In W.F. Straub (ed.), *Sport Psychology: An Analysis of Athletic Behavior*, Movement Publications, Ithaca, NY, pp. 236–249.
Hanin, Y.L. (1986) State trait anxiety research on sports in the USSR. In C.D. Spielberger and R. Diaz (eds), *Cross-cultural Anxiety (Vol. 3)*, Hemisphere, Washington, D.C., pp. 45–64.
Hanin, Y.L. (In Press) Individual zones of optimal functioning (IZOF) model: An idiographic approach to performance anxiety. In W.F. Straub (ed.), *Sport Psychology: An Analysis of Athlete Behaviour* (3rd edn), Movement Publications, Ithaca, NY.
Hanin, Y.L., and Syrjä, P. (1995a) Performance affect in junior ice hockey players: An application of the Individual Zones of Optimal Functioning model, *The Sport Psychologist*, **9**, 169–187.
Hanin, Y.L., and Syrjä, P. (1995b) Performance affect in soccer players: An application of the IZOF model, *International Journal of Sports Medicine*, **16**, 260–265.
Hanson, D.L. (1967) Cardiac response on participation in Little League baseball competition as determined by telemetry, *Research Quarterly*, **38**, 384–388.
Hanson, S.J., McCullagh, P., and Tonymon, P. (1992) The relationship of personality characteristics, life stress, and coping resources to athletic injury, *Journal of Sport and Exercise Psychology*, **14**, 262–272.

Hanton, S., and Jones, G. (1995) Antecedents of anxiety and confidence in elite competitive swimmers, *International Journal of Sport Psychology.*

Hardy, C.J., and Crace, R.K. (1991) Social support within sport, *Sport Psychology Training Bulletin*, **3**, 1–8.

Hardy, L. (1990) A catastrophe model of anxiety and performance. In J.G. Jones and L. Hardy (eds), *Stress and Performance in Sport*, Wiley, Chichester, pp. 81–106.

Hardy, L. (1996a) A test of catastrophe models of anxiety and sports performance against multidimensional anxiety theory models using the method of dynamic differences, *Anxiety, Stress and Coping: An International Journal*, **9**, 69–86.

Hardy, L. (1996b) Testing the predictions of the cusp catastrophe model of anxiety and performance, *The Sport Psychologist*, **10**, 140–156.

Hardy, L., and Callow, N. (1996) Kinaesthetic imagery and its interaction with visual imagery perspectives during the acquisition of a short gymnastics sequence. Manuscript in preparation.

Hardy, L., and Fazey, J.A. (1986) *Mental Preparation for Performance*, National Coaching Foundation, Leeds.

Hardy, L., and Fazey, J. (1990) *Mental Training*, National Coaching Foundation, Leeds.

Hardy, L., and Jones, J.G. (1990) Future directions for performance related research in sport psychology. In J.G. Jones and L. Hardy (eds), *Stress and Performance in Sport*, Wiley, Chichester, pp. 281–296.

Hardy, L., and Jones, G. (1994a) Current issues and future directions for performance-related research in sport psychology, *Journal of Sports Sciences*, **12**, 61–90.

Hardy, L., and Jones, G. (1994b) Sport Psychology. In M. Harries, L.J. Micheli, W.D. Stanish and C. Williams (eds), *Oxford Textbook of Sports Medicine*, Oxford University Press, Oxford.

Hardy, L., and Nelson, D. (1988) Self regulation training in sport and work, *Ergonomics*, **31**, 1673–1683.

Hardy, L., and Parfitt, C.G. (1991) A catastrophe model of anxiety and performance, *British Journal of Psychology*, **82**, 163–178.

Hardy, L., and Parfitt, G. (1994) The development of a model for the provision of psychological support to a national squad, *The Sport Psychologist*, **8**, 126–142.

Hardy, L., and Whitehead, R. (1984) Specific modes of anxiety and arousal, *Current Psychological Research and Reviews*, **3**, 14–24.

Hardy, L., and Wyatt, S. (1986) Immediate effects of imagery upon skillful motor performance. In D.G. Russell and D. Marks (eds), *Imagery* 2, Human Performance Associates, New Zealand.

Hardy, L., Maiden, D., and Sherry, K. (1986) Goal setting and performance anxiety, *Journal of Sport Sciences*, **4**, 223–234.

Hardy, L., Parfitt, C.G., and Pates, J. (1994) Performance catastrophes in sport: A test of the hysteresis hypothesis, *Journal of Sport Sciences*, **12**, 327–334.

Hardy, L., Swain, A.B.J., and Jones, G. (1996) An empirical test of the cusp and butterfly catastrophe models using basketball players. Manuscript in preparation.

Hardy, L., Mullen, R., and Jones, G. (in press) Knowledge and conscious control of motor actions under stress, *British Journal of Psychology.*

Harkins, S G., and Petty, R.E. (1982) Effects of task difficulty and task uniqueness on social loafing, *Journal of Personality and Social Psychology*, **43**, 1214–1229.

Harris, D.V., and Harris, B.L. (1984) *The Athlete's Guide To Sport Psychology: Mental Skills For Physical People*, Leisure Press, Champaign, Illinois.

Harris, J.L. (1988) Right-brain braining: Some reflections on the application of research on cerebral hemispheric specialization to education. In D.L. Molfese and S.J. Segalowitz (eds), *Brain Lateralization in Children*, Guildford, New York.

Harter, S. (1982) The Perceived Competence Scale for Children, *Child Development*, **53**, 87–97.
Harvey, N. (1988) *The Psychology of Action: Current Controversies*. In J. Claxton (ed.), Growth Points in Cognition, Routledge, London, pp. 66–90.
Hatfield, B.D., Landers, D.M., and Ray, W.J. (1984) Cognitive processes during self-paced motor performance: An electroencephalographic profile of skilled marksmen, *Journal of Sport Psychology*, **6**, 42–59.
Hatfield, B.D., Landers, D.M., and Ray, W.J. (1987) Cardiovascular CNS interactions during a self paced intentional state: Elite marksmanship performance, *Psychophysiology*, **24**, 542–549.
Hebb, D.O. (1955) Drives and the CNS (Conceptual Nervous System), *Psychological Review*, **62**, 243–254.
Heider, F. (1958) *The Psychology of Interpersonal Relations*, Wiley, New York.
Heil, J. (1985) The role of imagery in sport: as a 'training tool' and as a 'mode of thought'. Paper presented at the World Congress in Sport Psychology, Copenhagen.
Hemery, D. (1976) *Another Hurdle*, Heinemann, London.
Hemery, D. (1986) *The Pursuit of Sporting Excellence*. Collins, London.
Hemery, D. (1991) *Sporting Excellence: What makes a Champion* (2nd edn), Wiley, New York.
Highlen, P.S., and Bennett, B.B. (1979) Psychological characteristics of successful and unsuccessful elite wrestlers: An exploratory study, *Journal of Sport Psychology*, **1**, 123–137.
Highlen, P.S., and Bennett, B.B. (1983) Elite divers, wrestlers: A comparison between open and closed skilled athletes, *Journal of Sport Psychology*, **5**, 390–349.
Hockey, G.R.J., and Hamilton, P. (1983) The cognitive patterning of stress states. In G.R.J. Hockey (ed.), *Stress and Fatigue in Human Performance*, Wiley, Chichester, pp. 331–362.
Hollingsworth, B. (1975) Effects of performance goals and anxiety on learning a gross motor task, *Research Quarterly*, **46**, 162–168.
Homme, L.E. (1965) Perspectives in Psychology: XXIV Control of coverants, the operants of the mind. *Psychological Record*, **15**, 501–511.
Horn, T. (1984) The expectancy process: causes and consequences. In W. Straub and J. Williams (eds), *Cognitive Sport Psychology*, Sport Sciences Associates, Lansing, New York, pp. 199–211.
Housner, L.D. (1984) The role of visual imagery in recall of modelled motoric stimuli, *Journal of Sport Psychology*, **6**, 148–158.
Houston, B. (1987) Stress and Coping. In C. Snyder and C. Ford (eds), *Coping with Negative Life Events: Clinical and Social Psychological*, Plenum Press, New York, pp. 377–399.
Humphreys, M.S., and Revelle, W. (1984) Personality, motivation and performance: A theory of the relationship between individual differences and information processing, *Psychological Review*, **91**, 153–184.
Ievleva, L., and Orlick, T. (1991) Mental links to enhanced healing, *The Sport Psychologist*, **5**, 25–40.
Ingledew, D.K., Hardy, L., and Cooper, C.L. (1996) Do resources bolster coping and does coping buffer stress? An organisational study with longitudinal aspect and control for negative affectivity. Manuscript submitted for publication.
Jackson, G.M., and Eberly, D.A. (1982) Facilitation of performance on an arithmetic task as a result of the application of biofeedback procedure to suppress alpha wave activity, *Biofeedback and Self Regulation*, **7**, 211–221.

Jackson, J.M., and Williams, K.D. (1985) Social loafing on difficult tasks: Working collectively can improve performance, *Journal of Personality and Social Psychology*, **49**, 937–942.

Jackson, S.A. (1992) Athletes in flow: A qualitative investigation of flow states in elite figure skaters, *Journal of Applied Sport Psychology*, **4**, 161–180.

Jackson, S.A. (1994) *Athletes in Flow: The Psychology of Optimal Experience*. Doctoral dissertation, University of North Carolina Greensboro, University Microfilm Publications, Oregon.

Jacobson, E. (1930) Electrical measurement of neuromuscular states during mental activity, *American Journal of Physiology*, **94**, 22–34.

Jacobson, E. (1938) *Progressive Relaxation*, University of Chicago Press, Chicago, IL.

Jakeman, P.M., Winter, E.M., and Doust, J. (1994) A review of research in sport psychology, *Journal of Sport Sciences*, **12** (1), 33–60.

Jaskowski, P., Verleger, R., and Wascher, E. (1994) Response force and reaction time in a simple reaction task under time pressure, *Zeitschrift für Psychologie*, 202, 405–413.

Jick, T., and Payne, R.L. (1980) Stress at work, *Exchange: The Organisational Behaviour Teaching Journal*, **5**, 50–53.

Johnson, L., and Biddle, S.J. (1988) Persistence after failure: An exploratory look at 'learned helplessness' in motor performance, *British Journal of Physical Education Research Supplement*, **5**, 7–10.

Johnson, P. (1982) The functional equivalence of imagery and movement, *Quarterly Journal of Experimental Psychology*, **34A**, 349–365.

Johnston-O'Connor, E.J., and Kirschenbaum, D.S. (1986) Something succeeds like success: Positive self-monitoring for unskilled golfers, *Cognitive Therapy and Research*, **10**, 123–136.

Jones, E.E. (1979) The rocky road from acts to dispositions, *American Psychologist*, **34**, 107–117.

Jones, G. (1990) A cognitive perspective on the processes underlying the relationship between stress and performance in sport. In G. Jones and L. Hardy (eds), *Stress and Performance in Sport*, Wiley, Chichester, pp. 17–42.

Jones, G. (1991) Recent developments and current issues in competitive state anxiety research, *The Psychologist*, **4**, 152–155.

Jones, G. (1993) The role of performance profiling in cognitive behavioural interventions in sport, *The Sport Psychologist*, **7**, 160–172.

Jones, G. (1995a) Anxiety and performance: Research issues and developments. In S. Biddle (ed.), *Exercise and Sport Psychology: A European Perspective*, Human Kinetics, Champaign, IL.

Jones, G. (1995b) More than just a game: Research developments and issues in competitive anxiety in sport, *British Journal of Psychology*, **86**, 449–478.

Jones, G., and Cale, A. (1989) Relationship between multidimensional competitive state anxiety and cognitive and motor subcomponents of performance, *Journal of Sport Sciences*, **7**, 129–140.

Jones, G., and Cale, A. (in press) Goal difficulty, anxiety and performance. *Ergonomics*.

Jones, G., and Hanton, S. (1996) Interpretation of competitive anxiety symptoms and goal attainment expectancies, *Journal of Sport and Exercise Psychology*, **18**, 144–157.

Jones, J.G., and Hardy, L. (1989) Stress and cognitive functioning in sport, *Journal of Sport Sciences*, **7**, 41–63.

Jones, G., and Hardy, L. (1990a) Stress in sport: Experiences of some elite performers. In G. Jones and L. Hardy (eds), *Stress and Performance in Sport*, Wiley, Chichester, pp. 247–277.

Jones, G., and Hardy, L. (1990b) *Stress and Performance in Sport*, Wiley, Chichester.

Jones, G., and Swain, A.B.J. (1992) Intensity and direction dimensions of competitive anxiety and relationships with competitiveness, *Perceptual and Motor Skills*, **74**, 467–472.

Jones, G., and Swain, A.B.J. (1995) Predisposition to experience debilitative and facilititative anxiety in elite and nonelite performers, *The Sport Psychologist*, **9**, 201–211.

Jones, G., Swain, A.B.J., and Cale, A. (1990) Antecedents of multidimensional competitive state anxiety and self confidence in elite intercollegiate middle distance runners, *The Sport Psychologist*, **4**, 107–118.

Jones, G., Swain, A.B.J., and Cale, A. (1991) Gender differences in precompetition temporal patterning and antecedents of anxiety and self confidence, *Journal of Sport and Exercise Psychology*, **13**, 1–15.

Jones, G., Swain, A.B.J., and Hardy, L. (1993) Intensity and direction dimensions of competitive state anxiety and relationships with performance, *Journal of Sport Sciences*, **11**, 525–532.

Jones, G., Hanton, S., and Swain, A.B.J. (1994) Intensity and interpretation of anxiety symptoms in elite and non-elite sports performers, *Personal Individual Differences*, **17**, 657–663.

Jowdy, D.P., Murphy, S.M., and Durtschi, S. (1989) *An Assessment Of The Use Of Imagery By Elite Athletes: Athlete, Coach And Psychological Perspectives*, United States Olympic Committee, Colorado Springs, CO.

Kahneman, D. (1973) *Attention and Effort*, Prentice-Hall, Englewood Cliffs, NJ.

Kavanagh, D., and Hausfeld, S. (1986) Physical performance and self efficacy under happy and sad moods, *Journal of Sport Psychology*, **8**, 112–123.

Kazdin, A.E. (1978) Conceptual and assessment issues raised by self-efficacy theory. In S. Rachman (ed.), *Advances in Behaviour Research and Therapy. Volume 1*, Pergamon Press, Oxford, pp. 177–185.

Keast, D., Cameron, K., and Morton, A.R. (1988) Exercise and the immuno-response. *Sports Medicine*, **5**, 248–267.

Keele, S.W. (1973) *Attention and Human Performance*, Pacific Palisades, CA.

Kelley, B.C. (1994) A model of stress and burnout in collegiate coaches: Effects of gender and time of season, *Research Quarterly for Sport and Exercise*, **65**, 48–58.

Kelley, B.C., and Gill, D.L. (1993) An examination of personal/situational variables, stress appraisal, and burnout in collegiate teacher-coaches, *Research Quarterly for Sport and Exercise*, **64**, 94–102.

Kelley, H.H. (1983) Love and commitment. In H.H. Kelley, E. Bersceid, A. Christensen, J.H. Harvey, T.L. Huston, G. Levinger, E. McLintock, L.A. Peplau, D.R. Peterson (eds), *Close Relationships*, Freeman, New York, pp. 265–314.

Kelley, H.H., and Michela, J.L. (1980) Attribution theory and research, *Annual Review of Psychology*, **31**, 457–501.

Kerr, J.H. (1990) Stress in sport: Reversal theory. In J.G. Jones and L. Hardy (eds), *Stress and Performance in Sport*, Wiley, Chichester, pp. 107–131.

Kimura, D. (1973) The asymmetry of the human brain, *Scientific American*, **228**, 70–78.

Kingston, K.M., and Hardy, L. (1994a) When are some goals more beneficial than others?, *Journal of Sport Sciences*, **12**, 198–199.

Kingston, K.M., and Hardy, L. (1994b) Factors affecting the salience of outcome performance and process goals in golf. In A.J. Cochran and M.R. Farally (eds), *Science and Golf II*, Chapman and Hall, London, pp. 144–149.

Kirsch, I. (1985) Self-efficacy and expectancy: Old wine with new labels, *Journal of Personality and Social Psychology*, **49**, 824–830.

Kirschenbaum, D.S., and Bale, R.M. (1984) Cognitive–behavioural skills in sports. In W.F. Straub and J.M. Williams (eds), *Cognitive Sport Psychology*, Sport Science Associates, Lansing, New York.

Kirschenbaum, D.S., Tomarken, A.J., and Ordman, A.M. (1982) Specificity of planning and choice in adult self control, *Journal of Personality and Social Psychology*, **41**, 576–585.

Klinger, E., Bart, S.J., and Glass, R.A. (1981) Thought content and gap time in basketball, *Cognitive Therapy and Research*, **5**, 109–114.

Krane, V. (1990) *Anxiety and Athletic Performance: A Test of the Multidimensional Anxiety and Catastrophe Theories*. Unpublished doctoral thesis, University of North Carolina, Greensboro.

Krane, V. (1992) Conceptual and methodological considerations in sport anxiety research: From the inverted-U hypothesis to catastrophe theory, *Quest*, **44**, 72–87.

Krane, V. (1993) A practical application of the anxiety–performance relationship: The zone of optimal functioning hypothesis, *The Sport Psychologist*, **7**, 113–126.

Krane, V., and Williams, J.M. (1987) Performance and somatic anxiety, and confidence changes prior to competition, *Journal of Sport Behaviour*, **10**, 47–56.

Krohne, H.W. (1988) Coping research: Current theoretical and methodological developments, *The German Journal of Psychology*, **12**, 1–30.

Krohne, H.W., and Hindel, C. (1988) Trait anxiety, state anxiety, and coping behaviors as predictors of athletic performance, *Anxiety Research*, **1**, 225–235.

Kroll, W.P. (1971) *Perspectives in Physical Education*, Academic Press, New York.

Kroll, W. (1979) The stress of high performance athletics. In P. Klavora and J.V. Daniel (eds), *Coach, Athlete and Sport Psychologists*, Human Kinetics, Champaign, IL, pp. 211–219.

Kubler-Ross, E. (1969) *On Death and Dying*, MacMillan, New York.

Kuhn, T.S. (1962) *The Structure of Scientific Revolutions*, University of Chicago Press, Chicago, IL.

Kukla, K.J. (1976) The effects of progressive relaxation training upon athletic performance under stress, *Dissertation Abstracts International*, **37**, 63–92.

Lacey, J.I. (1967) Somatic response patterning of stress: Some revisions of activation theory. In M. Appley and R. Trumbell (eds), *Psychological Stress in Research*, Appleton, New York.

Lacey, B.B., and Lacey, J.I. (1970) Some autonomic central nervous system interrelationships. In P.Black (ed.), *Physical Correlates of Emotion*, Academic Press, NY.

Landers, D.M. (1981) Arousal, attention and skilled performance: Further considerations, *Quest*, **33**, 271–283.

Landers, D.M. (1983) Whatever happened to theory testing in sport psychology?, *Journal of Sport Psychology*, **5**, 77–90.

Landers, D.M. (1985) Psychophysiological assessment and biofeedback: Application for athletes in closed skill sport. In J. Sandweiss and S. Wolf (eds), *Biofeedback and Sport Science*, Plenum Press, NY, pp. 65–105.

Landers, D.M. (1994) Performance, stress and health: Overall reaction, *Quest*, **46**, 123–135.

Landers, D.M., and Boutcher, S.H. (1986) Arousal–performance relationships. In J.M. Williams (ed.), *Applied Sport Psychology*, Mayfield, Palo Alto, CA.

Landers, D.M., Christina, R., Hatfield, B.D., Daniels, S.F., and Doyle, L.A. (1980) Moving competitive shooting into the scientists' lab, *American Rifleman*, **128**, 36–37, 76–77.

Landers, D., Han, M., Salazar, W., Petruzzello, S., Kubitz, K., and Gannon, T. (in press) Effects of learning on electroencephalographic and electrocardiographic patterns in novice archers, *International Journal of Sport Psychology*.

Lane, J.F. (1980) Improving athletic performance through visuo-motor behavior rehearsal. In R.M. Suinn (ed.), *Psychology in Sport: Methods and Applications*, Burgess, Minneapolis, Minnesota.

Lang, P.J. (1977) Imagery in therapy: An information-processing analysis of fear, *Behavior Therapy*, **8**, 862–886.

Lang, P.J. (1979) A bio-informational theory of emotional imagery, *Psychophysiology*, **17**, 495–512.

Lang, P.J. (1984) Cognition in emotion: Concept and action. In C. Izard, J. Kagan and R. Zajonc (eds), *Emotion, Cognition and Behaviour*, Cambridge University Press, New York, pp. 192–225.

Lang, P.J., Kozak, M., Miller, G.A., Levin, D.N., and McLean, A. (1980) Emotional imagery: conceptual structure and pattern of somato-visceral response, *Psychophysiology*, **17**, 179–192.

Lang, P.J., Levin, D.N., Miller, G.A., and Kozak, J.J. (1983) Fear behavior, fear imagery, and the psychophysiology of emotion: The problem of affective response integration, *Journal of Abnormal Psychology*, **92**, 276–306.

Langer, E.J., and Imber, L.G. (1979) When practice makes imperfect: Debilitating effects of overlearning, *Journal of Personality and Social Psychology*, **37**, 2014–2024.

Lanning, W., and Hisanaga, B. (1983) A study of the relationship between the reduction of competition anxiety and an increase in athletic performance, *International Journal of Sport Psychology*, **14**, 219–227.

Latham, G.P., and Yukl, G.A. (1975) Assigned versus participative goal setting with educated and uneducated wood workers, *Journal of Applied Physiology*, **60**, 229–302.

Lazarus, R.S. (1966) *Psychological Stress and Coping Process*, McGraw-Hill, New York.

Lazarus, R.S. (1982) Thoughts on the relation between emotion and cognition, *American Psychologist*, **37**, 1019–1024.

Lazarus, R.S., and Folkman, S. (1984) *Stress Appraisal and Coping*, Springer, New York.

Lee, C. (1990) Psyching up for a muscular endurance task: Effect of image content on performance and mood state, *Journal of Sport and Exercise Psychology*, **12**, 66–73.

Lewthwaite, R. (1990) Threat perception in competitive trait anxiety: The endangerment of important goals, *Journal of Sport and Exercise Psychology*, **12**, 280–300.

Liebert, R.M., and Morris, L.W. (1967) Cognitive and emotional components of test anxiety: A distinction and some initial data, *Psychological Reports*, **20**, 975–978.

Lincoln, Y.S., and Guba, E.G. (1985) *Naturalistic inquiry*, Sage, Newbury Park, CA.

Lirgg, C.D., and Feltz, D.L. (1991) Teacher versus peer models revisited: Effects on motor performance, *Research Quarterly for Exercise and Sport*, **62**, 217–224.

Lirgg, C.D., and Feltz, D.L. (1994) Relationship of individual and collective efficacy to team performance, *Journal of Sport and Exercise Psychology*, **16** (supplement, S17).

Lobmeyer, D.L., and Wasserman, E.A. (1986) Preliminaries to free throw shooting: Superstitious behaviour, *Journal of Sport Behaviour*, **11**, 70–78.

Locke, E.A. (1966) The relationship of intentions to level of performance, *Journal of Applied Psychology*, **50**, 60–66.

Locke, E.A. (1968) Toward a theory of task motivation and incentives, *Organisational Behaviour and Human Performance*, **3**, 157–189.

Locke, E.A. (1991) Problems with goal-setting to sports – and their solution, *Journal of Sport and Exercise Psychology*, **13**, 311–316.

Locke, E.A., and Latham, G.P. (1985) The application of goal setting to sport, *Journal of Sport Psychology*, **7**, 205–222.

Locke, E.A., and Latham, G.P. (1990) *A Theory Of Goal-Setting And Task Performance*, Prentice-Hall, Englewood Cliffs, New Jersey.

Locke, E.A., Feren, D.B., McCaleb, V.M., Shaw, K.N., and Denney, A.T. (1980) The relative effectiveness of four methods of motivating employee performance. In K. Duncan and D. Wallis (eds), *Changes in Working Life*, Wiley, New York, pp. 363–388.
Locke, E.A., Shaw, K.N., Saari, L.M., and Latham, G.P. (1981) Goal setting and task performance (1969–1980), *Psychological Bulletin*, **96**, 125–152.
Locke, E.A., Frederick, E., Bobko, P., and Lee, C. (1984) Effect of self efficacy, goals and strategies on task performance, *Journal of Applied Psychology*, **69**, 241–251.
Logan, G.D. (1988) Toward an instance theory of automation, *Psychological Review*, **95**, 32–63.
Logan, G.D. (1990) Repetition priming and automaticity: Common underlying mechanisms, *Cognitive Psychology*, **22**, 1–35.
Louganis, G., and Marcus, E. (1995) *Breaking the surface*, Random House, NY.
Lowe, R., and McGrath, J.E. (1971) *Stress, arousal and performance: Some findings calling for a new theory*. Project Report, AF 1161–67, AFOSR.
Lutkus, A.D. (1975) The effect of 'imaging' on mirror drawing, *Bulletin of the Psychonomic Society*, **5**, 389–390.
Mace, R. (1990) Cognitive behavioural interventions in sport. In J.G. Jones and L. Hardy (eds), *Stress and Performance in Sport*, Wiley, Chichester, pp. 203–230.
Mace, R.D., and Carroll, D. (1985) The control of anxiety in sport: Stress Inoculation training prior to abseiling, *International Journal of Sport Psychology*, **16**, 165–175.
Mace, R.D., and Carroll, D. (1986) Stress inoculation training to control anxiety in sport: Two case studies in squash, *British Journal of Sports Medicine*, **20**, 115–117.
MacLeod, C. (1990) Mood disorders and cognition. In M.W. Eysenck (ed.), *Cognitive Psychology: An International Review*, Wiley, Chichester.
MacLeod, C., and Mathews, A. (1988) Anxiety and the allocation of attention to threat, *Quarterly Journal of Experimental Psychology*, **38a**, 659–670.
Madden, C.C., Kirkby, R.J., and McDonald, D. (1989) Coping styles of competitive middle distance runners, *International Journal of Sport Psychology*, **20**, 287–296.
Madden, C.C., Summers, J.J., and Brown, D.F. (1990) The influence of perceived stress on coping with competitive basketball, *International Journal of Sport Psychology*, **21**, 21–35.
Maehr, M.L., and Nicholls, J.G. (1980) Culture and achievement motivation: A second look. In N. Warren (ed.), *Studies in Cross-cultural Psychology*, Academic Press, New York, pp. 221–267.
Magnusson, D., and Ekehammar, B. (1975) Perceptions of and reaction to stressful situations, *Journal of Personality and Social Psychology*, **31**, 1147–1154.
Mahoney, M.J. (1979) Cognitive skills and athletic performance. In P.C. Kendall and S.D. Hollon (eds), *Cognitive Behaviour Interventions: Theory, Research and Procedure*, Academic Press, New York.
Mahoney, M.J., and Avener, M. (1977) Psychology of the elite athlete: An exploratory study, *Cognitive Therapy and Research*, **1**, 135–141.
Mahoney, M.J., Gabriel, T.J., and Perkins, T.S. (1987) Psychological skills and exceptional athletic performance, *The Sport Psychologist*, **1**, 181–199.
Manderlink, G., and Harockiewizc, J.M. (1984) Proximal versus distal goal setting and intrinsic motivation, *Journal of Personality and Social Psychology*, **47**, 918–928.
Marks, D., and Issac, A. (1992) *The Neuropsychological Basis of Imagery and Motor Processes*, Paper presented at the International Workshop on Imagery and Motor Processes, Beaumont Hall, Leicester.
Marsh, H.W., Cairns, L., Relich, J., Barnes, J., and Debus, R.L. (1984) The relationship between dimensions of self attribution and dimensions of self concept, *Journal of Educational Psychology*, **76**, 3–32.

Martens, R. (ed.), (1977) *Sport Competition Anxiety Test*, Human Kinetics, Champaign, IL.
Martens, R. (1979) About smocks and jocks, *Journal of Sport Psychology*, **1**, 94–99.
Martens, R. (1987) Science, knowledge, and sport psychology, *The Sport Psychologist*, **1**, 29–55.
Martens, R., Burton, D., Vealey, R.S., Bump, L.A., and Smith, D.E. (1990a) Development and validation of the Competitive State Anxiety Inventory-2. In R. Martens, R.S. Vealey, and D. Burton (eds), *Competitive Anxiety in Sport*, Human Kinetics, Champaign, IL, pp. 117–190.
Martens, R., Vealey, R.S., and Burton, D. (1990b) *Competitive Anxiety in Sport*, Human Kinetics, Champaign, IL.
Martin, J.J., and Gill, D.L. (1991) The relationships between competitive orientation, sport-confidence, self-efficacy, anxiety and performance, *Journal of Sport and Exercise Psychology*, **13**, 149–159.
Masters, R.S.W. (1992) Knowledge, knerves, and know-how: The role of explicit versus implicit knowledge in the breakdown of a complex motor skill under pressure, *British Journal of Psychology*, **83**, 343–358.
Maynard, I.W., and Cotton, P.C.J. (1993) An investigation of two stress management techniques in a field setting, *The Sport Psychologist*, 375–387.
Maynard, M.W., Hemmings, B., and Warwick-Evans, L. (1995a) The effects of a somatic intervention strategy on competitive state anxiety and performance in semiprofessional soccer players, *The Sport Psychologist*, **9**, 51–64.
Maynard, M.W., Smith, M.J., and Warwick-Evans, L. (1995b) The effects of a cognitive intervention strategy on competitive state anxiety and performance in semiprofessional soccer players, *Journal of Sport and Exercise Psychology*, **17**, 428–446.
McAuley, E. (1985) Modelling and Self-efficacy: A test of Bandura's model, *Journal of Sport Psychology*, **7**, 283–295.
McAuley, E. (1991) Efficacy, attributional and affective responses to exercise participation, *Journal of Sport and Exercise Psychology*, **13** (4), 382–393.
McAuley, E. (1992) Self-referent thought in sport and physical activity. In T. S. Horn (ed.), *Advances in Sport Psychology*, Human Kinetics, Champaign, IL, pp. 101–118.
McAuley, E., and Duncan, T.E. (1989) Causal attributions and affective reactions to disconfirming outcomes in motor performance, *Journal of Sport and Exercise Psychology*, **11**, 187–200.
McAuley, E., and Goss, J.B. (1983) Perceptions of causality in sport: An application of the causal dimension scale, *Journal of Sport Psychology*, **5**, 72–76.
McAuley, E., Duncan, T.E., and McElroy, M. (1989) Self efficacy cognitions and causal attributions for children's' motor performance: An exploratory investigation, *Journal of Genetic Psychology*, **150**, 65–73.
McCrae, R.R. (1984) Situational determinants of coping responses: Loss, threat, and challenge, *Journal of Personality and Social Psychology*, **46**, 919–928.
McGrath, J.E. (1970) A conceptual formation for research on stress. In J.E. McGrath (ed.), *Social and Psychological Factors in Stress*, Holt, Rinehart and Winston, New York, pp. 19–49.
McLeod, P. (1977) A dual task response modality effect: Support for multiprocessor models of attention, *Quarterly Journal of Experimental Psychology*, **29**, 651–667.
McNair, D.M., Lorr, M., and Droppelman, L.F. (1971) *Profile of Mood States Manual*, Educational and Industrial Testing Services, San Diego, CA.
Meacci, W.G., and Price, E.E. (1985) Acquisition of retention of golf putting skill through the relaxation, visualisation and body rehearsal intervention, *Research Quarterly for Exercise and Sport*, **56**, 176–179.

Meichenbaum, D. (1973) Cognitive factors in behavior modifications. Modifying what people say to themselves. In C. M. Franks and G. T. Wilson (eds), *Annual Review of Behavior Therapy: Theory and Practice*, Vol. 1, Bruner, Mazel, New York.

Meichenbaum, D. (1975) A self instructional approach to stress management: A proposal for stress inoculation training. In C.D. Spielberger and I.G. Sarason (eds), *Stress and Anxiety (Vol. 1)*, Hemisphere, Washington, DC.

Meichenbaum, D. (1977) *Cognitive Behaviour Modification: An Integrative Approach*, Plenum Press, New York.

Mento, A.J., Steel, R.P., and Karren, R.J. (1987) A meta-analytic study of the effects of goal setting on task performance: 1966–1984, *Organisational Behaviour and Human Decisions Processes*, **39**, 52–83.

Meyers, A.W., and Schlesser, R. (1980) A cognitive behavioural intervention for improving basketball performance, *Journal of Sport Psychology*, **2**, 69–73.

Meyers, A.W., Cooke, C.J., Cullen, J., and Liles, L. (1979) Psychological aspects of athletic competitors: A replication across sports, *Cognitive Therapy and Research*, **3**, 361–366.

Miller, D.T. (1976) Ego involvement and attributions for success and failure, *Journal of Personality and Social Psychology*, **34**, 901–906.

Miller, J.T., and McAuley, E. (1987) Effects of a goal-setting training program on basketball free-throw self-efficacy and performance, *The Sport Psychologist*, **1**, 103–113.

Minas, S.C. (1980) Mental practice of a complex perceptual-motor skill, *Journal of Human Studies*, **4**, 102–107.

Moore, W.E., and Stevenson, J.R. (1991) Understanding trust in the performance of complex automatic skills, *The Sport Psychologist*, **5**, 281–289.

Moore, W.E., and Stevenson, J.R. (1994) Training for trust in sport skills, *The Sport Psychologist*, **8**, 1–12.

Morgan, W.P. (1985) Affective beneficence of vigorous physical activity, *Medicine and Science in Sport and Exercise*, **17**, 94–100.

Morgan, W.P. (1988) Nightline transcripts, *Journal Graphics*, **267** (Broadway, New York), 1007.

Morgan, W.P., and Pollock, M.L. (1977) Psychological characterization of the elite distance runner, *Annals of the New York Academy of Science*, **301**, 382–403.

Morgan, W.P., Costill, D.L., Flynn, M.G., Raglin, J.S., and O'Connor, P.J. (1988) Mood disturbance following increased training in swimmers, *Medicine and Science in Sport and Exercise*, **20**, 408–414.

Moritz, S.E., Hall, C.R., and Martin, K. (1996) What are confident athletes imaging?: An examination of image content, *The Sport Psychologist*.

Morris, L.W., Davis, M.A., and Hutchings, C.H. (1981) Cognitive and emotional components of anxiety: Literature review and a revised worry–emotionality scale, *Journal of Educational Psychology*, **73**, 541–555.

Mullen, B., and Riordan, C.A. (1988) Self serving attributions for performance in naturalistic settings: A meta-analytical review, *Journal of Applied Social Psychology*, **18**, 3–22.

Mumford, P., and Hall, C. (1985) The effects of internal and external imagery on performing figures in figure skating, *Canadian Journal of Applied Sport Sciences*, **10**, 171–177.

Murphy, S.M. (1988) The on-site provision of sport psychology services at the 1987 U.S. Olympic Festival, *The Sport Psychologist*, **2**, 337–351.

Murphy, S.M. (1990) Models of imagery in sport psychology: A review, *Journal of Mental Imagery*, **14**, 153–172.

Murphy, S.M. (1994) Imagery interventions in sport, *Medicine and Science in Sports and Exercise*, **26**, 486–494.

Murphy, S.M. (1995) Transitions in competitive sport: Maximizing individual potential. In S.M. Murphy (ed.), *Sport Psychology Interventions*, Human Kinetics, Champaign, IL, pp. 334–346.

Murphy, S.M., and Jowdy, D.P. (1992) Imagery and Mental Practice. In T.S. Horn (ed.), *Advances in Sport Psychology*, Human Kinetics, Champaign, IL, pp. 222–250.

Murphy, S.M., and Woolfolk, R.L. (1987) The effects of cognitive interventions on competitive anxiety and performance on a fine motor skill accuracy task, *International Journal of Sport Psychology*, **18**, 152–166.

Murphy, S.M., Woolfolk, R.L., and Budney, A.J. (1988) The effects of emotive imagery on strength performance, *Journal of Sport and Exercise Psychology*, **10**, 334–345.

Murphy, S.M., Fleck, S.J., Dudley, G., and Callister, R. (1990) Psychological and performance concomitants of increased volume training in elite athletes, *Journal of Applied Sport Psychology*, **2** (1), 34–50.

Naatanen, R. (1973) The inverted-U relationship between activation and performance: a critical review. In S. Kornblum (ed.) *Attention and Performance IV*, Academic Press, New York.

Navon, D., and Gopher, D. (1979) On the economy of the human processing, *Psychological Review*, **86**, 214–255.

Neiss, R. (1988a) Reconceptualizing relaxation treatments: Psychobiological states in sports, *Clinical Psychology Review*, **8**, 139–159.

Neiss, R. (1988b) Reconceptualising arousal: Psychobiological states in motor performance, *Psychological Bulletin*, **103**, 345–366.

Neisser, U.N. (1976) *Cognition and Reality: Principles and Applications of Cognitive Psychology*, W.H. Freeman, San Francisco, CA.

Ness, R.G., and Patton, R.W. (1977) *The Effect of External Cue Manipulation upon Weight-lifting Performance*. Paper presented at the American Alliance of Health, Physical Education and Recreation. Seattle, WA.

Newman, M.A. (1992) Perspectives on the psychological dimension of goalkeeping; Case studies of two exceptional performers in soccer, *Performance Enhancement*, **1**, 71–105.

Nicholls, J.G. (1980) Striving to demonstrate and develop ability: A theory of achievement motivation. In W. Meyer and B. Weiner (Chair) *Attributional Approaches to Human Motivation*. Symposium conducted at the Center for Interdisciplinary Research. University of Bielefeld, West Germany.

Nicholls, J.G. (1984) Achievement motivation: Conceptions of ability, subjective experience, task choice and experience, *Psychological Review*, **91**, 328–346.

Nicholls, J.G. (1989) *The Competitive Ethos and Democratic Education*, Harvard University Press, Harvard.

Nicholls, J.G. (1992) The general and the specific in the development and expression of achievement motivation. In G.C. Roberts (ed.), *Motivation in Sport and Exercise*, Human Kinetics, Champaign, IL.

Nideffer, R.N. (1976) *The Inner Athlete: Mind Plus Muscle for Winning*, Crowell, NY.

Nideffer, R.M. (1986) Concentration and attention control training. In J.M. Williams (ed.), *Applied Sport Psychology*, Mayfield, Palo Alto, CA.

Nideffer, R.N. (1990) Use of test of attentional and interpersonal style on sport, *The Sport Psychologist*, **4**, 285–300.

Nideffer, R.N. (1993) Attention control training. In R.N. Singer, M. Murphey and L.K. Tennant (eds), *Handbook of Research in Sport Psychology*, MacMillan, New York.

Nideffer, R., and Deckner, C. (1970) A case study of improved athletic performance following use of relaxation procedures, *Perceptual and Motor Skills*, **30**, 821–822.

Noakes, T.D. (1986) *The Lore of Running*, Oxford University Press, Capetown.
Norman, D. (1969) Toward a theory of memory and attention, *Psychological Review*, **75**, 522–536.
Ogilvie, B., and Taylor, J. (1993) Career termination in sports: When the dream dies. In J.M. Williams (ed.), *Applied Sport Psychology*, Mayfield, Mountain View, CA, pp. 356–366.
Olness, K., Culbert, T., and Uden, D. (1988) Self regulation of salivary immunoglobulin A by children, *Paediatrics*, **83**, 66–71.
Orlick, T. (1986) *Psyching for Sport*, Human Kinetics, Champaign, IL.
Orlick, T., and Lee-Gartner, K. (1993) Going after the dream and reaching it: The Olympic downhill, *Performance Enhancement*, **1**, 110–122.
Orlick, T., and McCaffrey, N. (1991) Mental training with children in sport and life, *The Sport Psychologist*, **5**, 322–234.
Orlick, T., and Partington, J. (1987) The sport psychology consultant: Analysis of critical components as viewed by Canadian Olympic athletes, *The Sport Psychologist*, **1**, 4–17.
Orlick, T., and Partington, J. (1988) Mental links to excellence, *The Sport Psychologist*, **2**, 105–130.
Oshida, Y., Yamanouchi, K., Hayamizu, S., and Sato, Y. (1988) Effect of acute physical exercise on lymphocyte subpopulations in trained and untrained subjects, *International Journal of Sports Medicine*, **9**, 137–140.
Ost, L.G. (1988) Applied relaxation: Description of an effective coping technique, *Scandinavian Journal of Behaviour Therapy*, **17**, 83–96.
Oxendine, J.B. (1970) Emotional arousal and motor performance, *Quest*, **13**, 23–32.
Oxendine, J.B. (1984) *Psychology of Motor Learning*, Prentice-Hall, Englewood Cliffs, NJ.
Paikov, V.B. (1985) Means of restoration in the training of speed skaters, *Soviet Sports Review*, **20**, 9–12.
Paivio, A. (1971) *Imagery and Verbal Processes*, Holt, Rinehart and Winston, New York.
Paivio, A. (1985) Cognitive and motivational functions of imagery in human performance, *Canadian Journal of Applied Sport Sciences*, **10**, 22–28.
Parfitt, C.G., and Hardy, L. (1987) Further evidence for the differential effects of competitive anxiety upon a number of cognitive and motor sub-systems, *Journal of Sport Sciences*, **5**, 62–63.
Parfitt, C.G., and Hardy, L. (1993) The effects of competitive anxiety on memory span and rebound shooting tasks in basketball players, *Journal of Sport Sciences*, **11**, 517–524.
Parfitt, C.G., Jones, J.G., and Hardy, L. (1990) Multidimensional anxiety and performance. In J.G. Jones and L. Hardy (eds), *Stress and Performance in Sport*, Wiley, Chichester, pp. 43–80.
Parfitt, C.G., Hardy, L., and Pates, J. (1995) Somatic anxiety and physiological arousal: Their effects upon a high anaerobic, low memory demand task, *International Journal of Sport Psychology*, **26**, 196–213.
Parry-Billings, M., Blomstrand, E., McAndrew, N., and Newsholme, E.A. (1990) A communicational link between skeletal muscle, brain and cells of the immune system, *International Journal of Sports Medicine*, **11**, 122–128.
Partington, J., and Orlick, T. (1987) The sport psychology consultant: Olympic coaches' views, *The Sport Psychologist*, **1**, 95–102.
Patmore, A. (1986) *Sportsmen Under Stress*, Stanley Paul, London.
Patton, M.Q. (1990) *Qualitative evaluation and research methods* (2nd edn), Sage, Newbury Park, CA.

Pearson, L., and Jones, G. (1992) Emotional effects of sport injuries: Implications for physiotherapists, *Physiotherapy*, **78**, 762–770.
Pederson, P. (1986) The grief response and injury: A special challenge for athletes and athletic trainers, *Athletic Trainer*, **21**, 312–314.
Pendleton, L.R., Jones, J.G., and Jones, M. (1995) Goal difficulty and performance as a function of skill level, *Journal of Sports Science*, **13**, 71.
Pennebaker, J.W., and Lightner, J.M. (1980) Competition of internal and external information in exercise settings, *Journal of Personality and Social Psychology*, **39**, 165–174.
Perlin, L.I. (1991) The study of coping: An overview of problems and directions. In J. Eckenrode (ed.), *The Social Context of Coping*, Plenum Press, New York, pp. 261–276.
Peterson, C., Semmel, A., Von Baeyer, C., Abramson, L.Y., Metalsky, G.I., and Seligman, M.E.P. (1982) The attributional style questionnaire, *Cognitive Therapy and Research*, **6**, 287–299.
Platt, J.R. (1964) Strong inference, *Science*, **146**, 347–352.
Powell, G.E. (1973) Negative and positive mental practice in motor skill acquisition, *Perceptual Motor Skills*, **37**, 312.
Prapavessis, H., and Carron, A.V. (1988) Learned helplessness in sport, *The Sport Psychologist*, **2**, 189–201.
Prapavessis, H., and Grove, J.R. (1991) Precompetitive emotions and shooting performance: The mental health and zone of optimal functioning rationale, *The Sport Psychologist*, **5**, 223–234.
Predebon, J., and Docker, S.B. (1992) Free-throw shooting performance as a function of preshot routine, *Perceptual and Motor Skills*, **75**, 167–171.
Pribram, K.H., and McGuiness, D. (1975) Arousal, activation and effort in the control of attention, *Psychological Review*, **82**, 116–149.
Privette, G. (1984) *Experience Questionnaire*, University of West Florida, Pensacola, FL.
Raedeke, T.D., and Stein, G.L. (1994) Felt, arousal, thoughts, feelings and ski performance, *The Sport Psychologist*, **8**, 360–375.
Raglin, J. (1992) Anxiety and sport performance, *Exercise and Sport Science Review*, **20**, 243–274.
Raglin, J., and Morgan, W. (1988) Predicted and actual precompetition anxiety in college swimmers, *Journal of Swimming Research*, **4**, 5–7.
Ravizza, K. (1977) Peak experiences in sport, *Journal of Humanistic Psychology*, **17**, 35–40.
Ravizza, K. (1988) Gaining entry with athletic personnel for season-long consulting, *The Sport Psychologist*, **2**, 243–274.
Ravizza, K.H. (1993) An interview with Peter Vidmar, member of the 1994 US Olympic gymnastics team, *Contemporary Thought on Performance Enhancement*, **2**, 93–100.
Reason, J.T. (1979) Actions not as planned: The price of automation. In G. Underwood and R. Stevens (eds), *Aspects of Consciousness, Vol. 1: Psychological Issues*, Academic Press, London, pp. 67–89.
Reddy, J.K., Bai, A.J.L., and Rao, V.R. (1976) The effects of the Transcendental Meditation program on athletic performance. In D.J., and I. Farrow (eds), *Scientific Research on the Transcendental Meditation Program: Collected Papers. Vol. 1*, MERU Press, Weggis, Switzerland.
Reed, E.S. (1982) An outline of a theory of action systems, *Journal of Motor Behaviour*, **14**, 98–134.
Reese, W.L. (1980) *Dictionary of Philosophy and Religion*, Humanities, Atlantic Highlands, NJ.

Rejeski, W.J., Darracott, C., and Hutslar, S. (1979) Pygmalion in youth sports: A field study, *Journal of Sport Psychology*, **1**, 311–319.

Renger, R. (1993) A review of the Profile of Mood States (POMS) in the prediction of athletic success, *Journal of Applied Sport Psychology*, **5**, 78–84.

Revelle, W., and Michaels, E.J. (1976) The theory of achievement motivation revisited: The implication of inertial tendencies, *Psychological Review*, **83**, 394–404.

Richardson, A. (1967) Mental Practice: A review and discussion, *Research Quarterly*, **38**, 95–107.

Richardson, A. (1969) *Mental Imagery*, Springer, New York.

Ripol, W. (1993) The psychology of the swimming taper. *Contemporary Thought on Performance Enhancement*, **2**, 22–64.

Roberts, G.C. (1986) The growing child and the perception of competitive stress in sport. In G. Gleeson (ed.), *The Growing Child in Competitive Sport*, Hodder and Stoughton, London.

Rosin, L., and Nelson, W. (1983) The effects of rational and irrational self-verbalizations on performance efficiency and levels of anxiety, *Journal of Clinical Psychology*, **39**, 208–213.

Ross, S.L (1985) The effectiveness of mental practice in improving the performance of college trombonists, *Journal of Research in Music Education*, **33**, 221–230.

Rotella, R.J. (1985) Strategies for controlling anxiety and arousal. In L.K. Bunker, R.J. Rotella and A. Reilly (eds), *Sport Psychology*, McNaughton and Gunn, Ann Arbor, Michigan.

Rotella, R.J., Gansneder, B., Ojala, D., and Billing, J. (1980) Cognitions and coping strategies of elite skiers: An exploratory study of young developing athletes, *Journal of Sport Psychology*, **4**, 350–354.

Rotter, J.B. (1954) *Social Learning and Clinical Psychology*, Prentice-Hall, Englewood Cliffs, New York.

Rowley, A.J., Landers, D.M., Kyllo, L.B., and Etnier, J.L. (1995) Does the iceberg profile discriminate between successful and less successful athletes?, *Journal of Sport and Exercise Psychology*, **17**, 185–199.

Rubinstein, S.L. (1973) *Grundlagen der Allgemeinen Psychologie*, Volk und Wissen, Berlin.

Rudisill, M.E. (1988) The influence of causal dimension orientations and perceived competence on adults expectations, persistence, and the selection of causal dimensions, *International Journal of Sport Psychology*, **19**, 184–198.

Rudisill, M.E. (1989) Influence of perceived competence and causal dimension orientations on expectations, persistence and performance during perceived failure, *Research Quarterly for Exercise and Sport*, **60**, 166–175.

Rummelhart, D., McClelland, J.L. and PDP Research Group (1986) *Parallel Distributed Processing: Explorations in the Microstructure of Cognition*, MIT Press, Cambridge, MA.

Rusbult, C.E. (1980) Commitment and satisfaction in romantic associations: A test of the investment model, *Journal of Experimental Social Psychology*, **16**, 172–186.

Rusbult, C.E., and Farrell, D. (1983) A longitudinal test of the investment model: The development (and deterioration) of satisfaction and commitment in heterosexual involvements, *Journal of Personality and Social Psychology*, **45**, 101–117.

Rusbult, C.E., Johnson, D.J., and Morrow, G.D. (1986) Predicting satisfaction and commitment in adult romantic involvements: An assessment of the generalizability of the investment model, *Social Psychology Quarterly*, **49**, 81–89.

Rushall, B.S. (1984) The content of competition thinking. In W.F. Straub and J.M. Williams (eds), *Cognitive Sport Psychology*, Sport Science Associates, Lansing, NY, pp. 51–62.

Russell, D., and McAuley, E. (1986) Causal attributions, causal dimensions, and affective actions to success and failure, *Journal of Personality and Social Psychology*, **50**, 1174–1185.
Ryan, E.D., and Simons, J. (1982) Efficacy of mental imagery in enhancing mental practice of motor skills, *Journal of Sport Psychology*, **4**, 41–51.
Sackett, R.S. (1934) The influences of symbolic rehearsal upon the retention of a maze habit, *Journal of General Psychology*, **10**, 376–395.
Salazar, W., Landers, D., Petruzzello, S., Han, M.W., Crews, D., and Kubitz, K. (1990) Hemispheric asymmetry, cardiac response, and performance in elite archers, *Research Quarterly for Exercise and Sport*, **61**, 351–359.
Sanders, A.F. (1983) Towards a model of stress and human performance, *Acta Psychologica*, **53**, 64–97.
Sarason, I.G., Sarason, B.R., and Pierce, G.R. (1991) Social support, personality and performance, *Journal of Applied Sport Psychology*, **2**, 117–127.
Scallen, S. (1993) Collegiate swimmers and zones of optimal functioning, *Journal of Sport and Exercise Psychology*, **15** (Suppl), S68.
Scanlan, T.K., and Passer, M.W. (1978) Factors related to competitive stress among male youth sport participants, *Medicine and Science in Sport*, **10**, 103–108.
Scanlan, T.K., Ravizza, K., and Stein, G.L. (1989) An in-depth study of former elite figure skaters: I. Introduction to the project, *Journal of Sport and Exercise Psychology*, **11**, 54–64.
Scanlan, T.K., Stein, G.L., and Ravizza, K. (1991) An in-depth study of former elite figure skaters: 3. Sources of stress, *Journal of Sport and Exercise Psychology*, **13**, 102–120.
Scanlan, T.K., Carpenter, P.J., Schmidt, G.W., Simons, J.P., and Keller, B. (1993a) An introduction to the sport commitment model, *Journal of Sport and Exercise Psychology*, **15**, 1–15.
Scanlan, T.K., Simons, J.P., Carpenter, P.J., Schmidt, G.W., and Keeler, B. (1993b) The sport commitment model: Measurement developed for youth domains sport, *Journal of Sport and Exercise Psychology*, **15**, 16–38.
Schachter, S. (1964) The interaction of cognitive and physiological determinants of the emotional state. In L. Berkowitz (ed.), *Advances in Experimental Social Psychology (Vol. 1)*, Academic Press, New York.
Scheier, M.F., Weintraub, J.K., and Carver, C.S. (1986) Coping with stress: Divergent strategies of optimists and pessimists, *Journal of Personality and Social Psychology*, **51**, 1257–1264.
Schmid, A.B., and Peper, E. (1993) Training strategies for concentration. In J.M. Williams (ed.), *Applied Sport Psychology: Personal Growth to Peak Performance*, Mayfield, Mountain View, California.
Schmidt, G.W., and Stein, G.L. (1991) Sport commitment: A model integrating enjoyment dropout and burnout, *Journal of Sport and Exercise Psychology*, **8**, 254–265.
Schmidt, R.A. (1975) A schema theory of discrete motor skill learning, *Psychological Bulletin*, **76**, 92–104.
Schmidt, R.A. (1982) *Motor Control and Learning: A Behavioural Emphasis*, Human Kinetics, Champaign, IL.
Schmidt, R.A. (1988) *Motor Control and Learning: A Behavioural Emphasis*, Human Kinetics, Champaign, IL.
Schneider, W., and Shiffrin, R.M. (1977) Controlled and automated human processing I: Detection, search and attention, *Psychological Review*, **84**, 1–66.
Schneider, W., Dumais, S.T., and Shiffrin, R.M. (1984) Automatic and control processing and attention. In R.Parasurama and R. Davies (eds), *Varieties of Attention*, Academic Press, Orlando, FL, pp. 1–27.

Schomer, H. (1986) Mental strategies and the perception of the effort of marathon runners, *International Journal of Sport Psychology*, **17**, 41–59.
Schunk, D.H. (1983) Developing children's self-efficacy and skills: The roles of social comparative information and goal setting, *Contemporary Educational Psychology*, **8**, 76–86.
Schwartz, G.E., Davidson, R.J., and Goleman, D. (1978) Patterning of cognitive and somatic progress in the self-regulation of anxiety: Effects of meditation versus exercise, *Psychosomatic Medicine*, **40**, 321–328.
Seligman, M.E.P., Nolen-Hoeksema, S., Thornton, N., and Thornton, K.M. (1990) Explanatory style as a mechanism of disappointing athletic performance, *Psychological Science*, **1** (2), 143–146.
Selye, H. (1976) *The Stress of Life*, McGraw-Hill, New York.
Shaffer, L.H. (1975) Multiple attention in continuous verbal tasks. In P.M.A. Rabbit and S. Dornic (eds), *Attention and Performance, Vol. 5*, Academic Press, London.
Shapiro, K.L., and Lim, A. (1989) The impact of anxiety on visual attention to central and peripheral events, *Behaviour and Research Therapy*, **27**, 345–351.
Shavelson, R.J., and Webb, N.M. (1991) *Generalizability Theory: A Primer*, Sage, Newbury Park, CA.
Shelton, T.O., and Mahoney, M.J. (1978) The content and effect of 'psyching up' strategies in weight lifters, *Cognitive Therapy and Research*, **2**, 275–284.
Shepard, R.N., and Podgorny, P. (1978) Cognitive processes that resemble perceptual processes. In W.K. Estes (ed.), *Handbook of Learning and Cognitive Processes*, Vol. 5, Erlbaum, Hillsdale, NJ.
Shiffrin, R.M., and Schneider, W. (1977) Controlled and automatic human information processing II: Perceptual learning, automatic attending and a general theory. *Psychological Review*, **84**, 127–190.
Silva, J.M. (1982) Performance enhancement in sport environments through cognitive intervention, *Behaviour Modification*, **6**, 433–463.
Silva, J.M. (1989) Establishing professional standards and advancing applied sport psychology, *Journal of Applied Sport Psychology*, **1**, 160–165.
Silva, J.M. (1990) An analysis of training stress syndrome in competitive athletics, *Journal of Applied Sport Psychology*, **2** (1), 5–20.
Simon, J.A., and Martens, R. (1977) S.C.A.T. as a predictor of A-states in varying competitive situations. In D.M. Landers and R.W. Christina (eds), *Psychology of Motor Behaviour and Sport – 1976* (Vol. 2), Human Kinetics, Champaign, IL, pp. 146–156.
Singer, R.N., Lidor, R., and Cauragh, J.H. (1993) To be aware or not aware? What to think about while learning and performing a motor skill, *The Sport Psychologist*, **7**, 19–30.
Smith, R.E. (1980) A cognitive-affective approach to stress management training for athletes. In C.H. Nadeau, W.R. Halliwell, K.M. Newell, and G.C. Roberts (eds), *Psychology of Motor Behaviour in Sport – 1979*, Human Kinetics, Champaign, IL, pp. 54–72.
Smith, R.E. (1986) Toward a cognitive affective model of athletic burnout, *Journal of Sport Psychology*, **8**, 36–50.
Smith, R.E. (1988) The logic and design of case study research, *The Sport Psychologist*, **2**, 1–12.
Smith, R.E.(1989) Applied sport psychology in the age of accountability, *Journal of Applied Sport Psychology*, **1**, 166–180.
Smith, R.E., and Christensen, D.S. (1995) Psychological skills as predictors of performance and survival in professional baseball, *Journal of Sport and Exercise Psychology*, **17**, 399–415.

Smith, R.E., and Smoll, F.L. (1995) The coach as the focus of research and intervention in youth sports. In F.L. Smoll and R.E. Smith (eds), *Children and Youth in Sport: A Biopsychosocial Perspective*, Benchmark, Madison, WI, pp. 125–141.

Smith, R.E., Smoll, F.L., and Ptacek, J.T. (1990a) Conjunctive moderator variables in vulnerability and resiliency research: Life stress, social support, and coping skills in adolescent sport injuries, *Journal of Personality and Social Psychology*, **58**, 360–369.

Smith, R.E., Smoll, F.L., and Schutz, R.W. (1990b) Measurements and correlates of sport-specific cognitive and somatic trait anxiety, *Anxiety Research*, **2**, 263–280.

Smith, R.E., Schultz, R.W., Smoll, F.L., and Ptacek, J.T. (1995) Development and validation of a multidimensional measure of sport-specific psychological skills: The Athletic Coping Skills Inventory, *Journal of Sport and Exercise Psychology*, **17**, 379–398.

Smoll, F.L., and Smith, R.E. (1984) Leadership research in young athletes. In J. Silva III and R.S. Weinberg (eds), *Psychological Foundations of Sport*, Human Kinetics, Champaign, IL.

Solcova, I., and Tomanek, P. (1995) *Coping with Daily Stress: Effect of Hardiness*. Presentation made at the Stress and Anxiety Research Society Conference, Prague–Czech Republic.

Southard, D.L., and Miracle, A. (1993) Rhythmicity, ritual, and motor performance: A study of free throw shooting in basketball, *Journal of Sport Sciences*, **7**, 163–173.

Spelke, E., Hirst, W., and Neisser, U. (1976) Skills of divided attention, *Cognition*, **4**, 215–230.

Spielberger, C.S. (1966) Theory and research on anxiety. In C.S. Spielberger (ed.), *Anxiety and Behaviour*, Academic Press, New York, pp. 3–20.

Spielberger, C.S., Gorsuch, R.L., and Lushene, R.L. (1970) *Manual for the State-Trait Anxiety Inventory*, Consulting Psychologists, Palo Alto, CA.

Spink, K.S. (1990) Group cohesion and collective efficacy of volleyball teams, *Journal of Sport and Exercise Psychology*, **12**, 301–311.

Spink, K.S., and Roberts, G.L. (1980) Ambiguity of outcome and causal attributions, *Journal of Sport Psychology*, **2**, 237–244.

Start, K.B., and Richardson, A. (1964) Imagery and mental practice, *British Journal of Educational Psychology*, **34**, 280–284.

Steckler, A., McLeroy, K.R., Goodman, R.M., Bird, S.T., and McCormick, L. (1992) Toward integrating qualitative and quantitative methods: An introduction, *Health Education Quarterly*, **19**, 1–8.

Stedry, A.C., and Kay, E. (1966) The effect of goal difficulty on performance: A field experiment, *Behavioural Science*, **1**, 459–470.

Stern, R.M. (1976) Reaction time and heart rate between the GET SET and GO of simulated races, *Psychophysiology*, **13**, 149–154.

Sternberg, S. (1969) On the discovery of processing stages: Some extensions of Donders' method, *Acta Psychologica*, **30**, 276–315.

Stitcher, T. (1989) *The Effects Of Goal Setting On Peak Performance In A Competitive Athletic Setting*. Unpublished doctoral dissertation, North Texas State University, Denton.

Stone, A.A., Kennedy-Moore, E., Newman, M.G., Greenberg, M., and Neale, J.M. (1992) In B.N. Carpenter (ed.), *Personal Coping: Theory, Research, and Application*, Praeger, Westport, CT, pp. 14–29.

Stroop, J.P. (1935) Studies of interference in serial verbal reactions, *Journal of Personality and Social Psychology*, **18**, 643–662.

Suinn, R.M. (1972a) Behaviour rehearsal training for ski racers, *Behaviour Therapy*, **3**, 519–520.

Suinn, R.M. (1972b) Removing obstacles to learning and performance by visuo-motor behaviour rehearsal, *Behaviour Therapy*, **3**, 308–310.
Suinn, R.M. (1976) Visual motor behaviour rehearsal for adaptive behaviour. In J. Krumboltz and C. Thoresen (eds), *Counselling Methods*, Holt, New York.
Suinn, R.M. (1983) Imagery and sports. In A. A. Sheikh (ed.), *Imagery: Current Theory Research And Application*, Wiley, New York, pp. 507–534.
Summers, J.J., Miller, K., and Ford, S.K. (1991) Attentional style and basketball performance, *Journal of Sport and Exercise Psychology*, **13**, 239–253.
Swain, A.B.J., and Jones, G. (1992) Relationships between sport achievement orientation and competitive state anxiety, *The Sport Psychologist*, **6**, 42–54.
Swain, A.B.J., and Jones, G. (1993) Intensity and frequency dimensions of competitive state anxiety, *Journal of Sport Sciences*, **11**, 533–542.
Swain, A.B.J., and Jones, G. (1995) Goal attainment scaling: Effects of goal setting interventions on selected subcomponents of basketball performance, *Research Quarterly for Exercise and Sport*, **66**, 51–63.
Swain, A.B.J., and Jones, G. (1996) Explaining performance variance: The relative contribution of intensity and direction dimensions of competitive state anxiety, *Anxiety, Stress and Coping: An International Journal*, **9**, 1–18.
Swain, A.B.J., Thorpe, S.E., and Parfitt, G. (1995) Self-efficacy, collective efficacy and performance: The mediating role of group cohesion, *Journal of Sport Sciences*, **13**, 75–76.
Sweeney, P.D., Anderson, K., and Bailey, S. (1986) Attributional style in depression: A meta-analytic review, *Journal of Personality and Social Psychology*, **50**, 974–991.
Syer, J., and Connolly, C. (1984) *Sporting Body, Sporting Mind: An Athlete's Guide to Mental Training*, Cambridge University Press, Cambridge.
Tarshis, D. (1977) Tennis and the Mind, *Tennis Magazine*, New York.
Taylor, A.H., Daniel, J.V., Leith, L., and Burke, R.J. (1990) Perceived stress, psychological burnout and paths to turnover intentions among sport officials, *Journal of Applied Sport Psychology*, **2** (1), 84–97.
Tenenbaum, G., Pinchas, S., Elbaz, G., Bar-Eli, M., and Weinberg, R.S. (1991) Effect of goal proximity and goal specificity on muscular endurance performance, *Journal of Sport and Exercise Psychology*, **13**, 174–187.
Terry, P. (1995) The efficacy of mood state profiling with elite performers: A review and synthesis, *The Sport Psychologist*, **9**, 309–324.
Thayer, R.E. (1978) Toward a psychological theory of multidimensional activation, *Motivation and Emotion*, **2**, 1–34.
Thibaut, J.W., and Kelley, H.H. (1959) *The Social Psychology of Groups*, Wiley, New York.
Thomas, P. (1990) *An Overview of the Performance Enhancement Process in Applied Psychology*, United States Olympic Center, Colorado Springs, CO.
Treisman, A. (1964) Selective attention in man, *British Medical Bulletin*, **20**, 12–16.
Tubbs, M.E. (1986) Goal-setting. A meta-analytic examination of the empirical evidence, *Journal of Applied Psychology*, **71**, 474–483.
Tulving, E. (1983) *Elements of Episodic Memory*, Oxford University Press, Oxford.
Turner, P.E., and Raglin, J.S. (1991) Anxiety and performance in track and field athletes: A comparison of ZOF and inverted-U theories, *Medical Science in Sport and Exercise*, **23**, s119.
Turvey, M.T., and Kugler, D.N. (1984) An ecological approach to perception and action. In H.T.A. Whiting (ed.), *Human Motor Actions: Bernstein Reassessed*, North-Holland, Amsterdam, pp. 373–412.

Udry, E. (1995) *Athlete Injury Rehabilitation and Recovery: The Role of Emotions, Coping Strategies, and Social Support*. Unpublished doctoral dissertation, University of North Carolina, Greensboro.

Udry, E., and Gould, D. (1992) Mental preparation profiles: Helping skiers prepare mentally for performance success, *American Ski Coach*, **15**, 15–23.

Unestahl, L.E. (1983) *Inner Mental Training*, Veje Publications, Orebro, Sweden.

Ussher, M.H., and Hardy, L. (1986) The effect of competitive anxiety on a number of cognitive and motor subsystems, *Journal of Sport Sciences*, **4**, 232–233.

Vadocz, E.A., and Hall, C.R. (in press) The cognitive and motivational functions of images in the anxiety–performance relationship, *Journal of Applied Sport Psychology*.

Vallerand, R.J. (1987) Antecedents of self related affects in sport: Preliminary evidence on the intuitive-reflective appraisal model, *Journal of Sport Psychology*, **9**, 161–182.

Van der Molen, M.W., Somsen, R.J., Jennings, J.R., and Nieuwboer, R.T. (1987) A psychophysiological investigation of cognitive–energetic relations in human information processing: A heart rate/additive factors approach, *Acta Psychologica*, **66**, 251–289

Van Raalte, J.L., Brewer, B. W., Rivera, P.M., and Petitpas, A.J. (1994) The relationship between observable self-talk and competitive Junior tennis players' match performances, *Journal of Sport and Exercise Psychology*, **16**, 400–415.

Van Raalte, J.L., Brewer, B.W., Lewis, B.P., Linder, D.E., Wildman, G., and Kozimar, J. (in press) Cork! The effects of positive and negative self-talk on dart throwing performance, *Journal of Sport Behaviour*.

Van Schoyk, S.R., and Grasha, A.F. (1981) Attentional style variations and athletic ability: The advantages of a sport specific test, *Journal of Sport Psychology*, **3**, 149–165.

Vealey, R.S. (1986) Conceptualisation of sport confidence and competitive orientation: Preliminary investigation and instrument development, *Journal of Sport Psychology*, **8**, 221–246.

Vealey, R.S. (1988) Future directions in psychological skills training, *The Sport Psychologist*, **2**, 318–336.

Vealey, R. (1992) Personality and sport: A comprehensive view. In T.S. Horn (ed.), *Advances in Sport Psychology*, Human Kinetics, Champaign, IL, pp. 25–59.

Vealey, R. (1993) Imagery. In J. Williams (ed.), *Applied Sport Psychology: Personal to Peak Performance* (2nd edn), Mayfield, Palo Alto, CA, pp. 158–169.

Vealey, R. (1994) Knowledge development and implementation in sport psychology: A review of *The Sport Psychologist*, 1987–1992, *The Sport Psychologist*, **8**, 331–348.

Wang, M., and Landers, D. (1986) Cardiac response and hemispheric differentiation during archery performance: A psychophysiological investigation of attention, *Psychophysiology*, **23**, 469.

Watkins, D. (1986) Attributions in the New Zealand sports pages, *The Journal of Social Psychology*, **126**, 817–819.

Wehlage, D.F. (1980) Managing the emotional reaction to loss in athletics, *Athletic Training*, **15**, 144–146.

Weinberg, R.S. (1978) The effects of success and failure on the patterning of neuromuscular energy, *Journal of Motor Behaviour*, **10**, 53–61.

Weinberg, R.S. (1981) The relationship between mental preparation strategies and motor performance: A review and critique, *Quest*, **33**, 195–213.

Weinberg, R.S. (1986) Relationship between self-efficacy and cognitive strategies in enhancing endurance performance, *International Journal of Sport Psychology*, **17**, 280–293.

Weinberg, R.S. (1988) *The Mental Advantage: Developing Your Psychological Skills In Tennis*, Human Kinetics, Champaign, IL.

Weinberg, R.S. (1989a) Anxiety arousal and motor performance: Theory, research and applications. In D. Hackfort and C.D. Spielberger (eds), *Anxiety in Sports: An International Perspective*, Hemisphere, New York.

Weinberg, R.S. (1989b) Applied sport psychology: Issues and challenges, *Journal of Applied Sport Psychology*, **1**, 181–195.

Weinberg, R.S. (1993) Goal setting and motor performance: A review and critique. In G.C. Roberts (ed.), *Motivation in Sport and Exercise*, Human Kinetics, Champaign, IL.

Weinberg, R.S. (1994) Goal setting and performance in sport and exercise settings: A synthesis and critique, *Medicine and Science in Sports and Exercise*, **26**, 495–502.

Weinberg, R.S., and Hunt, V. (1976) The interrelationships between anxiety, motor performance, and electromyography, *Journal of Motor Behaviour*, **8**, 219–224.

Weinberg, R.S., and Jackson, A. (1990) Building self-efficacy in tennis players: A coach's perspective, *Journal of Sport and Exercise Psychology*, **12**, 164–174.

Weinberg, R.S., and Weigand, D. (1993) Goal-setting in sport and exercise: A reaction to Locke, *Journal of Sport and Exercise Psychology*, **15**, 88–96.

Weinberg, R.S., Gould, D., and Jackson, A. (1979) Expectations and performance: An empirical test of Bandura's self efficacy theory, *Journal of Sport Psychology*, **1**, 320–331.

Weinberg, R.S., Gould, D., and Jackson, A. (1980) Cognition and motor performance: Effect of psyching-up strategies three motor tasks, *Cognitive Therapy and Research*, **4**, 239–245.

Weinberg, R.S., Gould, D., and Jackson, A. (1981a) Relationship between the duration of the psych-up interval and strength performance, *Journal of Sport Psychology*, **3**, 166–170.

Weinberg, R.S., Gould, D., Yukelson, D., and Jackson, A. (1981b) The effect of pre-existing and manipulated self-efficacy on a competitive muscular endurance task, *Journal of Sport Psychology*, **3**, 345–354.

Weinberg, R.S., Smith, J., Jackson, A., and Gould, D. (1984) Effect of association, dissociation and positive self-talk on endurance performance, *Canadian Journal of Applied Sport Sciences*, **9**, 25–32.

Weinberg, R.S., Bruya, L.D., and Jackson, A. (1985) The effects of goal proximity and goal specificity on endurance performance, *Journal of Sport Psychology*, **7**, 296–305.

Weinberg, R.S., Bruya, L., Jackson, A., and Garland, H. (1987) Goal difficulty and endurance performance: A challenge to the goal attainability assumption, *Journal of Sport Behaviour*, **10**, 82–92.

Weinberg, R.S., Bruya, L.D., Longino, J., and Jackson, A. (1988) Effect of goal proximity and goal specificity on endurance performance of primary grade children, *Journal of Sport and Exercise Psychology*, **10**, 81–91.

Weinberg, R.S., Bruya, L., Garland, H., and Jackson, A. (1990) Effect of goal difficulty and positive reinforcement on endurance performance, *Journal of Sport Psychology*, **12**, 144–156.

Weinberg, R.S., Fowler, C., Jackson, A., Bagnall, J., and Bruya, L. (1991) Effect of goal difficulty on motor performance: A replication across tasks and subjects, *Journal of Sport and Exercise Psychology*, **13**, 160–173.

Weinberg, R.S., Grove, R., and Jackson, A. (1992) Strategies for building self-efficacy in tennis players: A comparative analysis of Australian and American coaches, *The Sport Psychologist*, **6**, 3–13.

Weiner, B. (1972) *Theories of Motivation: From Mechanism to Cognition*, Rand-McNally, Chicago, IL.

Weiner, B. (1979) A theory of motivation for some classroom experiences, *Journal of Educational Psychology*, **71**, 3–25.
Weiner, B. (1985) An attributional theory of achievement motivation and emotion, *Psychological Review*, **97**, 74–84.
Weiner, B. (1986) *An Attributional Theory of Achievement Motivation and Emotion*, Springer-Verlag, New York.
Weiss, M.R., and Chaumeton, N. (1992) Motivation orientations in sport. In T. Horn (ed.), *Advances in Sport Psychology*, Human Kinetics, Champaign, IL, pp. 61–99.
Weiss, T., Beyer, L., Hansen, E., Rost, R., and Paproth, A. (1987) Motor imagination: Dynamic of some neurophysiological correlates, *Neuroscience*, **22**, 511.
Weiss, M.R., Wiese, D.M., and Klint, K.A. (1989) Head over heels with success: The relationship between self-efficacy and performance in competitive youth gymnastics, *Journal of Sport and Exercise Psychology*, **11**, 444–451.
Weiss, M.R., McAuley, E., Ebbeck, V., and Wiese, D.M. (1990) Self esteem and causal attributes for children's physical and social competence in sport, *Journal of Sport and Exercise Psychology*, **12**, 21–26.
Whelan, J.P., Epkins, C.C., and Meyers, A.W. (1990) Arousal intervention for athletic performance: Influence of mental preparation and competitive experience, *Anxiety Research*, **2**, 293–307.
White, A., and Hardy, L. (1995) Use of different imagery perspectives on learning and performance of different motor skills. *British Journal of Psychology*, **86**, 169–180.
Whiting, H.T.A. (1987) Motor learning research. In L.-E. Unestahl (ed.), *Sport Psychology: Theory and Practice*, Veje Publications, Orebro, pp. 147–160.
Whiting, H.T.A., Vogt, S., and Vereijken, B. (1992) Human skill and motor control: Some aspects of the motor control-motor learning relation. In J.J. Summers (ed.), *Approaches to the Study of Motor Control and Motor Learning*, Elsevier, Amsterdam, pp. 81–111.
Wickens, C.D. (1980) The structure of attentional resources. In R. Nickerson and R. Pew (eds), *Attention and Performance VIII*, Erlbaum, Hillsdale, NJ, pp. 239–257.
Widmeyer, W.N., Carron, A.V., and Brawley, L.R. (1993) Group cohesion in sport and exercise. In R.N. Singer, N. Murphey, and L.K. Tennant (eds), *Handbook of Research of Sport Psychology*, MacMillan, New York, pp. 673–692.
Wiese-Bjornstal, D.M., and Smith, A.M. (1993) Counselling strategies for enhanced recovery of injured athletes within a team approach. In D. Pargman (ed.), *Psychosocial Bases of Sport Injuries*, Fitness Information Technology, Morgantown, WV, pp. 149–182.
Wiese, D.M., and Weiss, M.R. (1987) Psychological rehabilitation and the physical injury: Implications for the sports medicine team, *The Sport Psychologist*, **1**, 318–330.
Wiese, D.M., Weiss, M.R., and Yukelson, D.P. (1991) Sport psychology in the training room: A survey of athletic trainers, *The Sport Psychologist*, **5**, 15–24.
Wilkes, R.L., and Summers, J.J. (1984) Cognitions, mediating variables and strength performance, *Journal of Sport Psychology*, **6**, 351–359.
Williams, J.M., and Krane, V. (1993) Psychological characteristics of peak performance. In J.M. Williams (ed.), *Applied Sport Psychology: Personal Growth to Peak Performance*, Mayfield, Mountain View, CA, pp. 137–147.
Williams, K.D., Harkin, S.G., and Latane, B. (1981) Identifiability as a deterrent to social loafing: Two cheering experiments, *Journal of Personality and Social Psychology*, **40**, 303–311.
Williams, L.R.T. (1978) Transcendental meditation and mirror-tracing skill, *Perceptual and Motor Skills*, **46**, 371–378.
Williams, L.R.T., Lodge, B., and Reddish, P.A. (1977) *Research Quarterly*, **48**, 196–201.

Williams, M., and Davids, K. (1995) Declarative knowledge in sport: A by-product of expertise or a characteristic of expertise?, *Journal of Sport and Exercise Psychology*, **17**, 259–275.

Wine, J.D. (1971) Test anxiety and direction of attention, *Psychological Bulletin*, **76**, 92–104.

Wine, J.D. (1980) Cognitive-attentional theory of test anxiety. In I.G. Sarason (ed.), *Test Anxiety: Theory, Research and Applications*, Erlbaum, Hillsdale, NJ.

Wolpe, J. (1978) Self-efficacy theory and therapeutic change: A square peg for a round hole. In S. Rachman (ed.), *Advances in Behavior Research and Therapy. Volume 1*, Pergamon Press, Oxford.

Wood, R.E., Mento, A.J., and Locke, E.A. (1987) Task complexity as a moderator of goal effects: A meta-analysis, *Journal of Applied Psychology*, **72**, 416–425.

Woolfolk, R.L., Murphy, S.M., Gottesfeld, D., and Aitkin, D. (1985a) The effects of mental practice of task and mental depiction of task outcome on motor performance, *Journal of Sport Psychology*, **7**, 191–197.

Woolfolk, R.L., Parrish, W., and Murphy, S.M. (1985b) The effects of positive and negative imagery on motor skill performance, *Cognitive Therapy and Research*, **9**, 335–341.

Wrisberg, C.A., and Ragsdale, M.R. (1979) Cognitive demand and practice level: Factors in the mental practice of motor skills, *Journal of Human Movement Studies*, **5**, 201–208.

Yerkes, R.M., and Dodson, J.D. (1908) The relation of strength of stimulus to rapidity of habit formation, *Journal of Comparative Neurology and Psychology*, **18**, 459–482.

Zaichowsky, L.D., and Fuchs, C.Z. (1988) Biofeedback applications in exercise and athletic performance, *Exercise and Sport Science Review*, **16**, 381–421.

FIRST AUTHOR INDEX

SUBJECT INDEX

Lightning Source UK Ltd.
Milton Keynes UK
UKHW03f0341310518
323467UK00005B/200/P
6756009
9 780471 957874